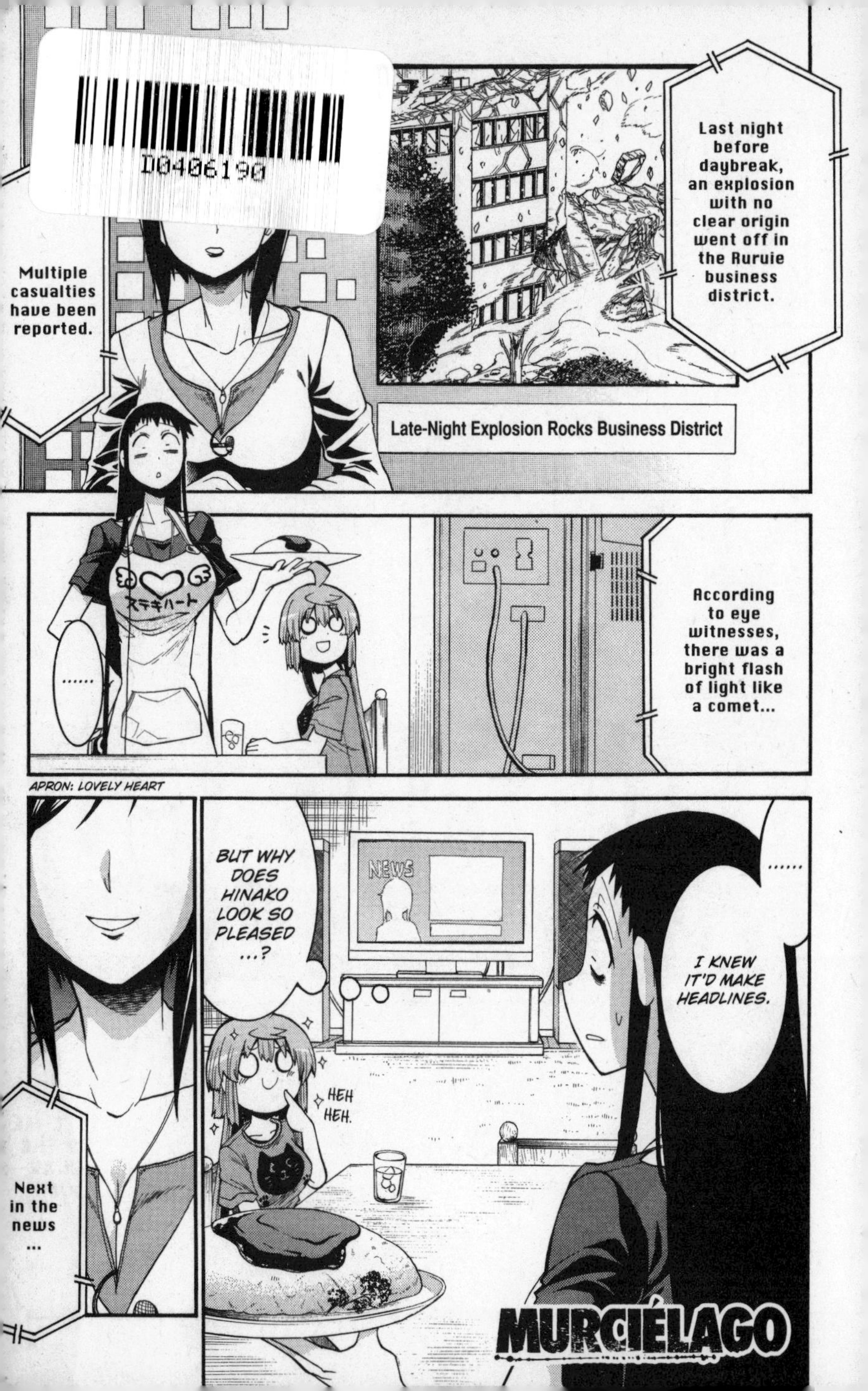

Last night before daybreak, an explosion with no clear origin went off in the Ruruie business district.
Late-Night Explosion Rocks Business District
Multiple casualties have been reported.
According to eye witnesses, there was a bright flash of light like a comet...
ステキハート
......
APRON: LOVELY HEART
......
I KNEW IT'D MAKE HEADLINES.
NEWS
BUT WHY DOES HINAKO LOOK SO PLEASED ...?
HEH HEH.
Next in the news ...
MURCIÉLAGO

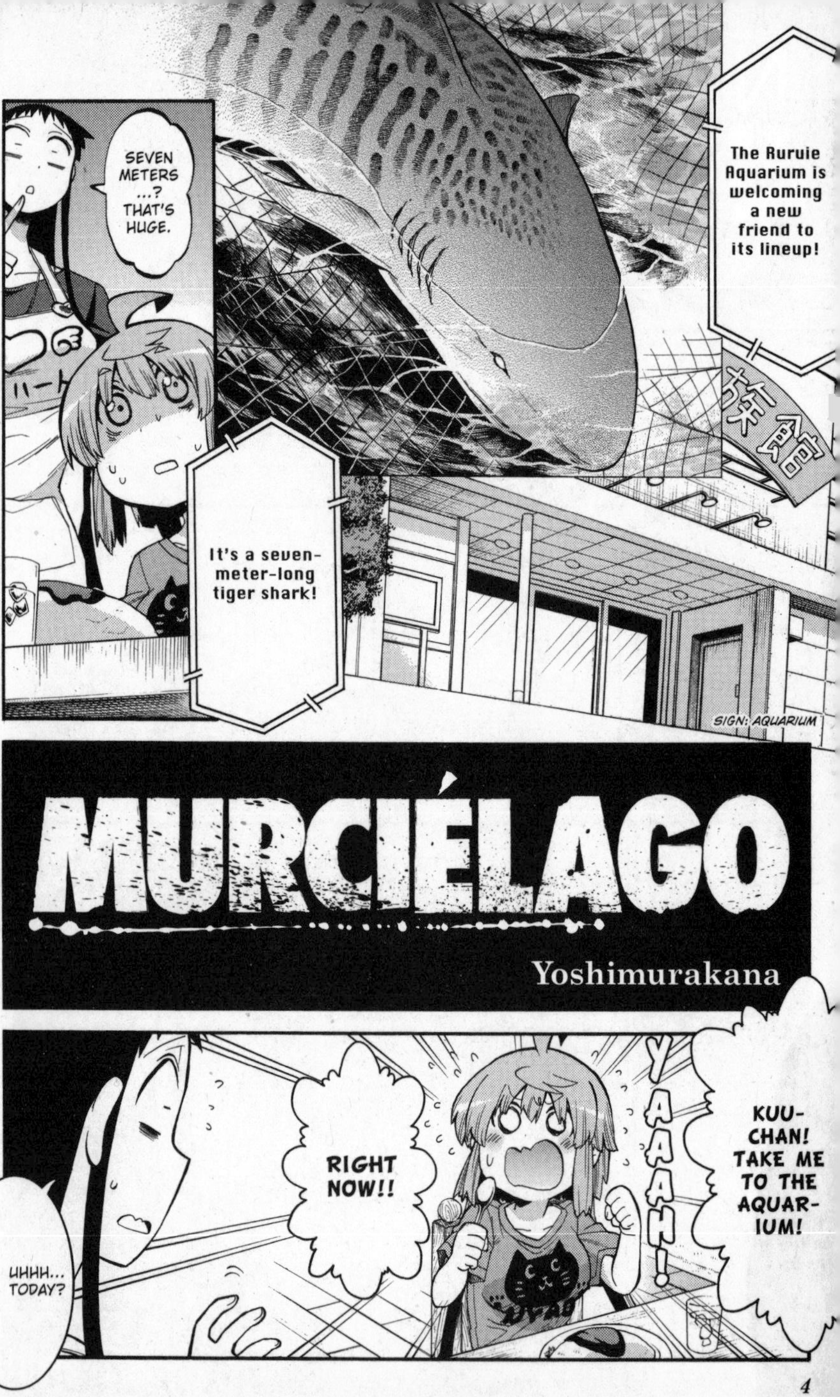
The Ruruie Aquarium is welcoming a new friend to its lineup!
It's a seven-meter-long tiger shark!
SIGN: AQUARIUM
SEVEN METERS ...? THAT'S HUGE.
MURCIÉLAGO
Yoshimurakana
KUU-CHAN! TAKE ME TO THE AQUARIUM!
YAAAAH!
RIGHT NOW!!
UHHH... TODAY?

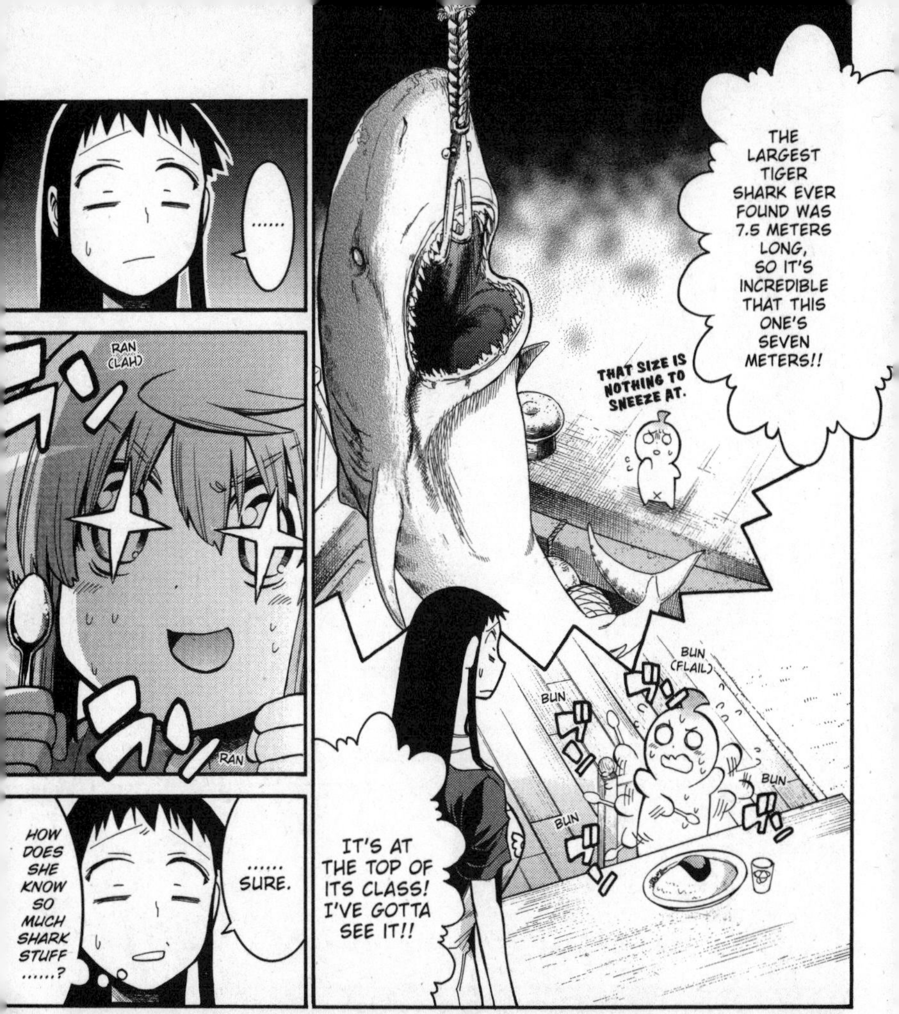
THE LARGEST TIGER SHARK EVER FOUND WAS 7.5 METERS LONG, SO IT'S INCREDIBLE THAT THIS ONE'S SEVEN METERS!!
THAT SIZE IS NOTHING TO SNEEZE AT.
BUN (FLAIL)
BUN
BUN
BUN
IT'S AT THE TOP OF ITS CLASS! I'VE GOTTA SEE IT!!
......
RAN (LAH)
RAN
...... SURE.
HOW DOES SHE KNOW SO MUCH SHARK STUFF ......?

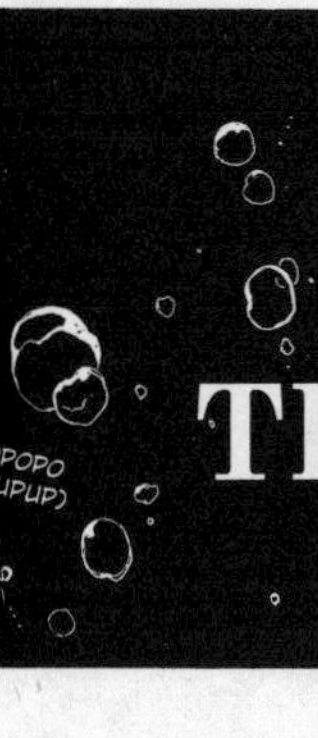
GOPOPO (GLUPUP)

Chapter 63

THE DEEP ONE

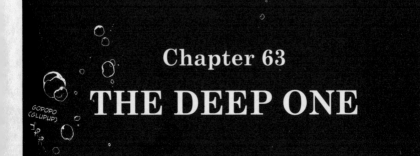

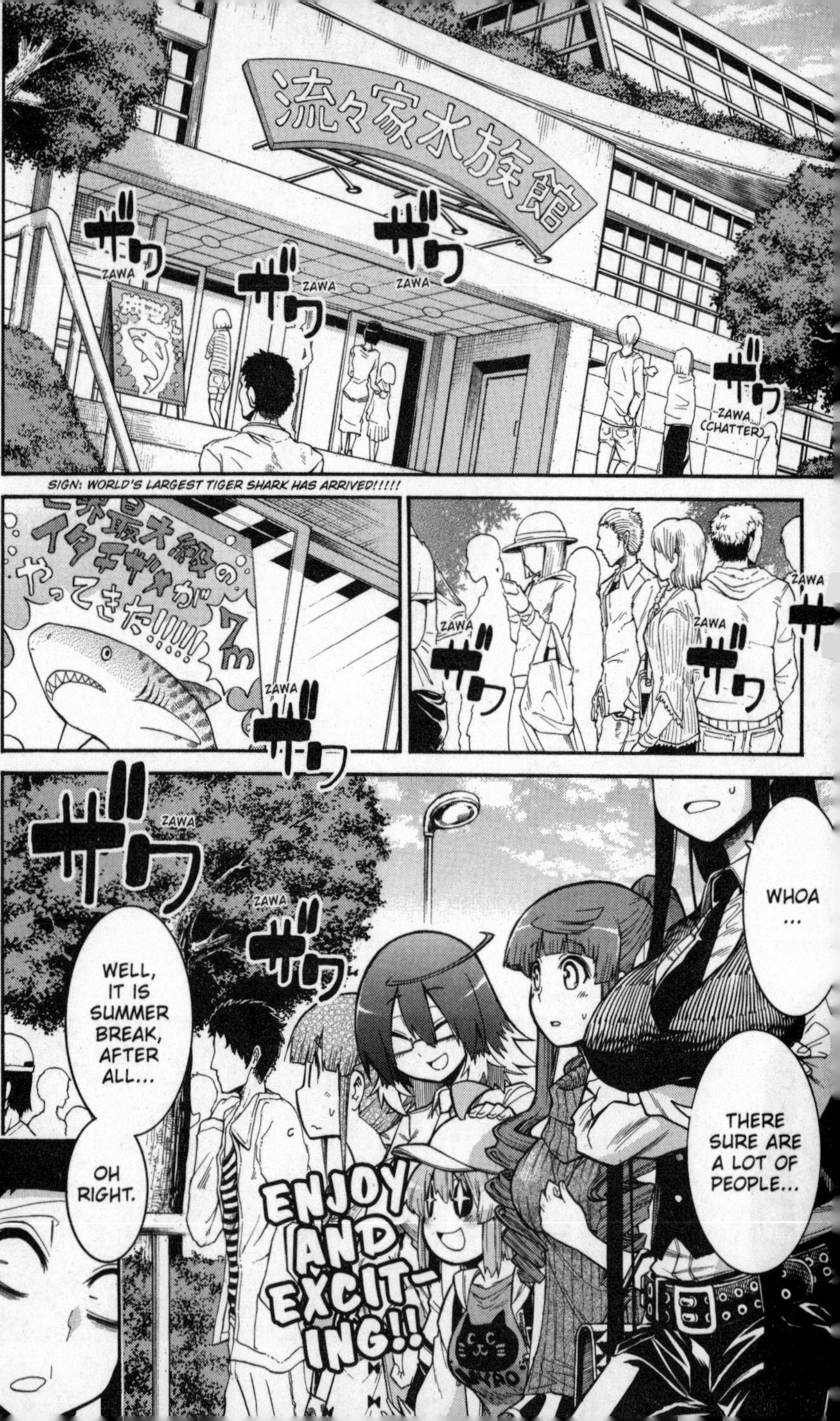
流々家水族館
ザワ ZAWA
ザワ ZAWA
ザワ ZAWA
ザワ ZAWA (CHATTER)
SIGN: WORLD'S LARGEST TIGER SHARK HAS ARRIVED!!!!!
ザ ZAWA
ザワ ZAWA
ザワ ZAWA
7m
ザワ ZAWA
WHOA...
THERE SURE ARE A LOT OF PEOPLE...
ザワ ZAWA
ザワ ZAWA
WELL, IT IS SUMMER BREAK, AFTER ALL...
OH RIGHT.
ENJOY AND EXCIT-ING!!

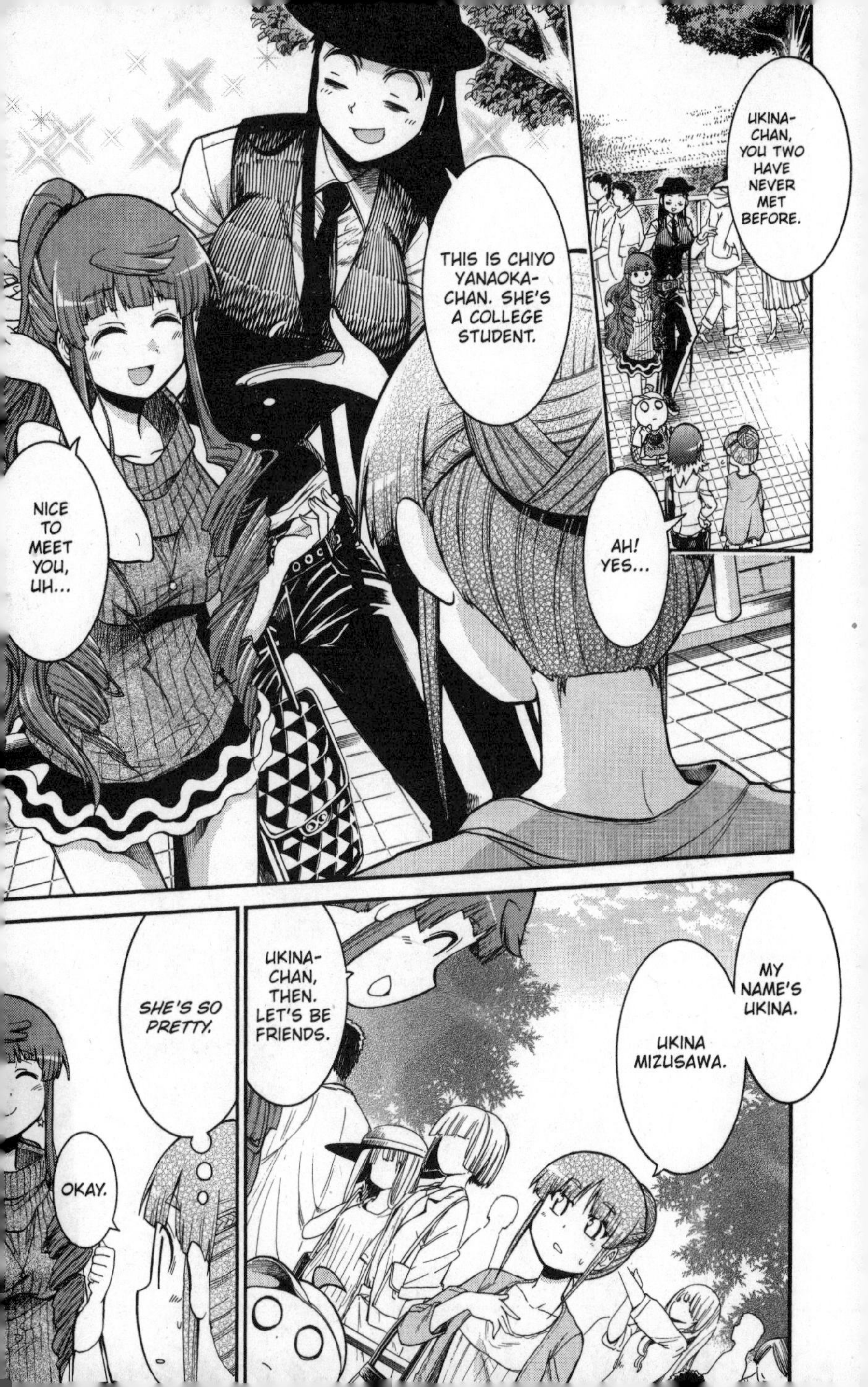
UKINA-CHAN, YOU TWO HAVE NEVER MET BEFORE.
AH! YES...
THIS IS CHIYO YANAOKA-CHAN. SHE'S A COLLEGE STUDENT.
NICE TO MEET YOU, UH...
MY NAME'S UKINA.
UKINA MIZUSAWA.
UKINA-CHAN, THEN. LET'S BE FRIENDS.
SHE'S SO PRETTY.
OKAY.

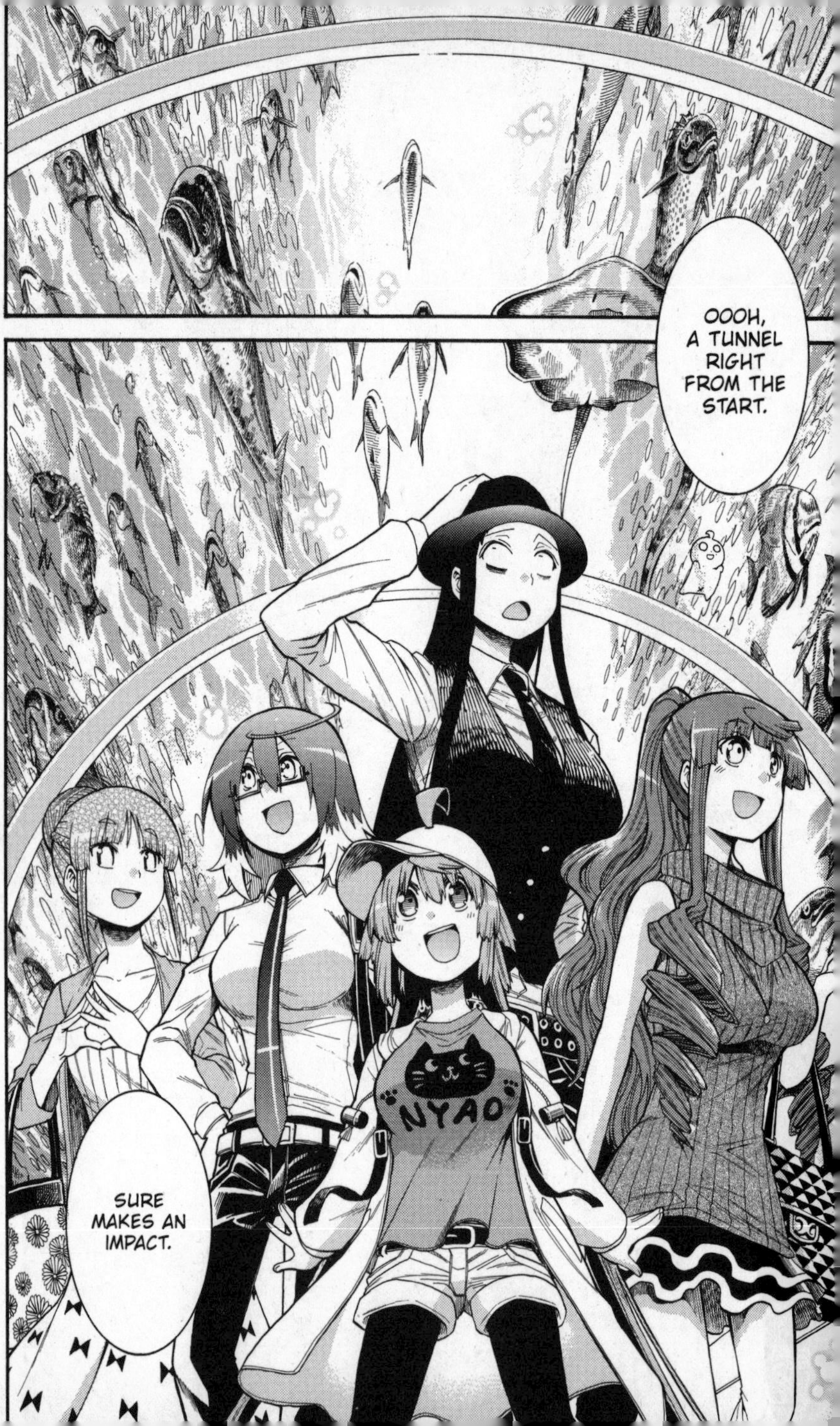
OOOH, A TUNNEL RIGHT FROM THE START.
SURE MAKES AN IMPACT.
NYAO

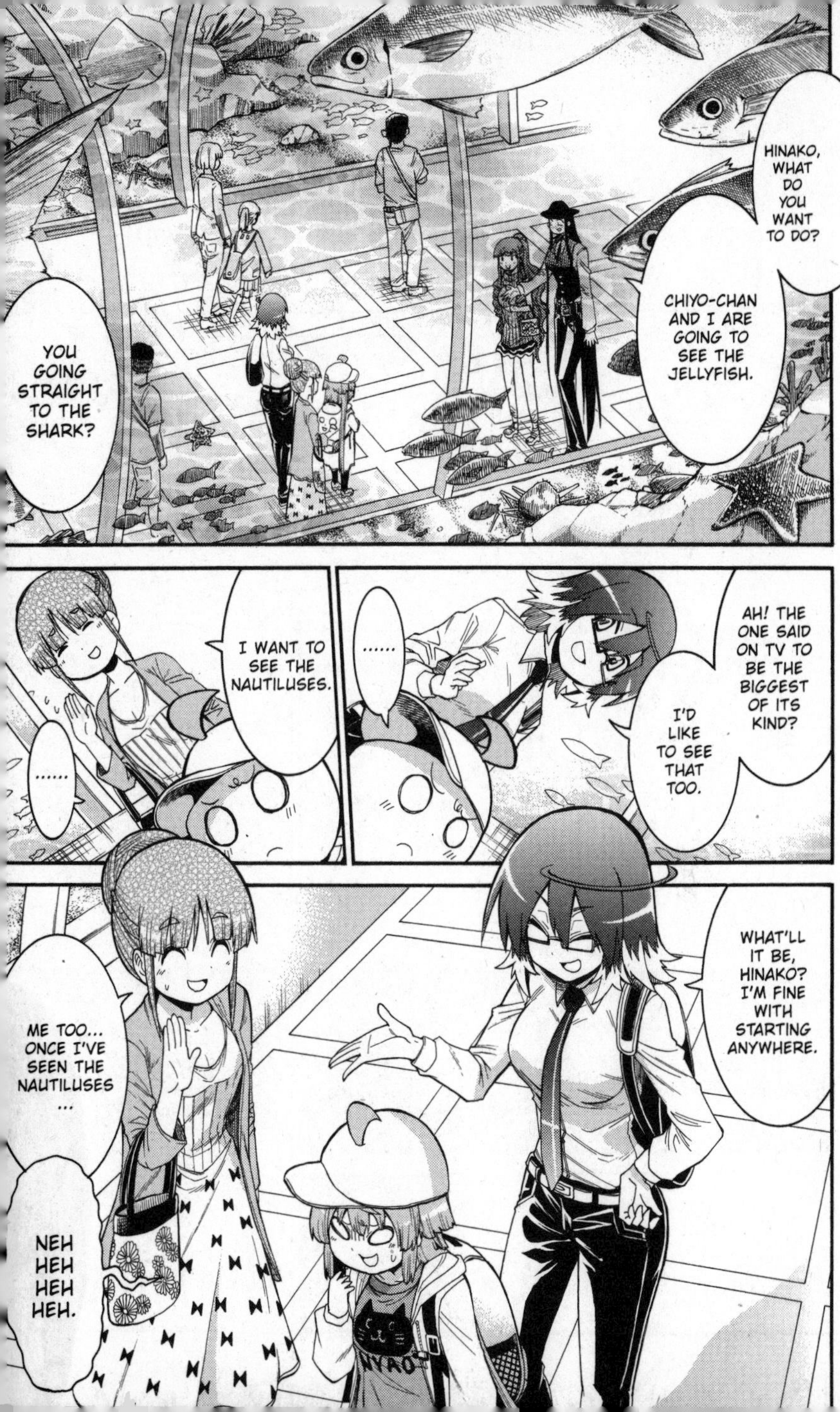
HINAKO, WHAT DO YOU WANT TO DO?
CHIYO-CHAN AND I ARE GOING TO SEE THE JELLYFISH.
YOU GOING STRAIGHT TO THE SHARK?
AH! THE ONE SAID ON TV TO BE THE BIGGEST OF ITS KIND?
I'D LIKE TO SEE THAT TOO.
......
I WANT TO SEE THE NAUTILUSES.
......
WHAT'LL IT BE, HINAKO? I'M FINE WITH STARTING ANYWHERE.
ME TOO... ONCE I'VE SEEN THE NAUTILUSES...
NEH HEH HEH HEH.

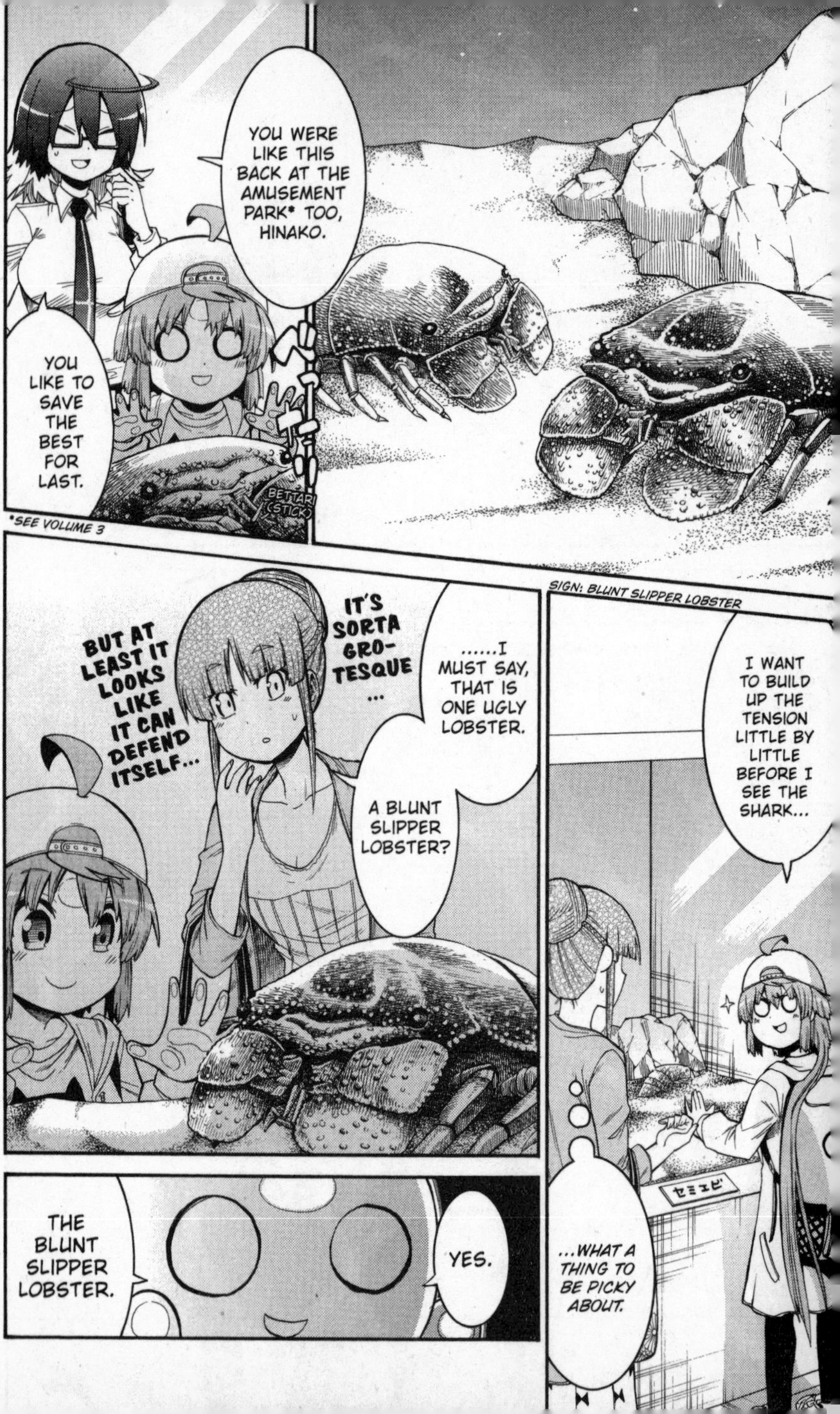
YOU WERE LIKE THIS BACK AT THE AMUSEMENT PARK* TOO, HINAKO.
YOU LIKE TO SAVE THE BEST FOR LAST.
BETTARI (STICK)
*SEE VOLUME 3
SIGN: BLUNT SLIPPER LOBSTER
I WANT TO BUILD UP THE TENSION LITTLE BY LITTLE BEFORE I SEE THE SHARK...
セミエビ
...WHAT A THING TO BE PICKY ABOUT.
......I MUST SAY, THAT IS ONE UGLY LOBSTER.
IT'S SORTA GRO-TESQUE...
BUT AT LEAST IT LOOKS LIKE IT CAN DEFEND ITSELF...
A BLUNT SLIPPER LOBSTER?
YES.
THE BLUNT SLIPPER LOBSTER.

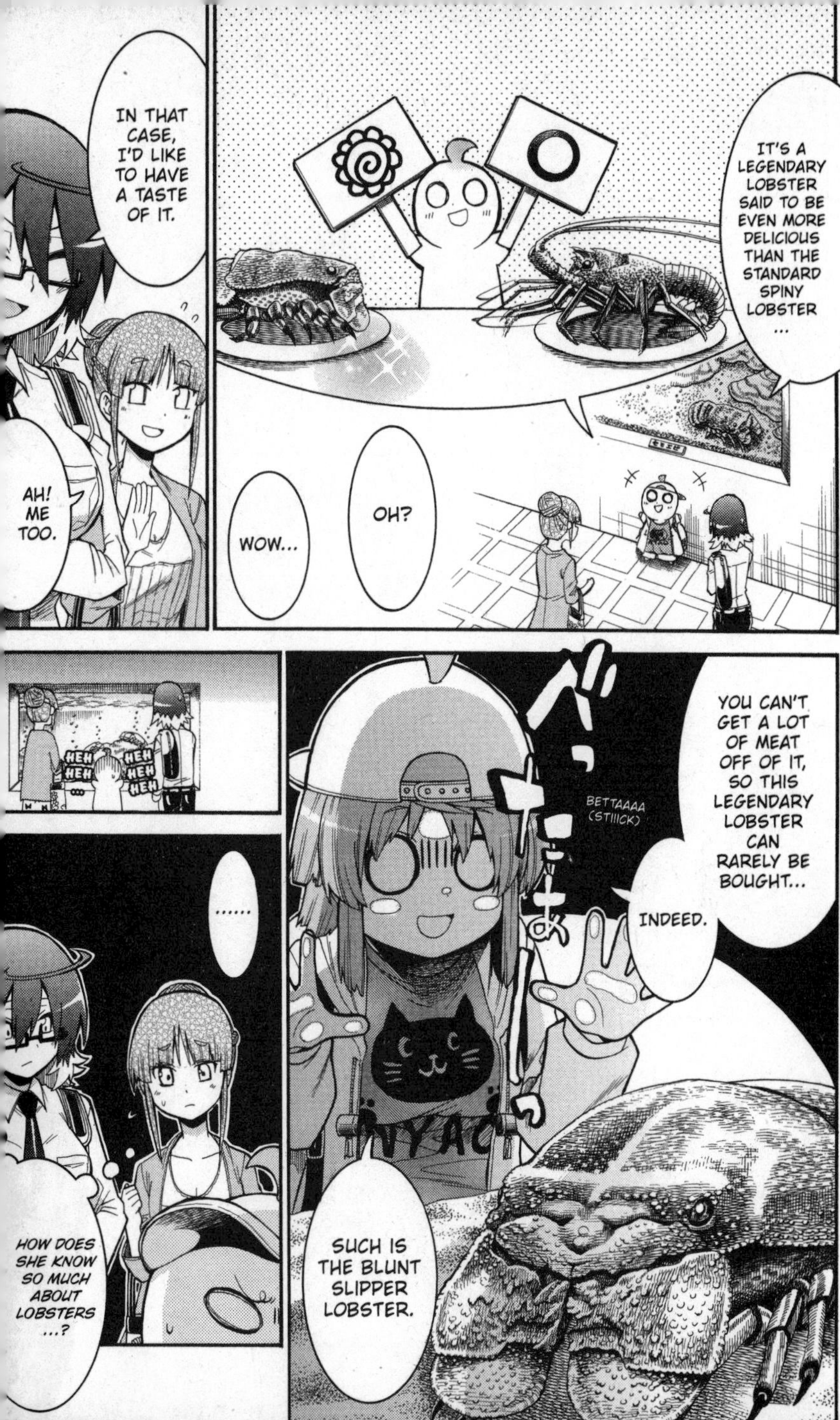
IT'S A LEGENDARY LOBSTER SAID TO BE EVEN MORE DELICIOUS THAN THE STANDARD SPINY LOBSTER ...
OH?
WOW...
IN THAT CASE, I'D LIKE TO HAVE A TASTE OF IT.
AH! ME TOO.
YOU CAN'T GET A LOT OF MEAT OFF OF IT, SO THIS LEGENDARY LOBSTER CAN RARELY BE BOUGHT...
BETTAAAA (STIIICK)
INDEED.
SUCH IS THE BLUNT SLIPPER LOBSTER.
HEH HEH HEH
HEH HEH
......
HOW DOES SHE KNOW SO MUCH ABOUT LOBSTERS ...?

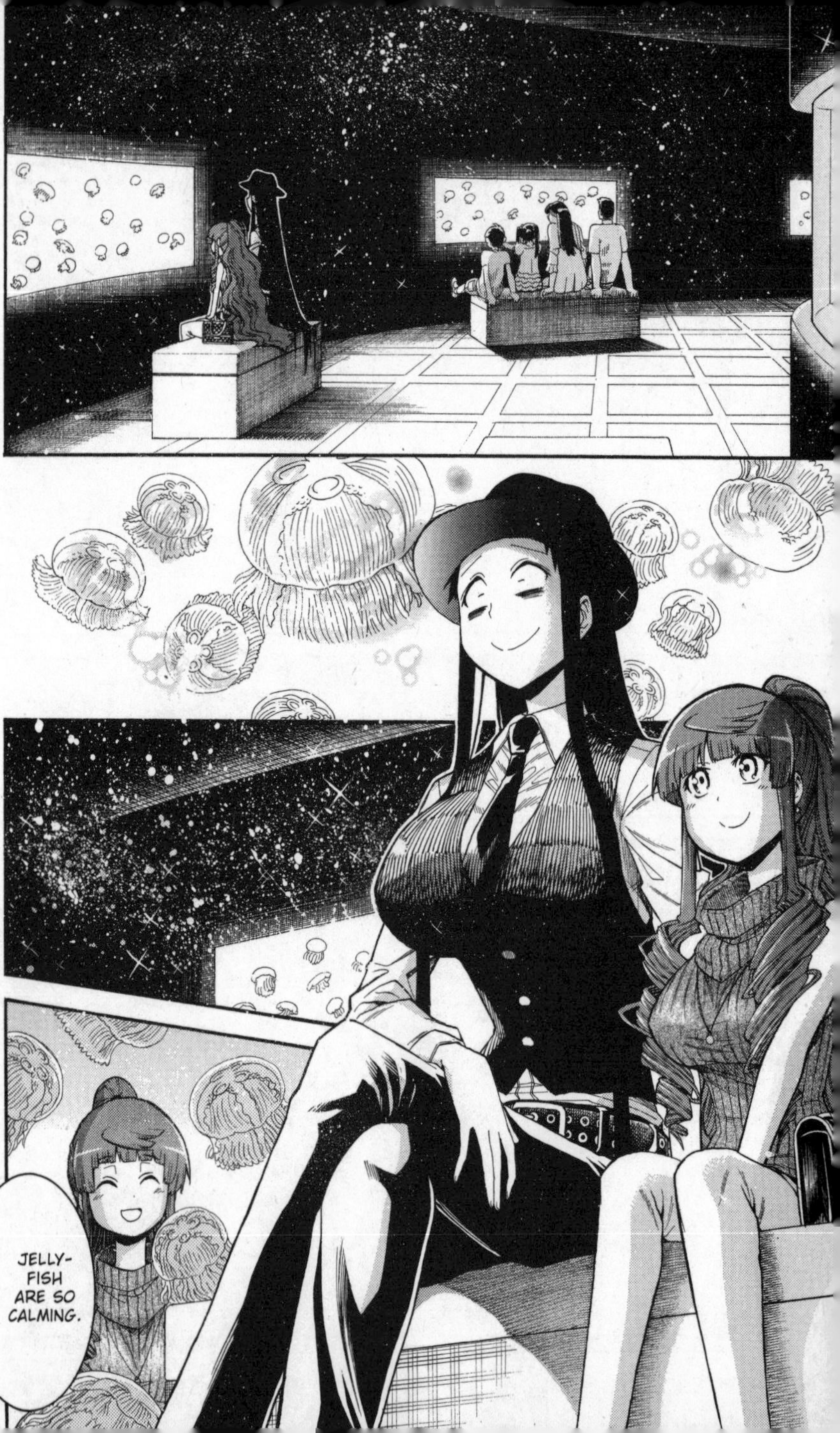
JELLY-FISH ARE SO CALMING.

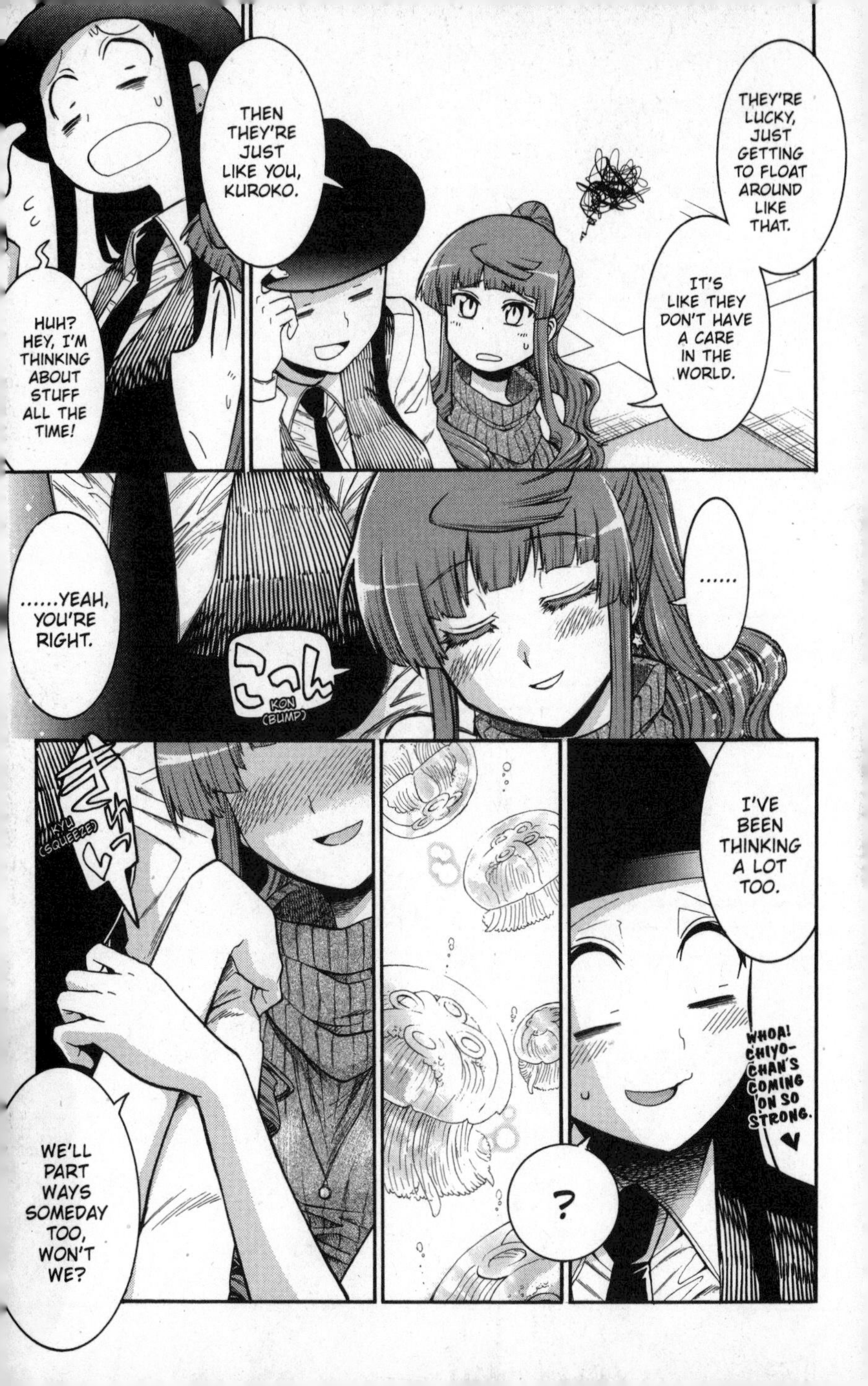
THEY'RE LUCKY, JUST GETTING TO FLOAT AROUND LIKE THAT.
IT'S LIKE THEY DON'T HAVE A CARE IN THE WORLD.
THEN THEY'RE JUST LIKE YOU, KUROKO.
HUH? HEY, I'M THINKING ABOUT STUFF ALL THE TIME!
......
......YEAH, YOU'RE RIGHT.
こつん
KON (BUMP)
I'VE BEEN THINKING A LOT TOO.
WHOA! CHIYO-CHAN'S COMING ON SO STRONG. ♥
?
きゅっ
KYU (SQUEEZE)
WE'LL PART WAYS SOMEDAY TOO, WON'T WE?

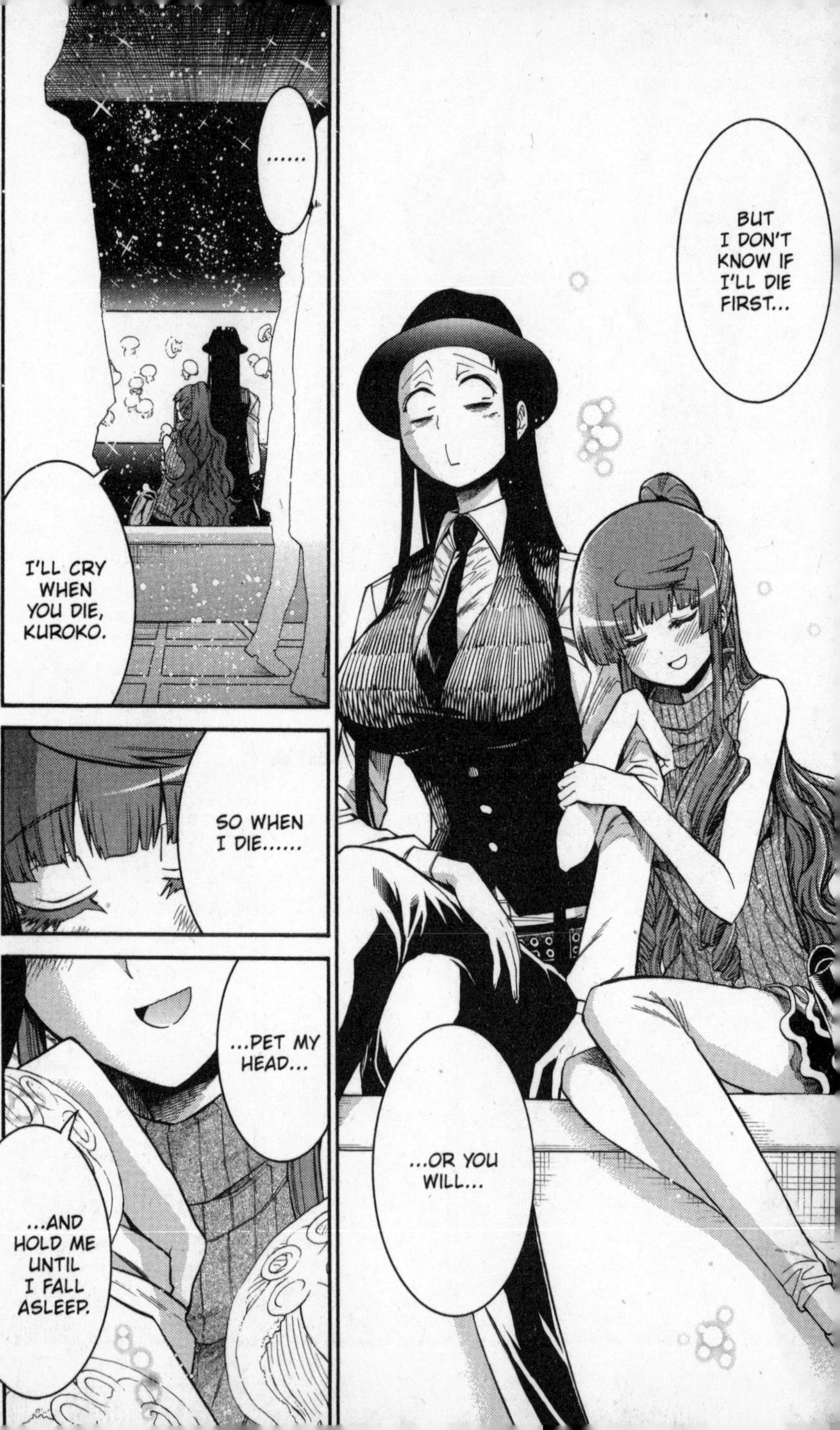
......
I'LL CRY WHEN YOU DIE, KUROKO.
SO WHEN I DIE......
...PET MY HEAD...
...AND HOLD ME UNTIL I FALL ASLEEP.
BUT I DON'T KNOW IF I'LL DIE FIRST...
...OR YOU WILL...

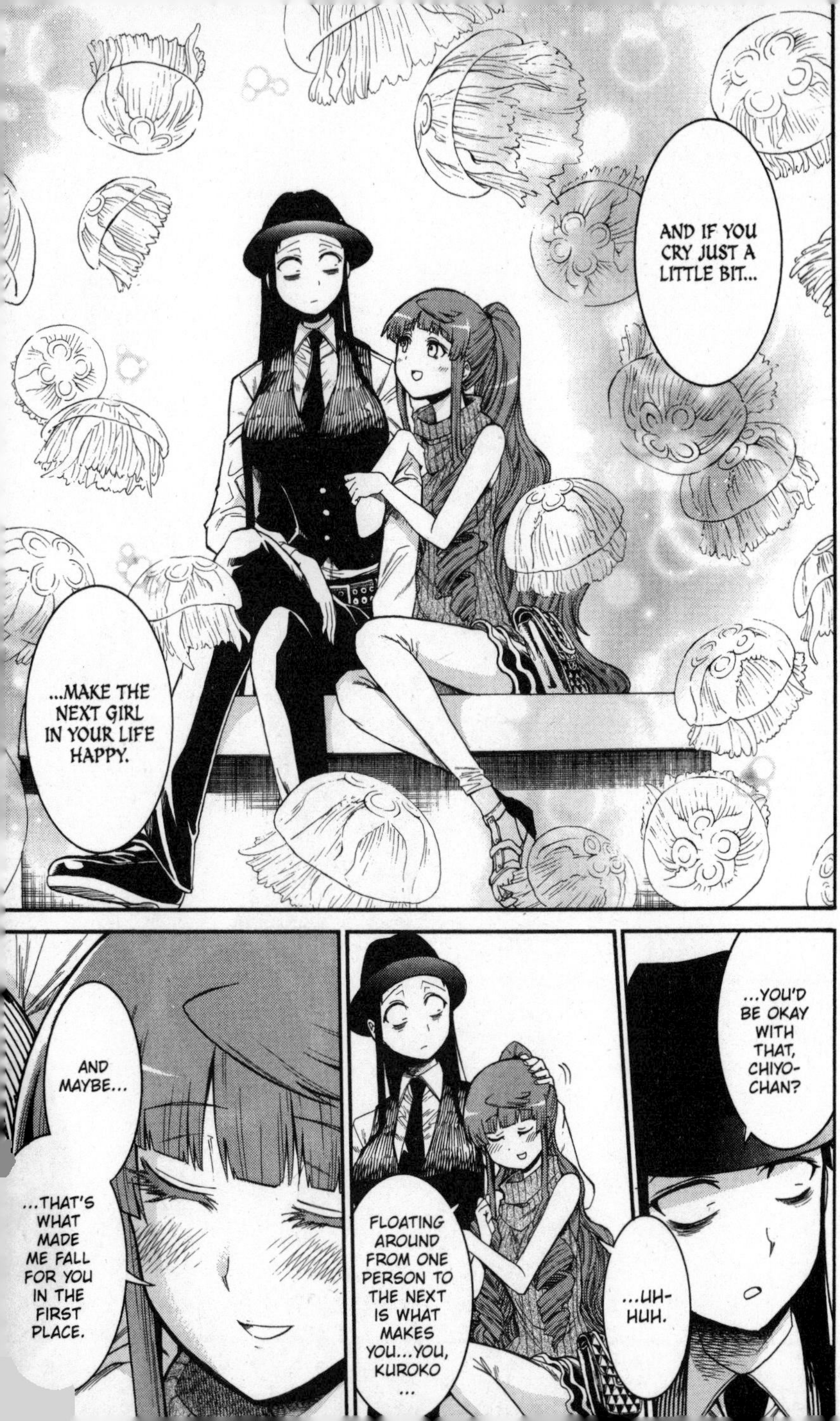
AND IF YOU CRY JUST A LITTLE BIT...
...MAKE THE NEXT GIRL IN YOUR LIFE HAPPY.
...YOU'D BE OKAY WITH THAT, CHIYO-CHAN?
...UH-HUH.
FLOATING AROUND FROM ONE PERSON TO THE NEXT IS WHAT MAKES YOU...YOU, KUROKO...
AND MAYBE...
...THAT'S WHAT MADE ME FALL FOR YOU IN THE FIRST PLACE.

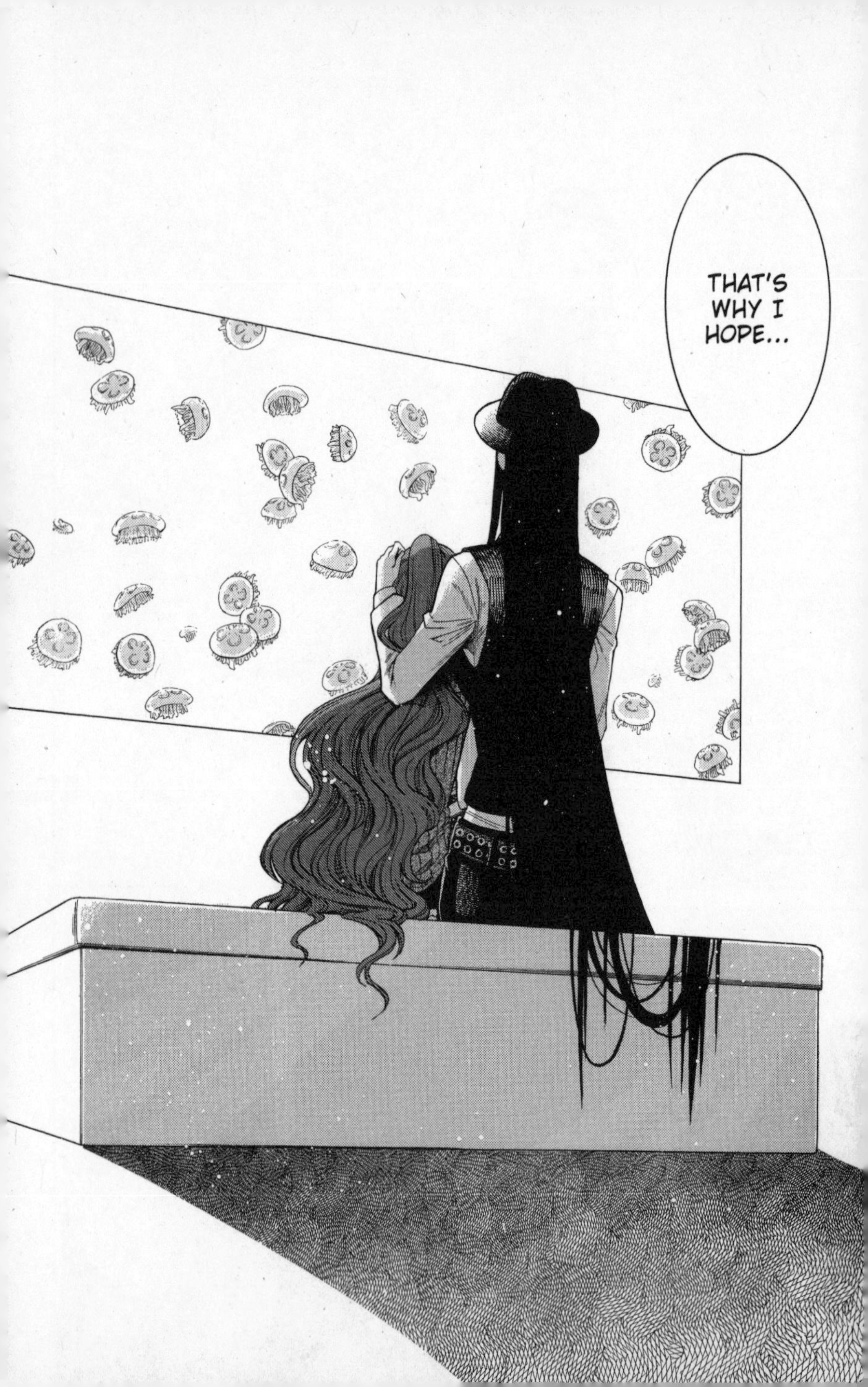
THAT'S WHY I HOPE...

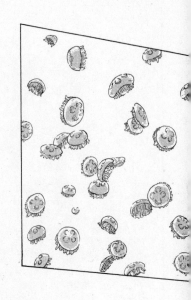

...YOU
NEVER
CHANGE.

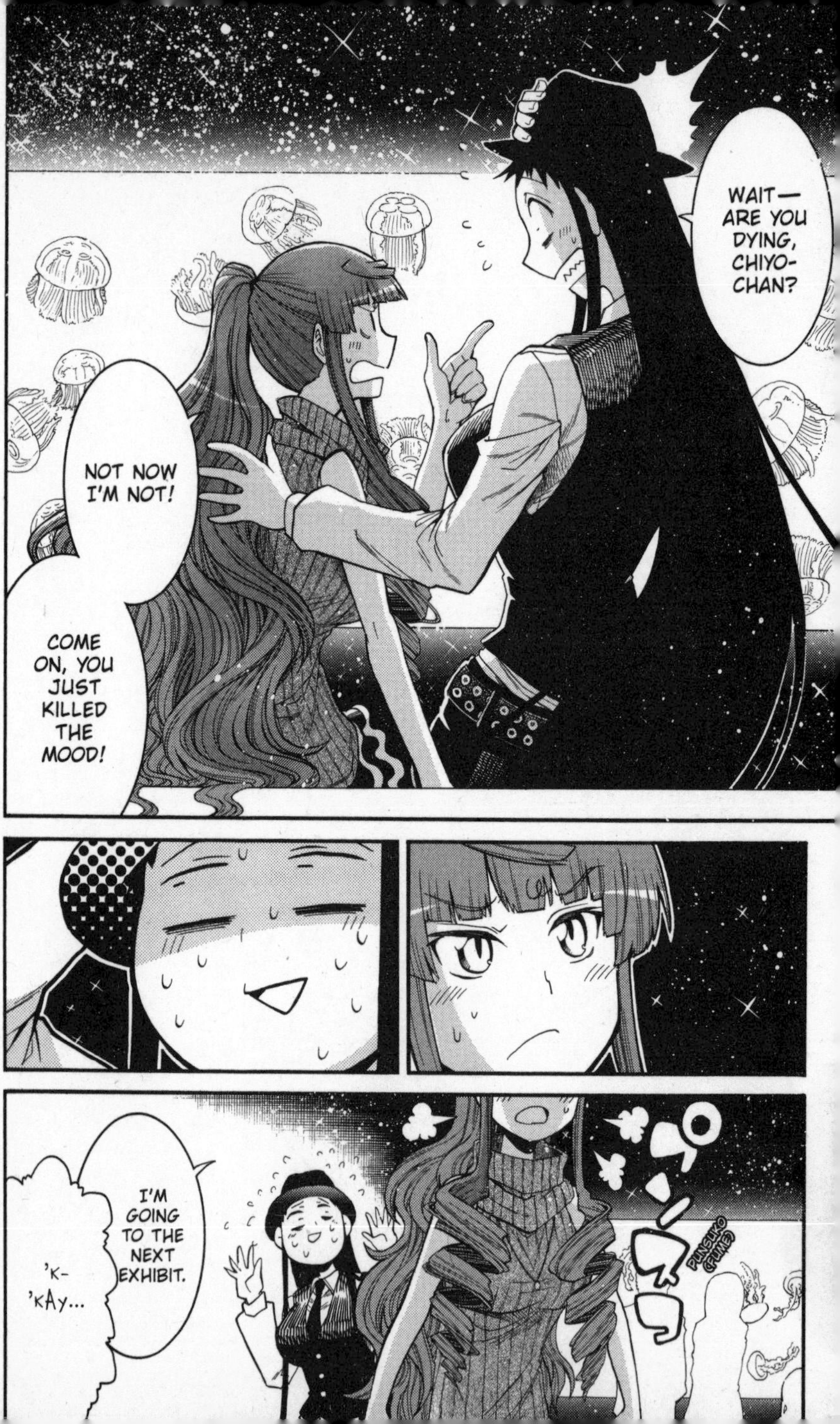
WAIT— ARE YOU DYING, CHIYO-CHAN?
NOT NOW I'M NOT!
COME ON, YOU JUST KILLED THE MOOD!
PUNSUKO (FUME)
I'M GOING TO THE NEXT EXHIBIT.
'K-'KAY...

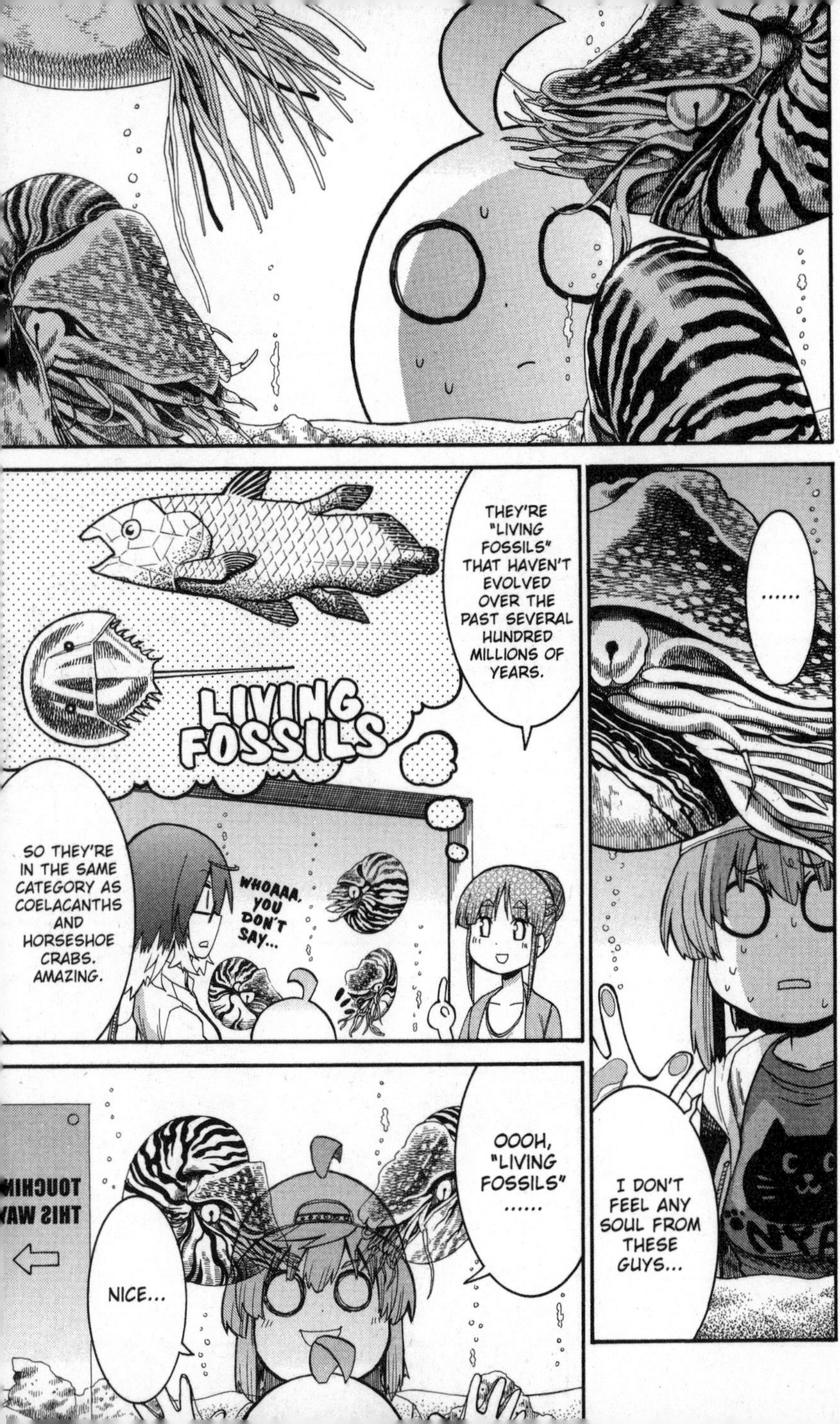
......
I DON'T FEEL ANY SOUL FROM THESE GUYS...
THEY'RE "LIVING FOSSILS" THAT HAVEN'T EVOLVED OVER THE PAST SEVERAL HUNDRED MILLIONS OF YEARS.
LIVING FOSSILS
WHOAAA, YOU DON'T SAY...
SO THEY'RE IN THE SAME CATEGORY AS COELACANTHS AND HORSESHOE CRABS. AMAZING.
OOOH, "LIVING FOSSILS" ......
NICE...

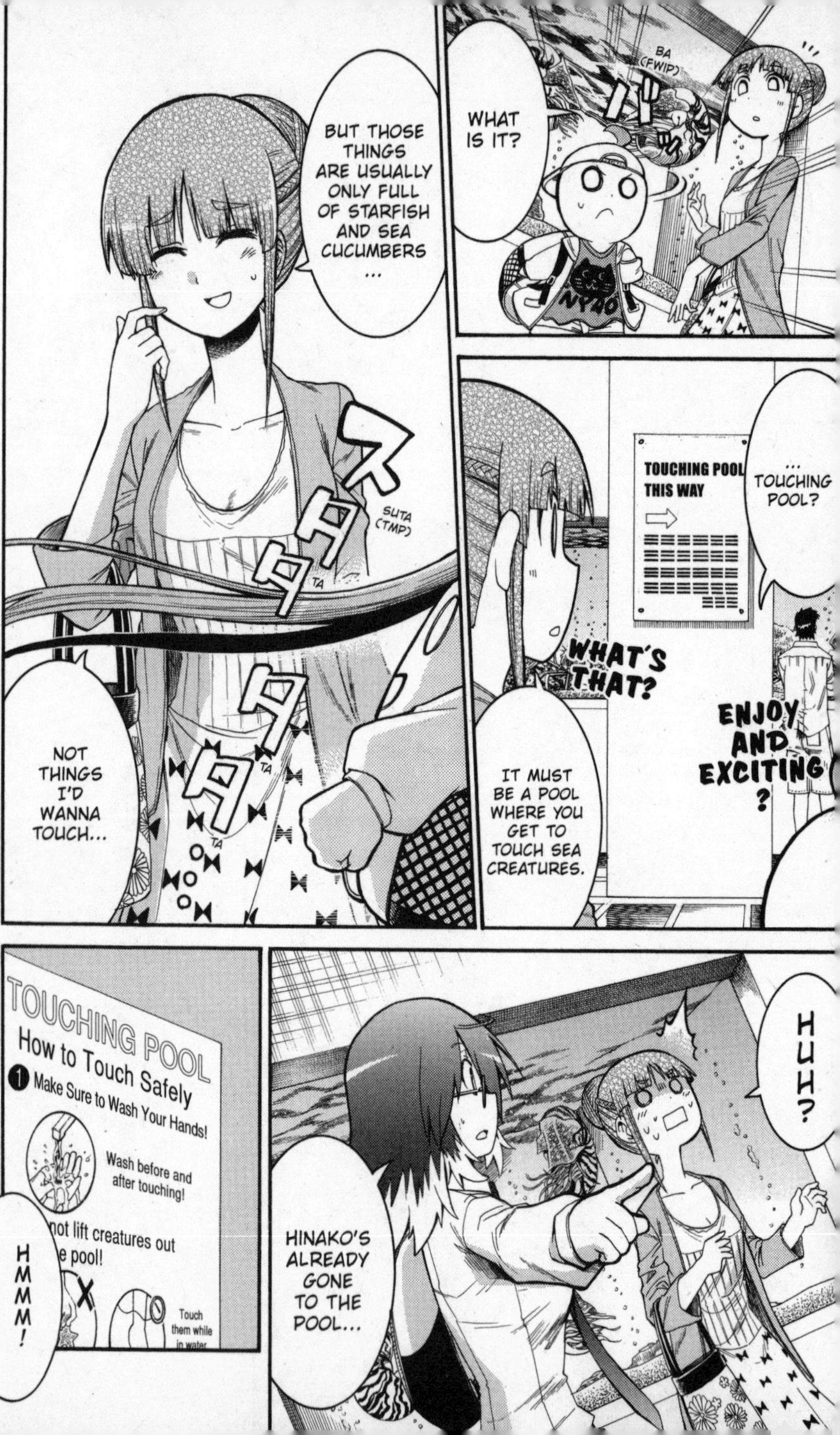
BA (FWIP)
WHAT IS IT?
... TOUCHING POOL?
TOUCHING POOL THIS WAY
WHAT'S THAT?
ENJOY AND EXCITING?
IT MUST BE A POOL WHERE YOU GET TO TOUCH SEA CREATURES.
BUT THOSE THINGS ARE USUALLY ONLY FULL OF STARFISH AND SEA CUCUMBERS ...
SUTA (TMP)
NOT THINGS I'D WANNA TOUCH...
HUH?
HINAKO'S ALREADY GONE TO THE POOL...
TOUCHING POOL
How to Touch Safely
1 Make Sure to Wash Your Hands!
Wash before and after touching!
not lift creatures out
e pool!
Touch them while in water
HMMM!

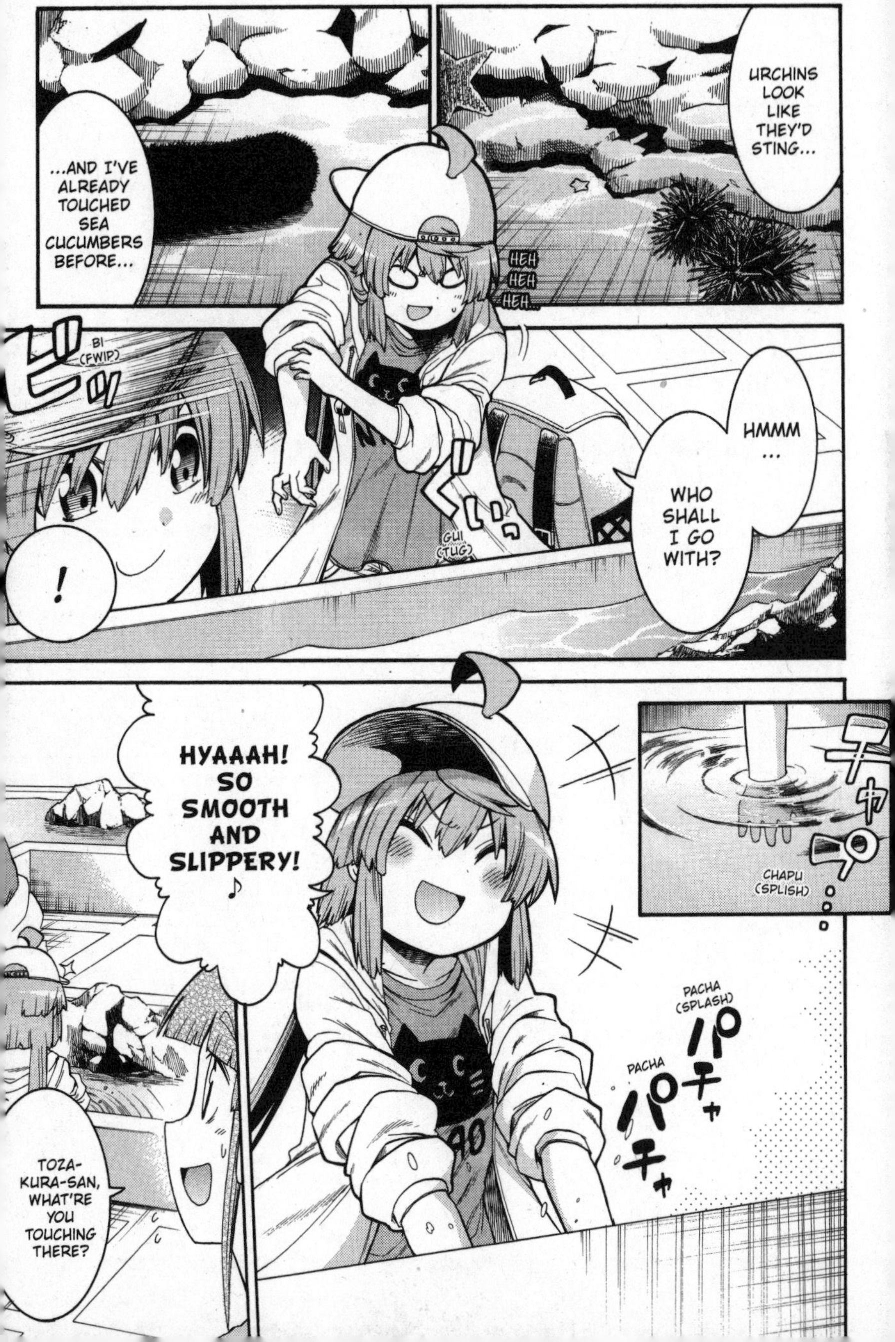
URCHINS LOOK LIKE THEY'D STING...
...AND I'VE ALREADY TOUCHED SEA CUCUMBERS BEFORE...
HEH HEH HEH...
HMMM... WHO SHALL I GO WITH?
GUI (TUG)
BI (FWIP)
!
CHAPU (SPLISH)
HYAAAH! SO SMOOTH AND SLIPPERY! ♪
PACHA (SPLASH)
PACHA
TOZA-KURA-SAN, WHAT'RE YOU TOUCHING THERE?

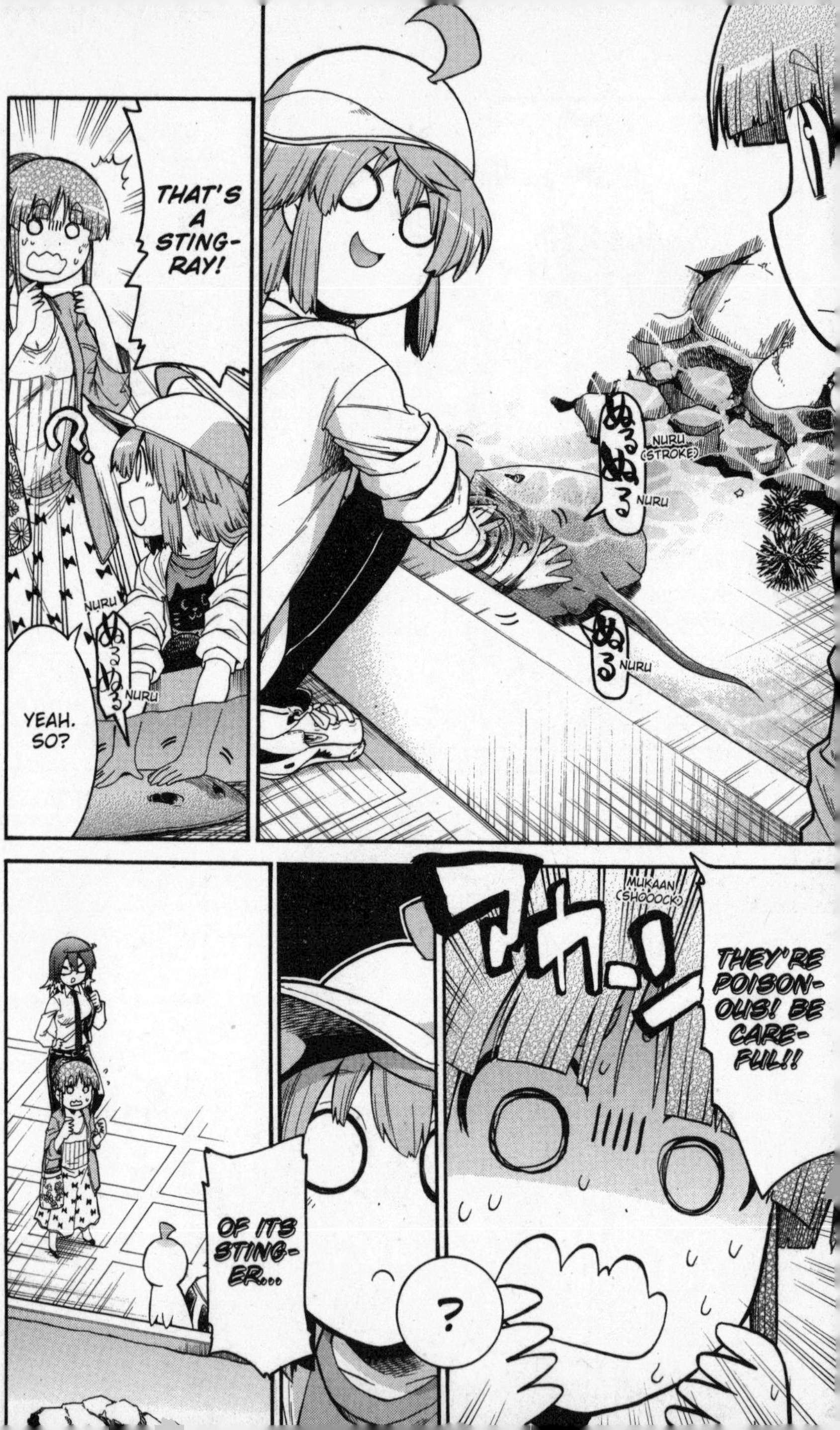

NURU (STROKE)
NURU
NURU
THAT'S A STING-RAY!
NURU
NURU
YEAH. SO?
MUKAAN (SHOOOCK)
THEY'RE POISON-OUS! BE CARE-FUL!!
?
OF ITS STING-ER...

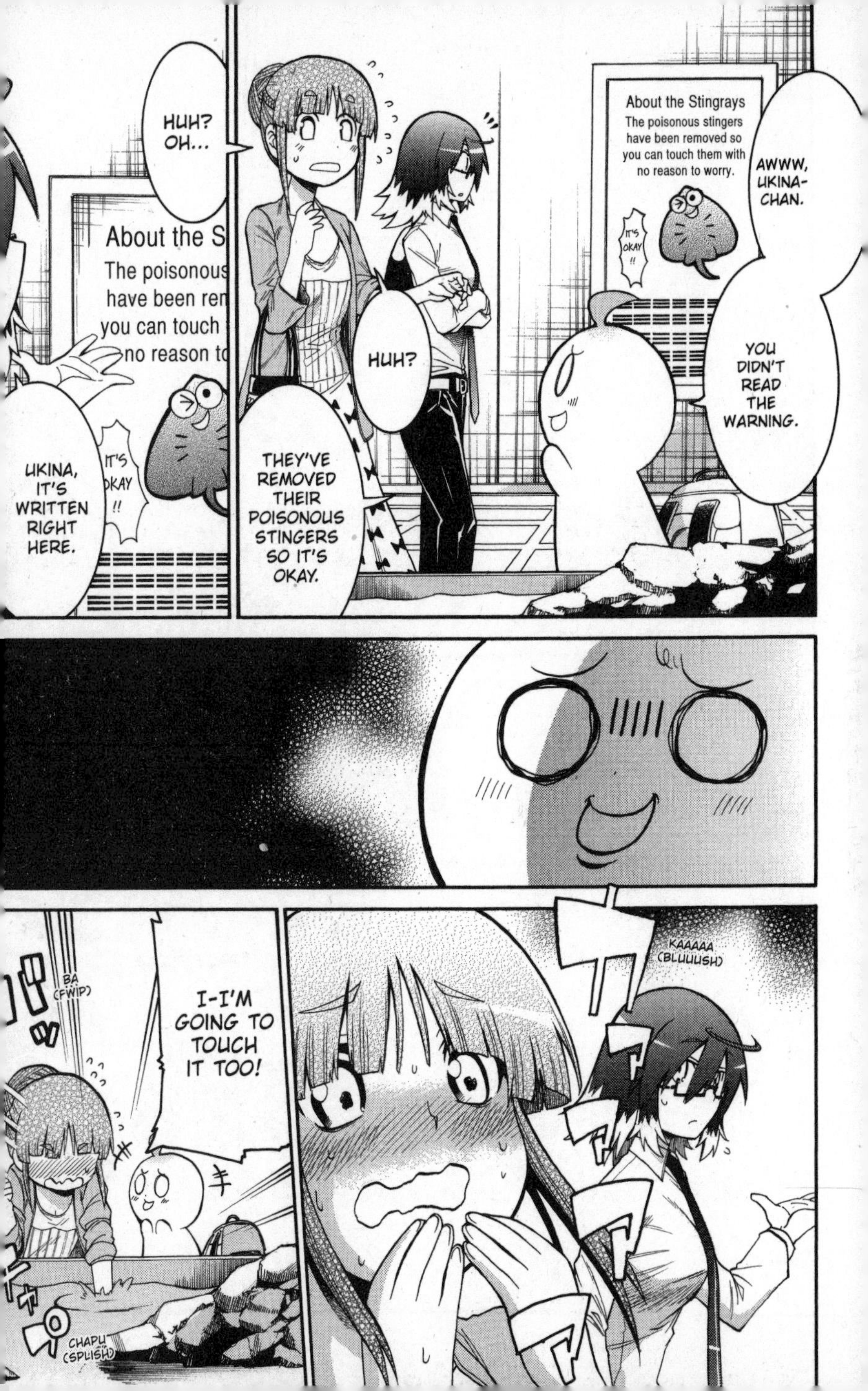
AWWW, UKINA-CHAN.
About the Stingrays
The poisonous stingers have been removed so you can touch them with no reason to worry.
IT'S OKAY !!
YOU DIDN'T READ THE WARNING.
HUH?
THEY'VE REMOVED THEIR POISONOUS STINGERS SO IT'S OKAY.
HUH? OH...
About the S
The poisonous
have been rem
you can touch
no reason to
UKINA, IT'S WRITTEN RIGHT HERE.
IT'S OKAY !!
KAAAAA (BLUUUSH)
I-I'M GOING TO TOUCH IT TOO!
BA (FWIP)
CHAPU (SPLISH)

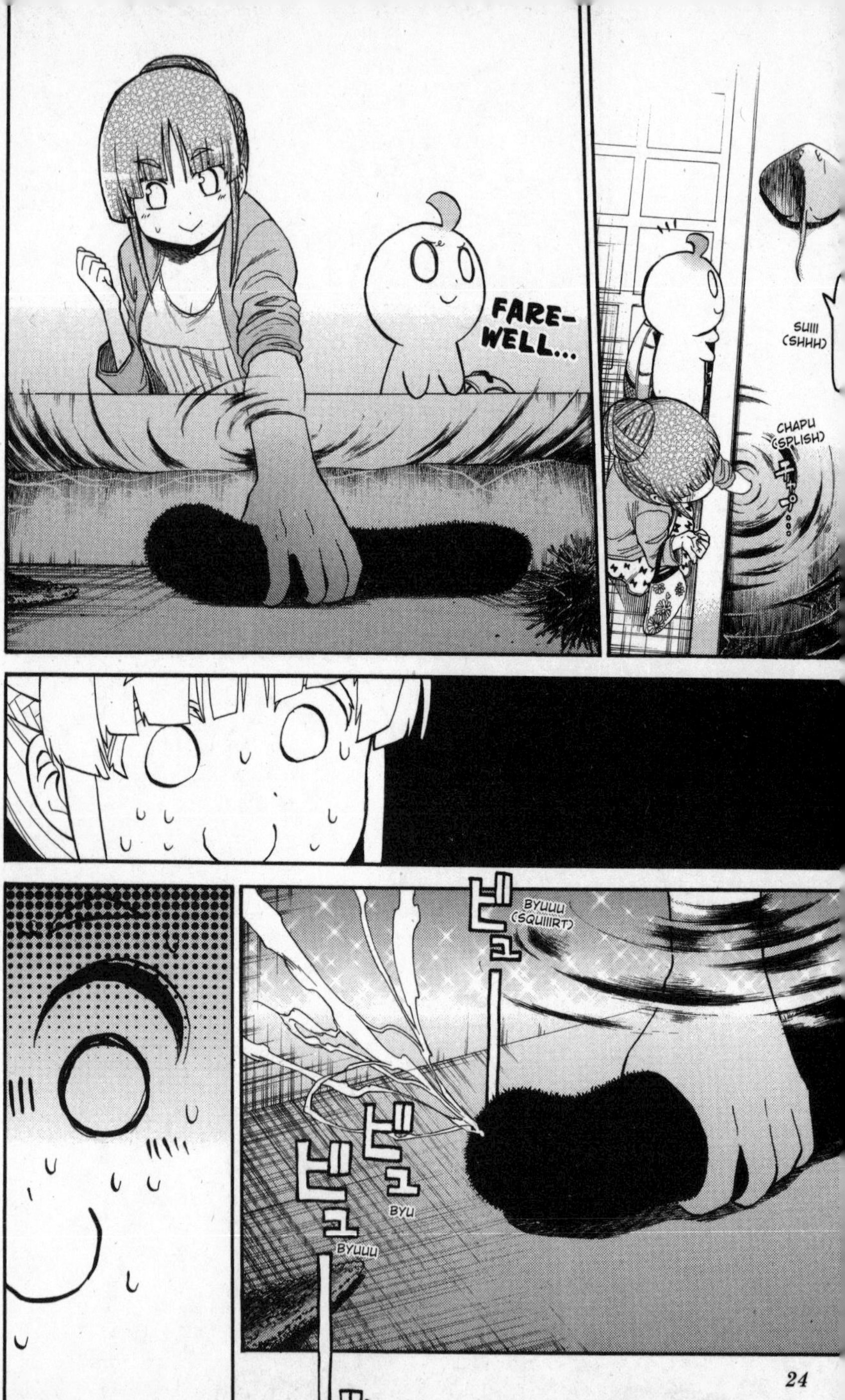
SUIII (SHHH)
CHAPU (SPLISH)
FARE-WELL...
BYUUU (SQUIIIRT)
BYU
BYUUU

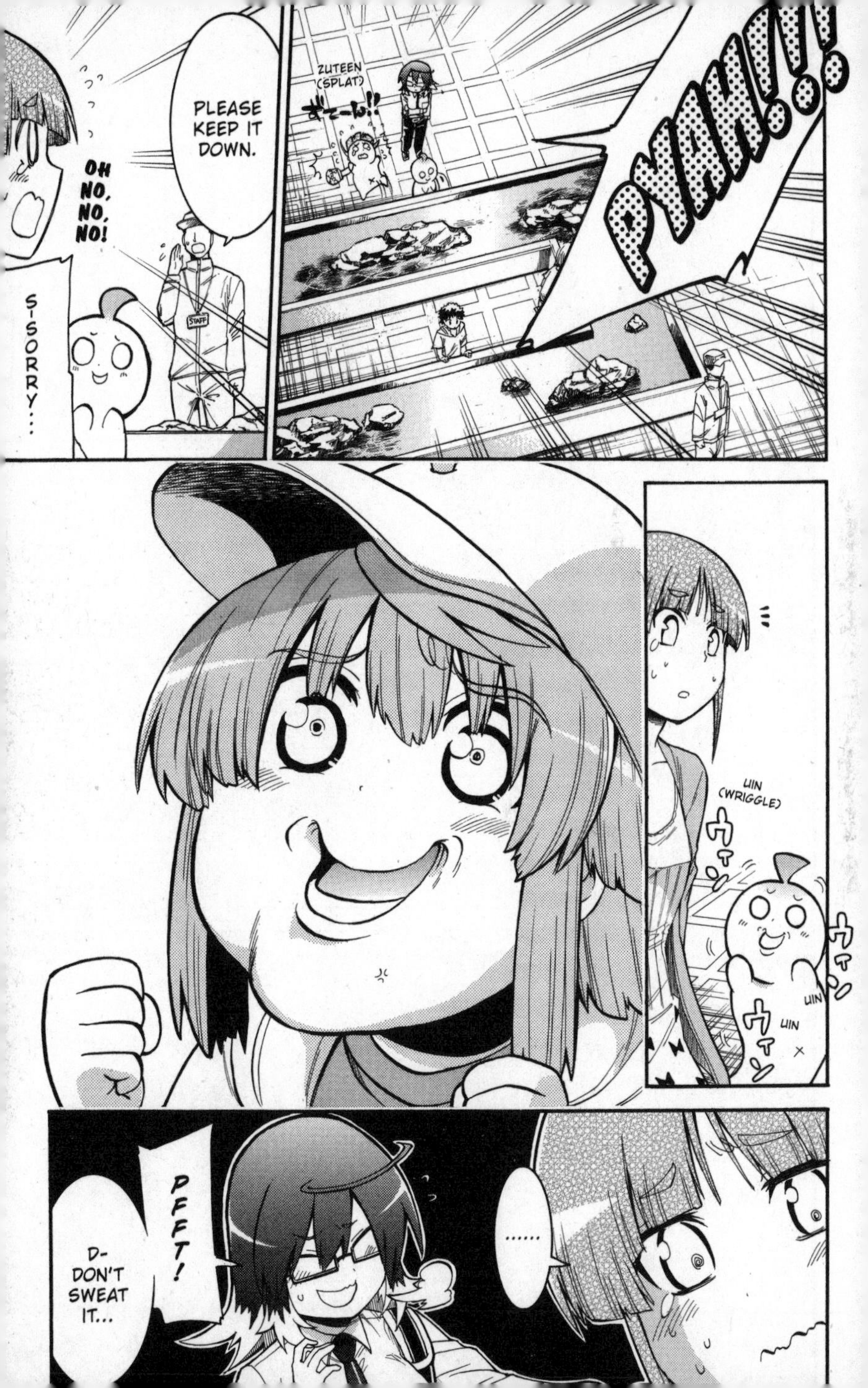
PYAH!?!
ZUTEEN (SPLAT)
PLEASE KEEP IT DOWN.
OH NO, NO, NO!
STAFF
S-SORRY...
UIN (WRIGGLE)
UIN
UIN
......
PFFT!
D-DON'T SWEAT IT...

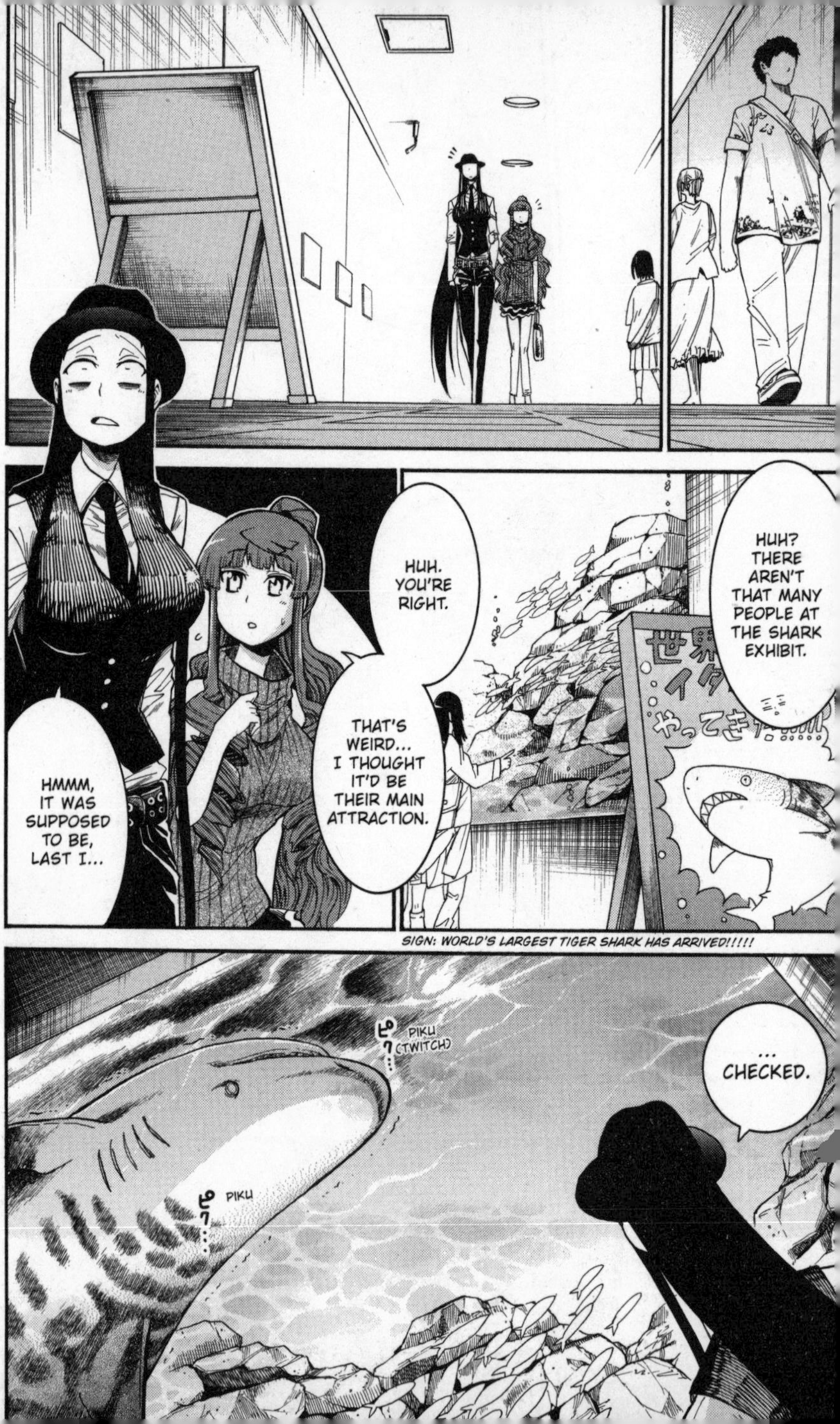

HUH? THERE AREN'T THAT MANY PEOPLE AT THE SHARK EXHIBIT.
SIGN: WORLD'S LARGEST TIGER SHARK HAS ARRIVED!!!!!
HUH. YOU'RE RIGHT.
THAT'S WEIRD... I THOUGHT IT'D BE THEIR MAIN ATTRACTION.
HMMM, IT WAS SUPPOSED TO BE, LAST I...
... CHECKED.
ピク… PIKU (TWITCH)
ピク… PIKU

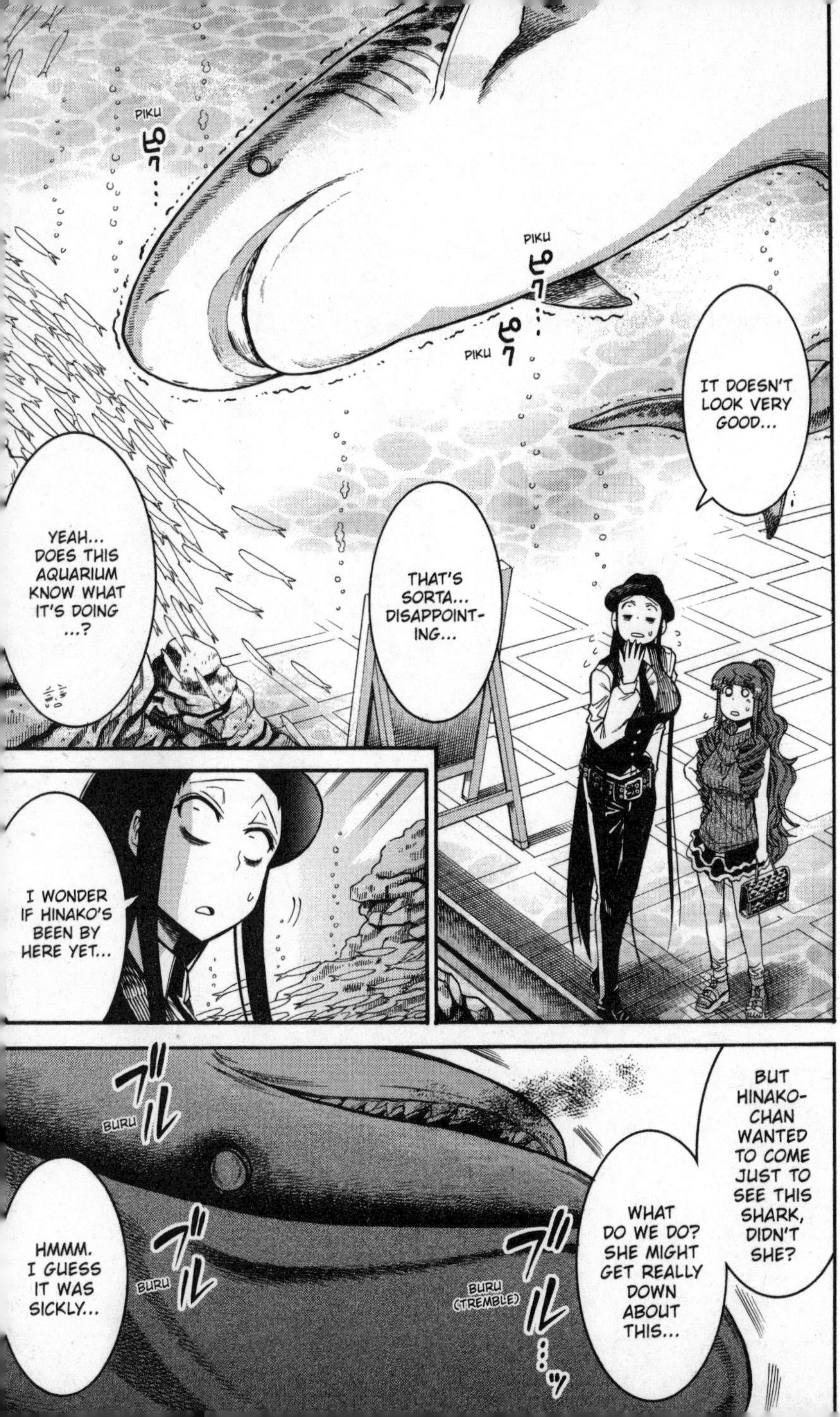
PIKU
PIKU
PIKU
IT DOESN'T LOOK VERY GOOD...
THAT'S SORTA... DISAPPOINTING...
YEAH... DOES THIS AQUARIUM KNOW WHAT IT'S DOING ...?
I WONDER IF HINAKO'S BEEN BY HERE YET...
BUT HINAKO-CHAN WANTED TO COME JUST TO SEE THIS SHARK, DIDN'T SHE?
WHAT DO WE DO? SHE MIGHT GET REALLY DOWN ABOUT THIS...
BURU (TREMBLE)
BURU
HMMM. I GUESS IT WAS SICKLY...
BURU

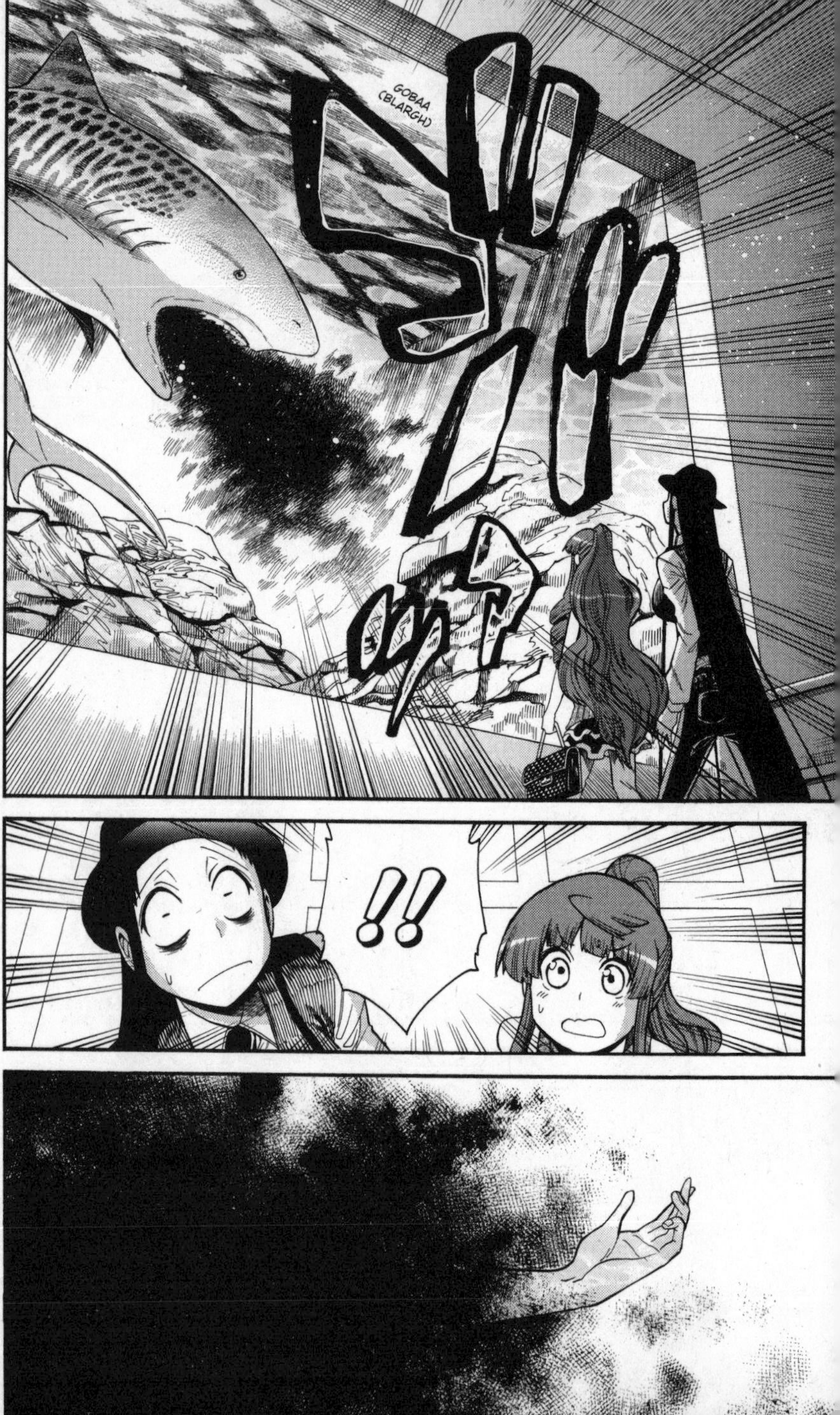
GOBAA
(BLARGH)
!!

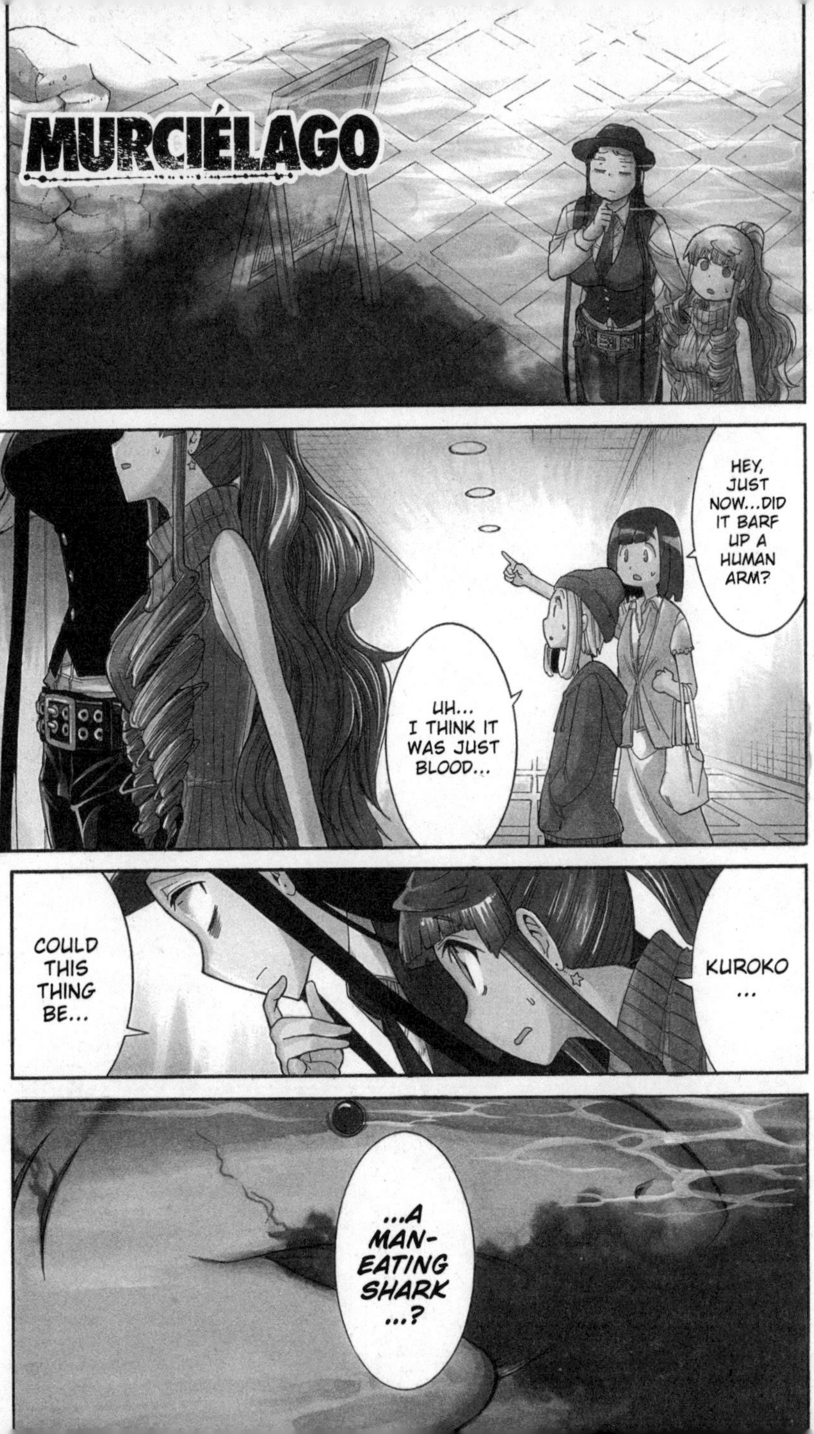
MURCIÉLAGO
HEY, JUST NOW...DID IT BARF UP A HUMAN ARM?
UH... I THINK IT WAS JUST BLOOD...
KUROKO...
COULD THIS THING BE...
...A MAN-EATING SHARK...?

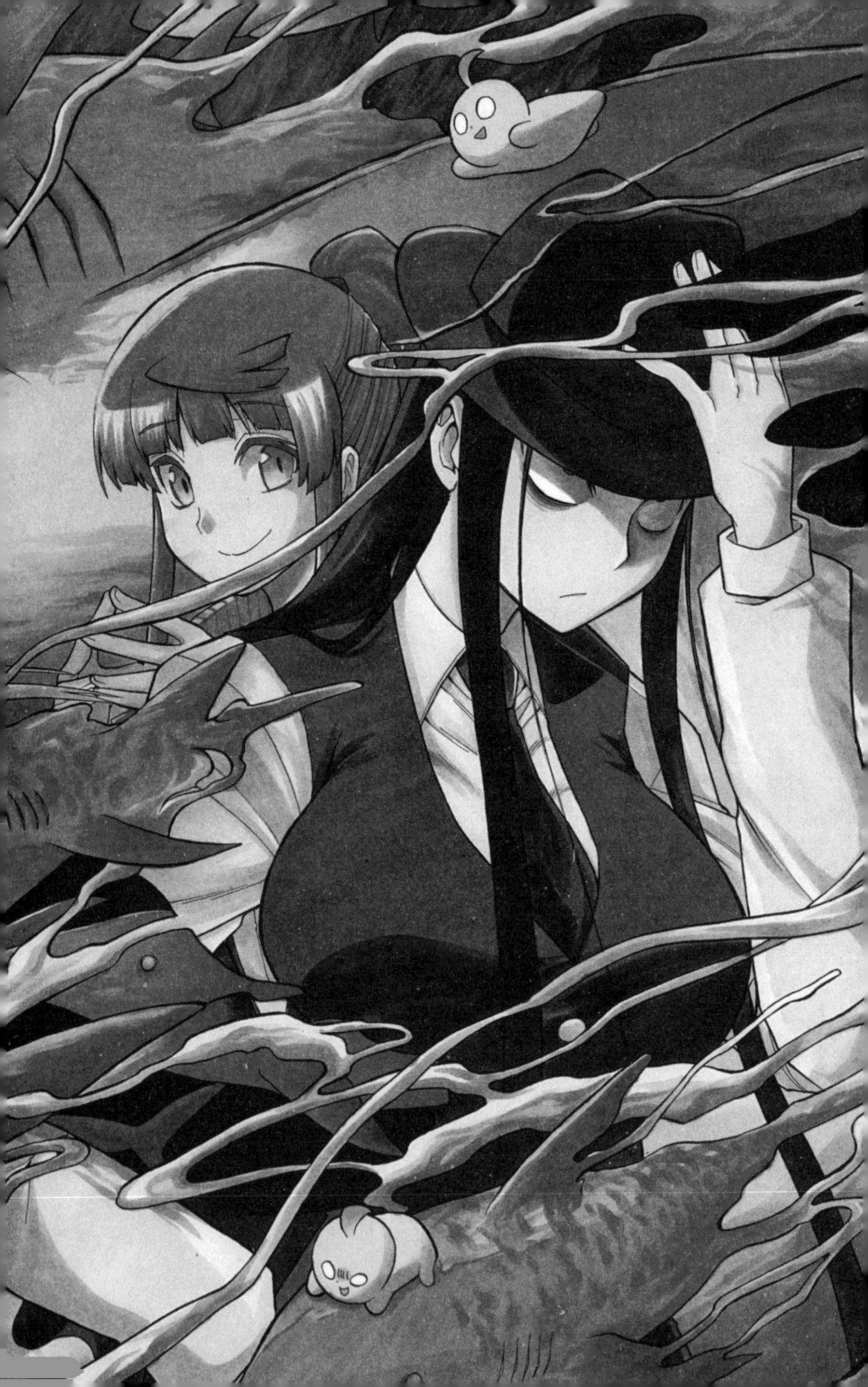

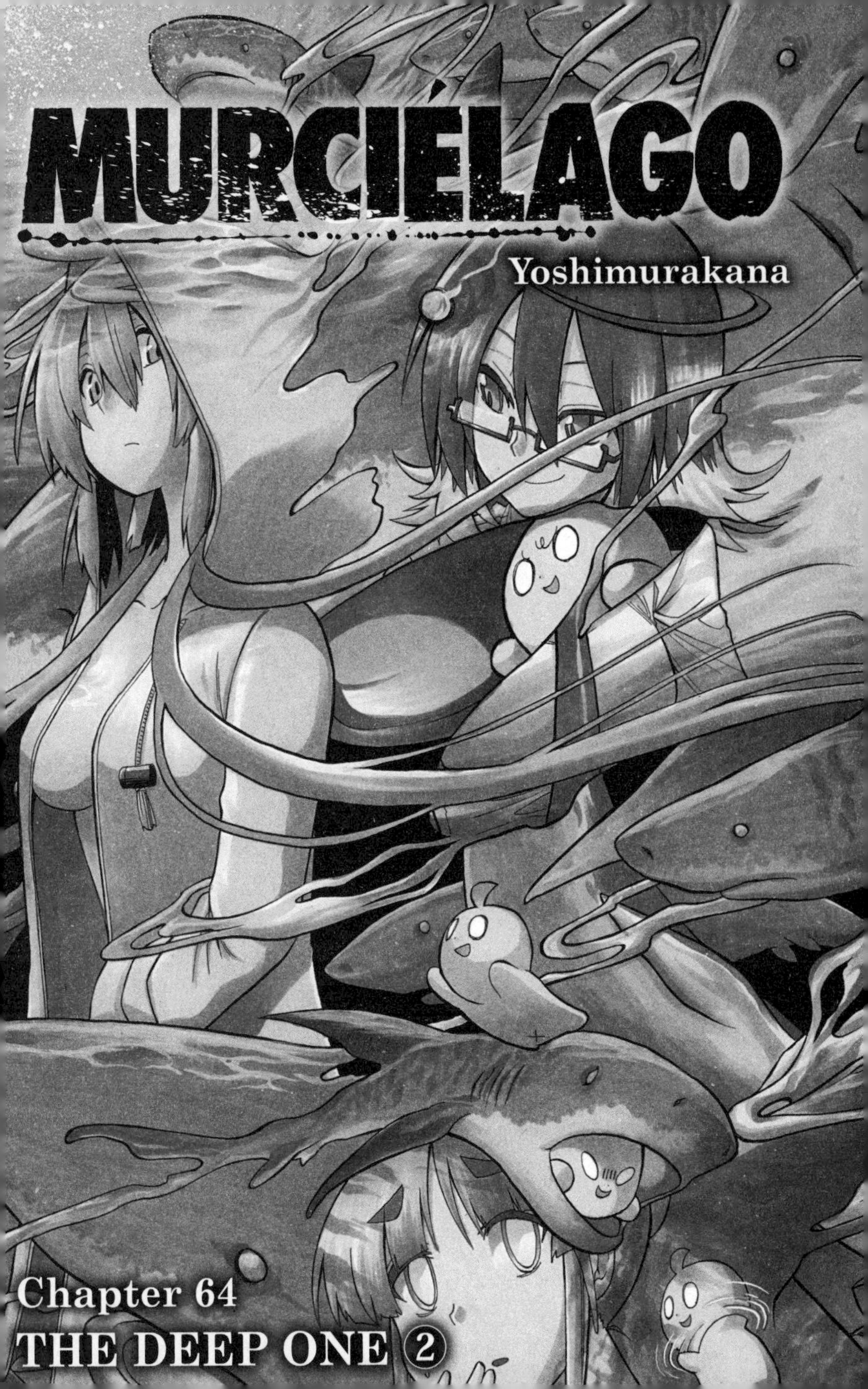
MURCIÉLAGO
Yoshimurakana
Chapter 64
THE DEEP ONE ②

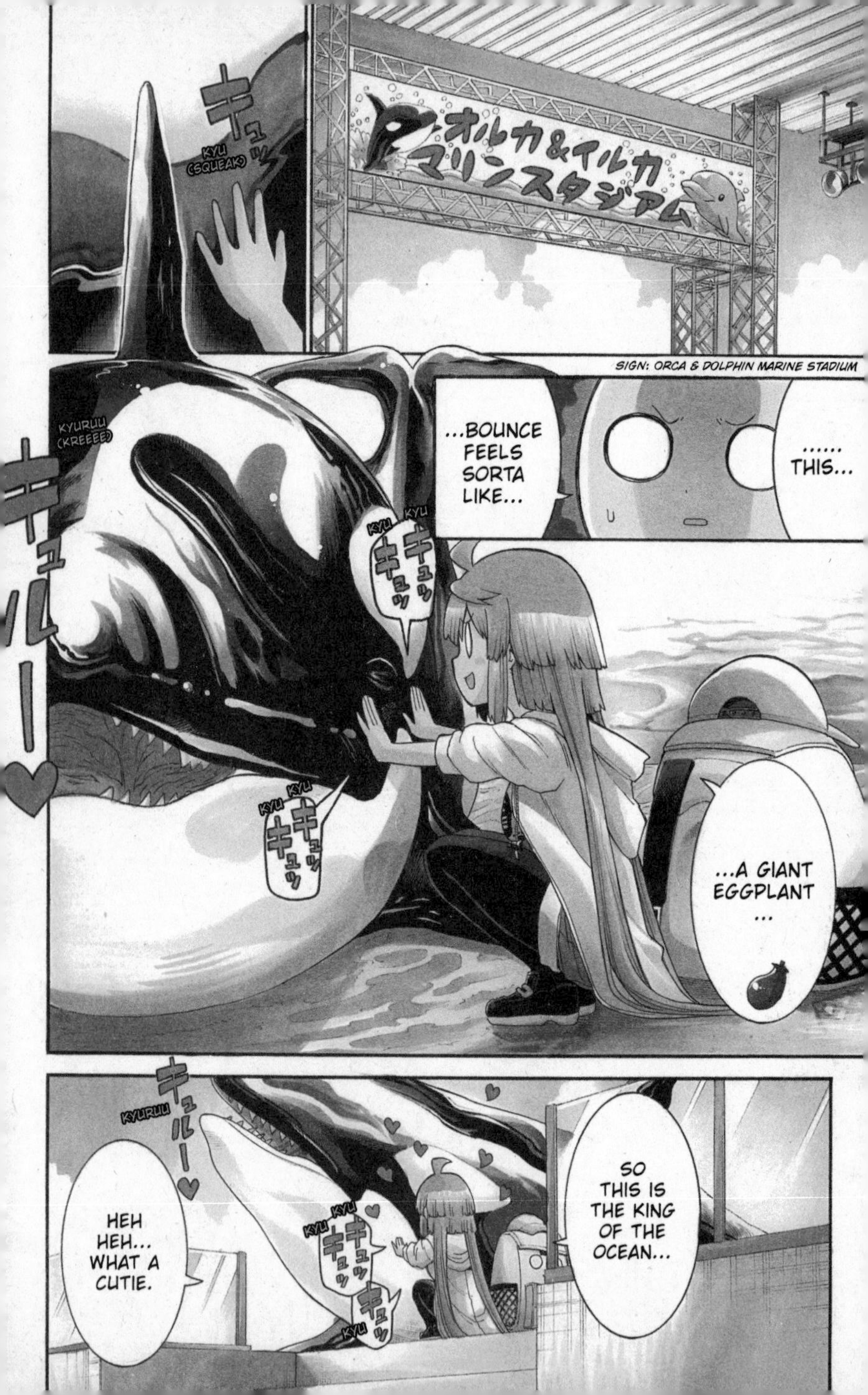
オルカ&イルカマリンスタジアム
キュッ
KYU (SQUEAK)
SIGN: ORCA & DOLPHIN MARINE STADIUM
...... THIS...
...BOUNCE FEELS SORTA LIKE...
...A GIANT EGGPLANT ...
キュッキュッ
KYU KYU
キュッキュッ
KYU KYU
キュルー♥
KYURUU (KREEEE)
SO THIS IS THE KING OF THE OCEAN...
キュッキュッ
KYU KYU
キュッ
KYU
HEH HEH... WHAT A CUTIE.
キュルー♥
KYURUU

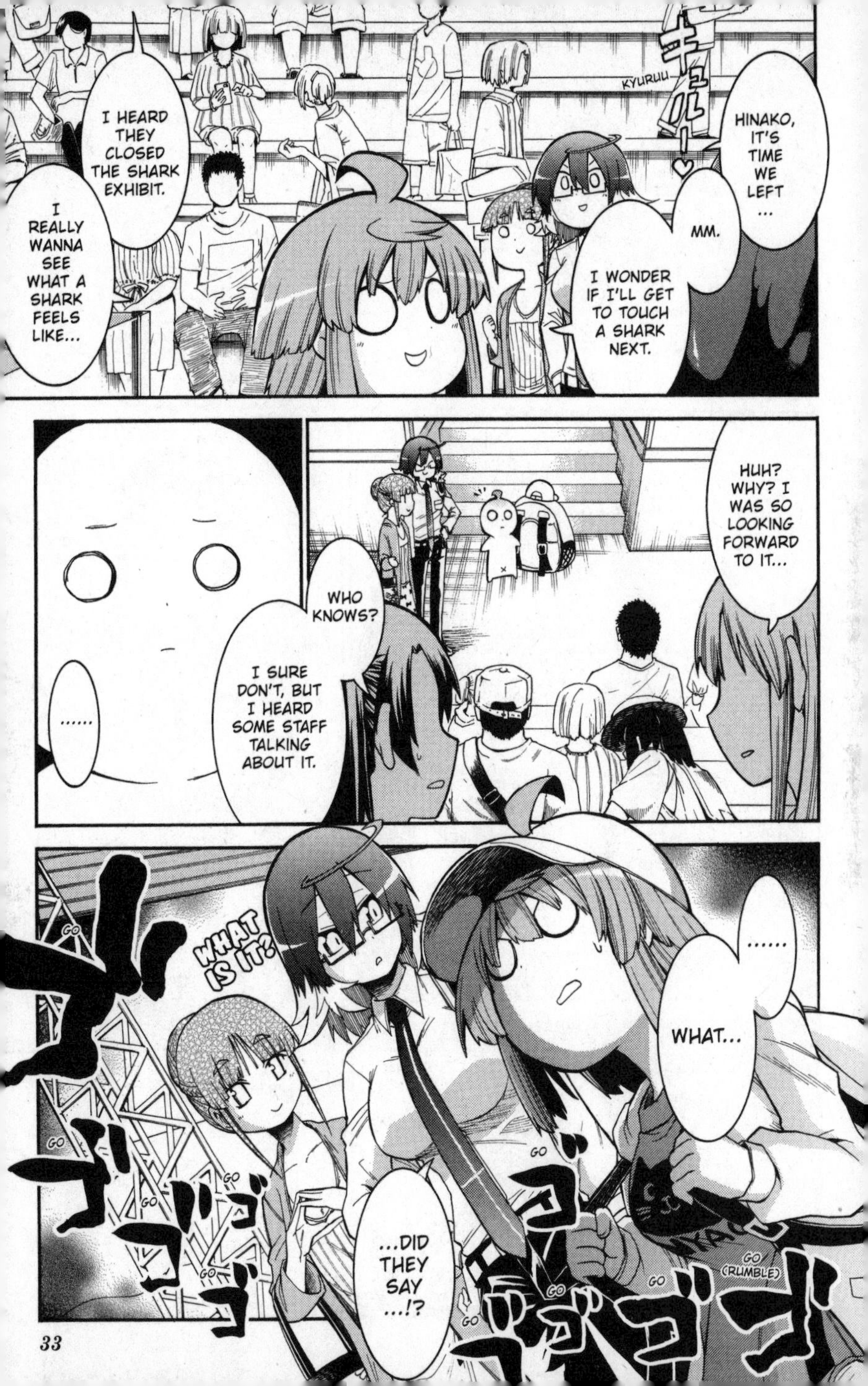
KYURUU
HINAKO, IT'S TIME WE LEFT...
MM.
I WONDER IF I'LL GET TO TOUCH A SHARK NEXT.
I HEARD THEY CLOSED THE SHARK EXHIBIT.
I REALLY WANNA SEE WHAT A SHARK FEELS LIKE...
HUH? WHY? I WAS SO LOOKING FORWARD TO IT...
WHO KNOWS?
I SURE DON'T, BUT I HEARD SOME STAFF TALKING ABOUT IT.
......
......
WHAT...
WHAT IS IT?
...DID THEY SAY ...!?
GO GO GO GO GO GO GO GO GO GO (RUMBLE)

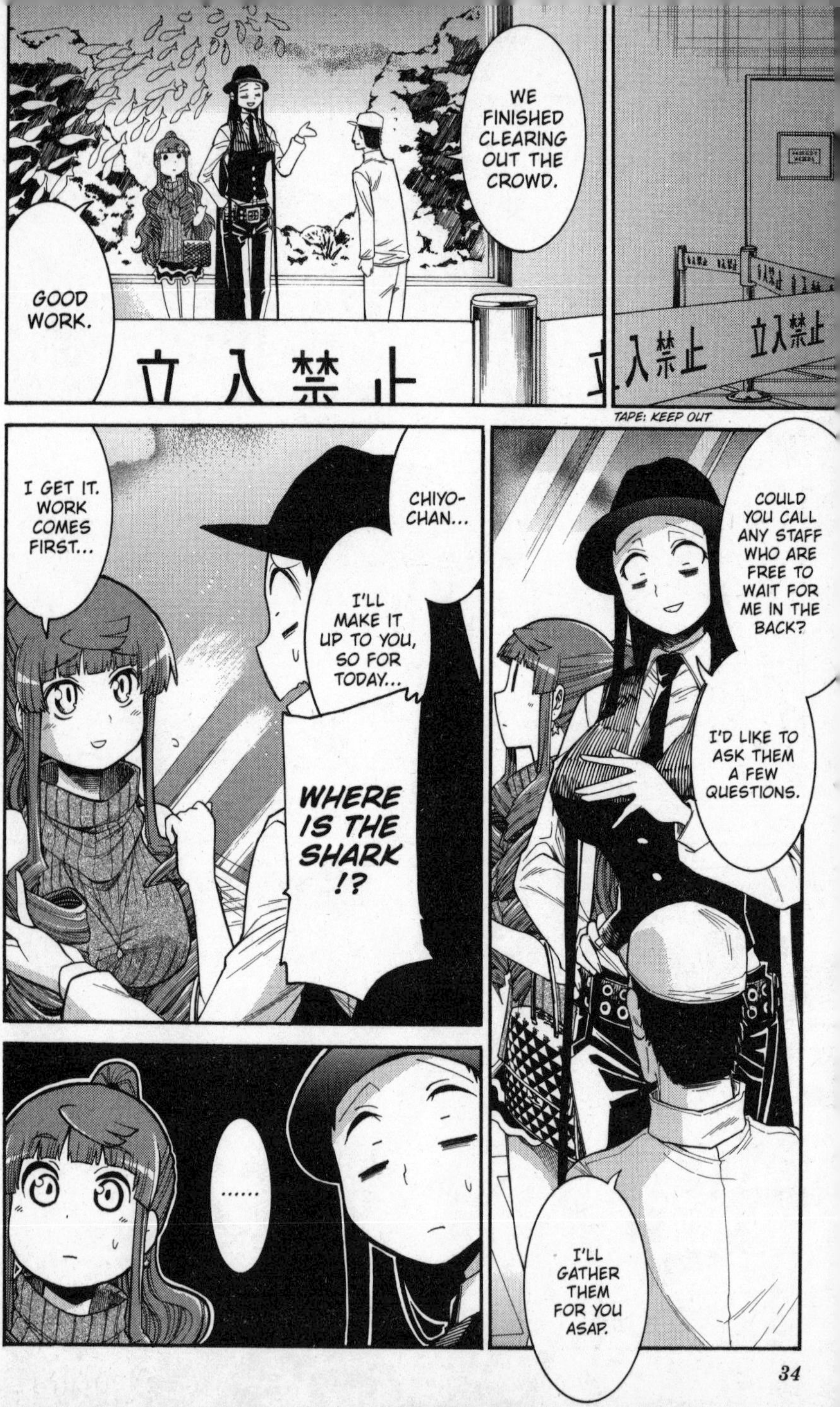
立入禁止
立入禁止
TAPE: KEEP OUT
WE FINISHED CLEARING OUT THE CROWD.
GOOD WORK.
立入禁止
COULD YOU CALL ANY STAFF WHO ARE FREE TO WAIT FOR ME IN THE BACK?
I'D LIKE TO ASK THEM A FEW QUESTIONS.
I'LL GATHER THEM FOR YOU ASAP.
CHIYO-CHAN...
I'LL MAKE IT UP TO YOU, SO FOR TODAY...
I GET IT. WORK COMES FIRST...
WHERE IS THE SHARK !?
......

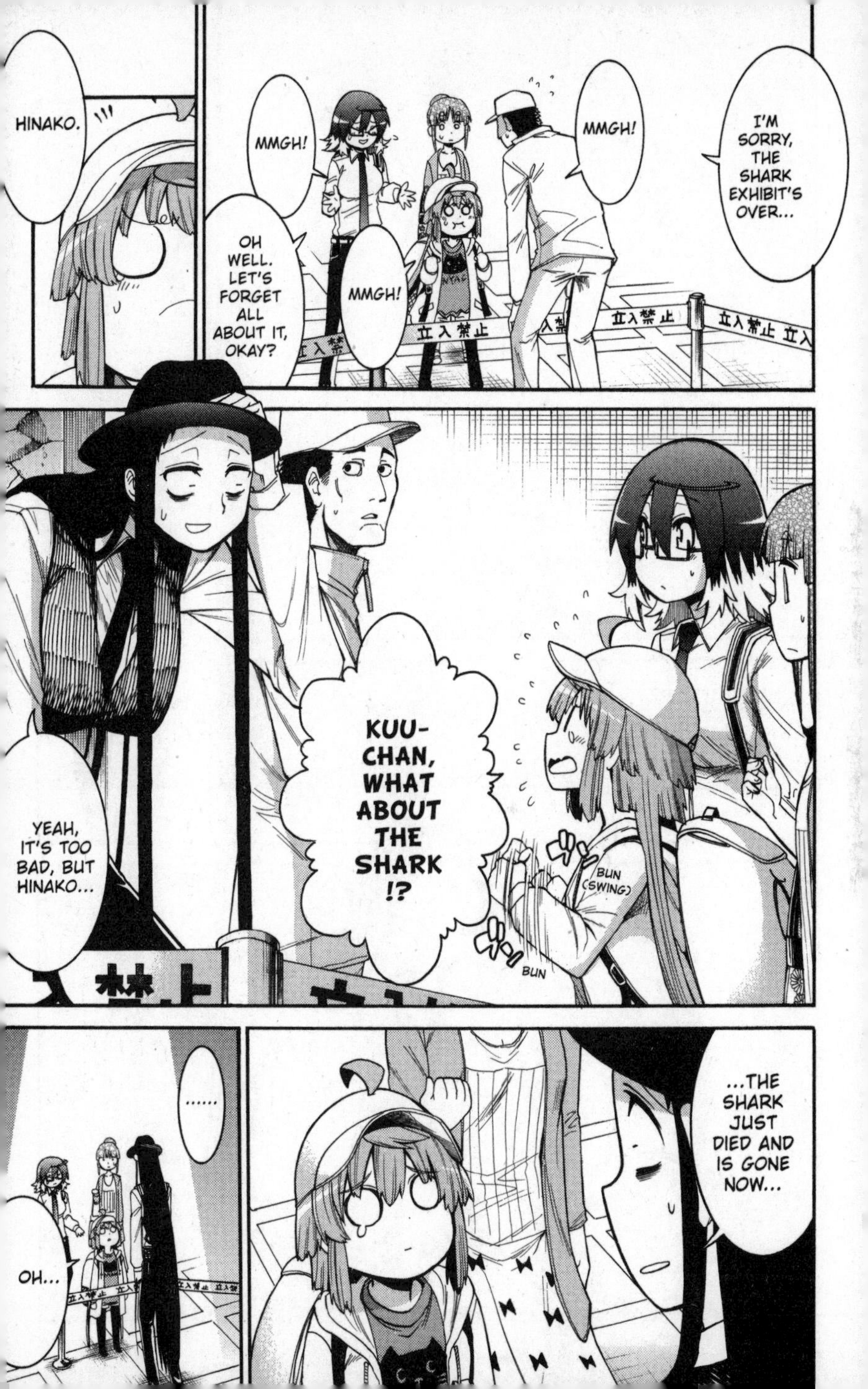
I'M SORRY, THE SHARK EXHIBIT'S OVER...
MMGH!
MMGH!
MMGH!
OH WELL. LET'S FORGET ALL ABOUT IT, OKAY?
HINAKO.
KUU-CHAN, WHAT ABOUT THE SHARK!?
BUN (SWING)
BUN
YEAH, IT'S TOO BAD, BUT HINAKO...
...THE SHARK JUST DIED AND IS GONE NOW...
......
OH...

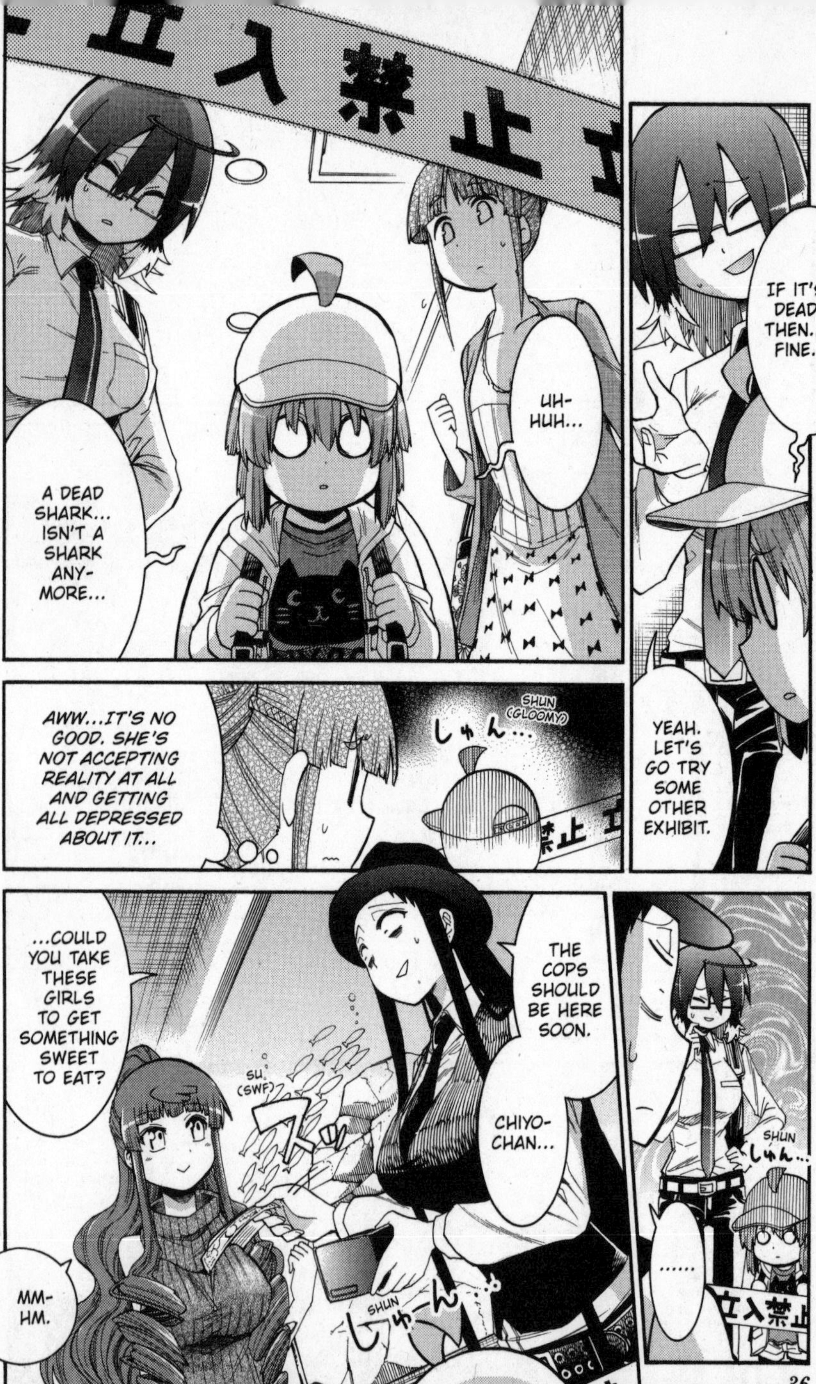
IF IT'S DEAD THEN... FINE.
YEAH. LET'S GO TRY SOME OTHER EXHIBIT.
立入禁止
UH-HUH...
A DEAD SHARK... ISN'T A SHARK ANY-MORE...
SHUN (GLOOMY)
しゅん...
AWW...IT'S NO GOOD. SHE'S NOT ACCEPTING REALITY AT ALL AND GETTING ALL DEPRESSED ABOUT IT...
SHUN
しゅん...
......
立入禁止
THE COPS SHOULD BE HERE SOON.
CHIYO-CHAN...
...COULD YOU TAKE THESE GIRLS TO GET SOMETHING SWEET TO EAT?
SU (SWF)
スッ
MM-HM.
SHUN
しゅーん

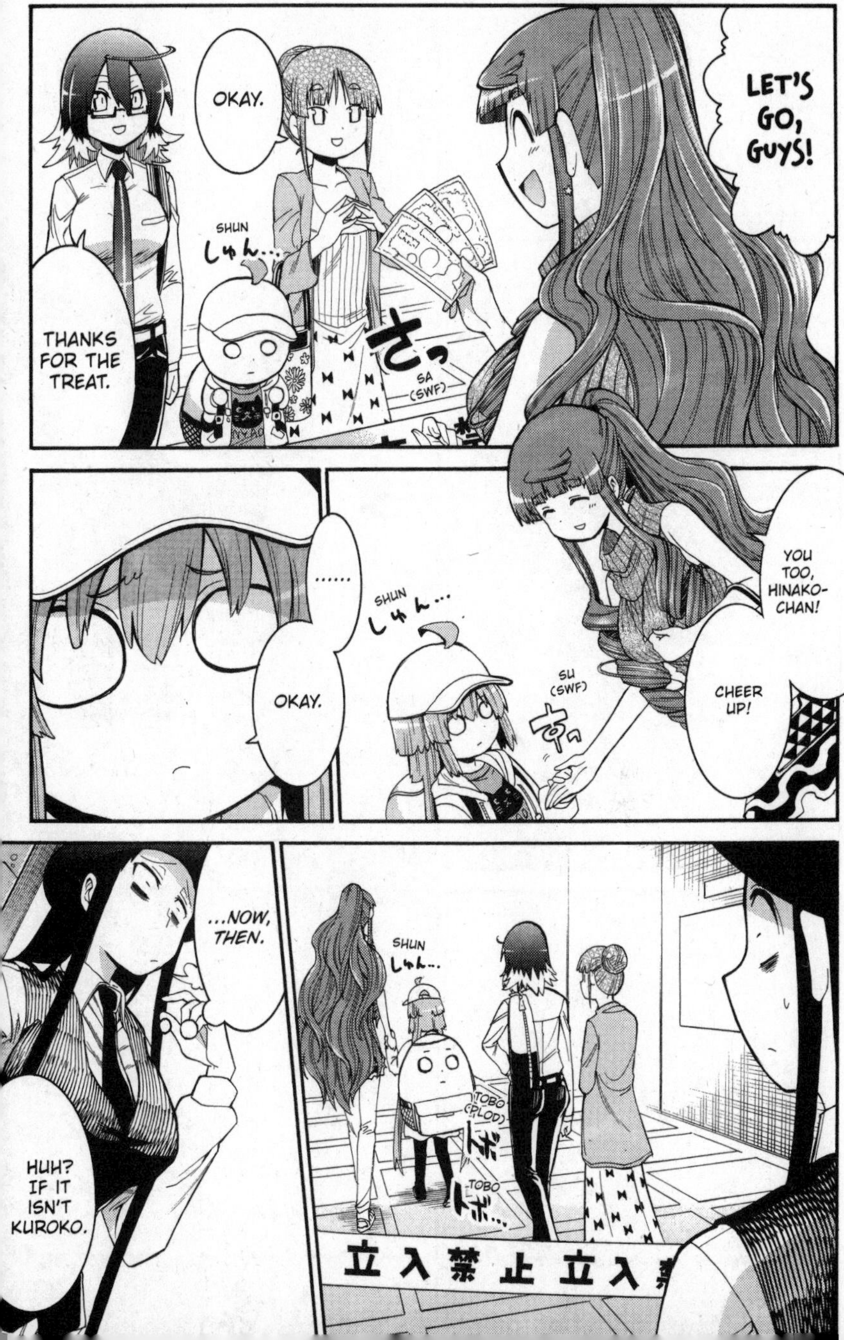
LET'S GO, GUYS!
OKAY.
SHUN
しゅん…
さっ
SA (SWF)
THANKS FOR THE TREAT.
YOU TOO, HINAKO-CHAN!
CHEER UP!
SU (SWF)
すっ
SHUN
しゅん…
OKAY.
……
SHUN
しゅん…
TOBO (PLOD)
トボ
TOBO
トボ…
立入禁止立入
…NOW, THEN.
HUH? IF IT ISN'T KUROKO.

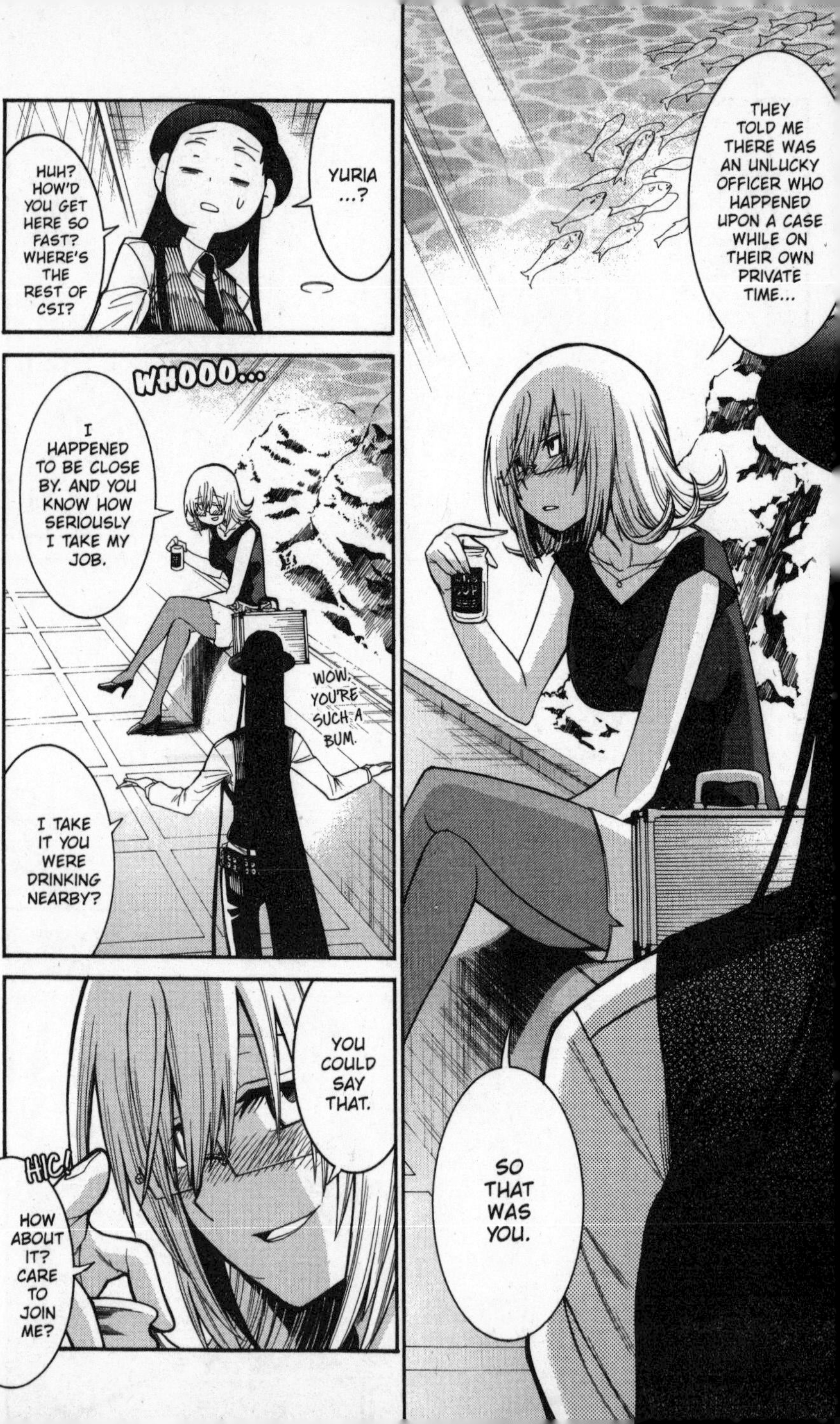
THEY TOLD ME THERE WAS AN UNLUCKY OFFICER WHO HAPPENED UPON A CASE WHILE ON THEIR OWN PRIVATE TIME...
SO THAT WAS YOU.
YURIA ...?
HUH? HOW'D YOU GET HERE SO FAST? WHERE'S THE REST OF CSI?
WHOOO...
I HAPPENED TO BE CLOSE BY. AND YOU KNOW HOW SERIOUSLY I TAKE MY JOB.
WOW, YOU'RE SUCH A BUM.
I TAKE IT YOU WERE DRINKING NEARBY?
YOU COULD SAY THAT.
HIC!
HOW ABOUT IT? CARE TO JOIN ME?

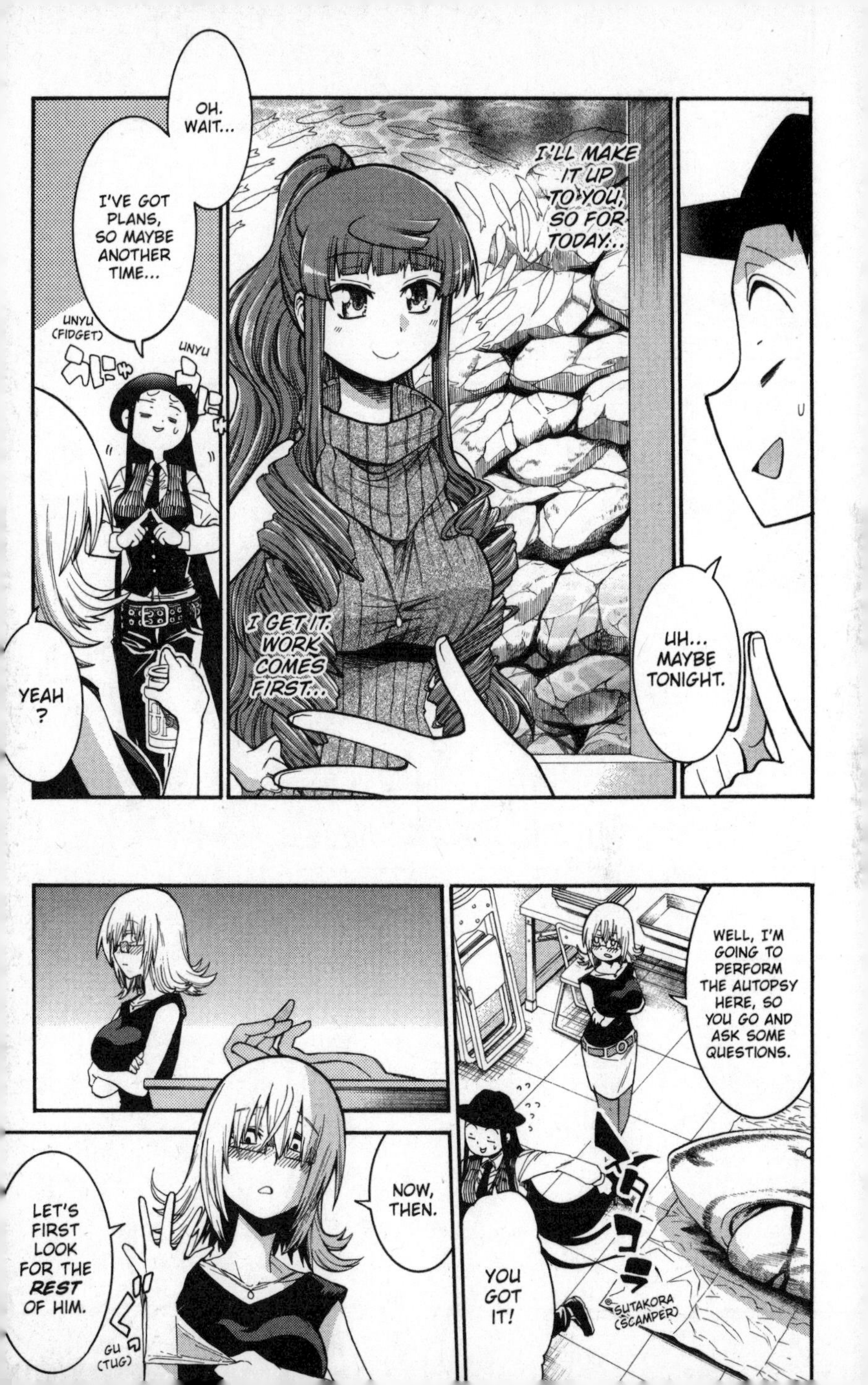
UH... MAYBE TONIGHT.
I'LL MAKE IT UP TO YOU, SO FOR TODAY...
I GET IT. WORK COMES FIRST...
OH. WAIT...
I'VE GOT PLANS, SO MAYBE ANOTHER TIME...
UNYU (FIDGET)
UNYU
YEAH?
WELL, I'M GOING TO PERFORM THE AUTOPSY HERE, SO YOU GO AND ASK SOME QUESTIONS.
YOU GOT IT!
SUTAKORA (SCAMPER)
NOW, THEN.
LET'S FIRST LOOK FOR THE ***REST*** OF HIM.
GU (TUG)

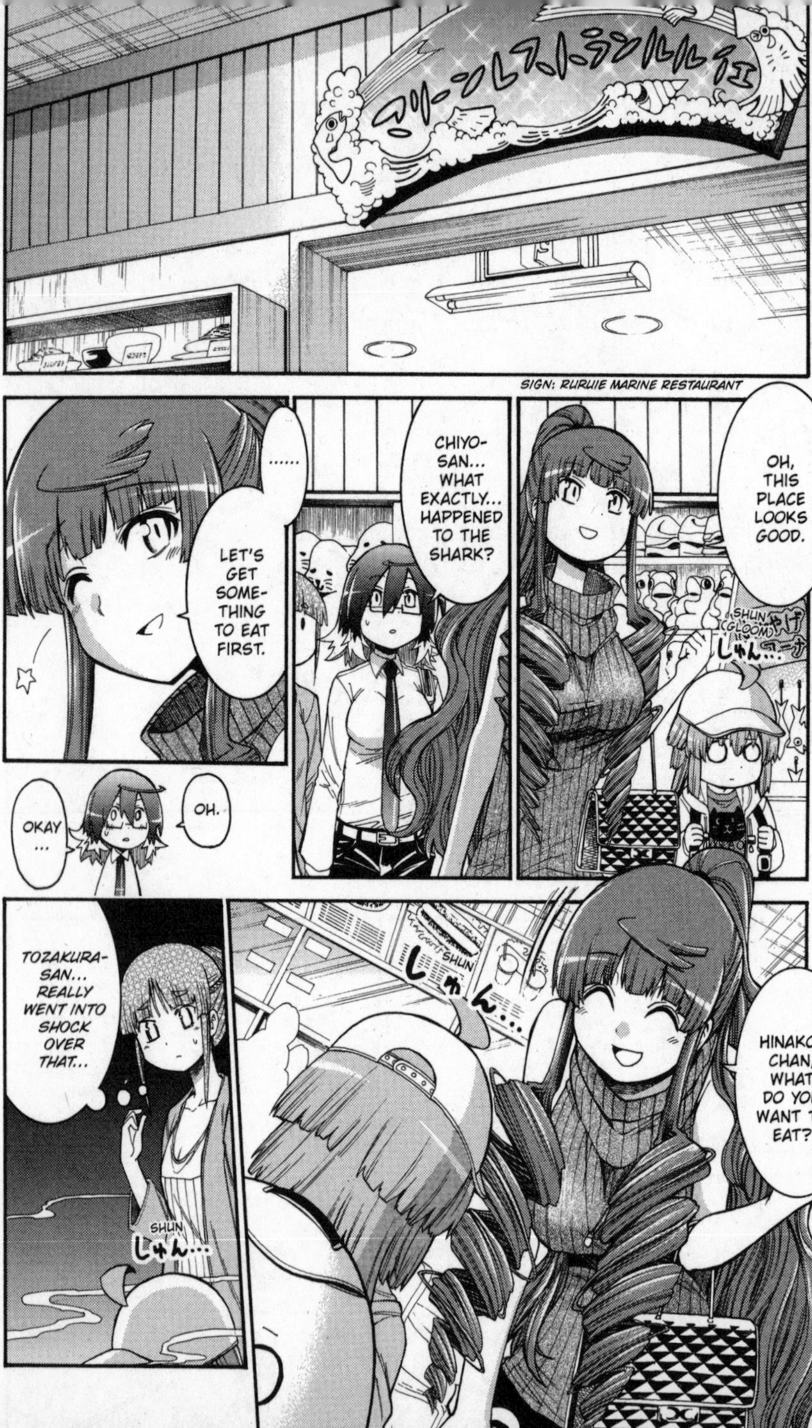
SIGN: RURUIE MARINE RESTAURANT
OH, THIS PLACE LOOKS GOOD.
SHUN (GLOOM)
しゅん…
CHIYO-SAN... WHAT EXACTLY... HAPPENED TO THE SHARK?
......
LET'S GET SOMETHING TO EAT FIRST.
OH.
OKAY...
HINAKO-CHAN, WHAT DO YOU WANT TO EAT?
SHUN
しゅん…
TOZAKURA-SAN... REALLY WENT INTO SHOCK OVER THAT...
SHUN
しゅん…

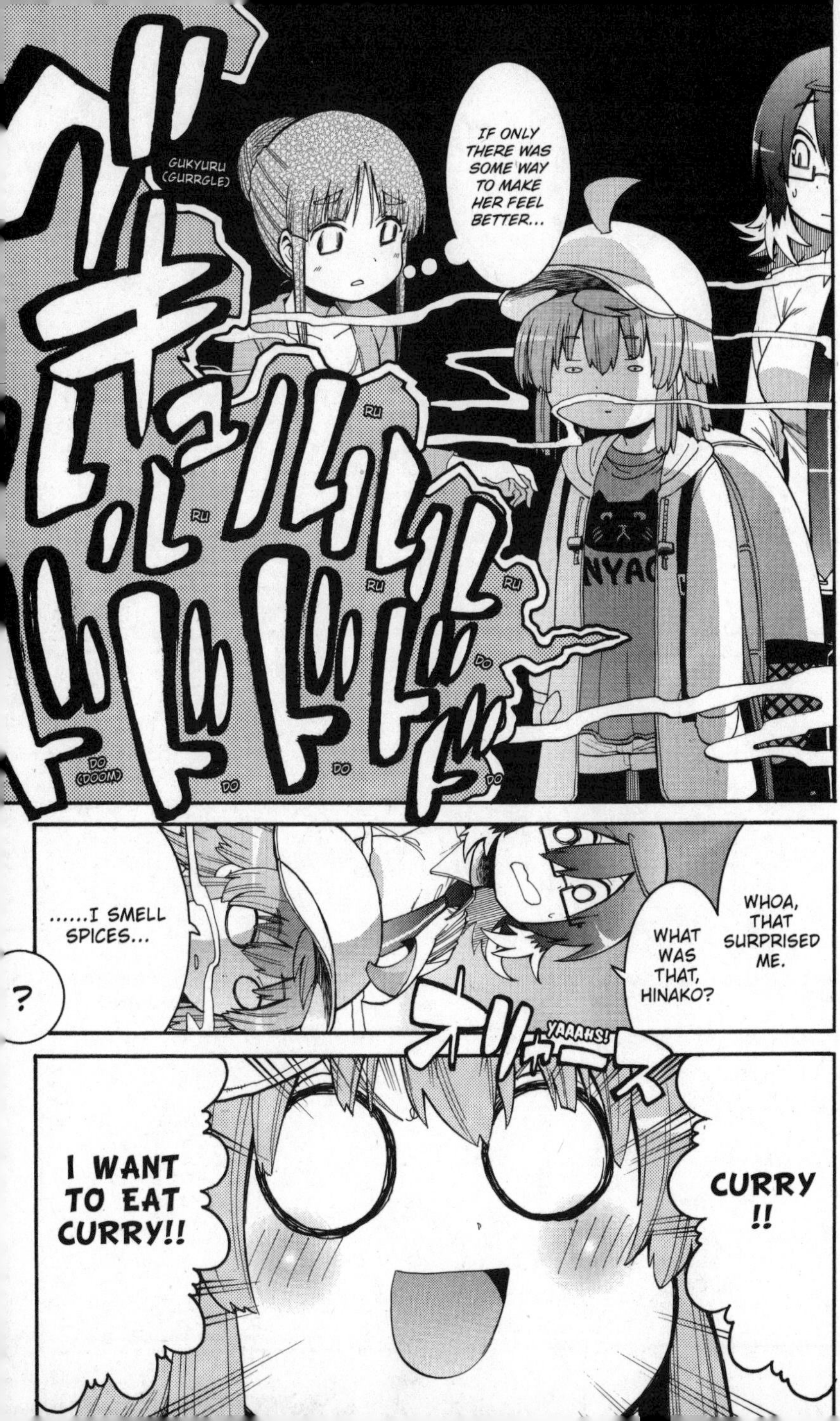
IF ONLY THERE WAS SOME WAY TO MAKE HER FEEL BETTER...
GUKYURU (GURRGLE)
RU
RU
RU
RU
DO
DO
DO
DO (DOOM)
DO
WHOA, THAT SURPRISED ME.
WHAT WAS THAT, HINAKO?
......I SMELL SPICES...
?
YAAAHS!
CURRY !!
I WANT TO EAT CURRY!!

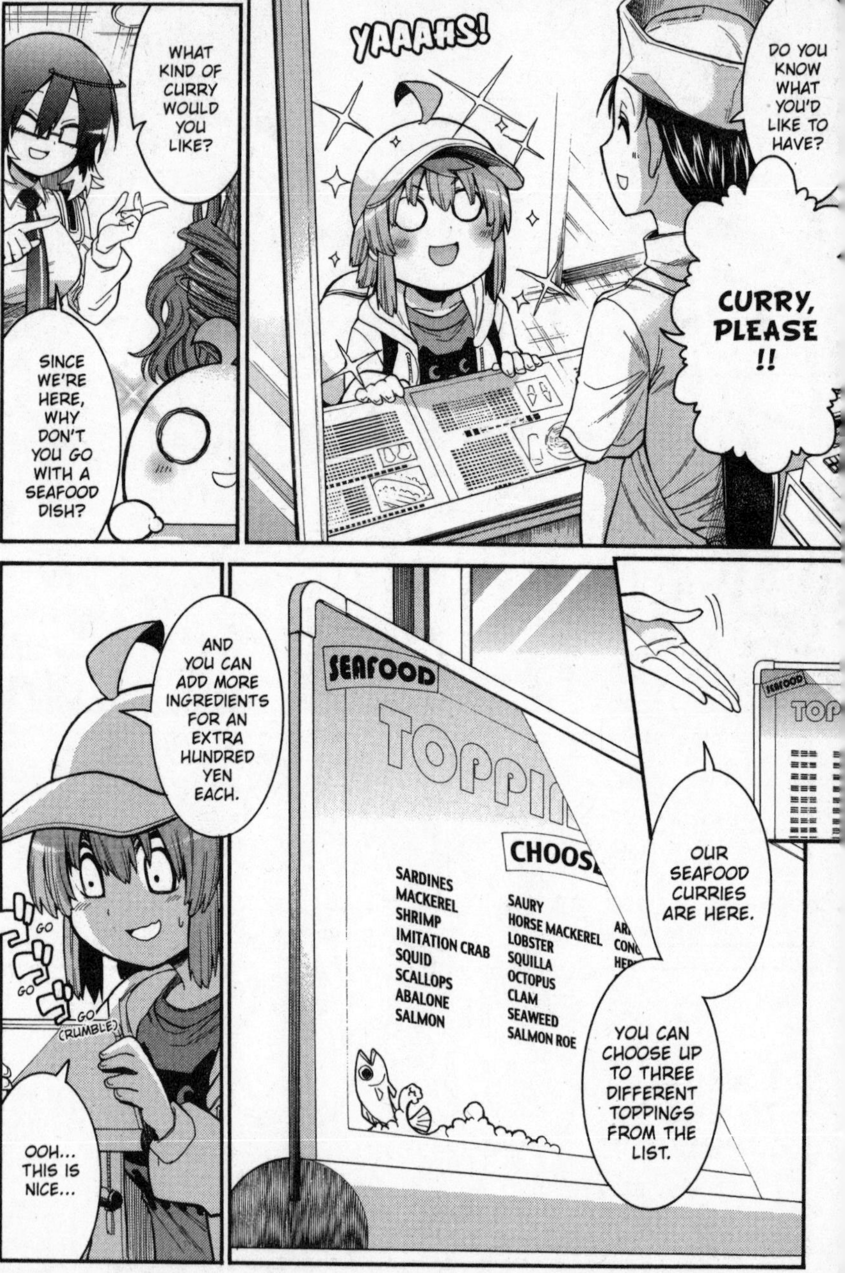
DO YOU KNOW WHAT YOU'D LIKE TO HAVE?
CURRY, PLEASE!!
YAAAHS!
WHAT KIND OF CURRY WOULD YOU LIKE?
SINCE WE'RE HERE, WHY DON'T YOU GO WITH A SEAFOOD DISH?
OUR SEAFOOD CURRIES ARE HERE.
YOU CAN CHOOSE UP TO THREE DIFFERENT TOPPINGS FROM THE LIST.
SEAFOOD
SARDINES
MACKEREL
SHRIMP
IMITATION CRAB
SQUID
SCALLOPS
ABALONE
SALMON
SAURY
HORSE MACKEREL
LOBSTER
SQUILLA
OCTOPUS
CLAM
SEAWEED
SALMON ROE
AND YOU CAN ADD MORE INGREDIENTS FOR AN EXTRA HUNDRED YEN EACH.
GO GO GO (RUMBLE)
OOH... THIS IS NICE...

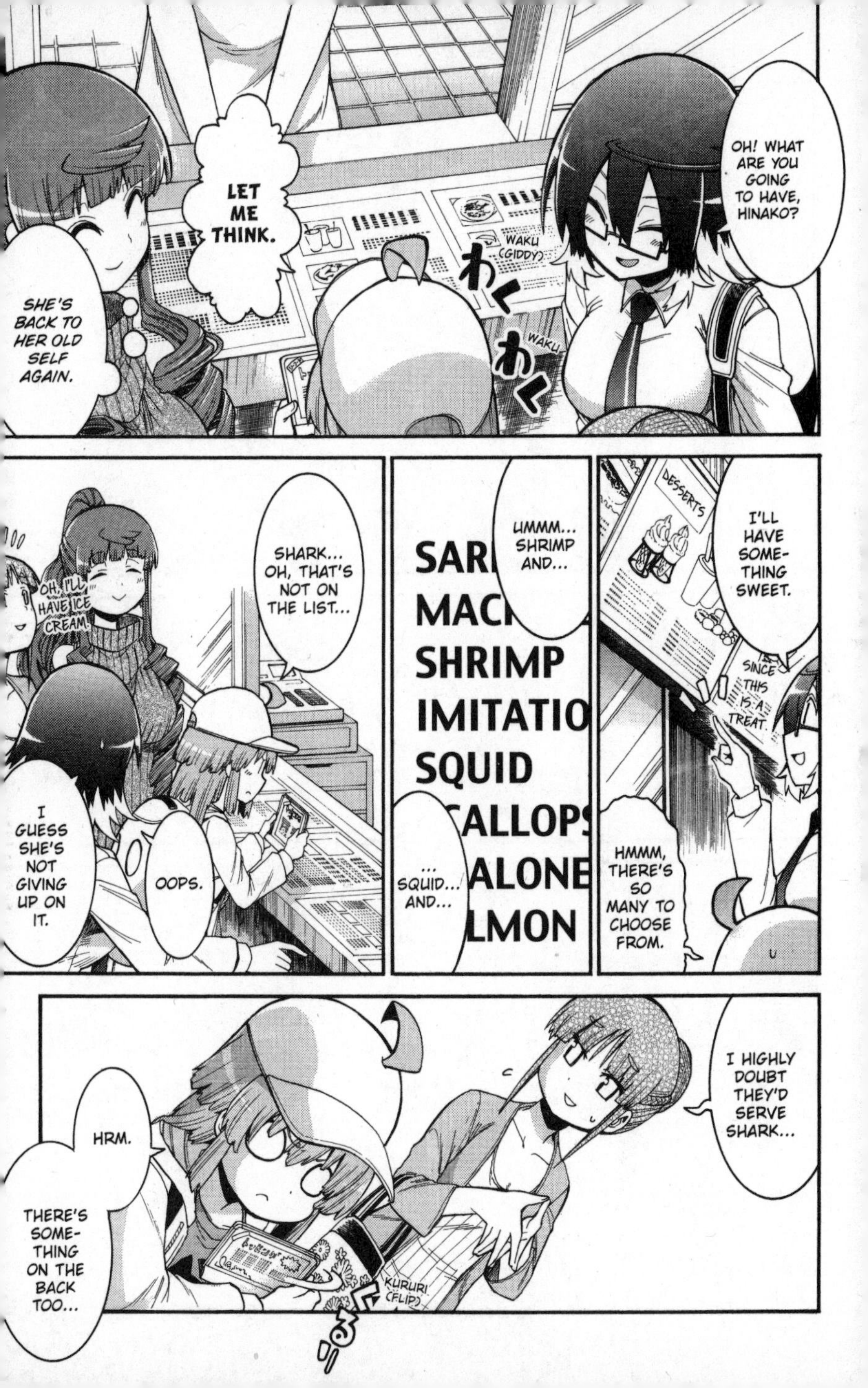
OH! WHAT ARE YOU GOING TO HAVE, HINAKO?
WAKU (GIDDY)
WAKU
LET ME THINK.
SHE'S BACK TO HER OLD SELF AGAIN.
I'LL HAVE SOME-THING SWEET.
DESSERTS
SINCE THIS IS A TREAT.
HMMM, THERE'S SO MANY TO CHOOSE FROM.
UMMM... SHRIMP AND...
SARI
MACK
SHRIMP
IMITATIO
SQUID
CALLOPS
ALONE
LMON
...SQUID... AND...
SHARK... OH, THAT'S NOT ON THE LIST...
OH, I'LL HAVE ICE CREAM.
OOPS.
I GUESS SHE'S NOT GIVING UP ON IT.
I HIGHLY DOUBT THEY'D SERVE SHARK...
HRM.
KURURI (FLIP)
THERE'S SOME-THING ON THE BACK TOO...

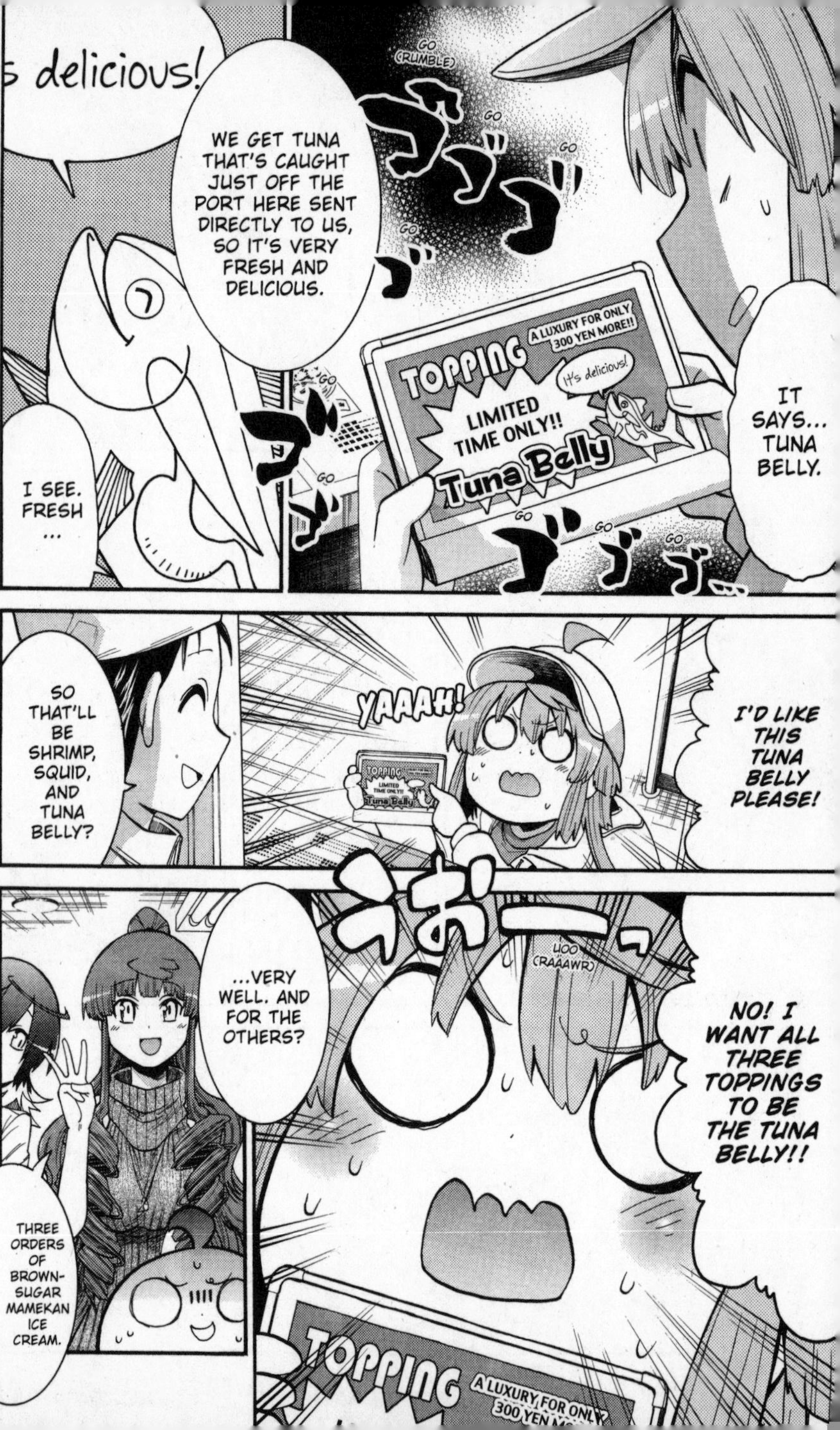
IT SAYS... TUNA BELLY.
GO (RUMBLE)
GO
GO
GO
TOPPING
A LUXURY FOR ONLY 300 YEN MORE!!
LIMITED TIME ONLY!!
It's delicious!
Tuna Belly
GO
GO
GO
GO
GO
s delicious!
WE GET TUNA THAT'S CAUGHT JUST OFF THE PORT HERE SENT DIRECTLY TO US, SO IT'S VERY FRESH AND DELICIOUS.
I SEE. FRESH ...
I'D LIKE THIS TUNA BELLY PLEASE!
YAAAH!
SO THAT'LL BE SHRIMP, SQUID, AND TUNA BELLY?
UOO (RAAAWR)
NO! I WANT ALL THREE TOPPINGS TO BE THE TUNA BELLY!!
TOPPING
A LUXURY FOR ONLY 300 YEN MO
...VERY WELL. AND FOR THE OTHERS?
THREE ORDERS OF BROWN-SUGAR MAMEKAN ICE CREAM.

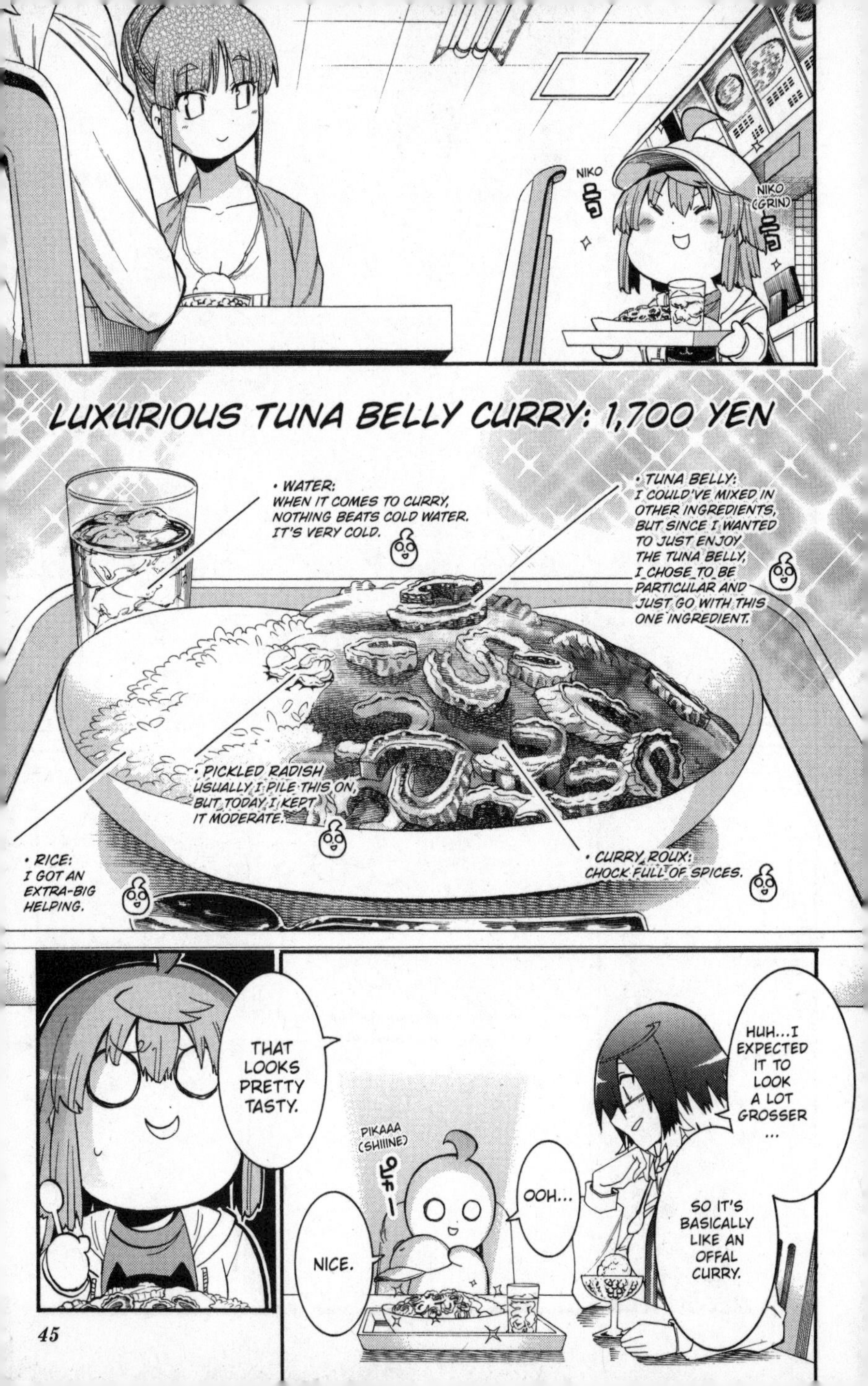
NIKO (GRIN)
NIKO
LUXURIOUS TUNA BELLY CURRY: 1,700 YEN
• TUNA BELLY: I COULD'VE MIXED IN OTHER INGREDIENTS, BUT SINCE I WANTED TO JUST ENJOY THE TUNA BELLY, I CHOSE TO BE PARTICULAR AND JUST GO WITH THIS ONE INGREDIENT.
• WATER: WHEN IT COMES TO CURRY, NOTHING BEATS COLD WATER. IT'S VERY COLD.
• CURRY ROUX: CHOCK FULL OF SPICES.
• PICKLED RADISH USUALLY I PILE THIS ON, BUT TODAY I KEPT IT MODERATE.
• RICE: I GOT AN EXTRA-BIG HELPING.
HUH...I EXPECTED IT TO LOOK A LOT GROSSER...
SO IT'S BASICALLY LIKE AN OFFAL CURRY.
OOH...
PIKAAA (SHIIINE)
NICE.
THAT LOOKS PRETTY TASTY.

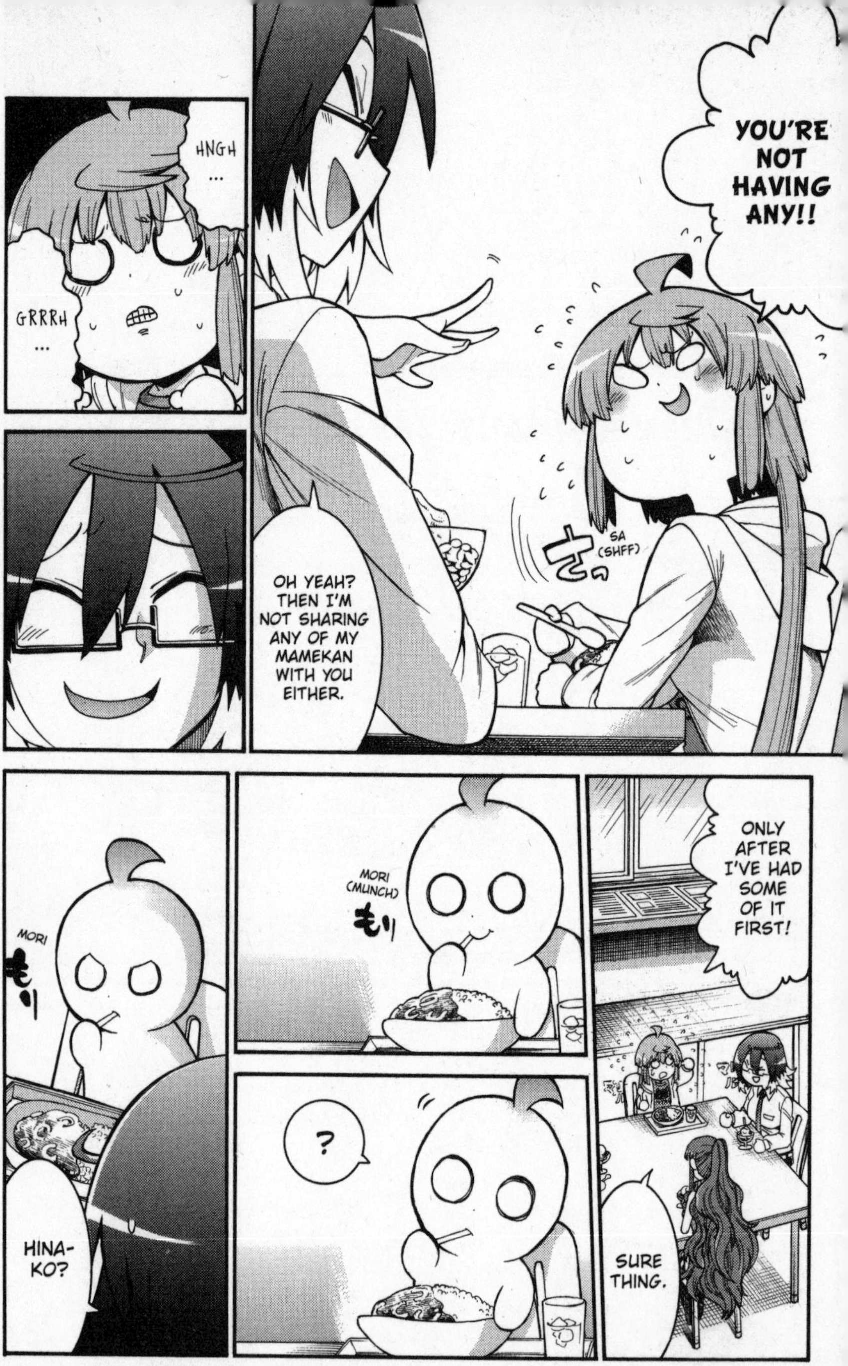
YOU'RE NOT HAVING ANY!!
SA (SHFF)
OH YEAH? THEN I'M NOT SHARING ANY OF MY MAMEKAN WITH YOU EITHER.
HNGH ...
GRRRH ...
ONLY AFTER I'VE HAD SOME OF IT FIRST!
SURE THING.
MORI (MUNCH)
?
MORI
HINA-KO?

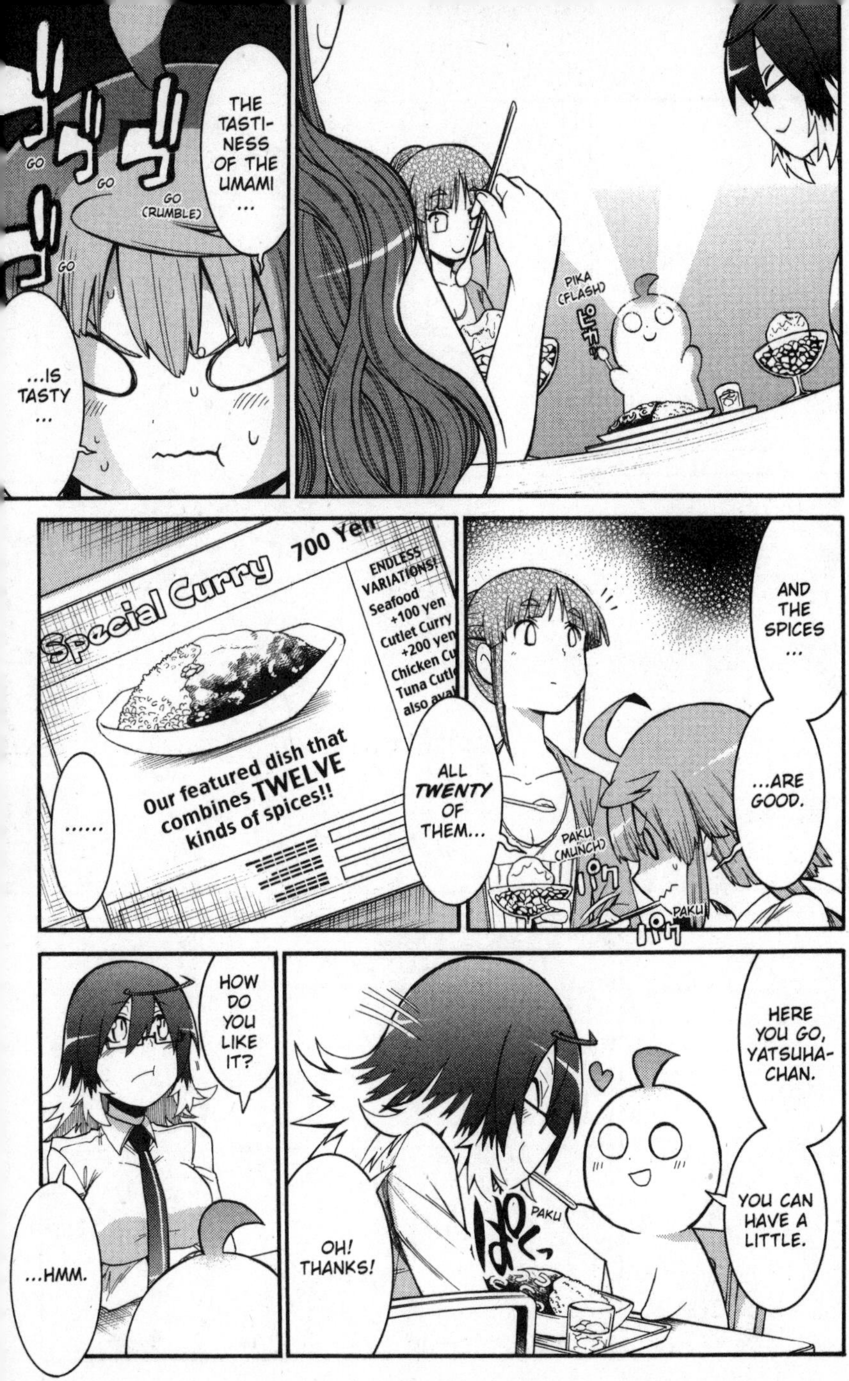
PIKA (FLASH)
THE TASTINESS OF THE UMAMI ...
GO GO GO (RUMBLE) GO
...IS TASTY ...
AND THE SPICES ...
...ARE GOOD.
ALL *TWENTY* OF THEM...
PAKU (MUNCH)
PAKU
Special Curry 700 Yen
ENDLESS VARIATIONS!
Seafood +100 yen
Cutlet Curry +200 yen
Our featured dish that combines TWELVE kinds of spices!!
......
HERE YOU GO, YATSUHA-CHAN.
YOU CAN HAVE A LITTLE.
PAKU
OH! THANKS!
HOW DO YOU LIKE IT?
...HMM.

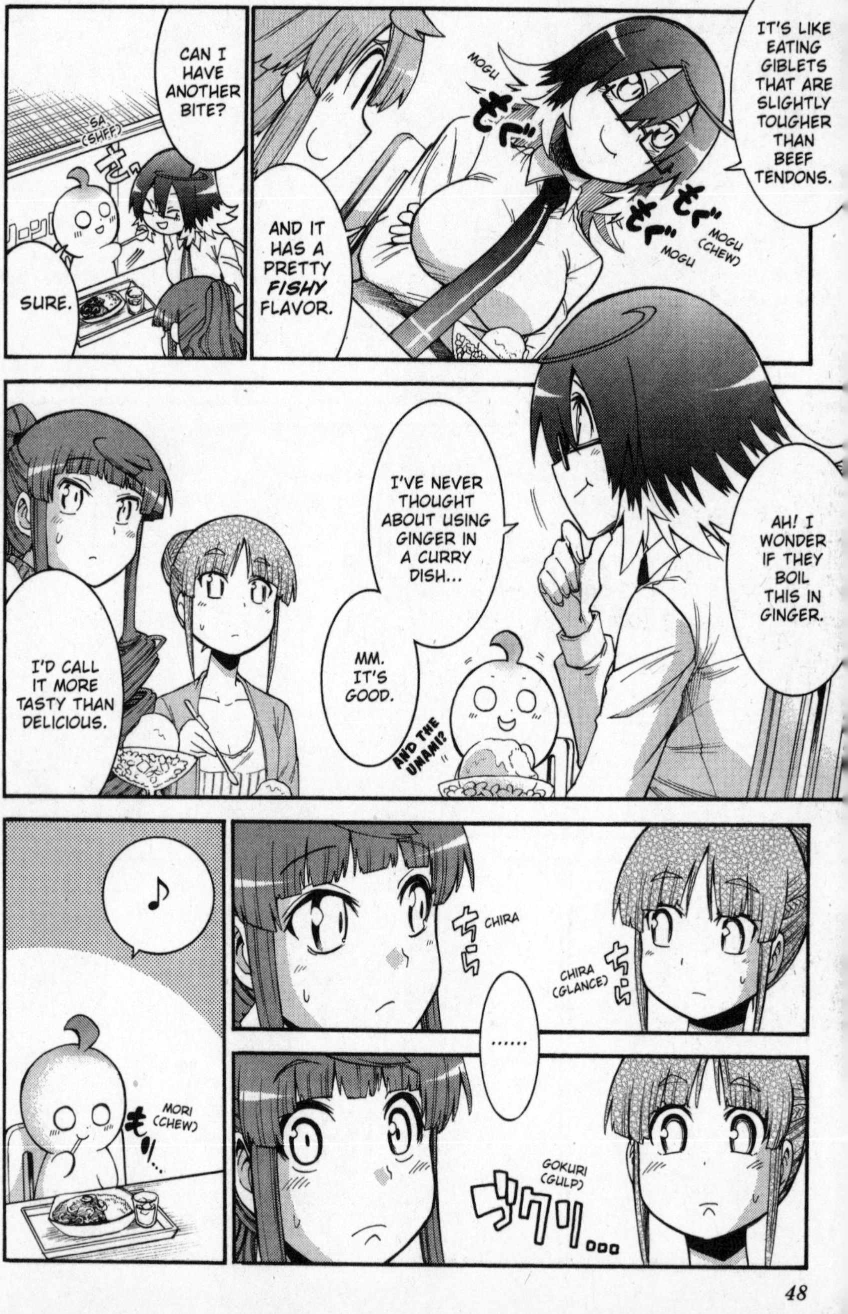
IT'S LIKE EATING GIBLETS THAT ARE SLIGHTLY TOUGHER THAN BEEF TENDONS.
MOGU
MOGU (CHEW) MOGU
AND IT HAS A PRETTY *FISHY* FLAVOR.
CAN I HAVE ANOTHER BITE?
SA (SHFF)
SURE.
AH! I WONDER IF THEY BOIL THIS IN GINGER.
I'VE NEVER THOUGHT ABOUT USING GINGER IN A CURRY DISH...
MM. IT'S GOOD.
AND THE UMAMI?
I'D CALL IT MORE TASTY THAN DELICIOUS.
CHIRA (GLANCE)
CHIRA
......
GOKURI (GULP)
♪
MORI (CHEW)

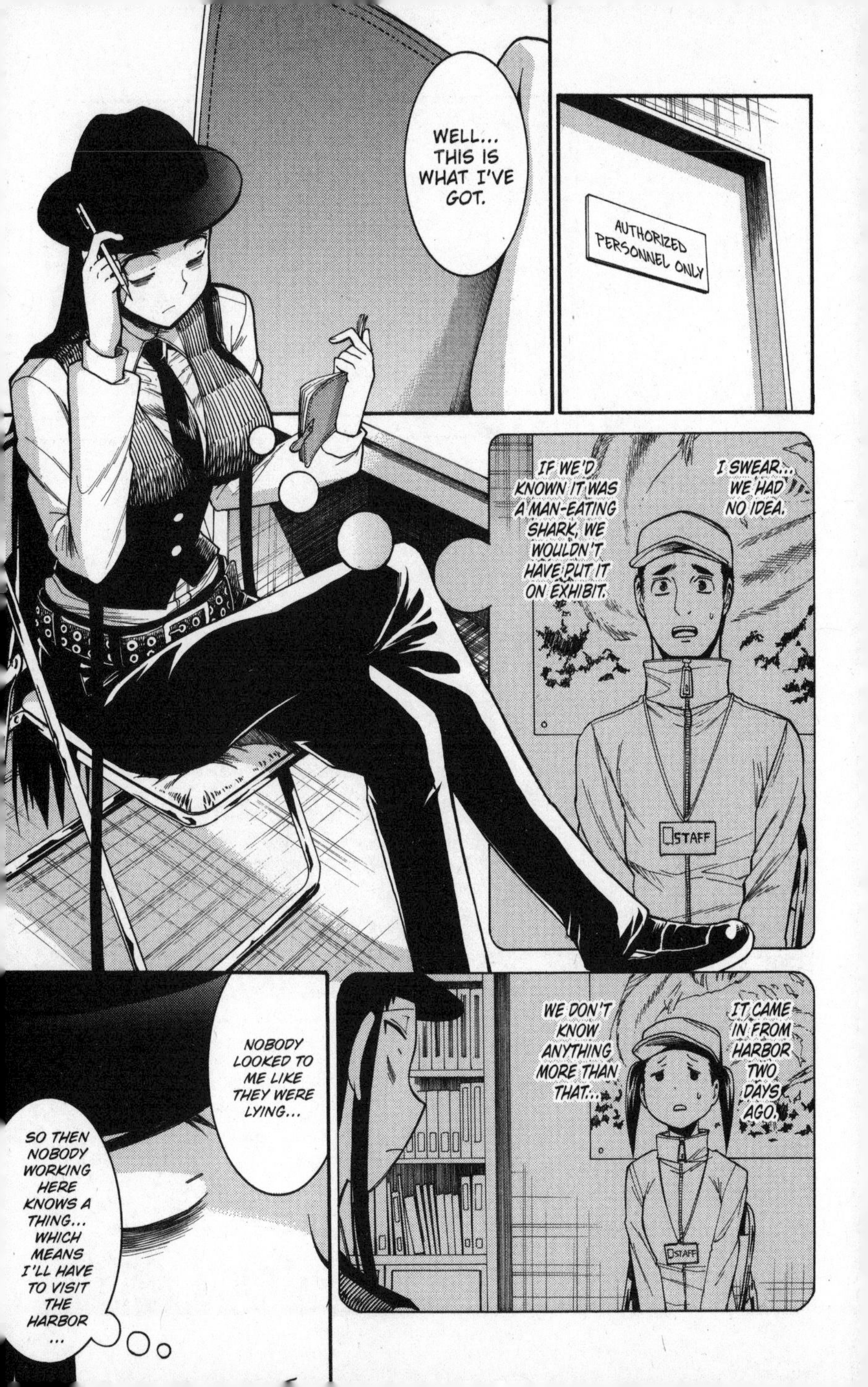
AUTHORIZED PERSONNEL ONLY
I SWEAR... WE HAD NO IDEA.
IF WE'D KNOWN IT WAS A MAN-EATING SHARK, WE WOULDN'T HAVE PUT IT ON EXHIBIT.
STAFF
WELL... THIS IS WHAT I'VE GOT.
IT CAME IN FROM HARBOR TWO DAYS AGO.
WE DON'T KNOW ANYTHING MORE THAN THAT...
STAFF
NOBODY LOOKED TO ME LIKE THEY WERE LYING...
SO THEN NOBODY WORKING HERE KNOWS A THING... WHICH MEANS I'LL HAVE TO VISIT THE HARBOR ...

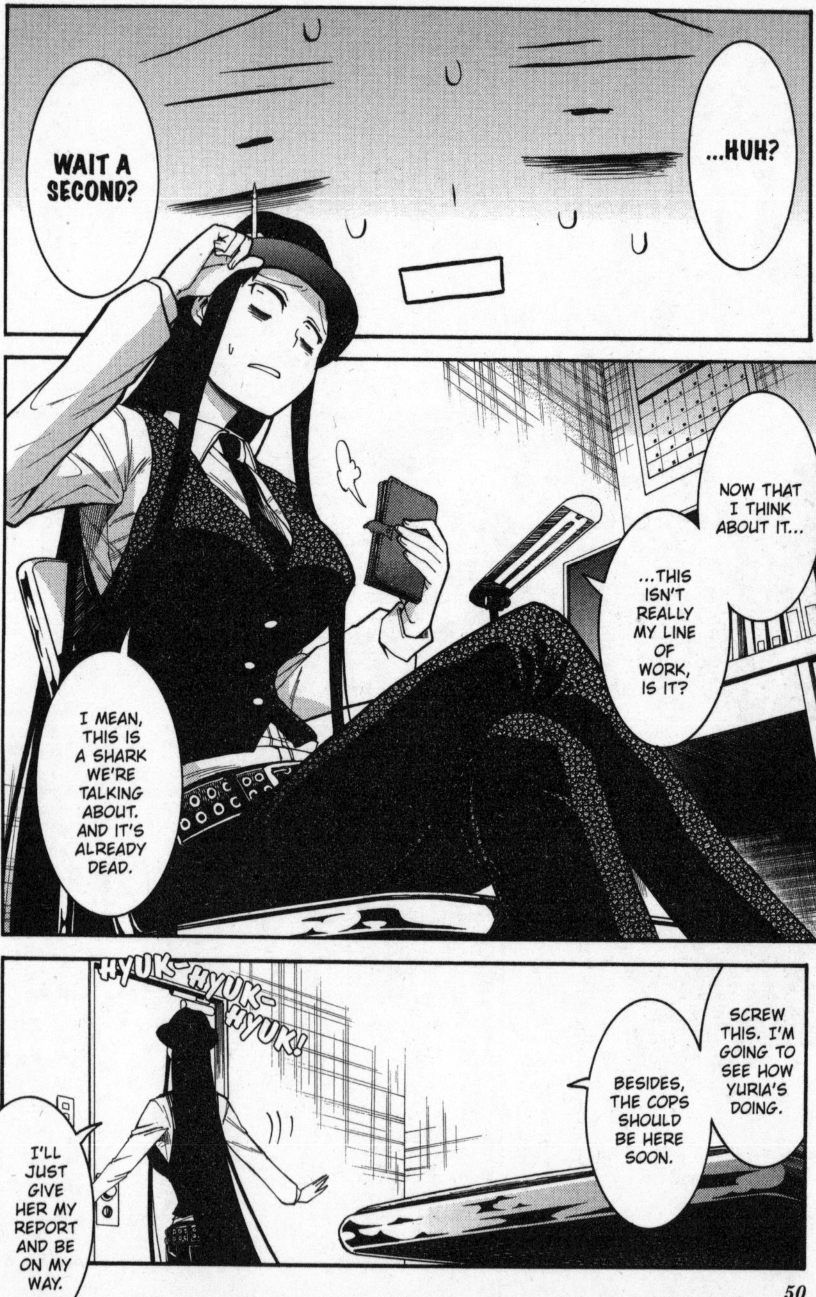
...HUH?
WAIT A SECOND?
NOW THAT I THINK ABOUT IT...
...THIS ISN'T REALLY MY LINE OF WORK, IS IT?
I MEAN, THIS IS A SHARK WE'RE TALKING ABOUT. AND IT'S ALREADY DEAD.
SCREW THIS. I'M GOING TO SEE HOW YURIA'S DOING.
BESIDES, THE COPS SHOULD BE HERE SOON.
HYUK-HYUK-HYUK!
I'LL JUST GIVE HER MY REPORT AND BE ON MY WAY.

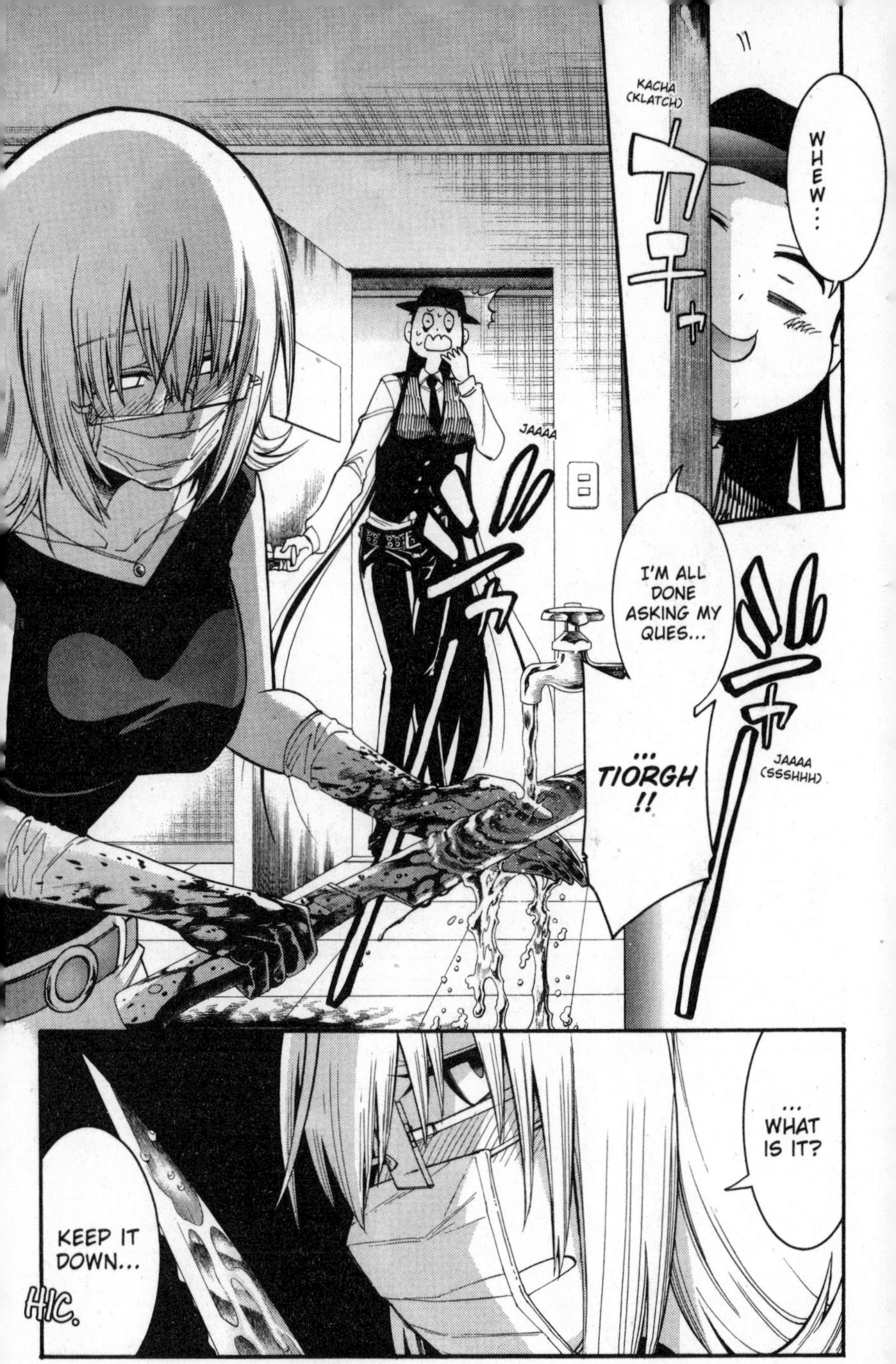
WHEW...
KACHA (KLATCH)
I'M ALL DONE ASKING MY QUES...
...TIÖRGH!!
JAAAA (SSSHHH)
JAAAA
...WHAT IS IT?
KEEP IT DOWN...
HIC.

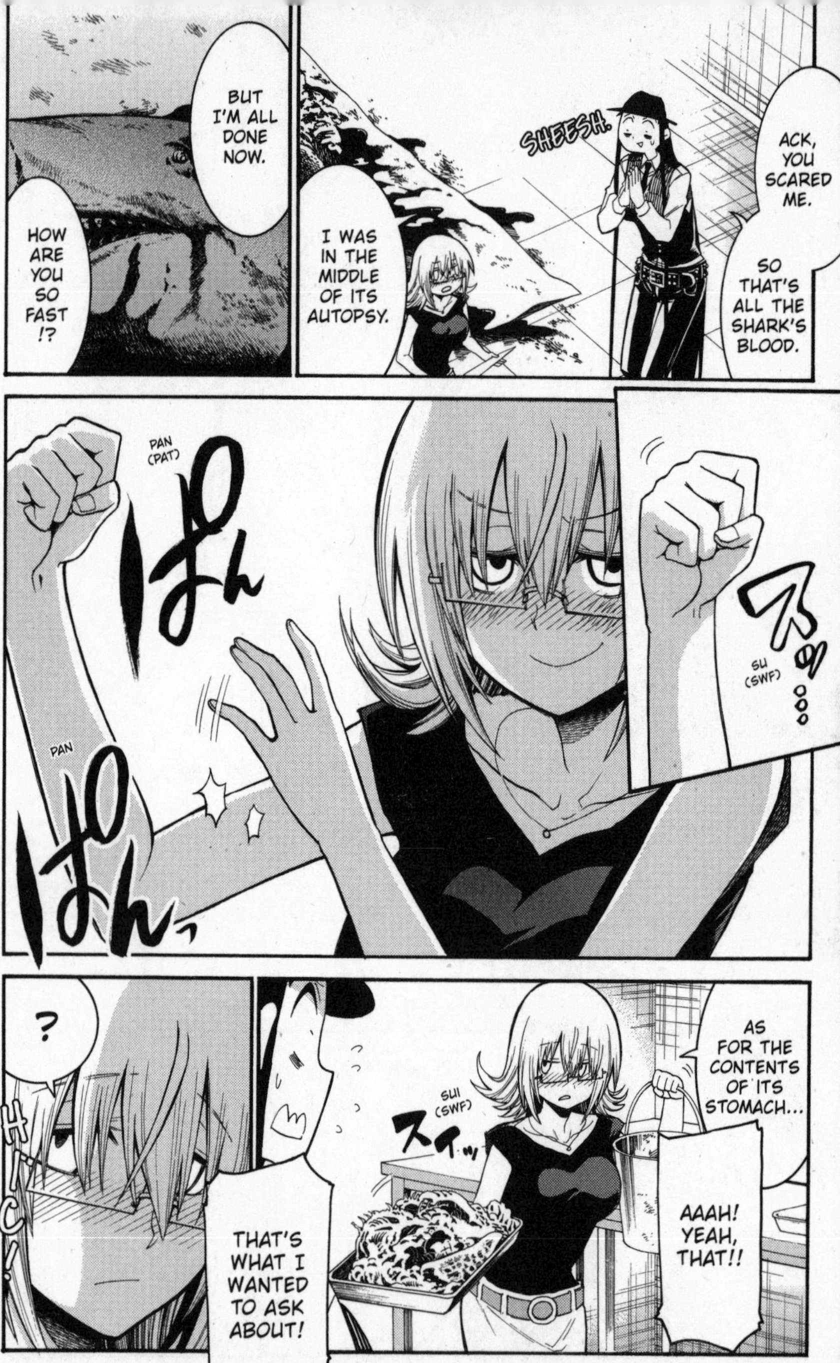
SHEESH.
ACK, YOU SCARED ME.
SO THAT'S ALL THE SHARK'S BLOOD.
I WAS IN THE MIDDLE OF ITS AUTOPSY.
BUT I'M ALL DONE NOW.
HOW ARE YOU SO FAST!?
SU (SWF)
PAN (PAT)
PAN
AS FOR THE CONTENTS OF ITS STOMACH...
SUI (SWF)
AAAH! YEAH, THAT!!
THAT'S WHAT I WANTED TO ASK ABOUT!
?
HIC!

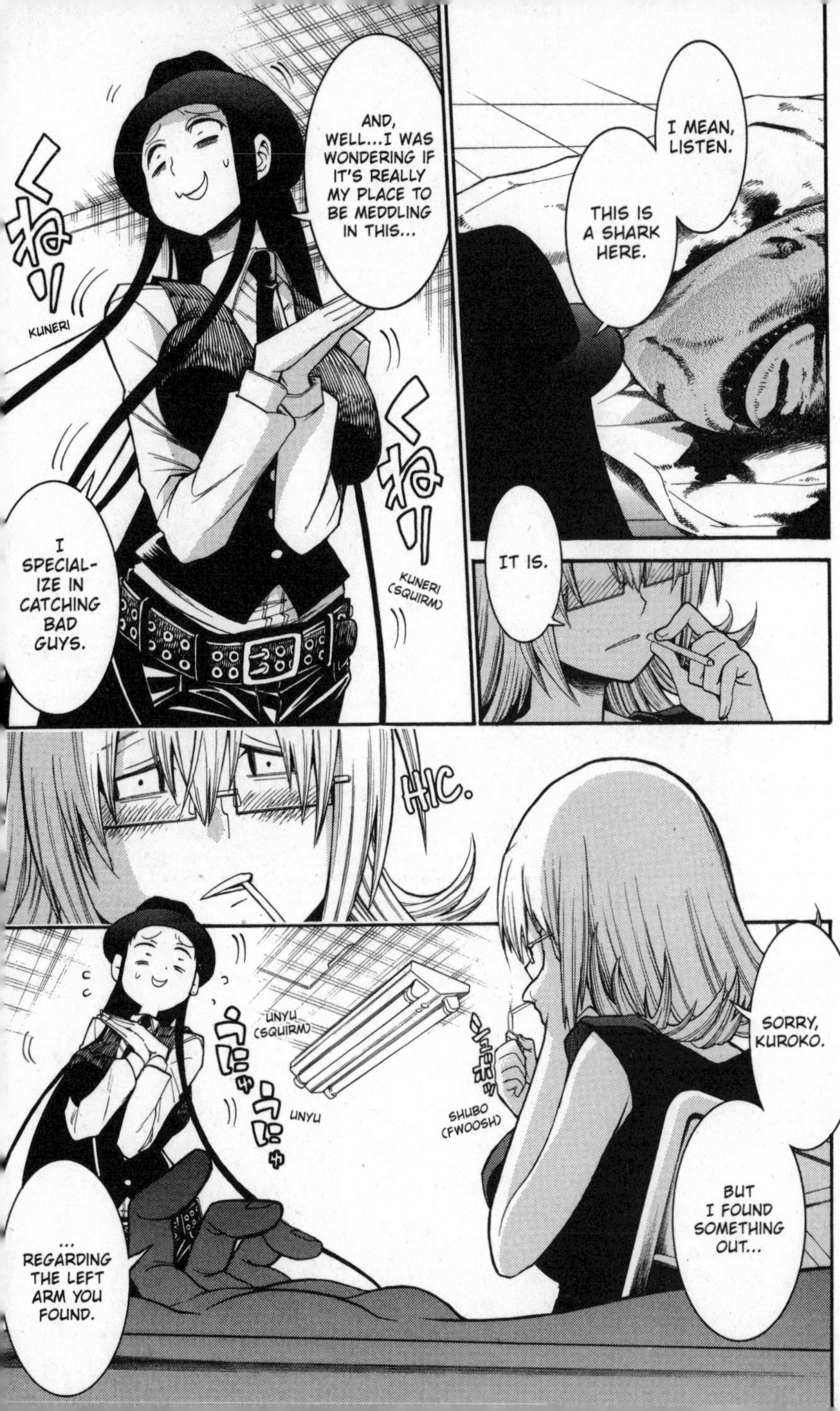

I MEAN, LISTEN.
THIS IS A SHARK HERE.
IT IS.
AND, WELL...I WAS WONDERING IF IT'S REALLY MY PLACE TO BE MEDDLING IN THIS...
くねり
KUNERI
くねり
KUNERI (SQUIRM)
I SPECIAL-IZE IN CATCHING BAD GUYS.
HIC.
SORRY, KUROKO.
BUT I FOUND SOMETHING OUT...
しゅぼっ
SHUBO (FWOOSH)
うにゅ
UNYU (SQUIRM)
うにゅ
UNYU
...REGARDING THE LEFT ARM YOU FOUND.

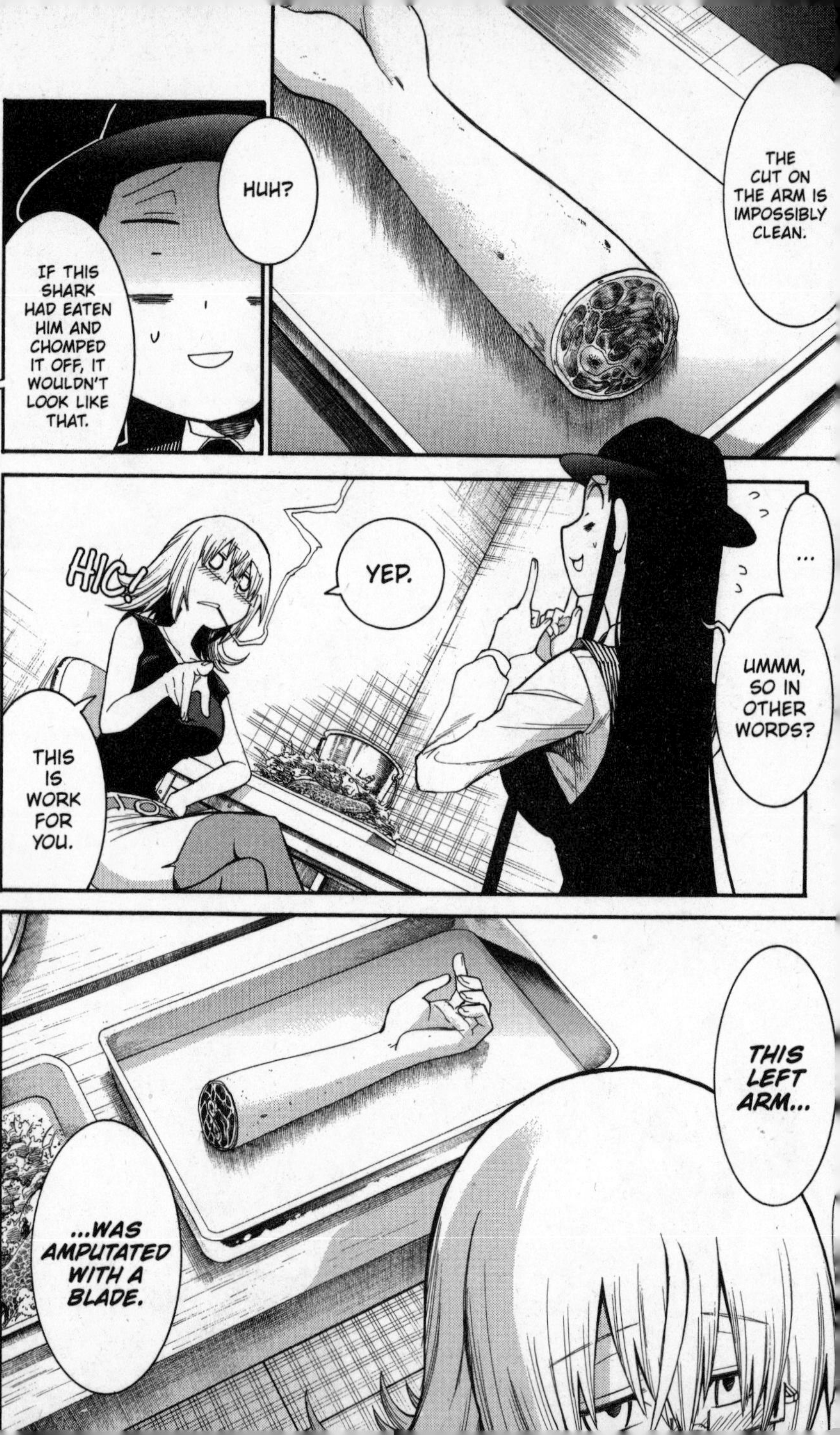
THE CUT ON THE ARM IS IMPOSSIBLY CLEAN.
HUH?
IF THIS SHARK HAD EATEN HIM AND CHOMPED IT OFF, IT WOULDN'T LOOK LIKE THAT.
...
UMMM, SO IN OTHER WORDS?
YEP.
HIC!
THIS IS WORK FOR YOU.
THIS LEFT ARM...
...WAS AMPUTATED WITH A BLADE.

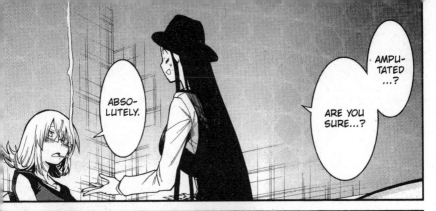

AMPUTATED...?
ARE YOU SURE...?
ABSOLUTELY.
THEN, UH, WELL... HUH...
MAYBE IT'S A SHARK WITH SPECIAL SUPER-SHARP TEETH!
ITS TEETH ARE NORMAL.
......

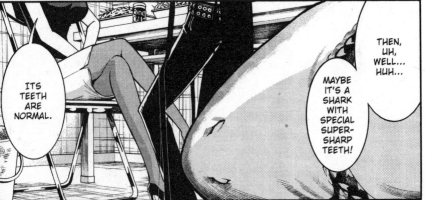

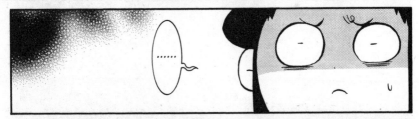

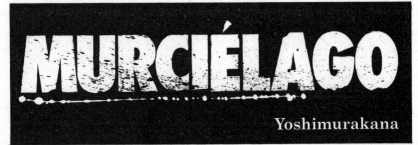

MURCIÉLAGO

Yoshimurakana

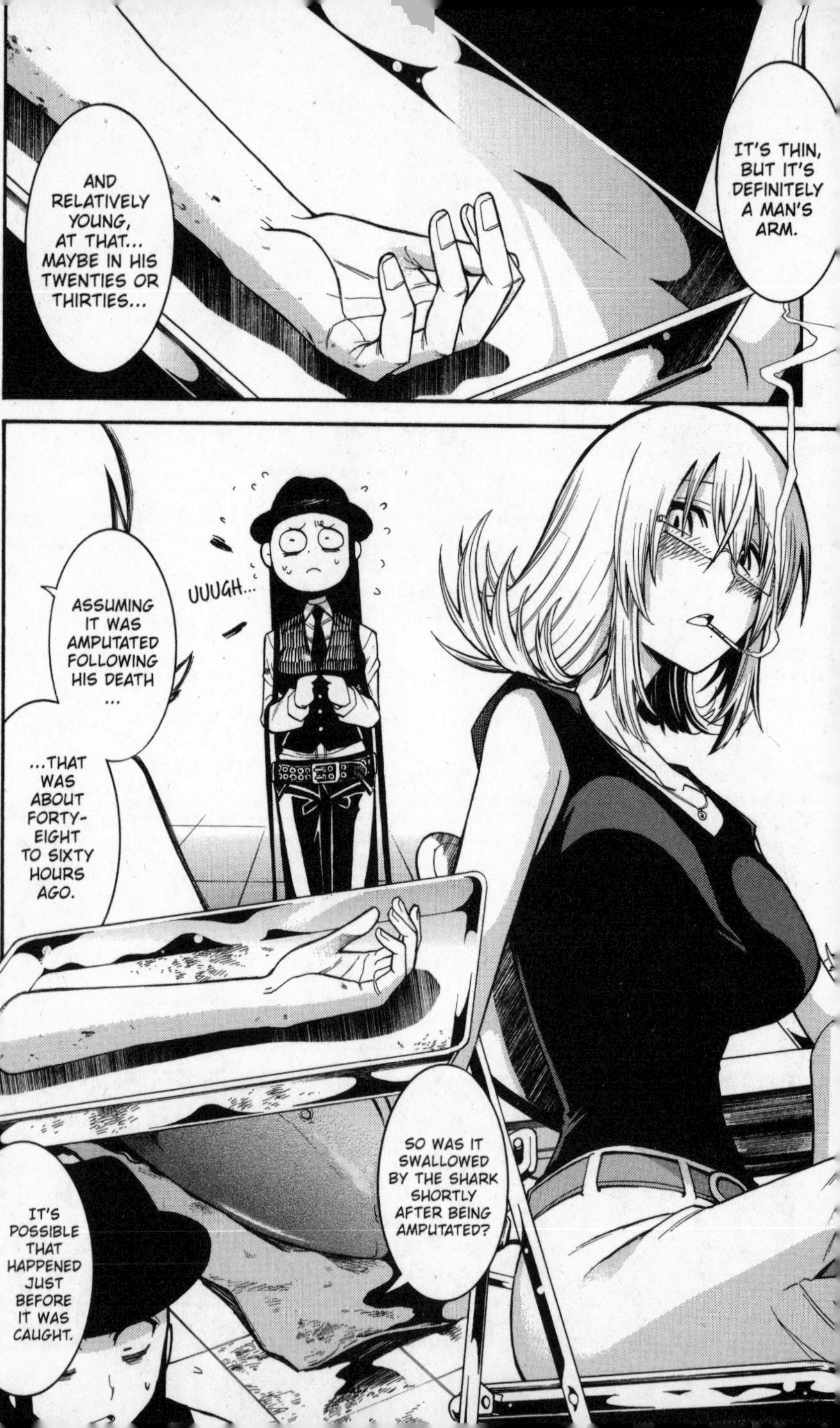
IT'S THIN, BUT IT'S DEFINITELY A MAN'S ARM.
AND RELATIVELY YOUNG, AT THAT... MAYBE IN HIS TWENTIES OR THIRTIES...
UUUGH...
ASSUMING IT WAS AMPUTATED FOLLOWING HIS DEATH...
...THAT WAS ABOUT FORTY-EIGHT TO SIXTY HOURS AGO.
SO WAS IT SWALLOWED BY THE SHARK SHORTLY AFTER BEING AMPUTATED?
IT'S POSSIBLE THAT HAPPENED JUST BEFORE IT WAS CAUGHT.

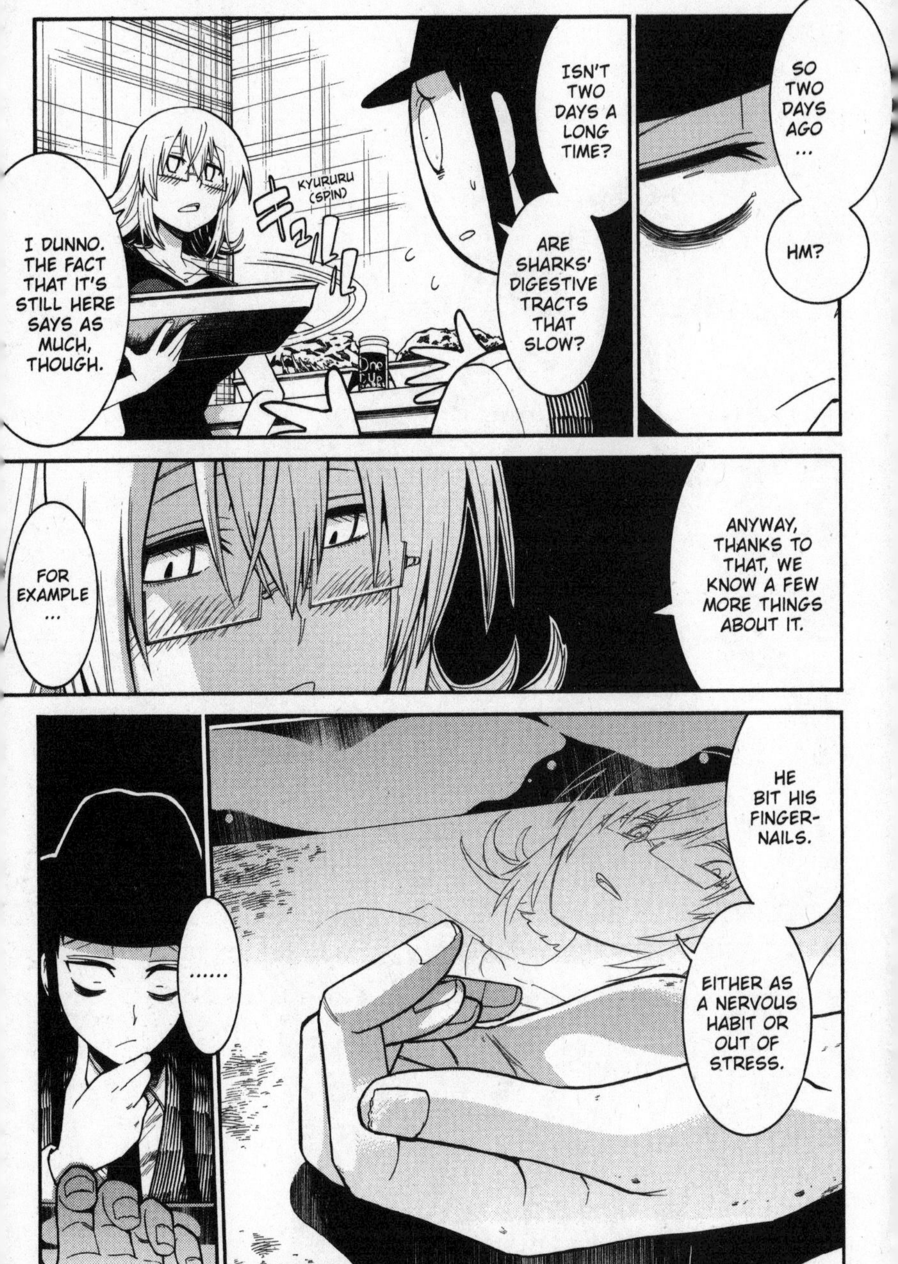
SO TWO DAYS AGO ...
HM?
ISN'T TWO DAYS A LONG TIME?
ARE SHARKS' DIGESTIVE TRACTS THAT SLOW?
KYURURU (SPIN)
I DUNNO. THE FACT THAT IT'S STILL HERE SAYS AS MUCH, THOUGH.
ANYWAY, THANKS TO THAT, WE KNOW A FEW MORE THINGS ABOUT IT.
FOR EXAMPLE ...
HE BIT HIS FINGER-NAILS.
EITHER AS A NERVOUS HABIT OR OUT OF STRESS.
......

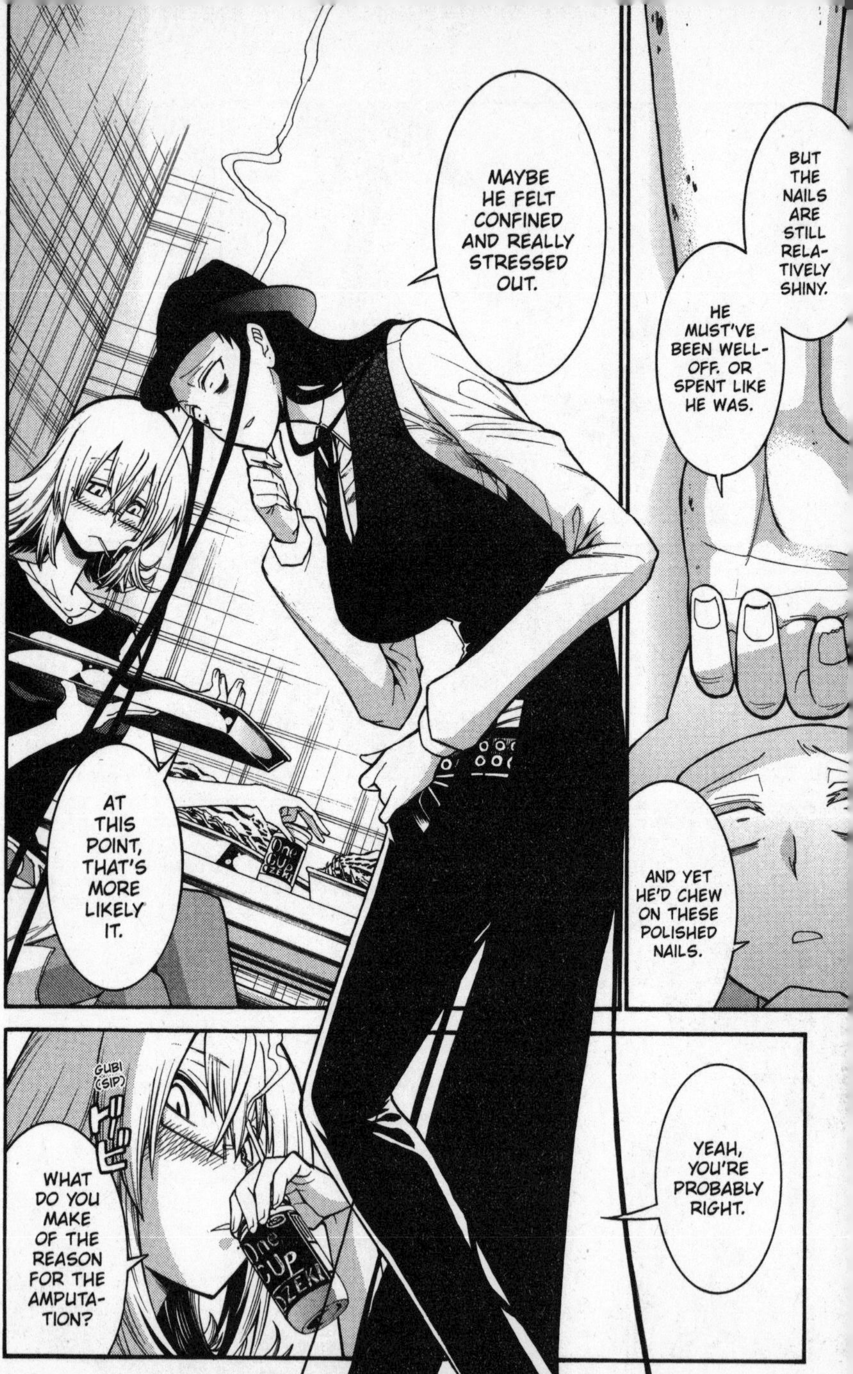
BUT THE NAILS ARE STILL RELATIVELY SHINY.
HE MUST'VE BEEN WELL-OFF. OR SPENT LIKE HE WAS.
AND YET HE'D CHEW ON THESE POLISHED NAILS.
MAYBE HE FELT CONFINED AND REALLY STRESSED OUT.
AT THIS POINT, THAT'S MORE LIKELY IT.
YEAH, YOU'RE PROBABLY RIGHT.
GUBI (SIP)
WHAT DO YOU MAKE OF THE REASON FOR THE AMPUTATION?

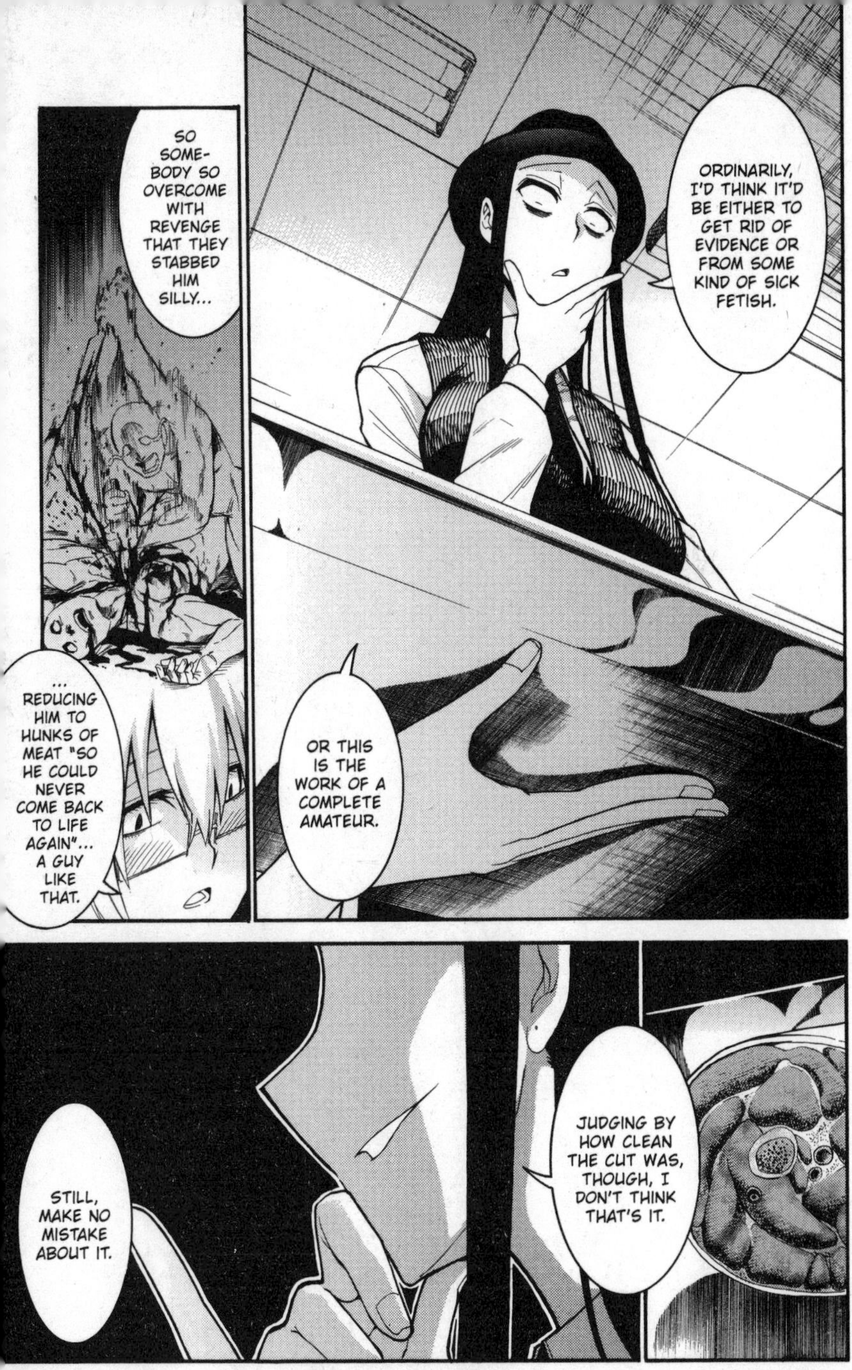
ORDINARILY, I'D THINK IT'D BE EITHER TO GET RID OF EVIDENCE OR FROM SOME KIND OF SICK FETISH.
OR THIS IS THE WORK OF A COMPLETE AMATEUR.
SO SOME-BODY SO OVERCOME WITH REVENGE THAT THEY STABBED HIM SILLY...
...REDUCING HIM TO HUNKS OF MEAT "SO HE COULD NEVER COME BACK TO LIFE AGAIN"... A GUY LIKE THAT.
JUDGING BY HOW CLEAN THE CUT WAS, THOUGH, I DON'T THINK THAT'S IT.
STILL, MAKE NO MISTAKE ABOUT IT.

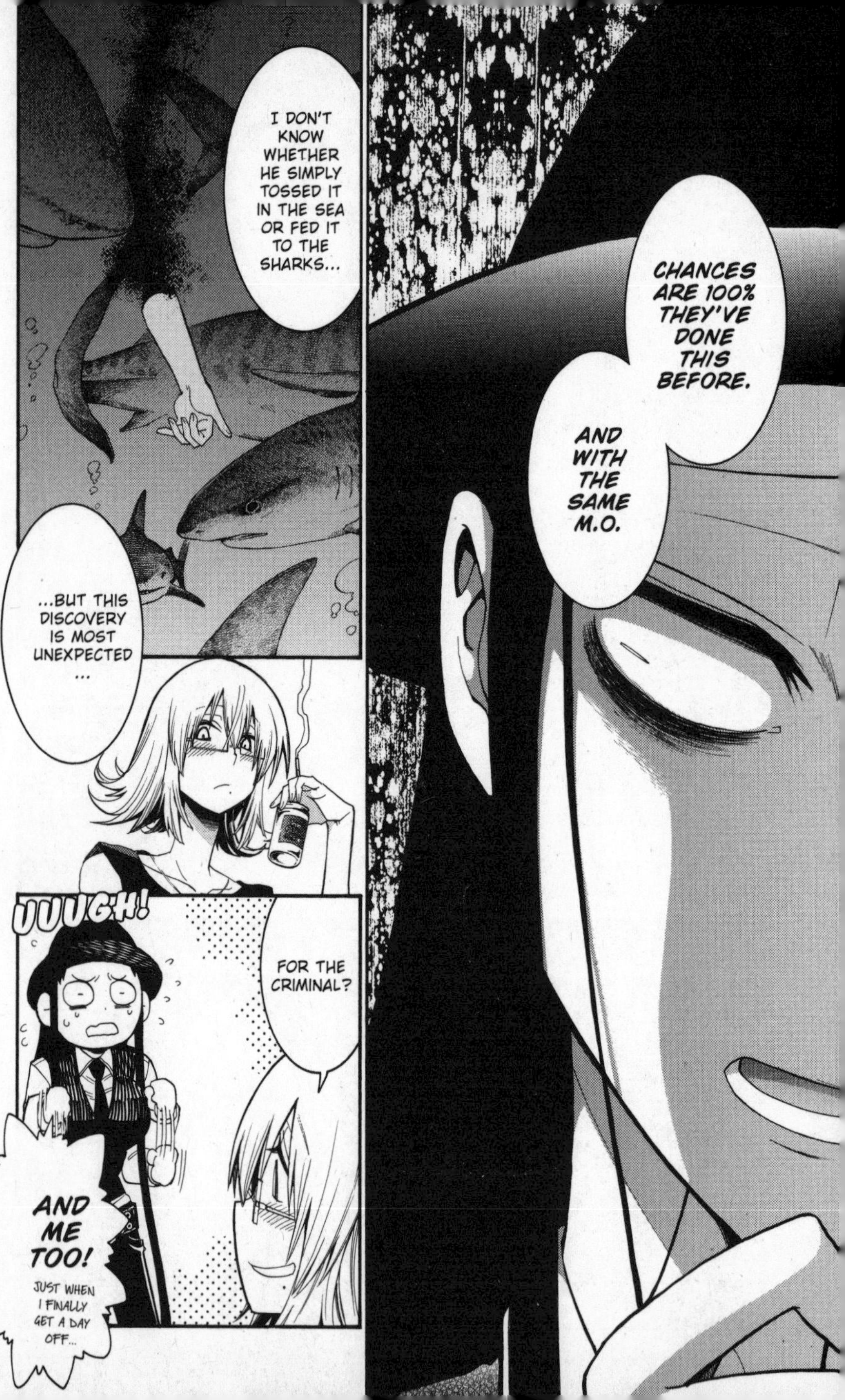
CHANCES ARE 100% THEY'VE DONE THIS BEFORE.
AND WITH THE SAME M.O.
I DON'T KNOW WHETHER HE SIMPLY TOSSED IT IN THE SEA OR FED IT TO THE SHARKS...
...BUT THIS DISCOVERY IS MOST UNEXPECTED...
FOR THE CRIMINAL?
UUUGH!
AND ME TOO!
JUST WHEN I FINALLY GET A DAY OFF...

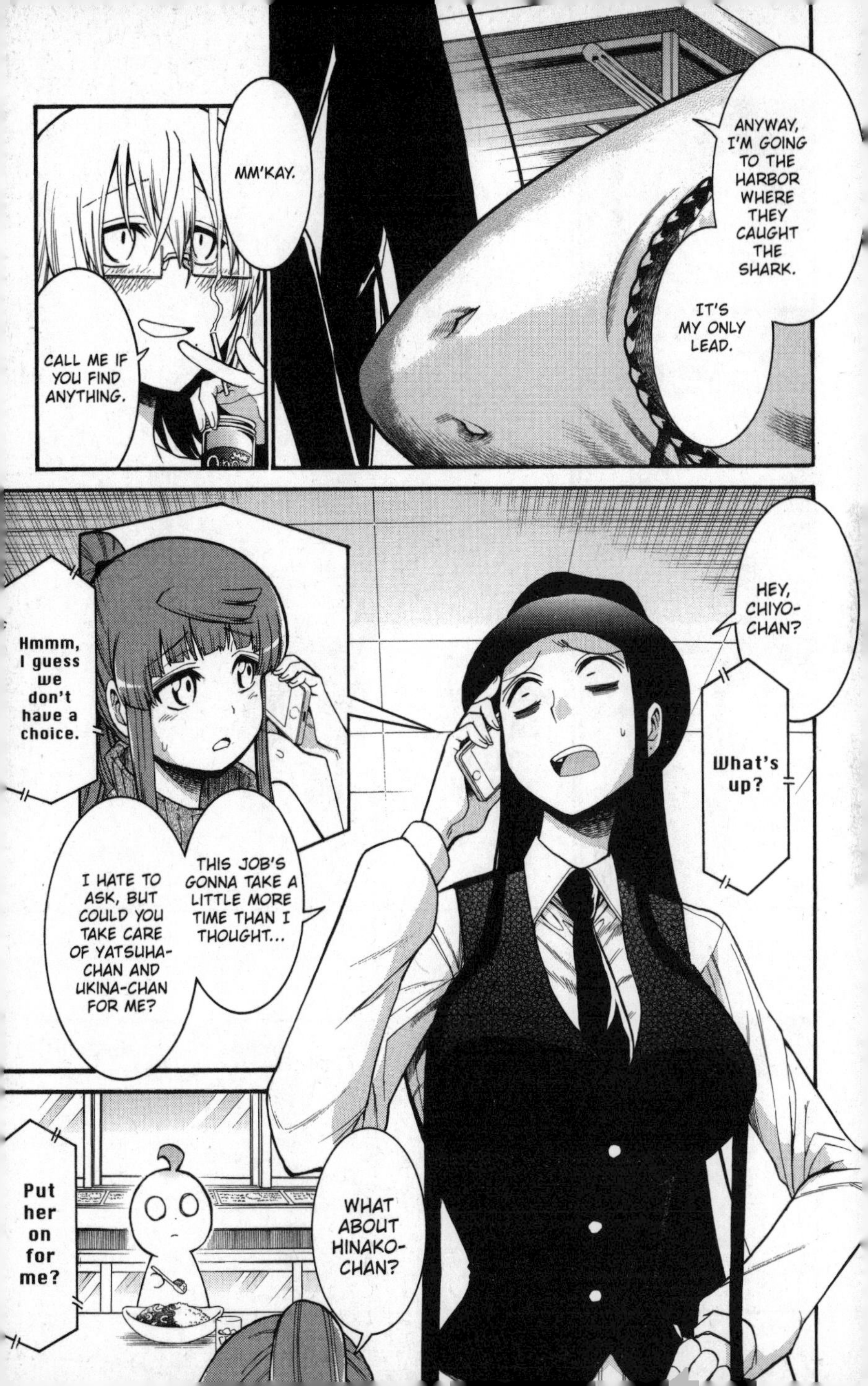
ANYWAY, I'M GOING TO THE HARBOR WHERE THEY CAUGHT THE SHARK.
IT'S MY ONLY LEAD.
MM'KAY.
CALL ME IF YOU FIND ANYTHING.
HEY, CHIYO-CHAN?
What's up?
THIS JOB'S GONNA TAKE A LITTLE MORE TIME THAN I THOUGHT...
I HATE TO ASK, BUT COULD YOU TAKE CARE OF YATSUHA-CHAN AND UKINA-CHAN FOR ME?
Hmmm, I guess we don't have a choice.
WHAT ABOUT HINAKO-CHAN?
Put her on for me?

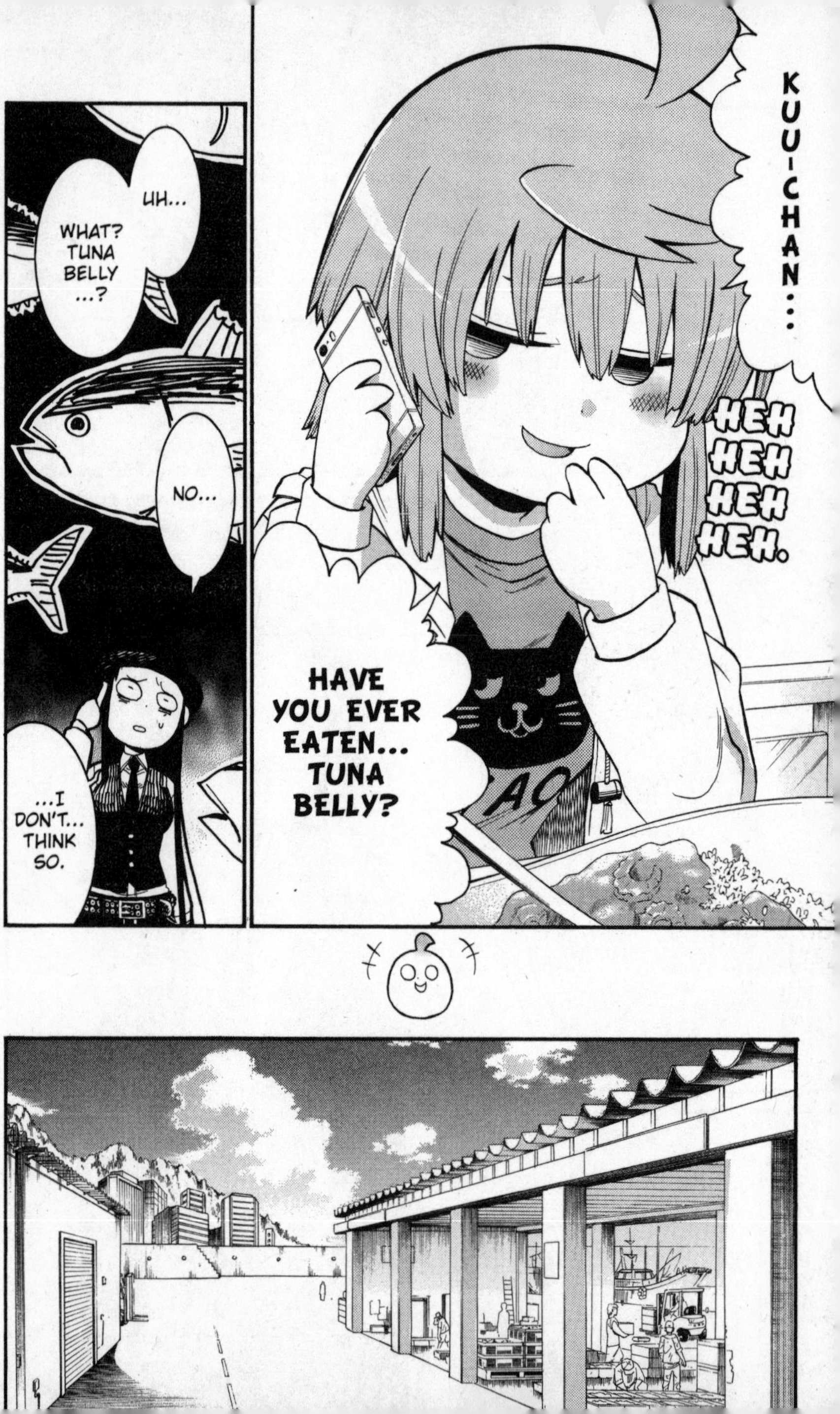
KUUICHAN...
HEH HEH HEH HEH.
HAVE YOU EVER EATEN... TUNA BELLY?
UH...
WHAT? TUNA BELLY ...?
NO...
...I DON'T... THINK SO.

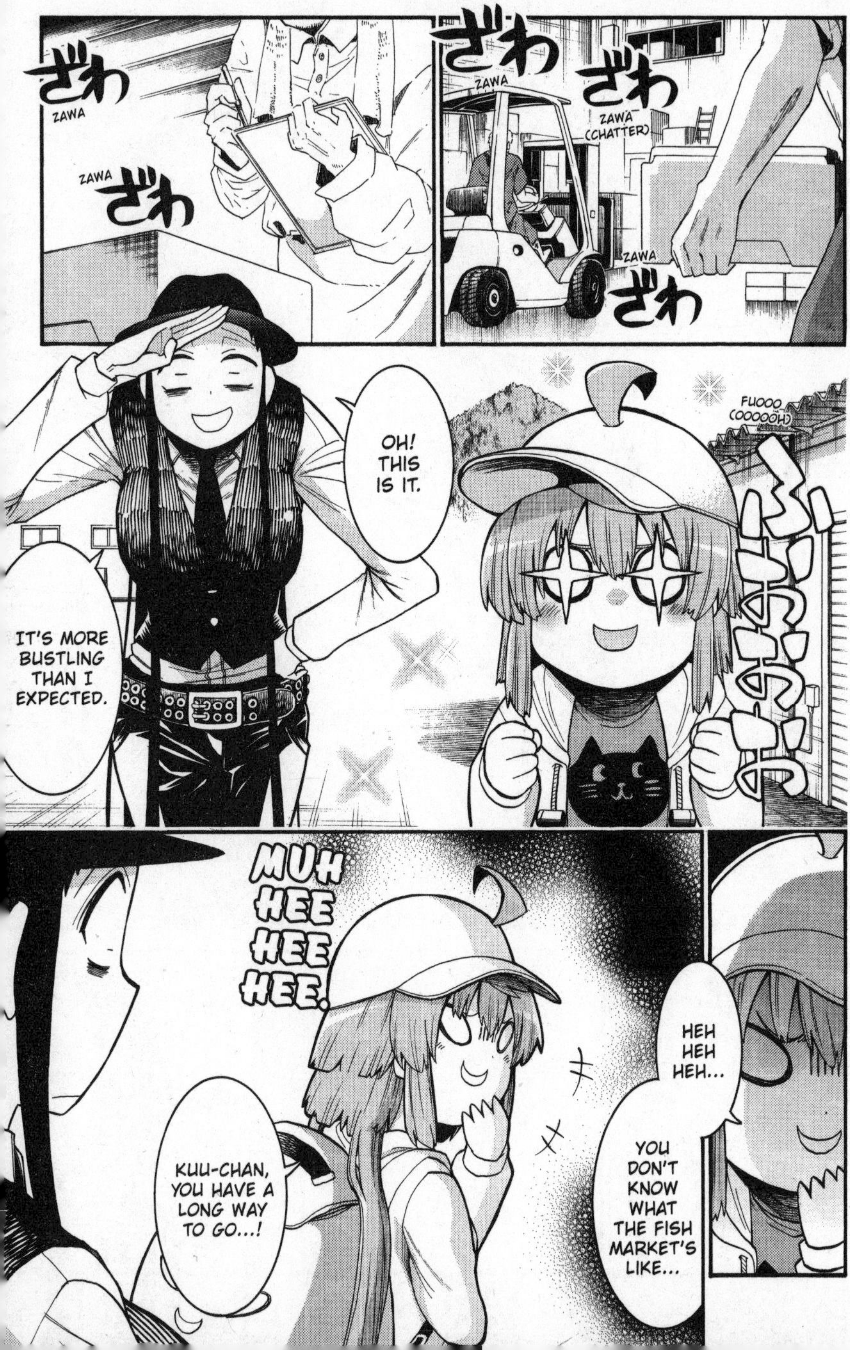
ざわ
ZAWA
ざわ
ZAWA (CHATTER)
ZAWA
ざわ
ざわ
ZAWA
ZAWA
ざわ
FUOOO (OOOOOH)
OH! THIS IS IT.
IT'S MORE BUSTLING THAN I EXPECTED.
HEH HEH HEH...
YOU DON'T KNOW WHAT THE FISH MARKET'S LIKE...
MUH HEE HEE HEE.
KUU-CHAN, YOU HAVE A LONG WAY TO GO...!

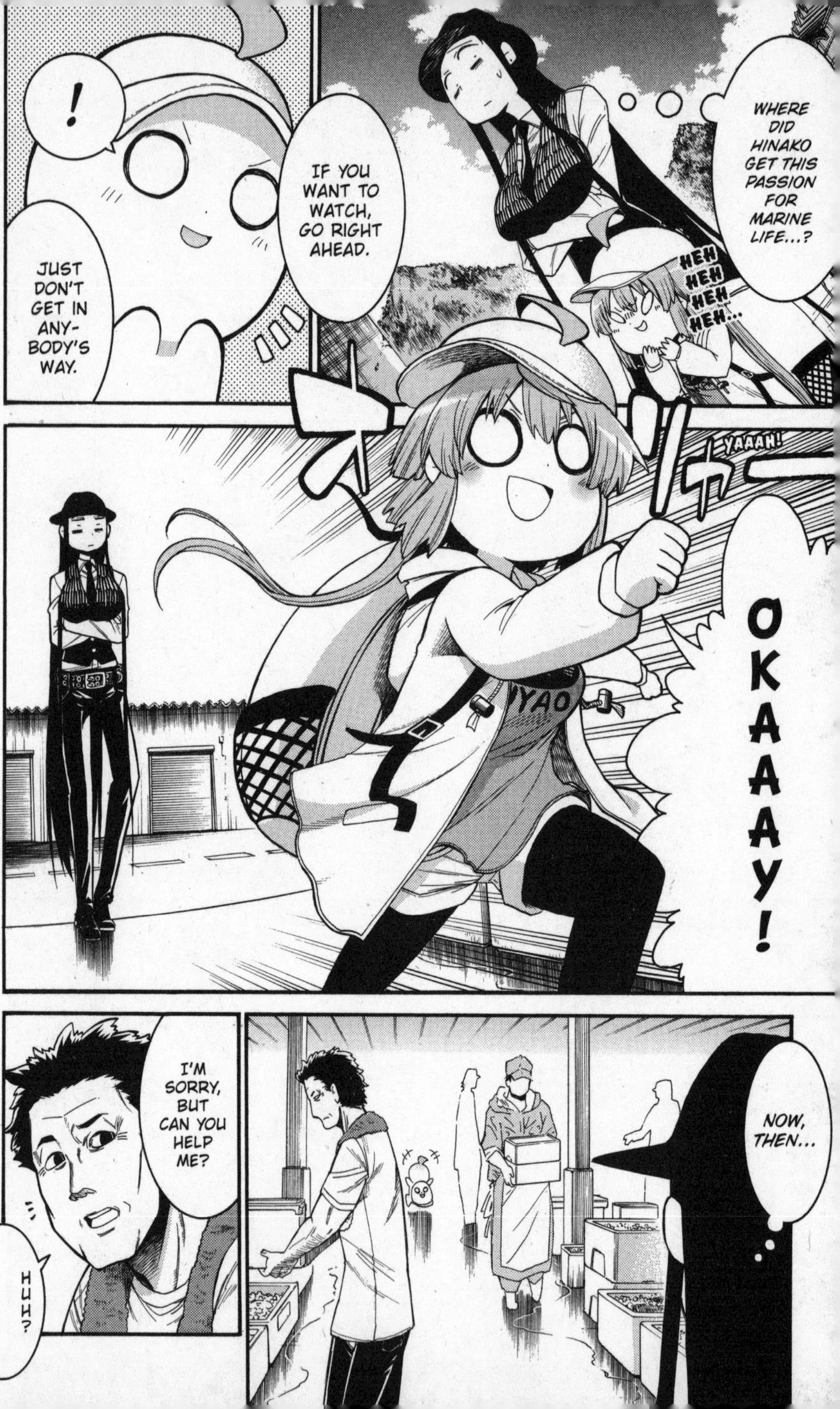
WHERE DID HINAKO GET THIS PASSION FOR MARINE LIFE...?
HEH HEH HEH HEH...
!
IF YOU WANT TO WATCH, GO RIGHT AHEAD.
JUST DON'T GET IN ANY-BODY'S WAY.
YAAAH!
OKAAAAY!
NOW, THEN...
I'M SORRY, BUT CAN YOU HELP ME?
HUH?

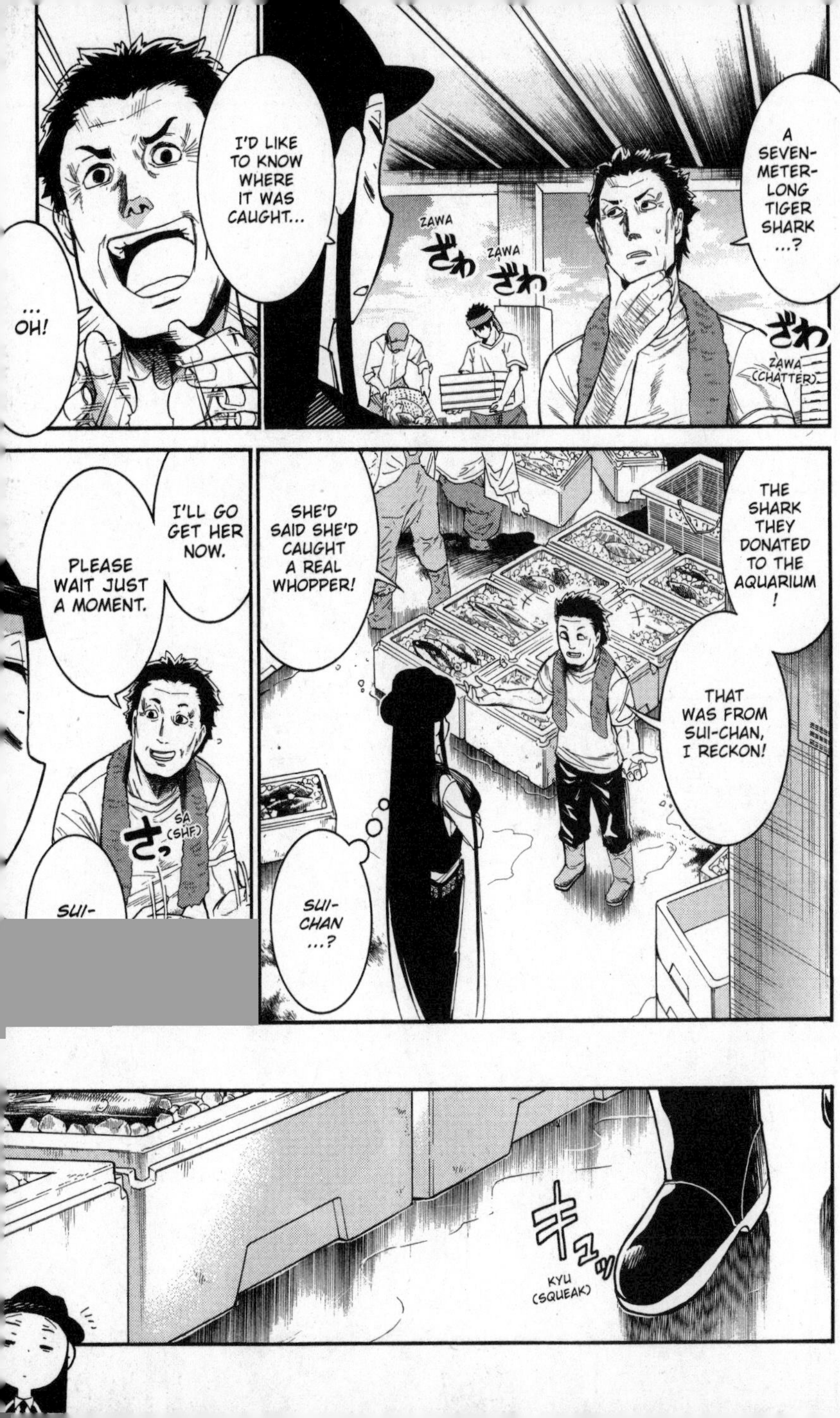
A SEVEN-METER-LONG TIGER SHARK ...?
ZAWA ざわ
ZAWA ざわ
ざわ ZAWA (CHATTER)
I'D LIKE TO KNOW WHERE IT WAS CAUGHT...
... OH!
THE SHARK THEY DONATED TO THE AQUARIUM!
THAT WAS FROM SUI-CHAN, I RECKON!
SHE'D SAID SHE'D CAUGHT A REAL WHOPPER!
SUI-CHAN ...?
I'LL GO GET HER NOW.
PLEASE WAIT JUST A MOMENT.
さっ SA (SHF)
SUI-
キュッ KYU (SQUEAK)

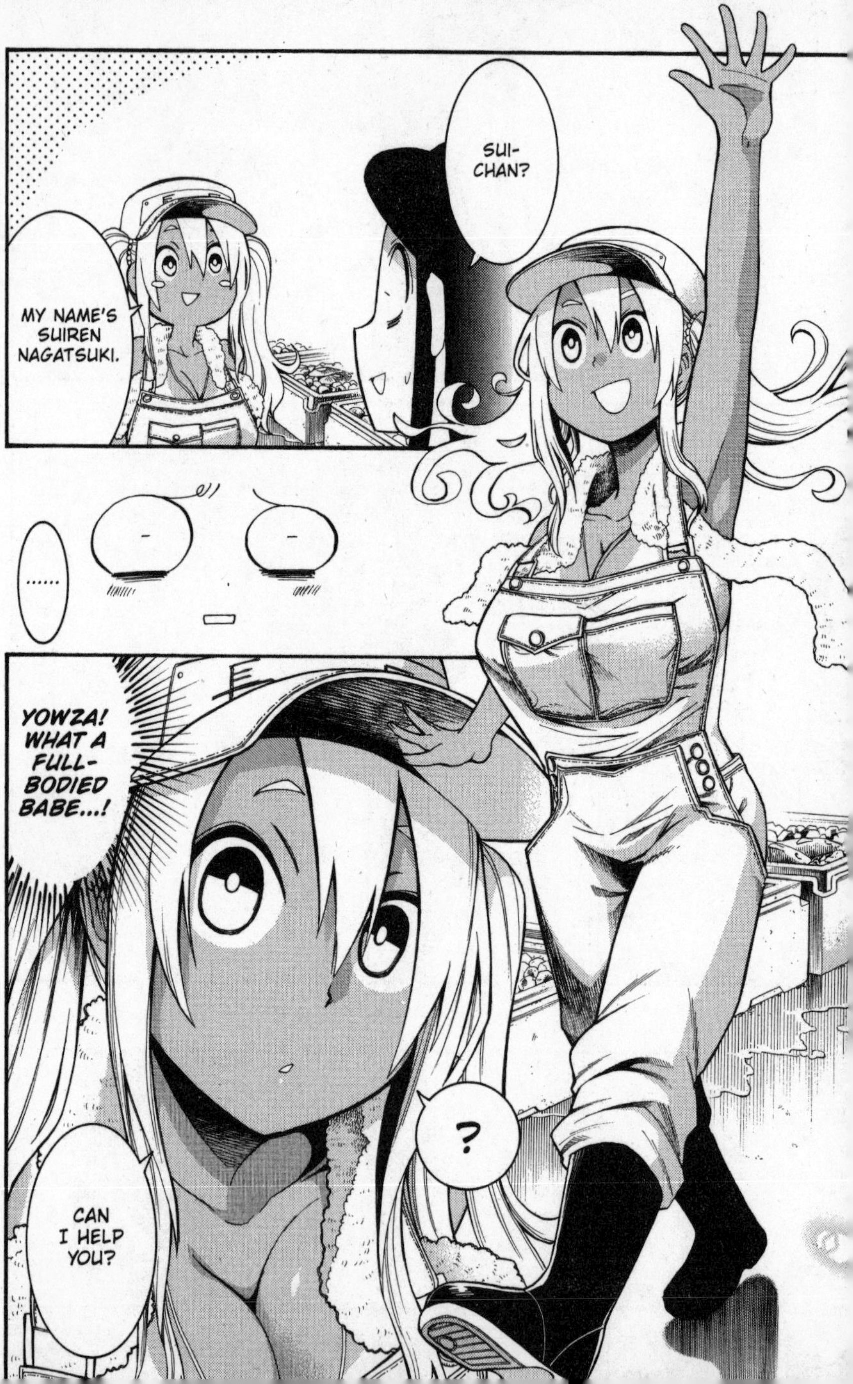
SUI-CHAN?
MY NAME'S SUIREN NAGATSUKI.
......
?
YOWZA! WHAT A FULL-BODIED BABE...!
CAN I HELP YOU?

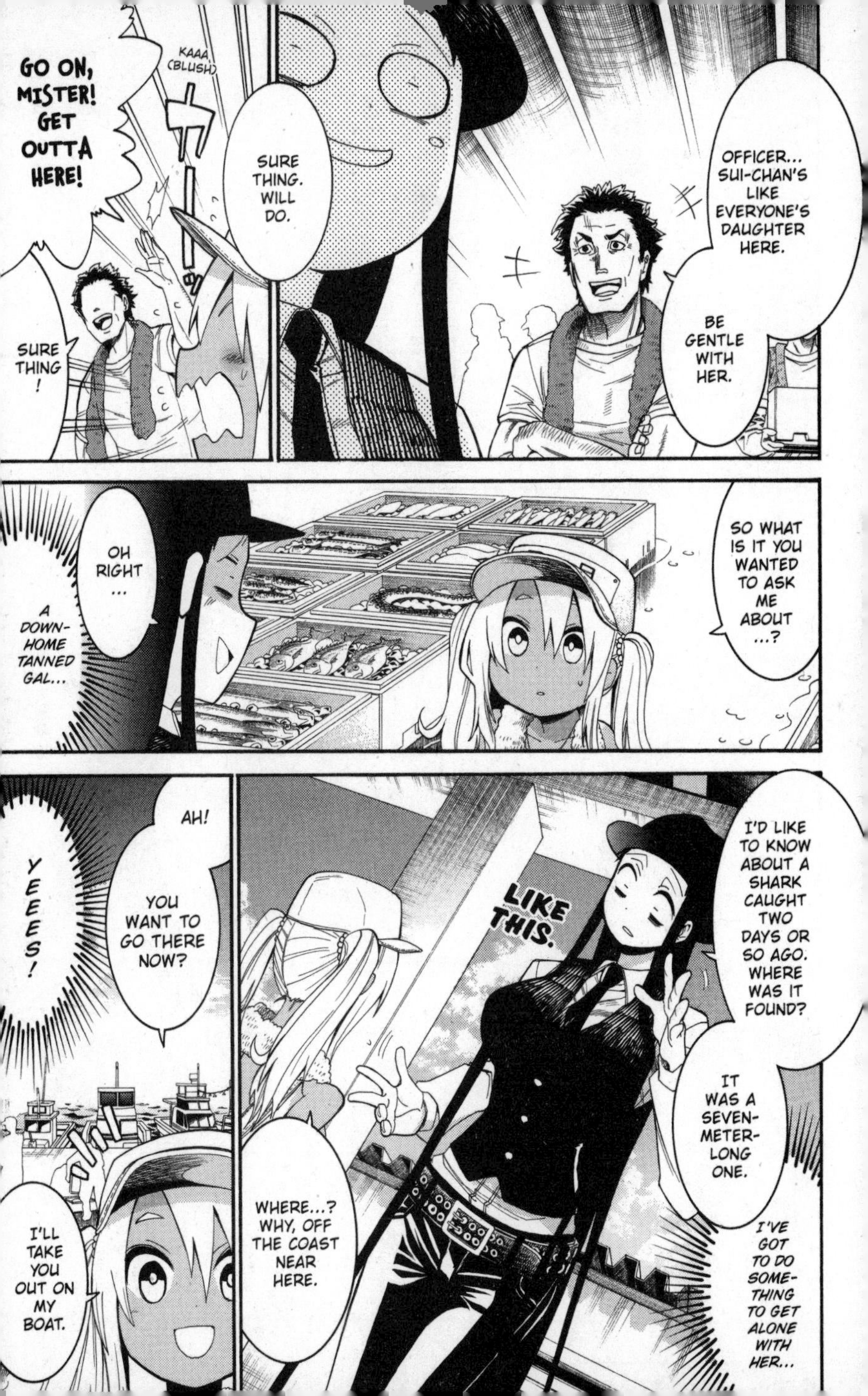
OFFICER... SUI-CHAN'S LIKE EVERYONE'S DAUGHTER HERE.
BE GENTLE WITH HER.
SURE THING. WILL DO.
KAAA (BLUSH)
GO ON, MISTER! GET OUTTA HERE!
SURE THING!
SO WHAT IS IT YOU WANTED TO ASK ME ABOUT...?
OH RIGHT...
A DOWN-HOME TANNED GAL...
I'D LIKE TO KNOW ABOUT A SHARK CAUGHT TWO DAYS OR SO AGO. WHERE WAS IT FOUND?
LIKE THIS.
IT WAS A SEVEN-METER-LONG ONE.
I'VE GOT TO DO SOMETHING TO GET ALONE WITH HER...
WHERE...? WHY, OFF THE COAST NEAR HERE.
AH!
YEEEES!
YOU WANT TO GO THERE NOW?
I'LL TAKE YOU OUT ON MY BOAT.

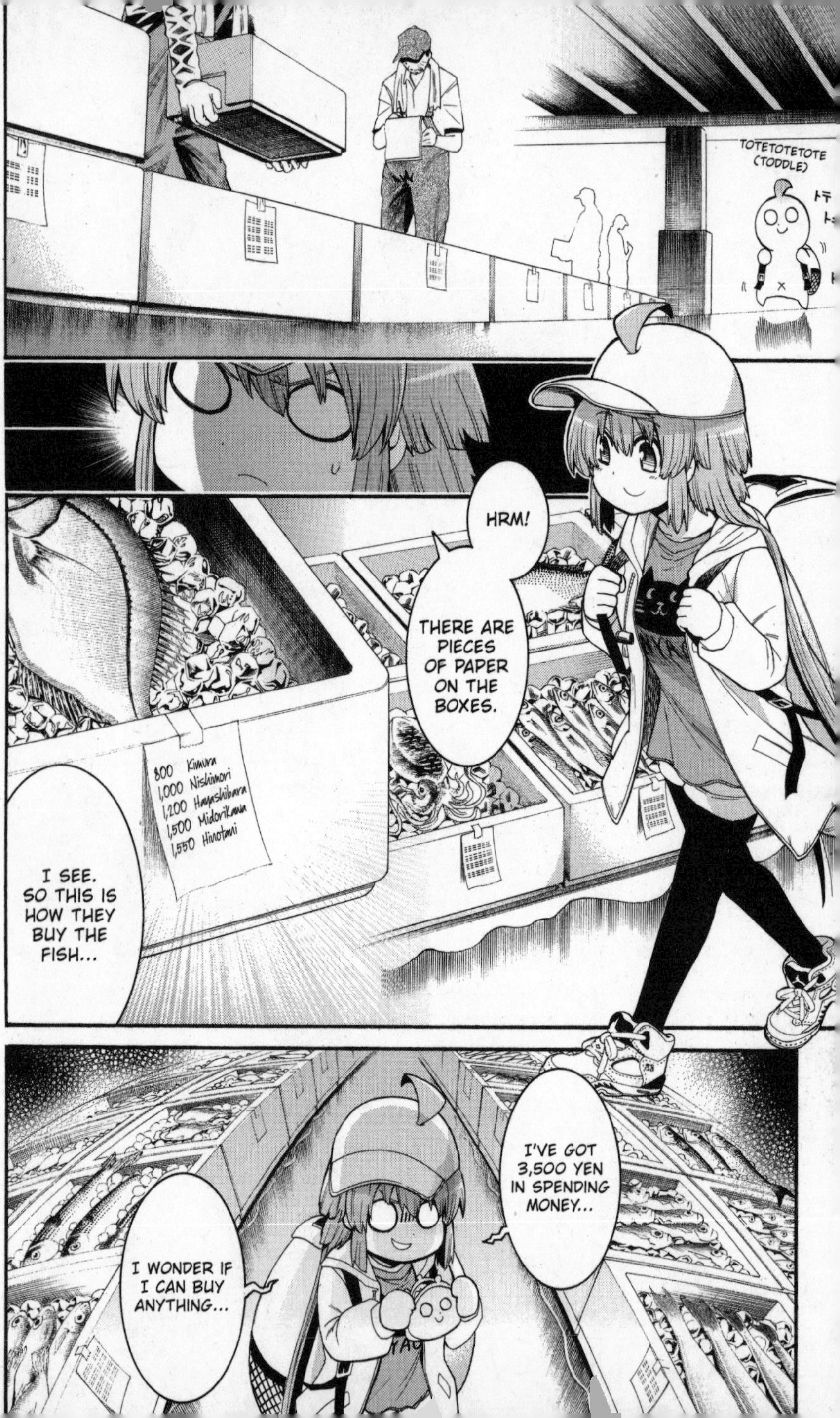
TOTETOTETOTE (TODDLE)
HRM!
THERE ARE PIECES OF PAPER ON THE BOXES.
800 Kimura
1,000 Nishimori
1,200 Hayashibara
1,500 Midorikawa
1,550 Hinotani
I SEE. SO THIS IS HOW THEY BUY THE FISH...
I'VE GOT 3,500 YEN IN SPENDING MONEY...
I WONDER IF I CAN BUY ANYTHING...

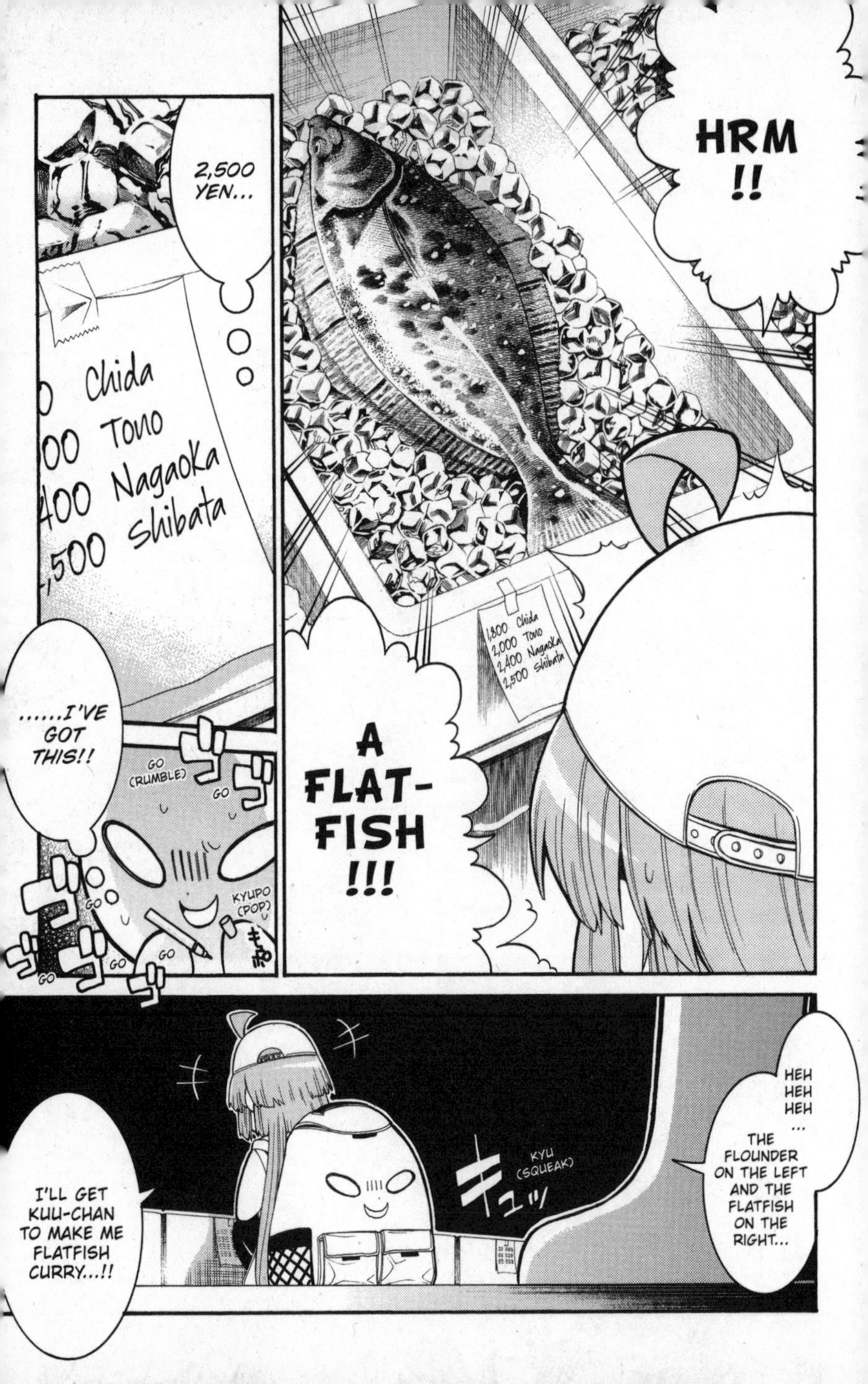
HRM!!
1,800 Chida
2,000 Tono
2,400 Nagaoka
2,500 Shibata
A FLAT-FISH!!!
2,500 YEN...
0 Chida
00 Tono
400 Nagaoka
,500 Shibata
......I'VE GOT THIS!!
GO (RUMBLE)
GO
GO
KYUPO (POP)
GO
GO
GO
HEH HEH HEH... THE FLOUNDER ON THE LEFT AND THE FLATFISH ON THE RIGHT...
KYU (SQUEAK)
I'LL GET KUU-CHAN TO MAKE ME FLATFISH CURRY...!!

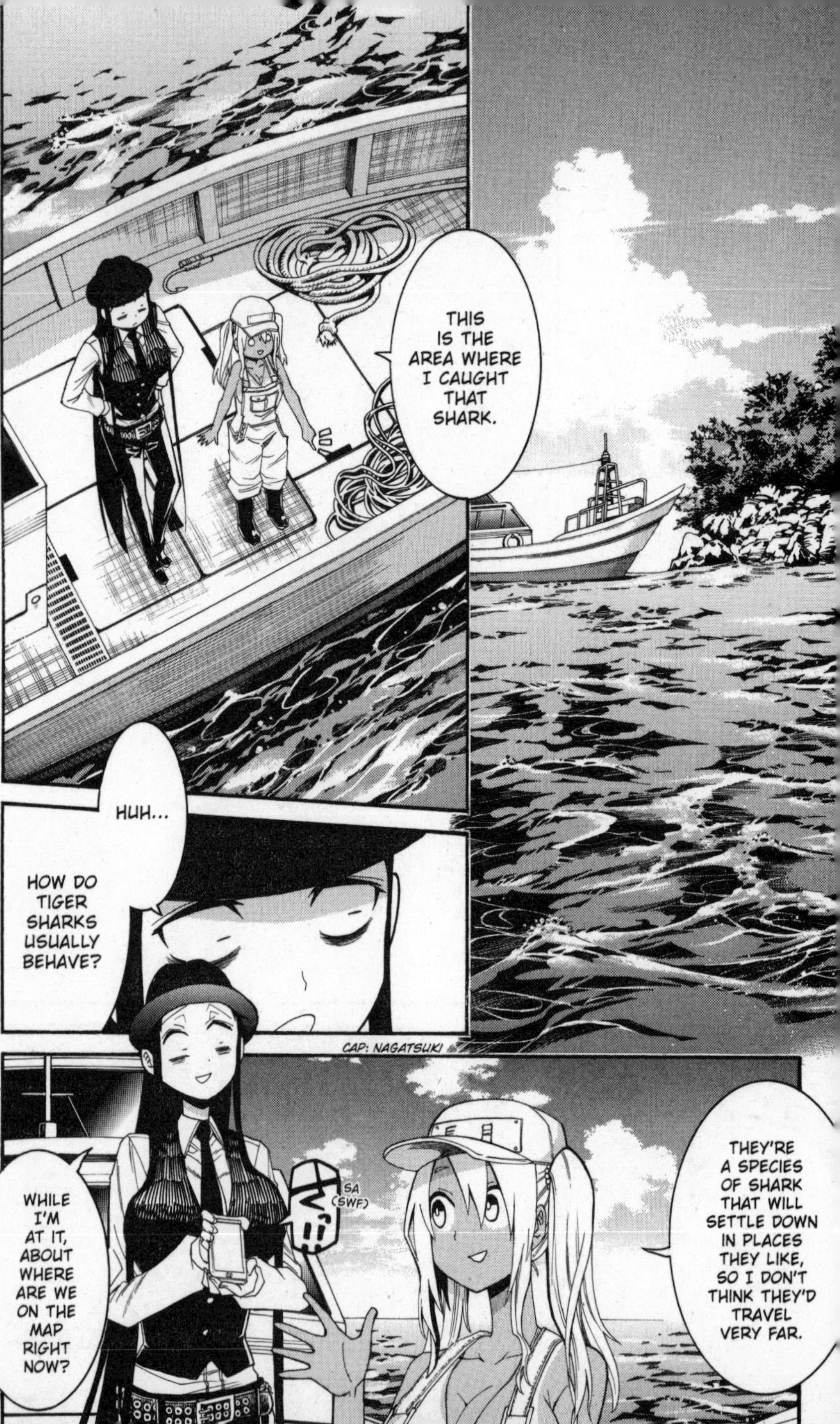
THIS IS THE AREA WHERE I CAUGHT THAT SHARK.
HUH...
HOW DO TIGER SHARKS USUALLY BEHAVE?
CAP: NAGATSUKI
THEY'RE A SPECIES OF SHARK THAT WILL SETTLE DOWN IN PLACES THEY LIKE, SO I DON'T THINK THEY'D TRAVEL VERY FAR.
SA (SWF)
WHILE I'M AT IT, ABOUT WHERE ARE WE ON THE MAP RIGHT NOW?

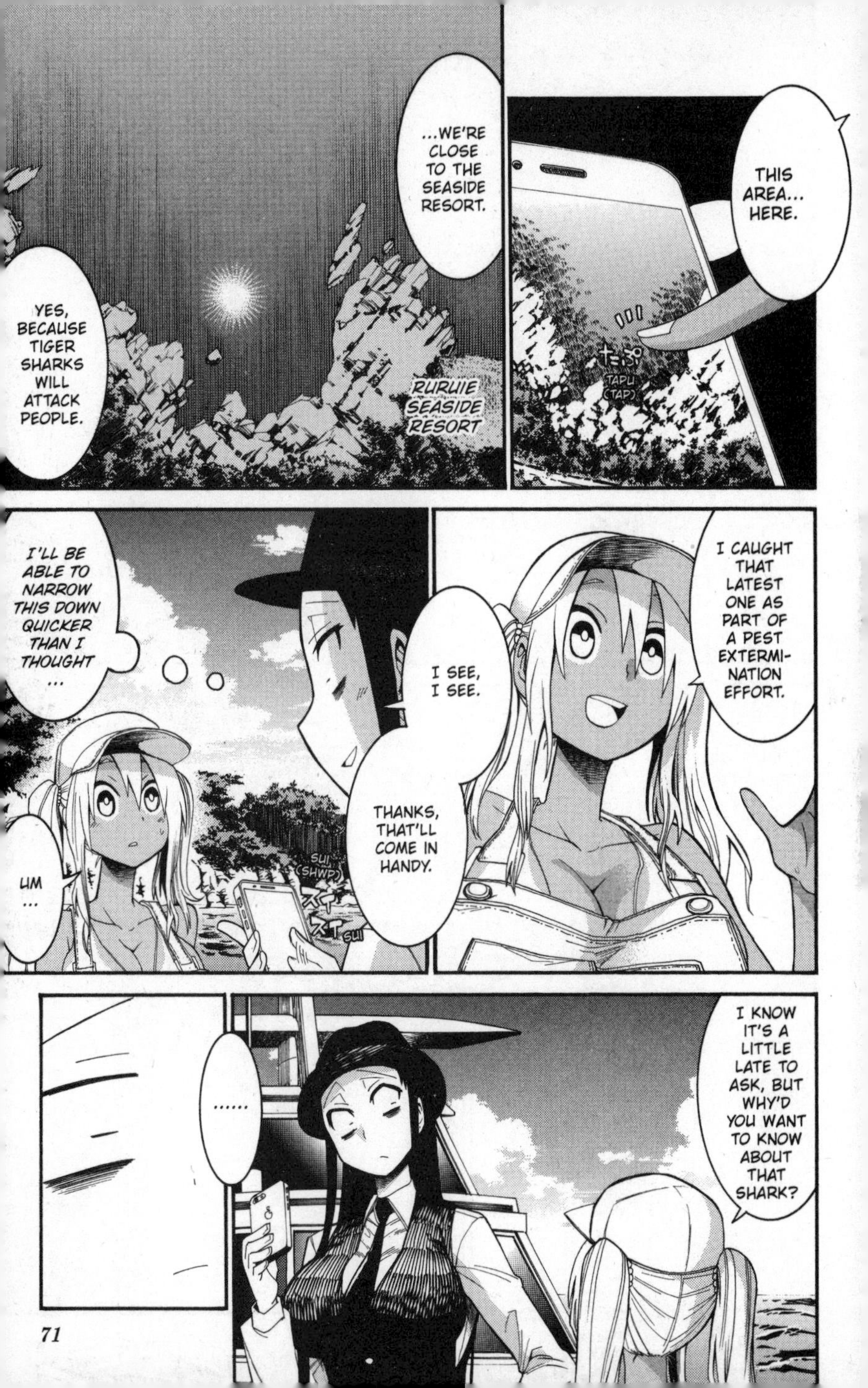
THIS AREA... HERE.
TAPU (TAP)
...WE'RE CLOSE TO THE SEASIDE RESORT.
RURUIE SEASIDE RESORT
YES, BECAUSE TIGER SHARKS WILL ATTACK PEOPLE.
I CAUGHT THAT LATEST ONE AS PART OF A PEST EXTERMI-NATION EFFORT.
I SEE, I SEE.
THANKS, THAT'LL COME IN HANDY.
SUI (SHWD)
SUI
I'LL BE ABLE TO NARROW THIS DOWN QUICKER THAN I THOUGHT ...
UM ...
I KNOW IT'S A LITTLE LATE TO ASK, BUT WHY'D YOU WANT TO KNOW ABOUT THAT SHARK?
......

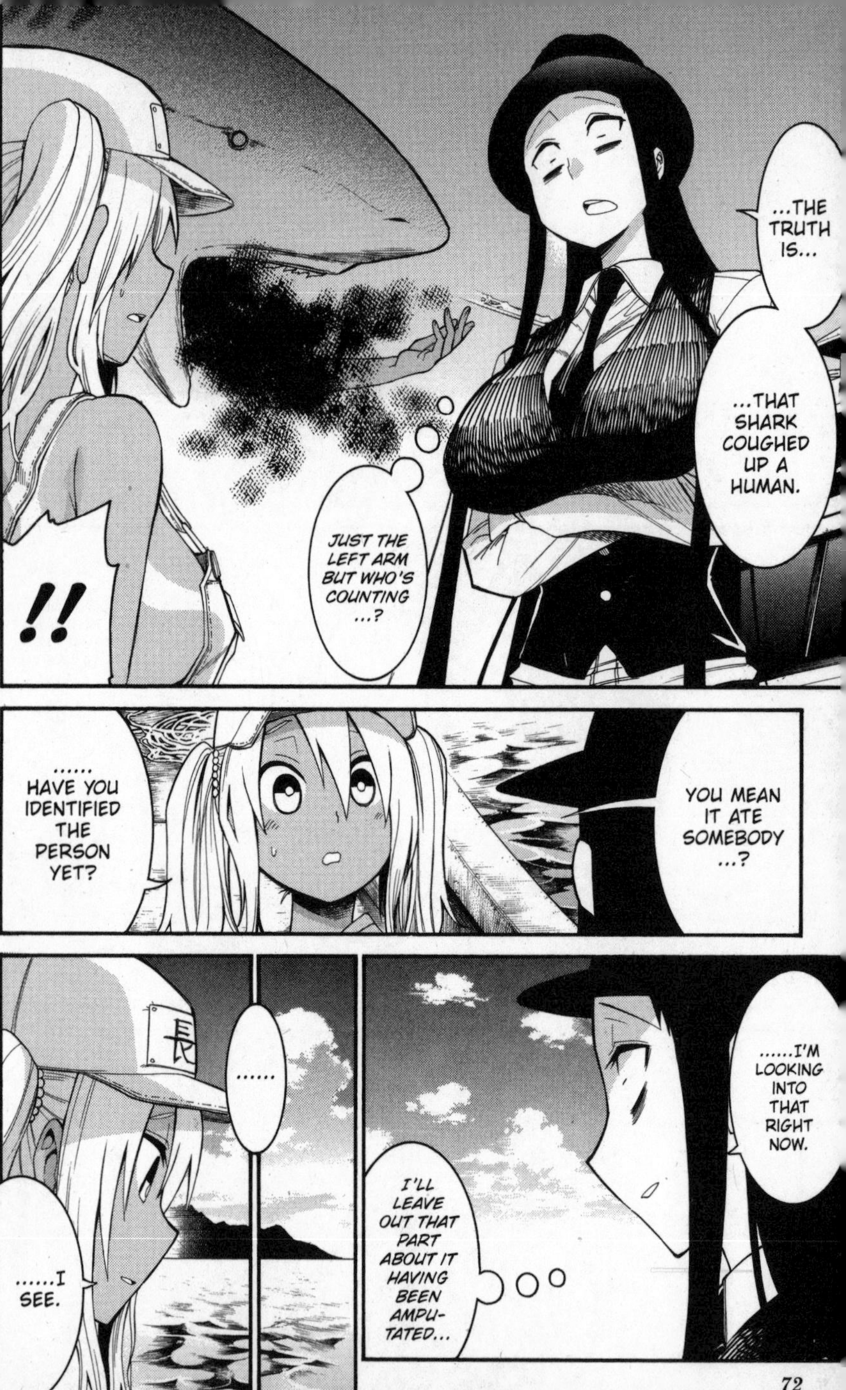
...THE TRUTH IS...
...THAT SHARK COUGHED UP A HUMAN.
JUST THE LEFT ARM BUT WHO'S COUNTING ...?
!!
YOU MEAN IT ATE SOMEBODY ...?
...... HAVE YOU IDENTIFIED THE PERSON YET?
......I'M LOOKING INTO THAT RIGHT NOW.
I'LL LEAVE OUT THAT PART ABOUT IT HAVING BEEN AMPUTATED...
......
......I SEE.

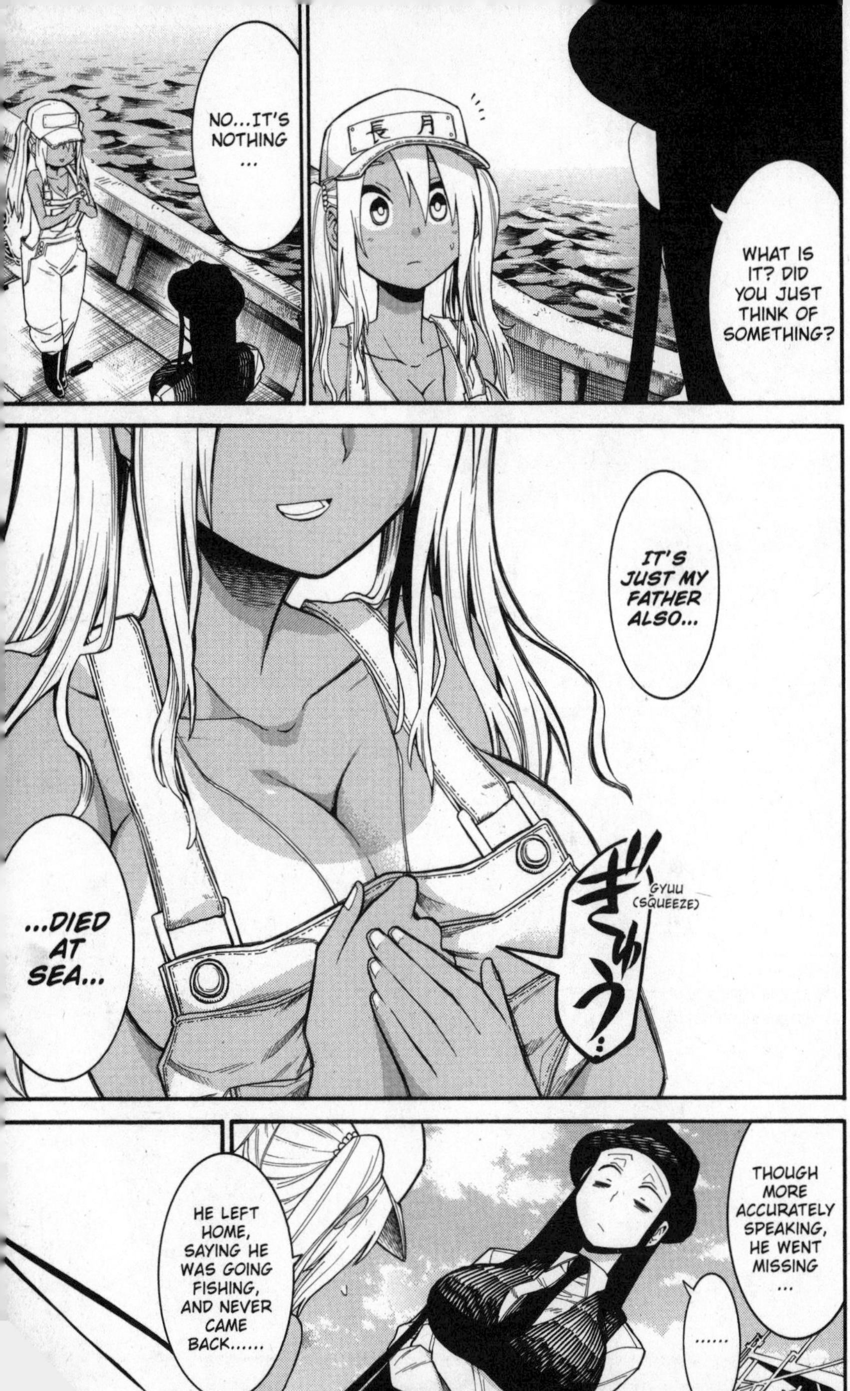
WHAT IS IT? DID YOU JUST THINK OF SOMETHING?
長月
NO...IT'S NOTHING ...
IT'S JUST MY FATHER ALSO...
ぎゅう!!
GYUU (SQUEEZE)
...DIED AT SEA...
THOUGH MORE ACCURATELY SPEAKING, HE WENT MISSING ...
......
HE LEFT HOME, SAYING HE WAS GOING FISHING, AND NEVER CAME BACK......

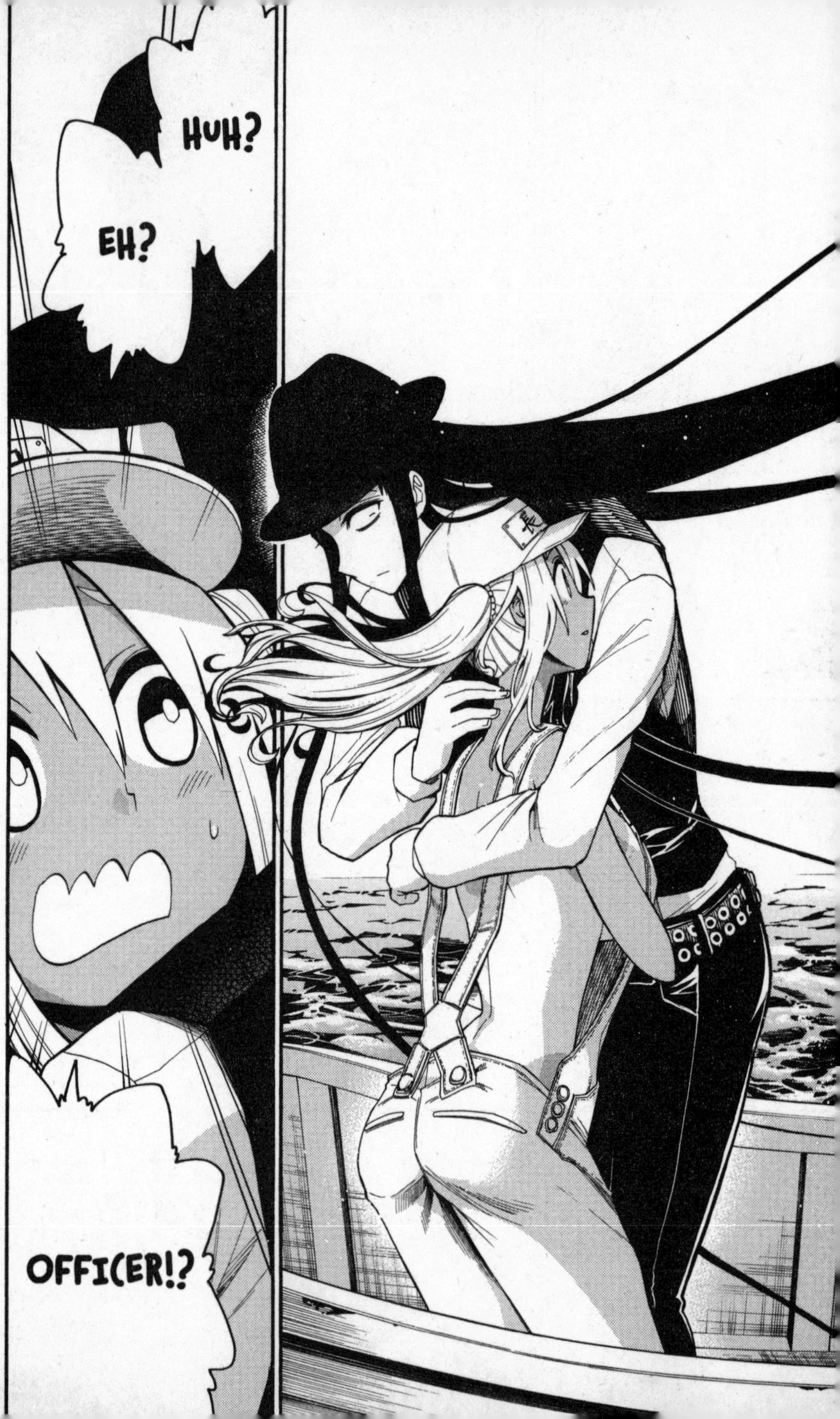
HUH?
EH?
OFFICER!?

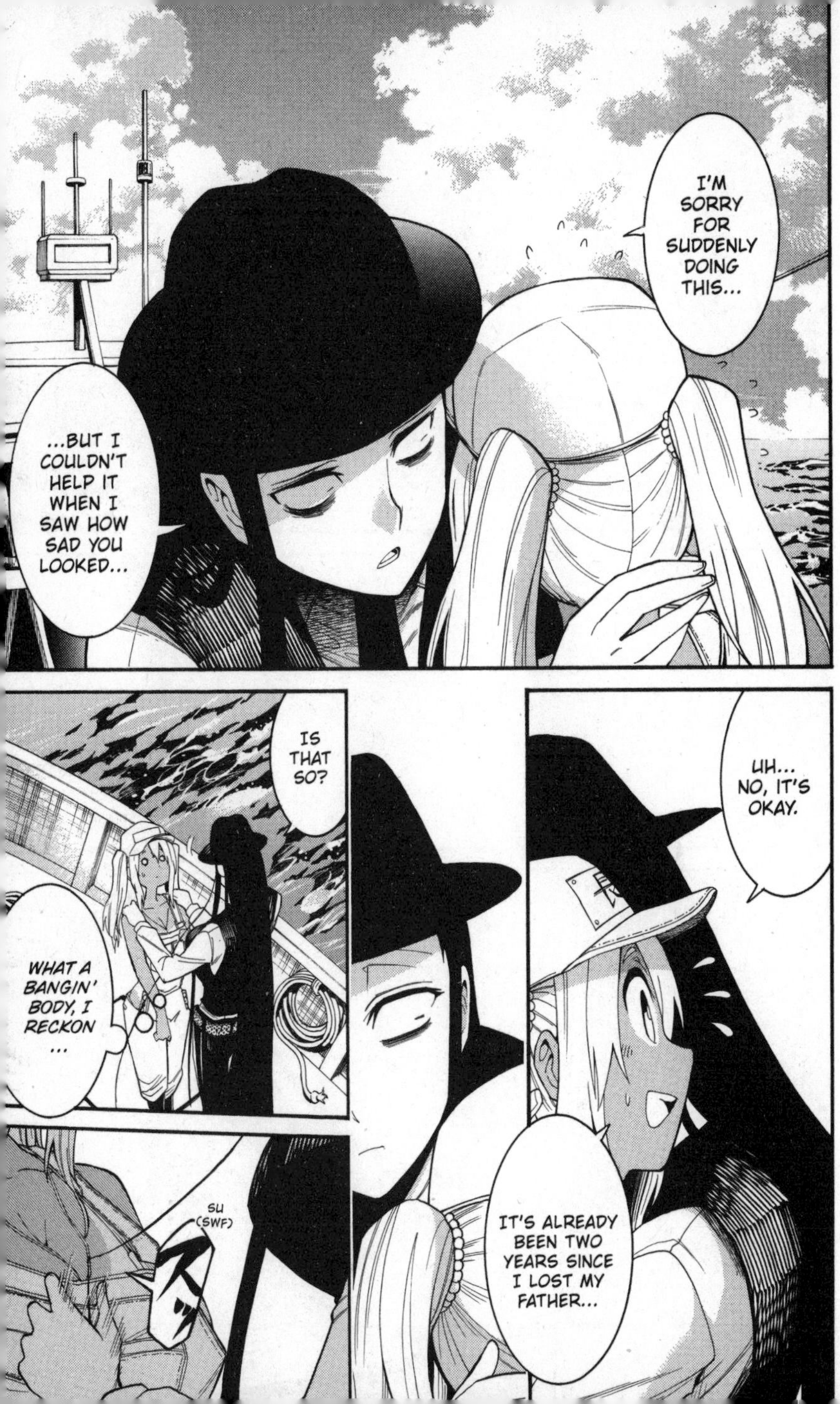
I'M SORRY FOR SUDDENLY DOING THIS...
...BUT I COULDN'T HELP IT WHEN I SAW HOW SAD YOU LOOKED...
UH... NO, IT'S OKAY.
IT'S ALREADY BEEN TWO YEARS SINCE I LOST MY FATHER...
IS THAT SO?
WHAT A BANGIN' BODY, I RECKON...
SU (SWF)

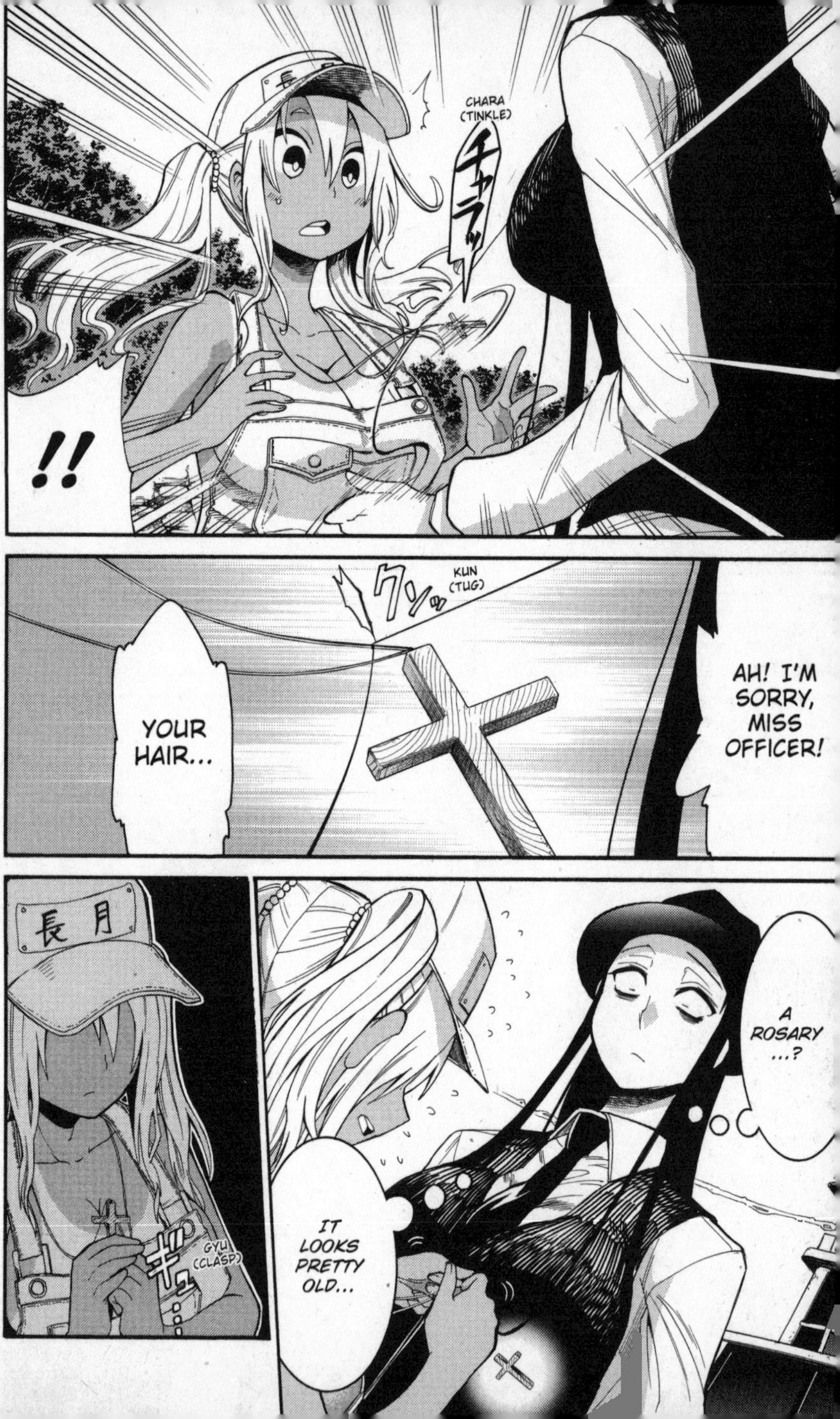
長
CHARA (TINKLE)
チャラッ
!!
AH! I'M SORRY, MISS OFFICER!
KUN (TUG)
クンッ
YOUR HAIR...
A ROSARY ...?
IT LOOKS PRETTY OLD...
長月
GYU (CLASP)
ギュ

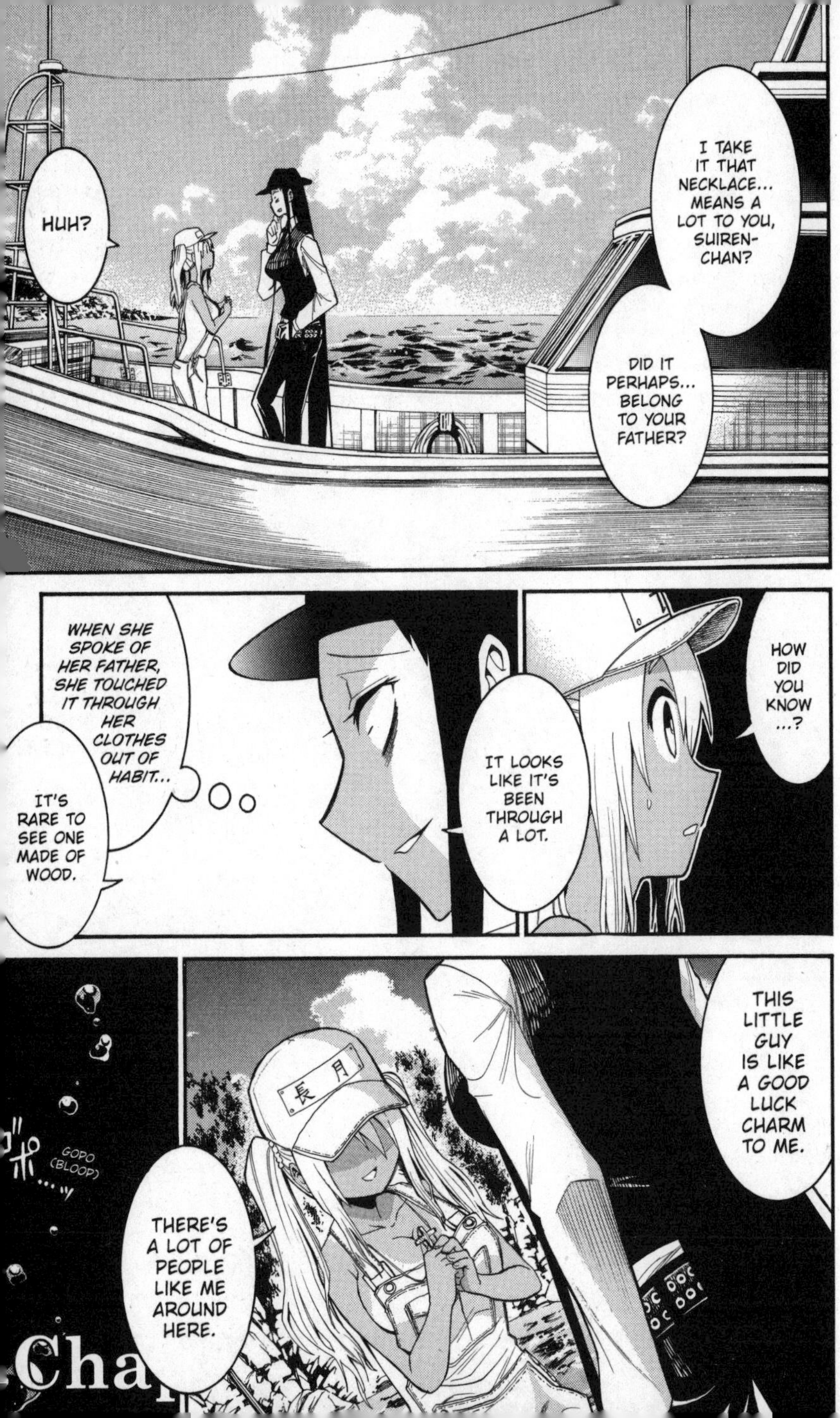
I TAKE IT THAT NECKLACE... MEANS A LOT TO YOU, SUIREN-CHAN?
DID IT PERHAPS... BELONG TO YOUR FATHER?
HUH?
HOW DID YOU KNOW ...?
IT LOOKS LIKE IT'S BEEN THROUGH A LOT.
WHEN SHE SPOKE OF HER FATHER, SHE TOUCHED IT THROUGH HER CLOTHES OUT OF HABIT...
IT'S RARE TO SEE ONE MADE OF WOOD.
THIS LITTLE GUY IS LIKE A GOOD LUCK CHARM TO ME.
長月
THERE'S A LOT OF PEOPLE LIKE ME AROUND HERE.
GOPO (BLOOP)
Chap

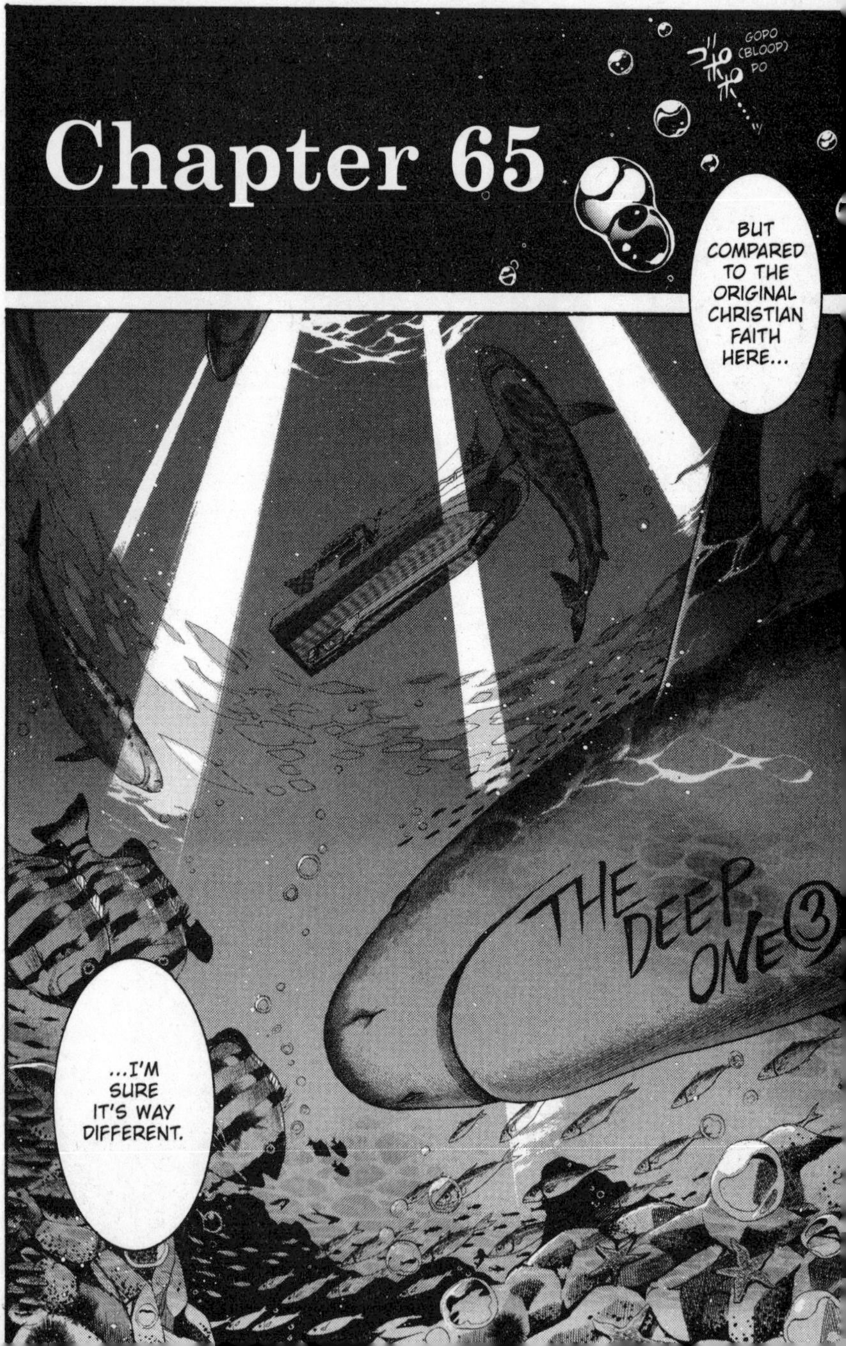

ゴポポ…
GOPO (BLOOP) PO
Chapter 65
BUT COMPARED TO THE ORIGINAL CHRISTIAN FAITH HERE...
THE DEEP ONE ③
...I'M SURE IT'S WAY DIFFERENT.

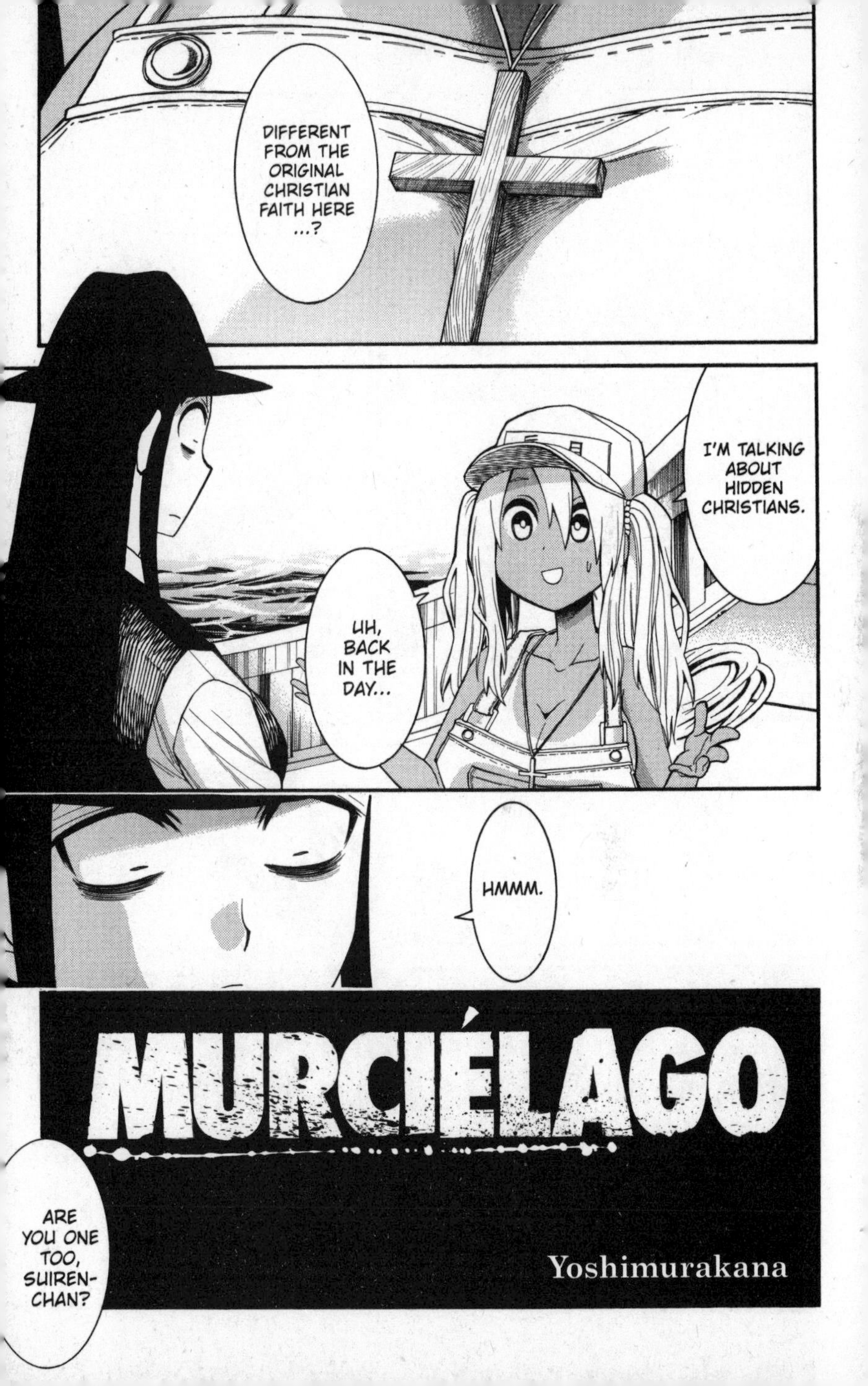
DIFFERENT FROM THE ORIGINAL CHRISTIAN FAITH HERE ...?
I'M TALKING ABOUT HIDDEN CHRISTIANS.
UH, BACK IN THE DAY...
HMMM.
MURCIÉLAGO
Yoshimurakana
ARE YOU ONE TOO, SUIREN-CHAN?

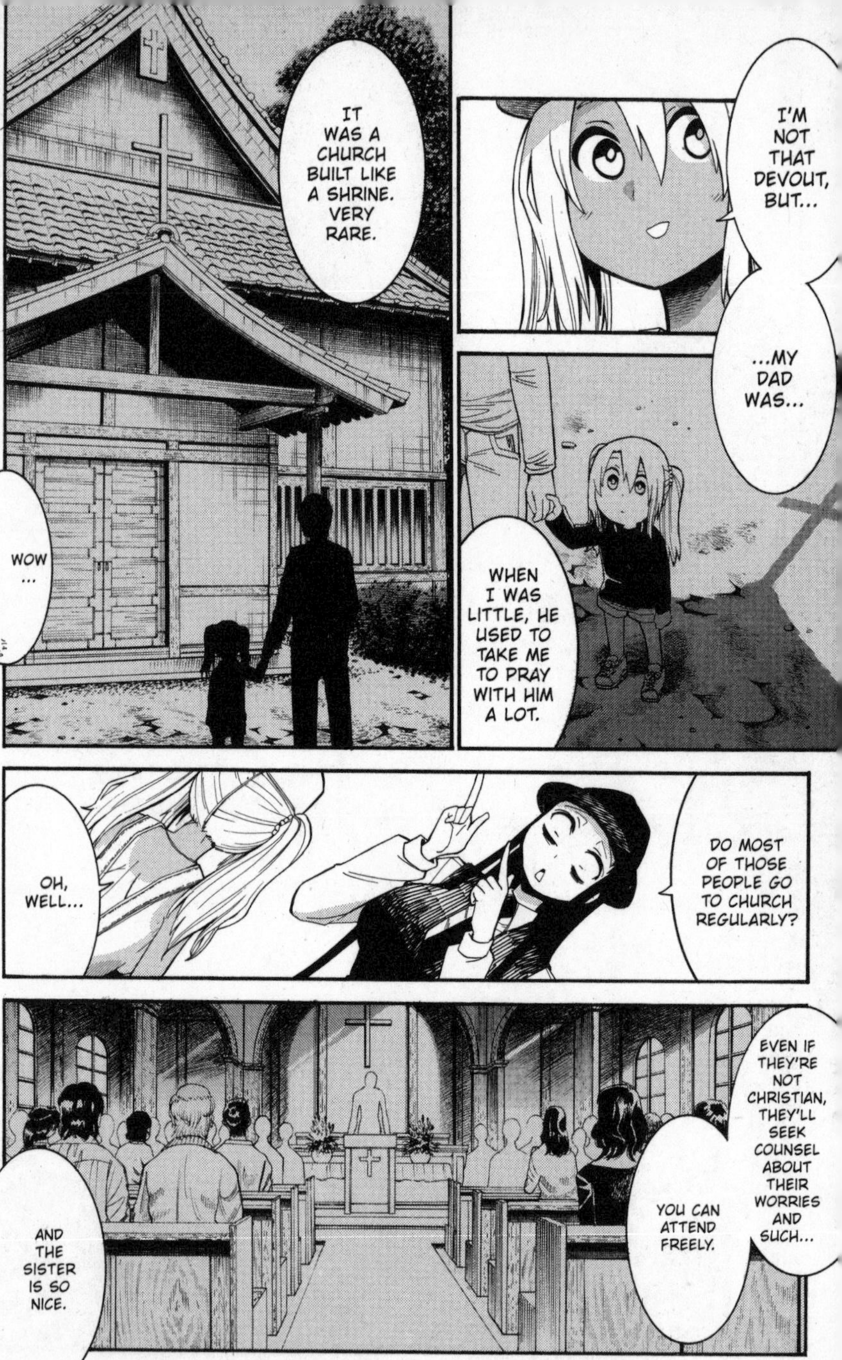
I'M NOT THAT DEVOUT, BUT...
...MY DAD WAS...
WHEN I WAS LITTLE, HE USED TO TAKE ME TO PRAY WITH HIM A LOT.
IT WAS A CHURCH BUILT LIKE A SHRINE. VERY RARE.
WOW...
DO MOST OF THOSE PEOPLE GO TO CHURCH REGULARLY?
OH, WELL...
EVEN IF THEY'RE NOT CHRISTIAN, THEY'LL SEEK COUNSEL ABOUT THEIR WORRIES AND SUCH...
YOU CAN ATTEND FREELY.
AND THE SISTER IS SO NICE.

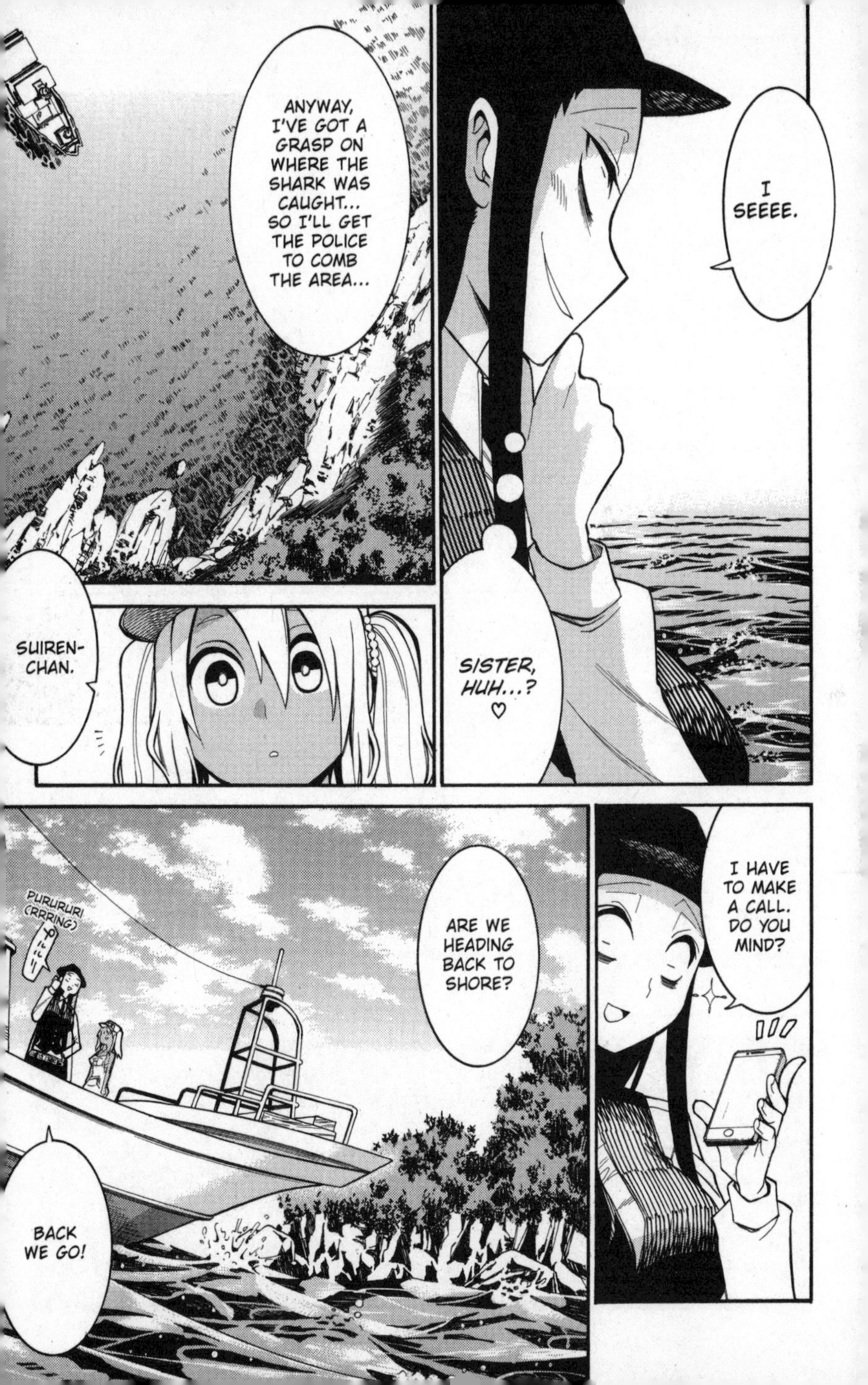
I SEEEE.
SISTER, HUH...? ♡
ANYWAY, I'VE GOT A GRASP ON WHERE THE SHARK WAS CAUGHT... SO I'LL GET THE POLICE TO COMB THE AREA...
SUIREN-CHAN.
I HAVE TO MAKE A CALL. DO YOU MIND?
ARE WE HEADING BACK TO SHORE?
PURURURI (RRRING)
BACK WE GO!

WHERE'D YOU COME FROM, KID?

1,800 Chida
2,000 Tono
2,400 Nagaoka
2,500 Shibata
3,500 Hinako

HMMM...

......ARE YOU LOST?

YOU CAN'T JUST ADD YOUR NAME TO THE LIST.

Chapter 66
THE DEEP ONE ④

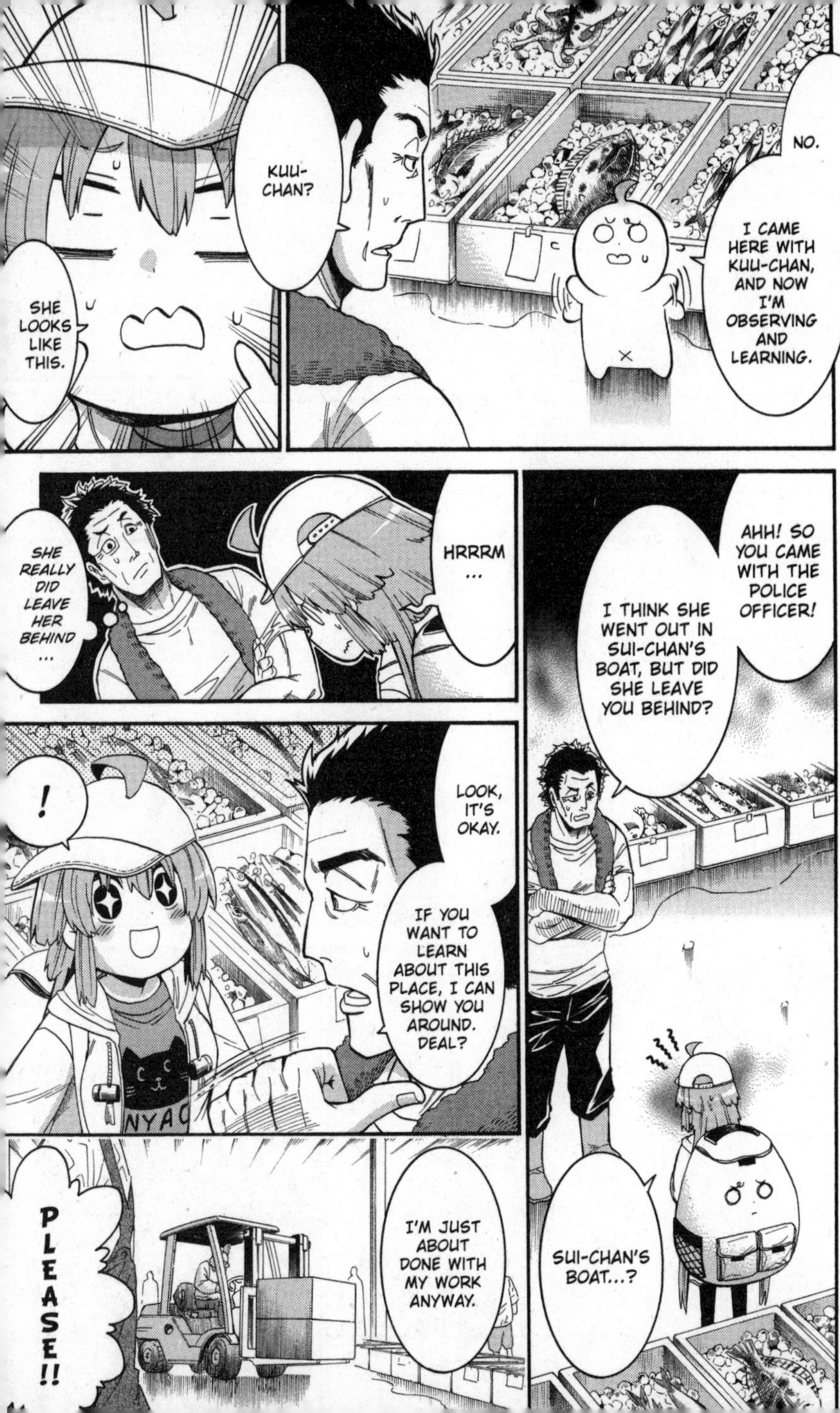
NO.
I CAME HERE WITH KUU-CHAN, AND NOW I'M OBSERVING AND LEARNING.
KUU-CHAN?
SHE LOOKS LIKE THIS.
AHH! SO YOU CAME WITH THE POLICE OFFICER!
I THINK SHE WENT OUT IN SUI-CHAN'S BOAT, BUT DID SHE LEAVE YOU BEHIND?
SUI-CHAN'S BOAT...?
HRRRM...
SHE REALLY DID LEAVE HER BEHIND...
LOOK, IT'S OKAY.
IF YOU WANT TO LEARN ABOUT THIS PLACE, I CAN SHOW YOU AROUND. DEAL?
!
I'M JUST ABOUT DONE WITH MY WORK ANYWAY.
PLEASE!!

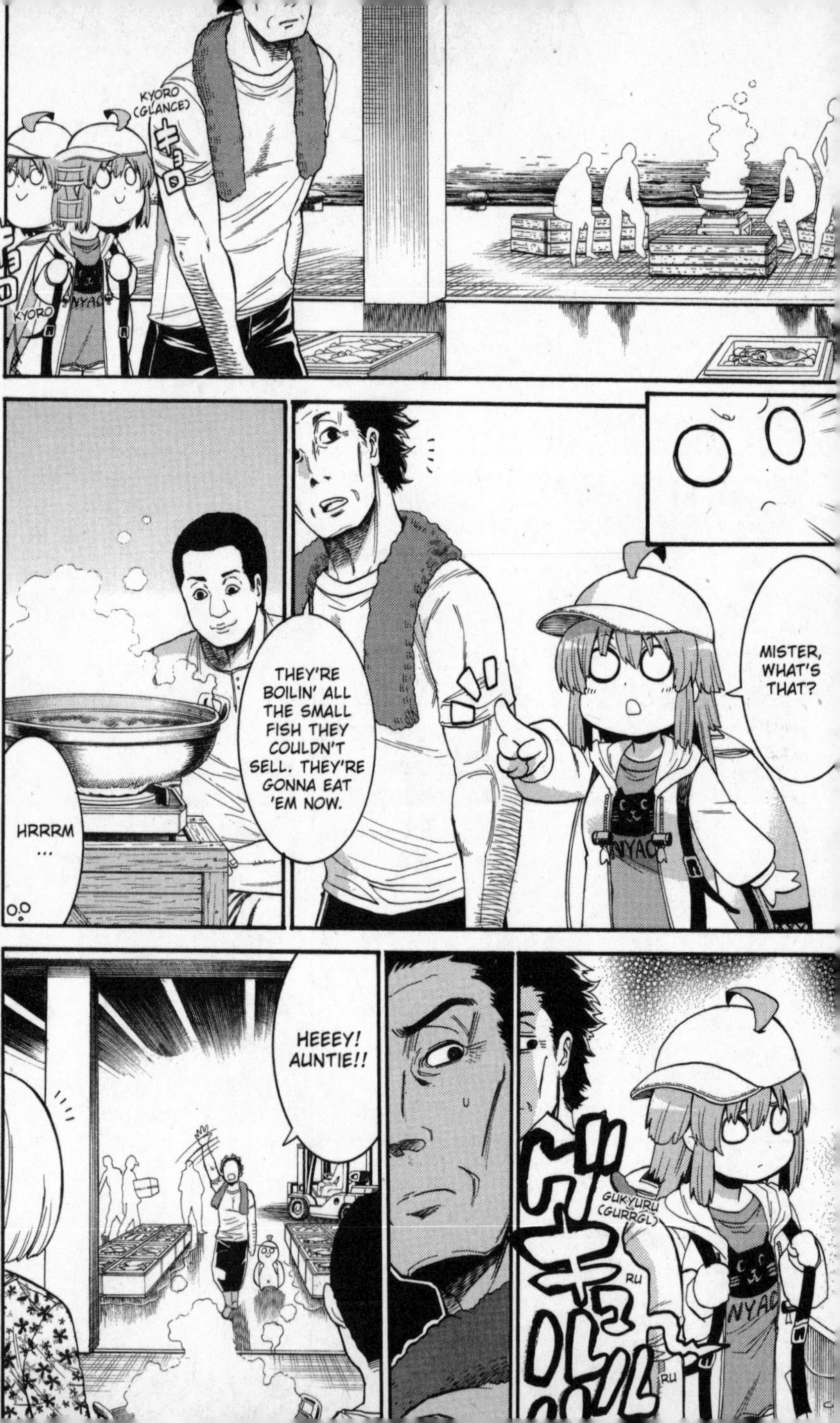
KYORO (GLANCE)
KYORO
MISTER, WHAT'S THAT?
THEY'RE BOILIN' ALL THE SMALL FISH THEY COULDN'T SELL. THEY'RE GONNA EAT 'EM NOW.
HRRRM ...
GUKYURU (GURRGL)
RU
RU
HEEEY! AUNTIE!!

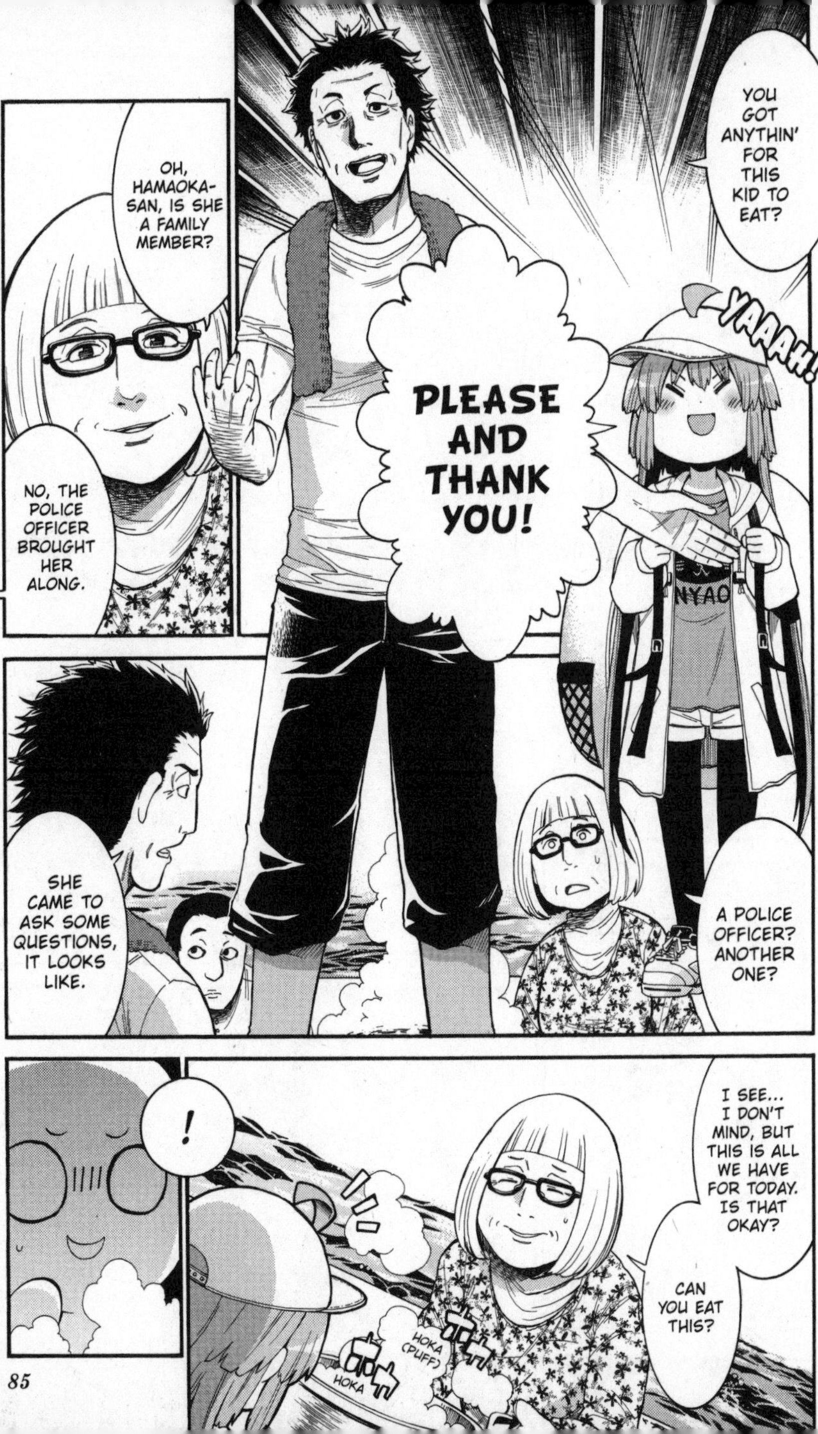
YOU GOT ANYTHIN' FOR THIS KID TO EAT?
YAAAAH!
PLEASE AND THANK YOU!
OH, HAMAOKA-SAN, IS SHE A FAMILY MEMBER?
NO, THE POLICE OFFICER BROUGHT HER ALONG.
A POLICE OFFICER? ANOTHER ONE?
SHE CAME TO ASK SOME QUESTIONS, IT LOOKS LIKE.
I SEE... I DON'T MIND, BUT THIS IS ALL WE HAVE FOR TODAY. IS THAT OKAY?
CAN YOU EAT THIS?
HOKA (PUFF)
HOKA
!

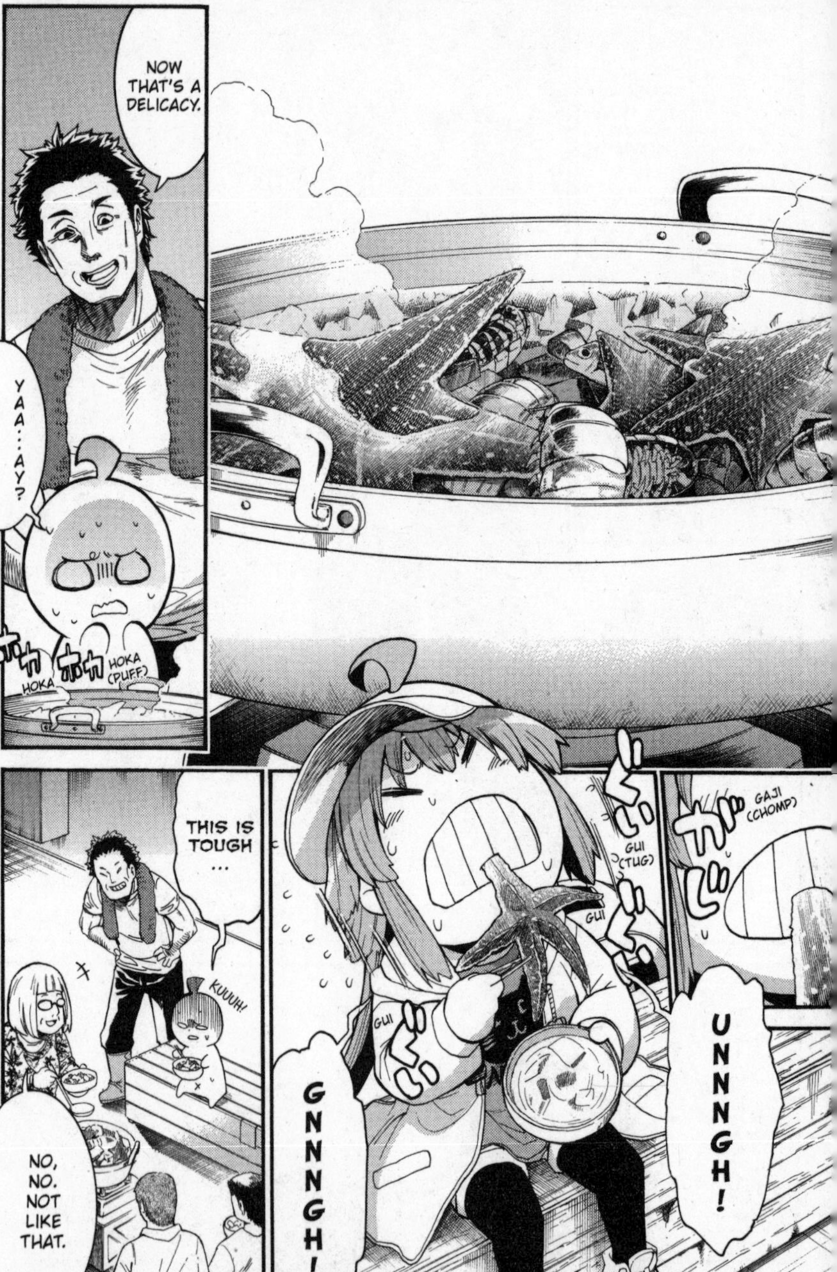
NOW THAT'S A DELICACY.
YAA...AY?
HOKA
HOKA (PUFF)
GAJI (CHOMP)
UNNNGH!
GUI (TUG)
GUI
GUI
GNNNGH!
THIS IS TOUGH...
KUUUH!
NO, NO. NOT LIKE THAT.

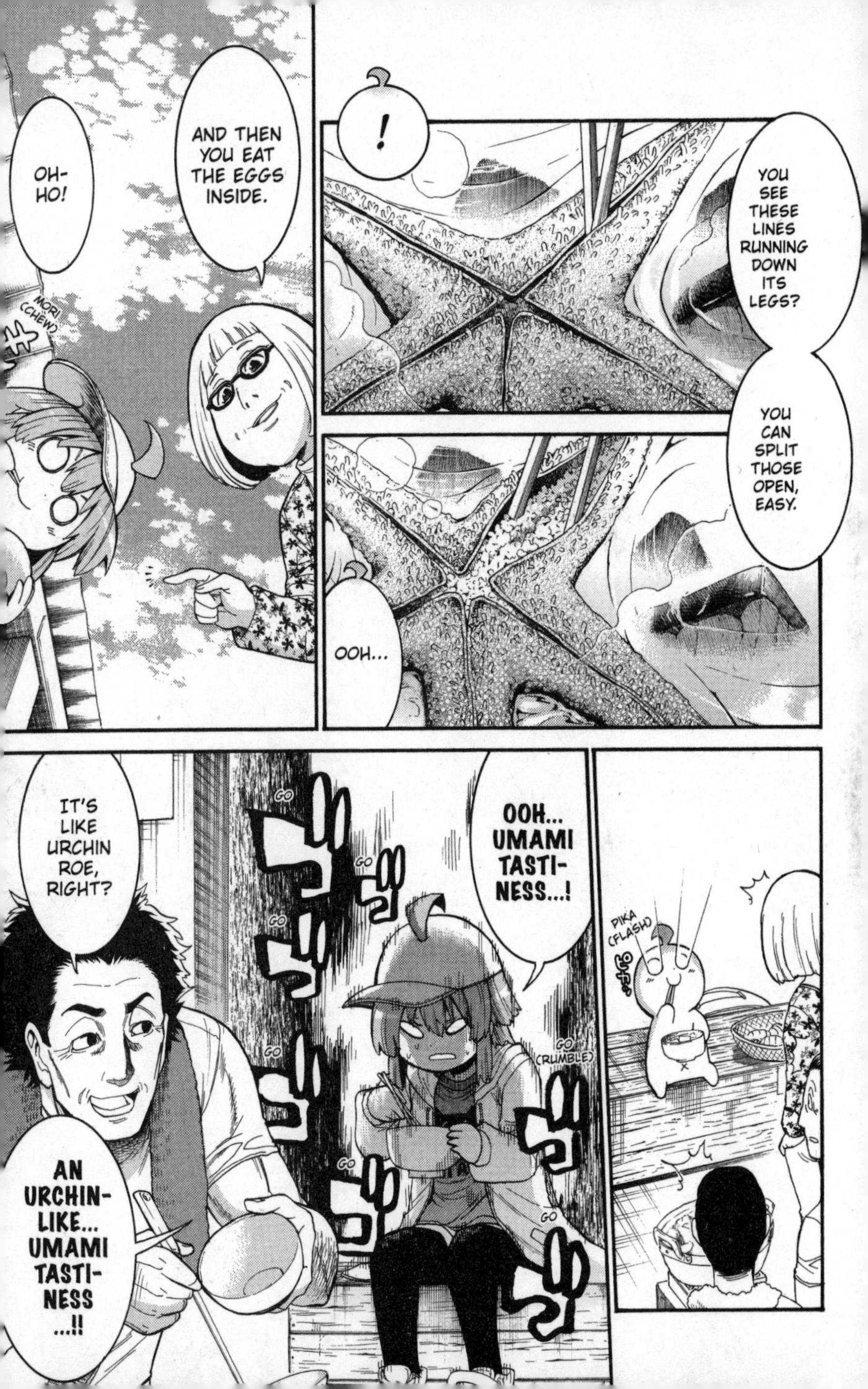
!
YOU SEE THESE LINES RUNNING DOWN ITS LEGS?
YOU CAN SPLIT THOSE OPEN, EASY.
OOH...
AND THEN YOU EAT THE EGGS INSIDE.
OH-HO!
MORI (CHEW)
PIKA (FLASH)
OOH... UMAMI TASTI-NESS...!
GO
GO
GO
GO (RUMBLE)
GO
GO
GO
IT'S LIKE URCHIN ROE, RIGHT?
AN URCHIN-LIKE... UMAMI TASTI-NESS ...!!

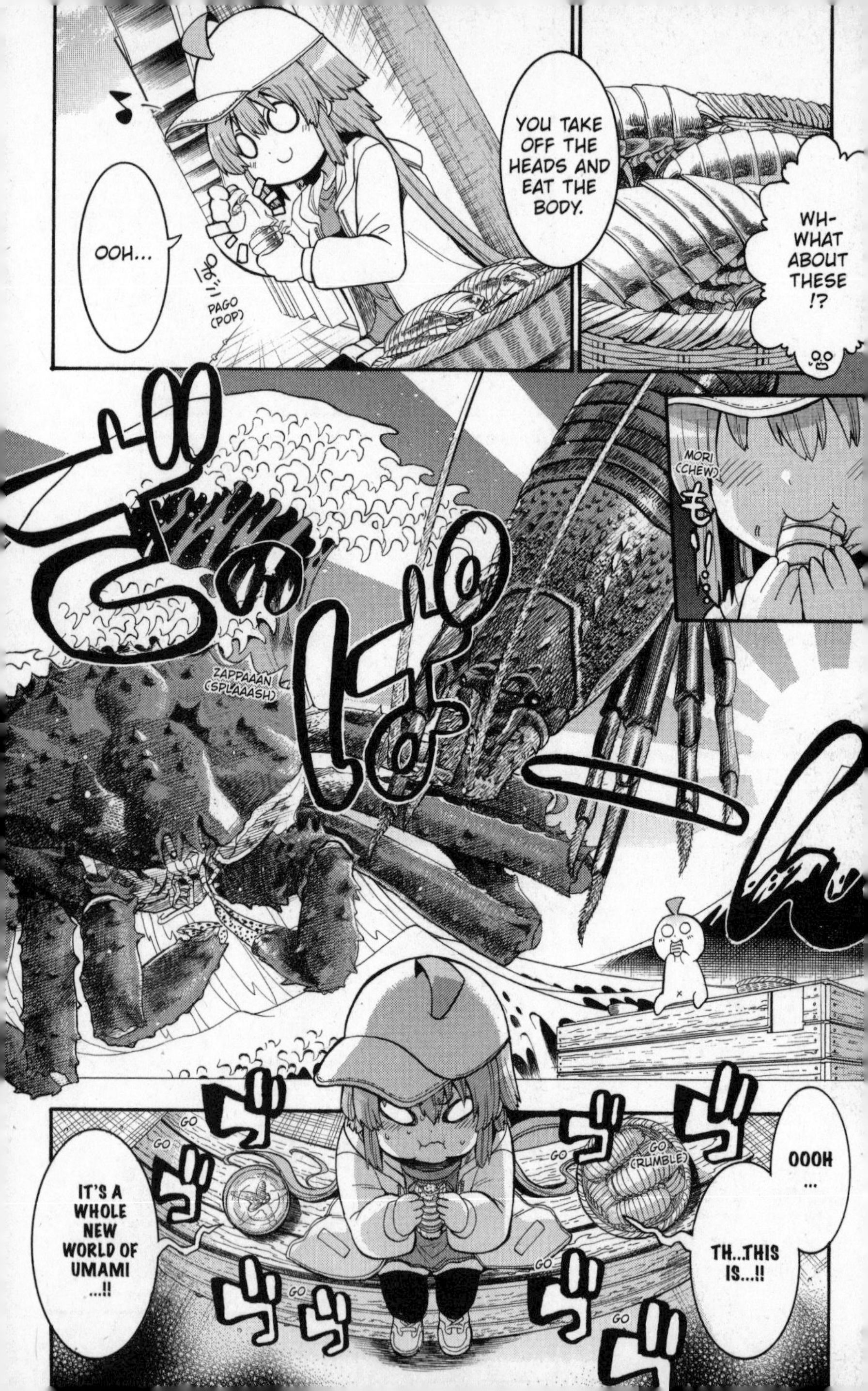
WH-WHAT ABOUT THESE !?
YOU TAKE OFF THE HEADS AND EAT THE BODY.
PAGO (POP)
OOH...
MORI (CHEW)
ZAPPAAAN (SPLAAAASH)
OOOH ...
TH...THIS IS...!!
GO (RUMBLE)
GO
GO
GO
GO
GO
GO
IT'S A WHOLE NEW WORLD OF UMAMI ...!!

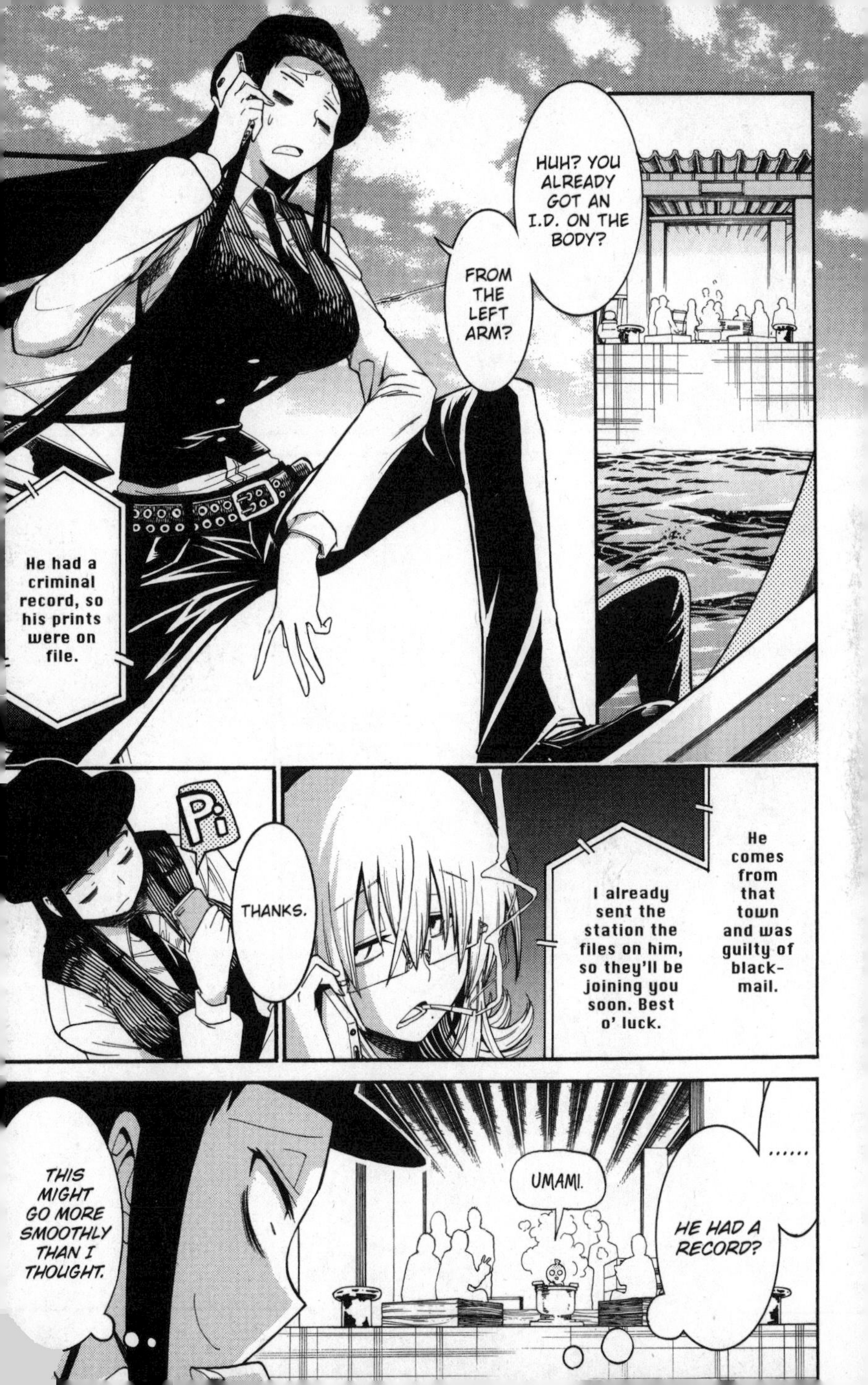
HUH? YOU ALREADY GOT AN I.D. ON THE BODY?
FROM THE LEFT ARM?
He had a criminal record, so his prints were on file.
He comes from that town and was guilty of black-mail.
I already sent the station the files on him, so they'll be joining you soon. Best o' luck.
Pi
THANKS.
......
HE HAD A RECORD?
UMAMI.
THIS MIGHT GO MORE SMOOTHLY THAN I THOUGHT.

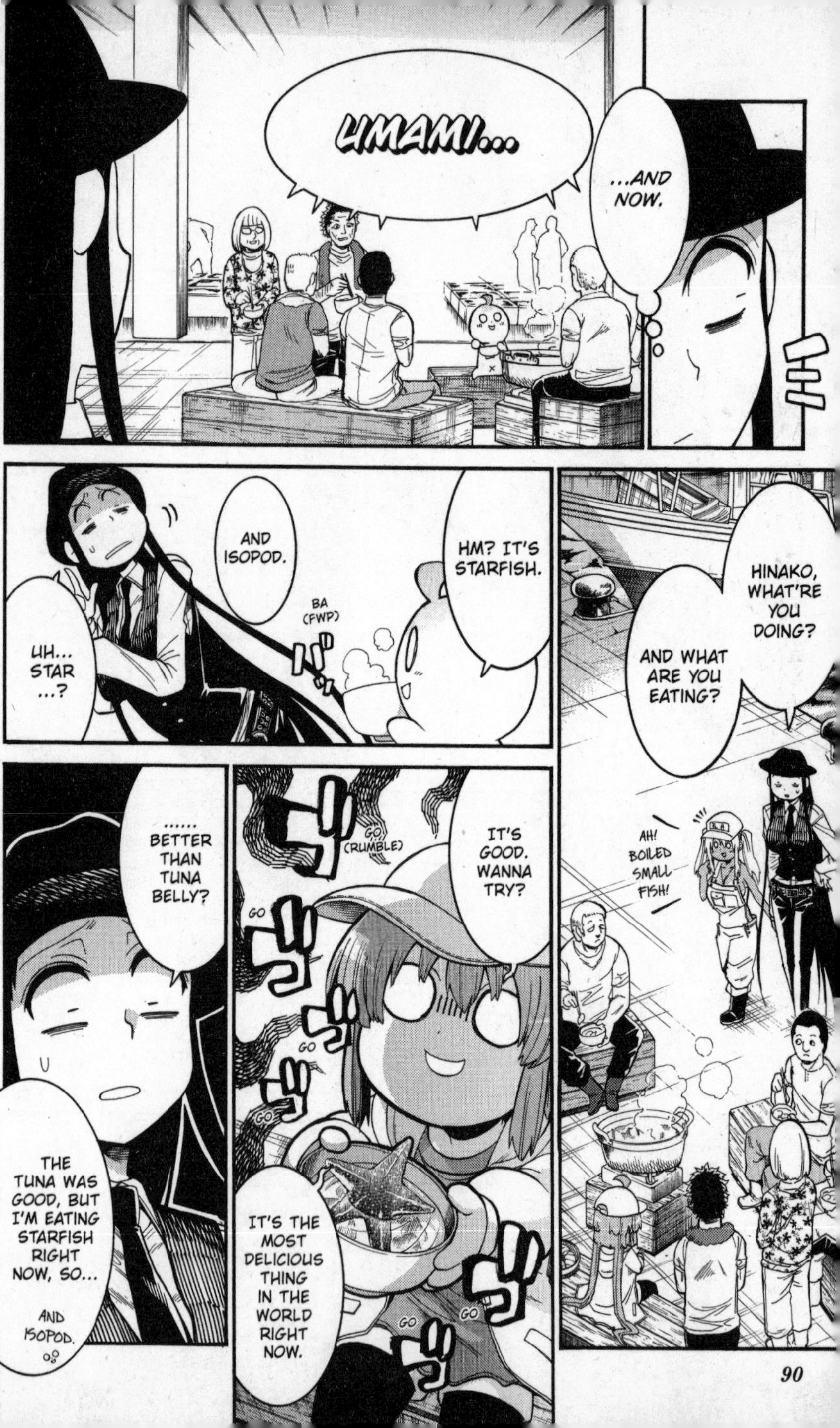
...AND NOW.
UMAMI...
HINAKO, WHAT'RE YOU DOING?
AND WHAT ARE YOU EATING?
AH! BOILED SMALL FISH!
HM? IT'S STARFISH.
BA (FWP)
AND ISOPOD.
UH... STAR ...?
IT'S GOOD. WANNA TRY?
GO (RUMBLE)
GO
GO
GO
IT'S THE MOST DELICIOUS THING IN THE WORLD RIGHT NOW.
GO
GO
...... BETTER THAN TUNA BELLY?
THE TUNA WAS GOOD, BUT I'M EATING STARFISH RIGHT NOW, SO...
AND ISOPOD.

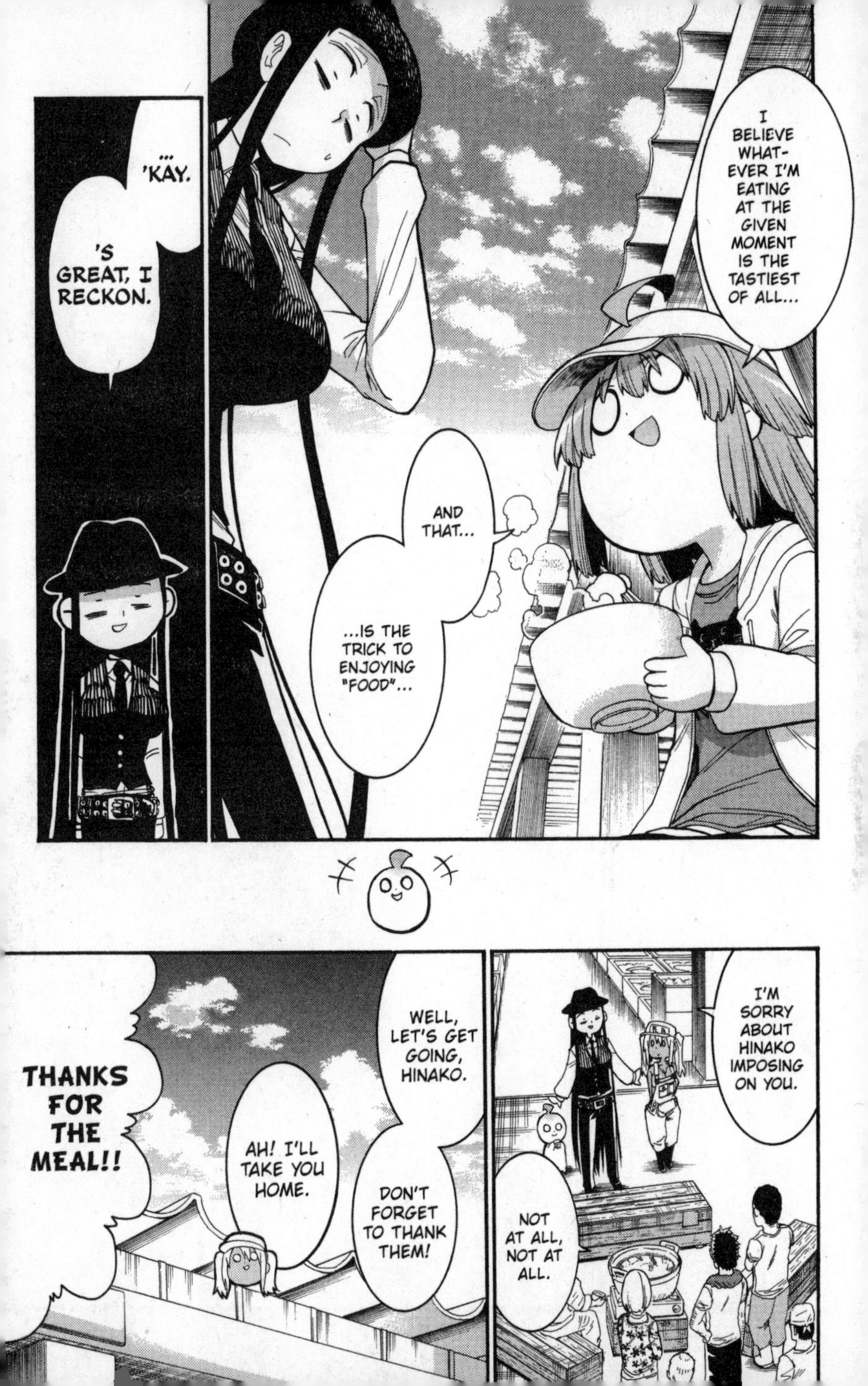
I BELIEVE WHATEVER I'M EATING AT THE GIVEN MOMENT IS THE TASTIEST OF ALL...
AND THAT...
...IS THE TRICK TO ENJOYING "FOOD"...
... 'KAY.
'S GREAT, I RECKON.
I'M SORRY ABOUT HINAKO IMPOSING ON YOU.
NOT AT ALL, NOT AT ALL.
WELL, LET'S GET GOING, HINAKO.
DON'T FORGET TO THANK THEM!
AH! I'LL TAKE YOU HOME.
THANKS FOR THE MEAL!!

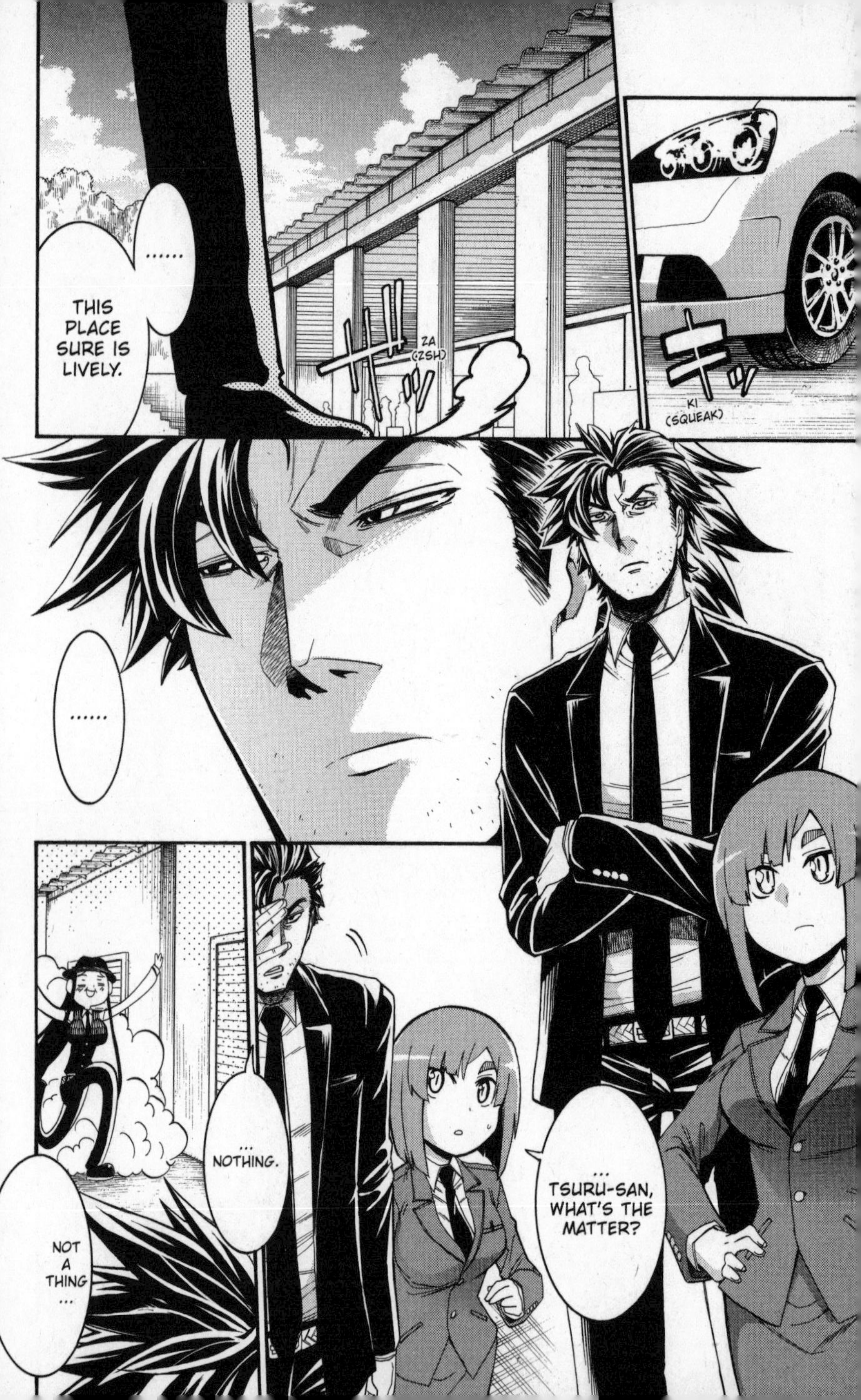
KI (SQUEAK)
ZA (ZSH)
......
THIS PLACE SURE IS LIVELY.
......
... TSURU-SAN, WHAT'S THE MATTER?
... NOTHING.
NOT A THING ...

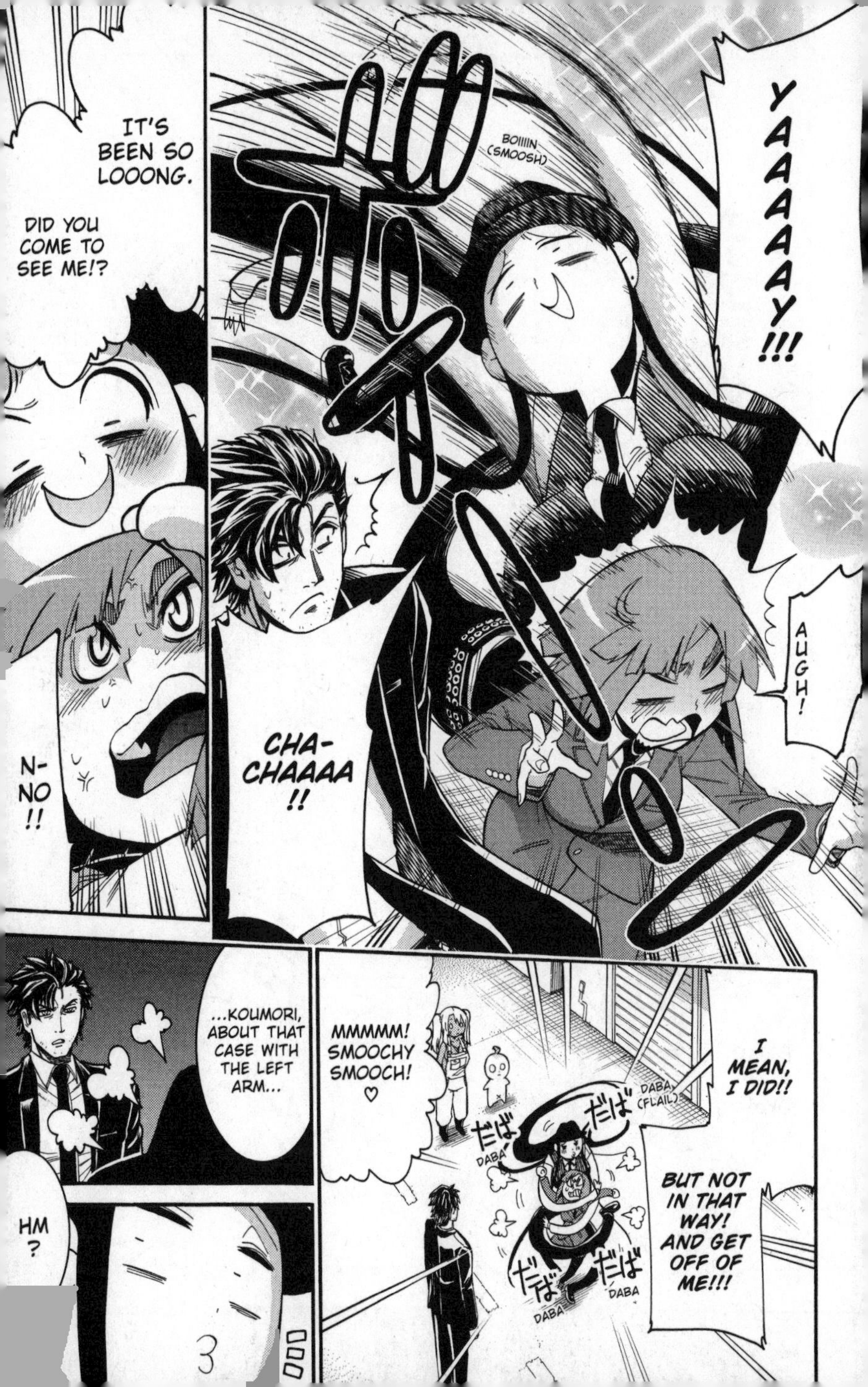
YAAAAAAY!!!
BOIIIIN (SMOOSH)
AUGH!
CHA-CHAAAAA!!
IT'S BEEN SO LOOONG.
DID YOU COME TO SEE ME!?
N-NO!!
I MEAN, I DID!!
MMMMM! SMOOCHY SMOOCH! ♡
DABA (FLAIL)
DABA
DABA
DABA
BUT NOT IN THAT WAY! AND GET OFF OF ME!!!
...KOUMORI, ABOUT THAT CASE WITH THE LEFT ARM...
HM?

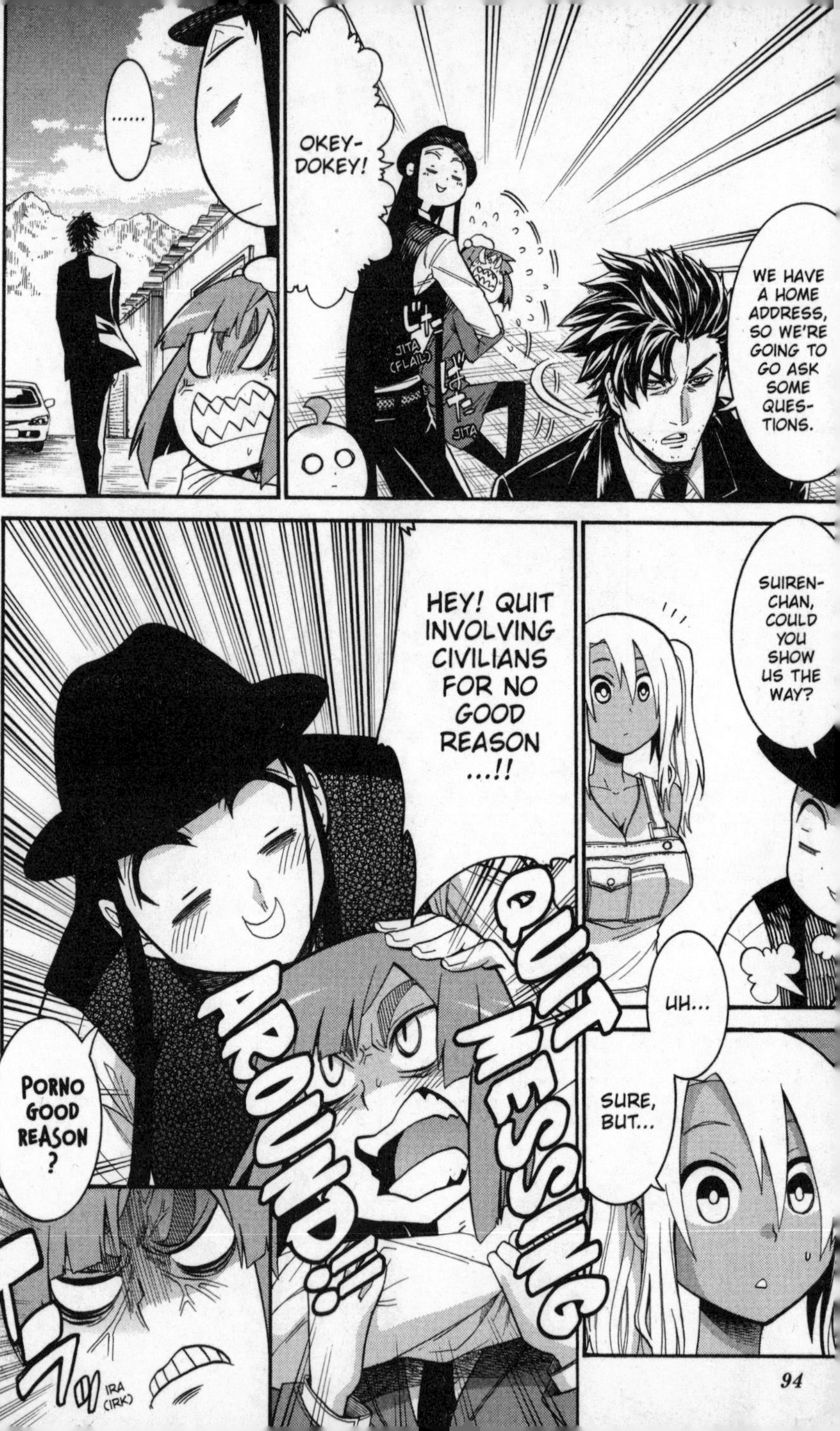
WE HAVE A HOME ADDRESS, SO WE'RE GOING TO GO ASK SOME QUES-TIONS.
OKEY-DOKEY!
JITA (FLAIL)
JITA
......
SUIREN-CHAN, COULD YOU SHOW US THE WAY?
UH...
SURE, BUT...
HEY! QUIT INVOLVING CIVILIANS FOR NO GOOD REASON ...!!
QUIT MESSING AROUND!!
PORNO GOOD REASON ?
IRA (IRK)

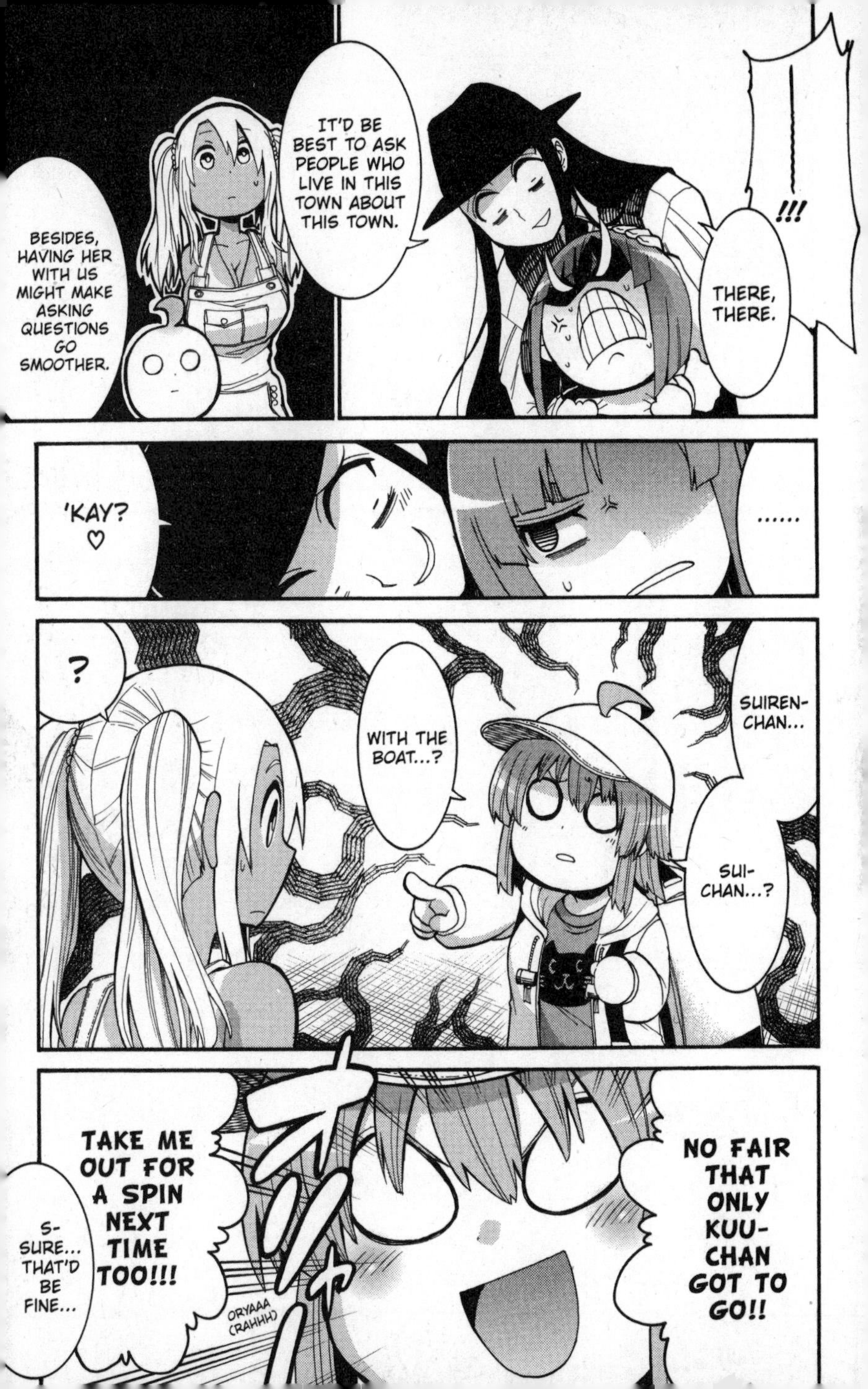
——!!!
IT'D BE BEST TO ASK PEOPLE WHO LIVE IN THIS TOWN ABOUT THIS TOWN.
THERE, THERE.
BESIDES, HAVING HER WITH US MIGHT MAKE ASKING QUESTIONS GO SMOOTHER.
......
'KAY? ♡
SUIREN-CHAN...
SUI-CHAN...?
WITH THE BOAT...?
?
NO FAIR THAT ONLY KUU-CHAN GOT TO GO!!
TAKE ME OUT FOR A SPIN NEXT TIME TOO!!!
ORYAAA (RAHHH)
S-SURE... THAT'D BE FINE...

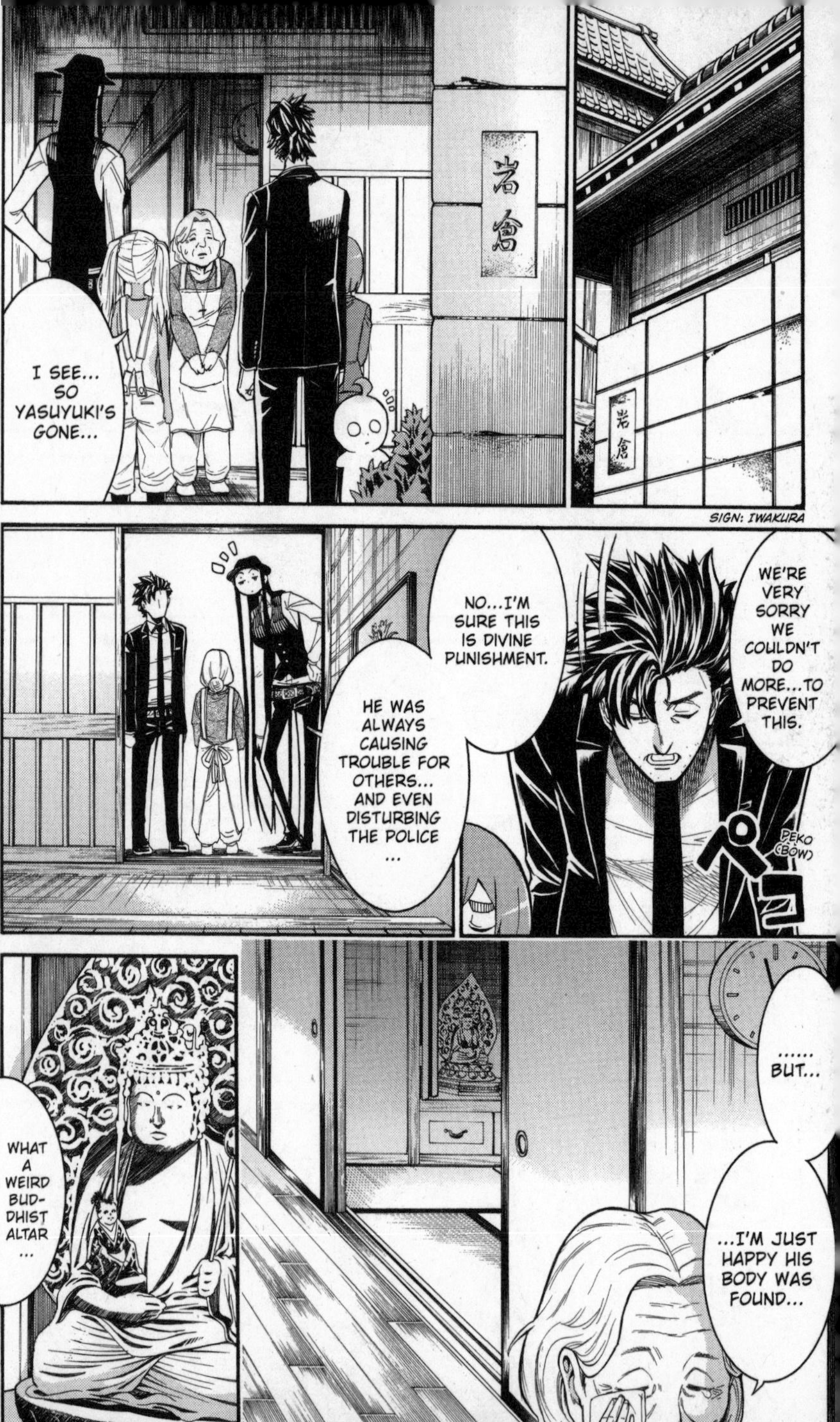
岩倉
岩倉
SIGN: IWAKURA
I SEE... SO YASUYUKI'S GONE...
WE'RE VERY SORRY WE COULDN'T DO MORE...TO PREVENT THIS.
PEKO (BOW)
NO...I'M SURE THIS IS DIVINE PUNISHMENT.
HE WAS ALWAYS CAUSING TROUBLE FOR OTHERS... AND EVEN DISTURBING THE POLICE ...
...... BUT...
...I'M JUST HAPPY HIS BODY WAS FOUND...
WHAT A WEIRD BUD-DHIST ALTAR ...

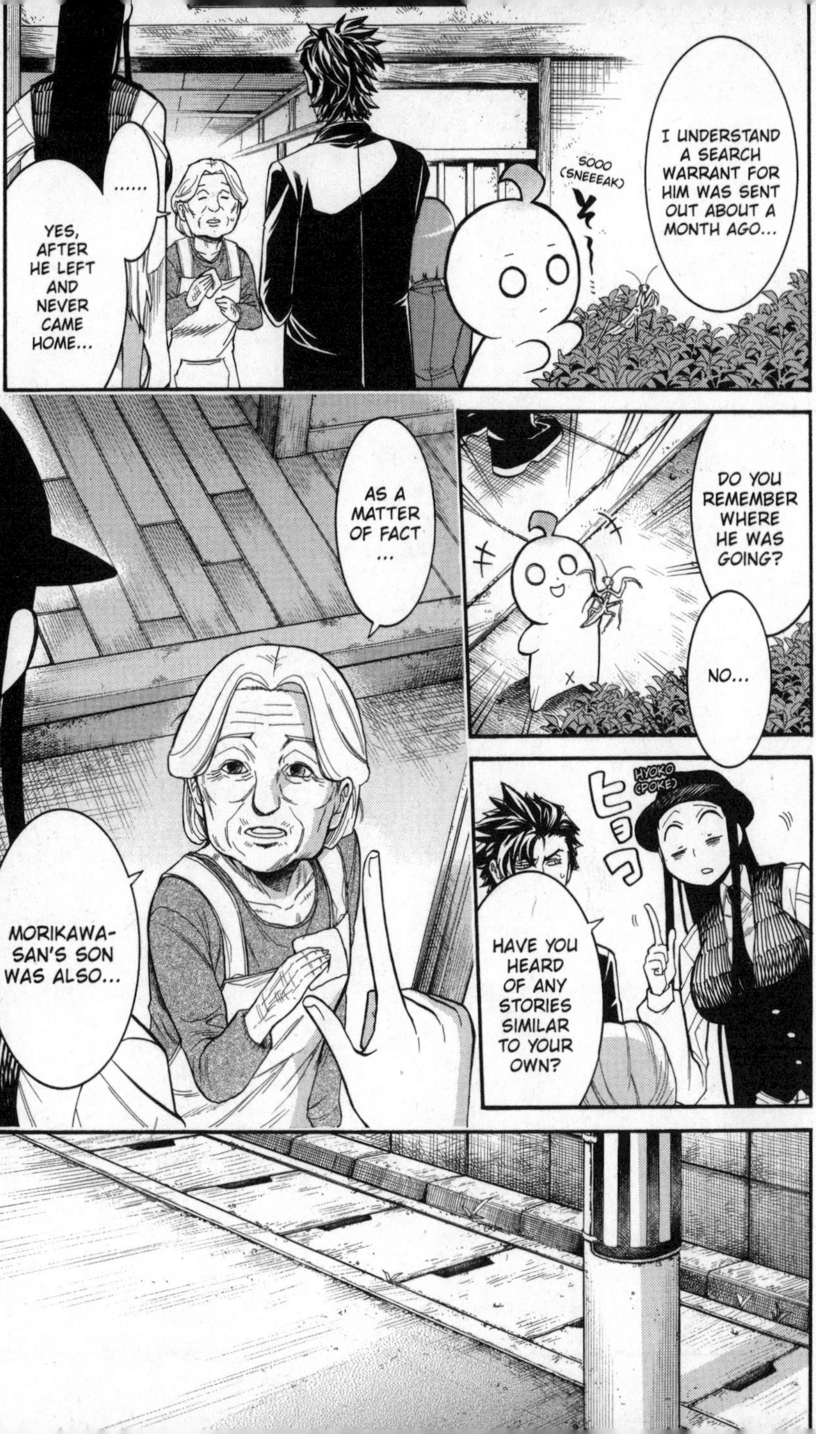
I UNDERSTAND A SEARCH WARRANT FOR HIM WAS SENT OUT ABOUT A MONTH AGO...
SOOO (SNEEEAK)
......
YES, AFTER HE LEFT AND NEVER CAME HOME...
DO YOU REMEMBER WHERE HE WAS GOING?
NO...
HYOKO (POKE)
HAVE YOU HEARD OF ANY STORIES SIMILAR TO YOUR OWN?
AS A MATTER OF FACT ...
MORIKAWA-SAN'S SON WAS ALSO...

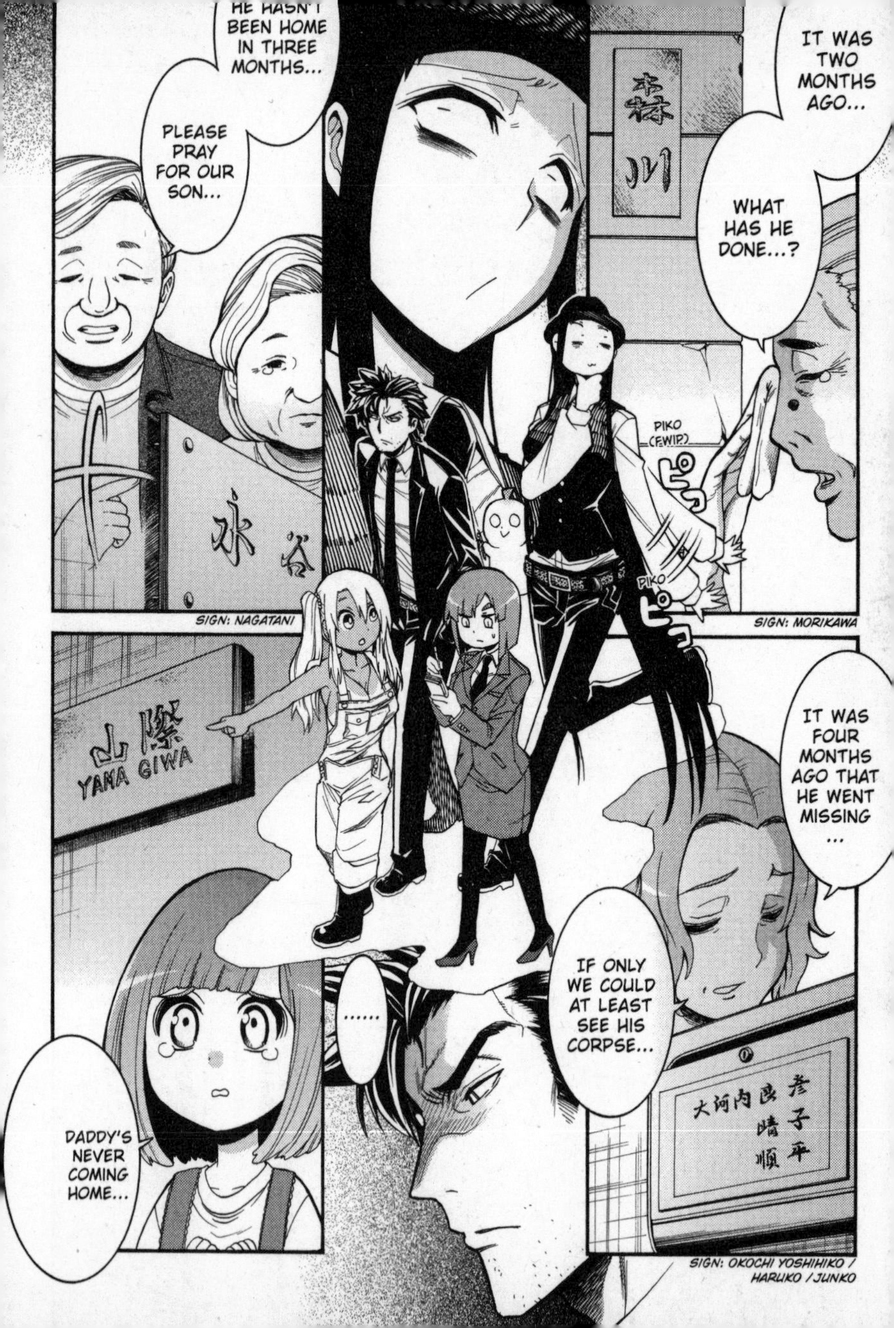
IT WAS TWO MONTHS AGO...
WHAT HAS HE DONE...?
PIKO (FWIP)
PIKO
SIGN: MORIKAWA
HE HASN'T BEEN HOME IN THREE MONTHS...
PLEASE PRAY FOR OUR SON...
SIGN: NAGATANI
IT WAS FOUR MONTHS AGO THAT HE WENT MISSING...
IF ONLY WE COULD AT LEAST SEE HIS CORPSE...
SIGN: OKOCHI YOSHIHIKO / HARUKO / JUNKO
......
YAMA GIWA
DADDY'S NEVER COMING HOME...

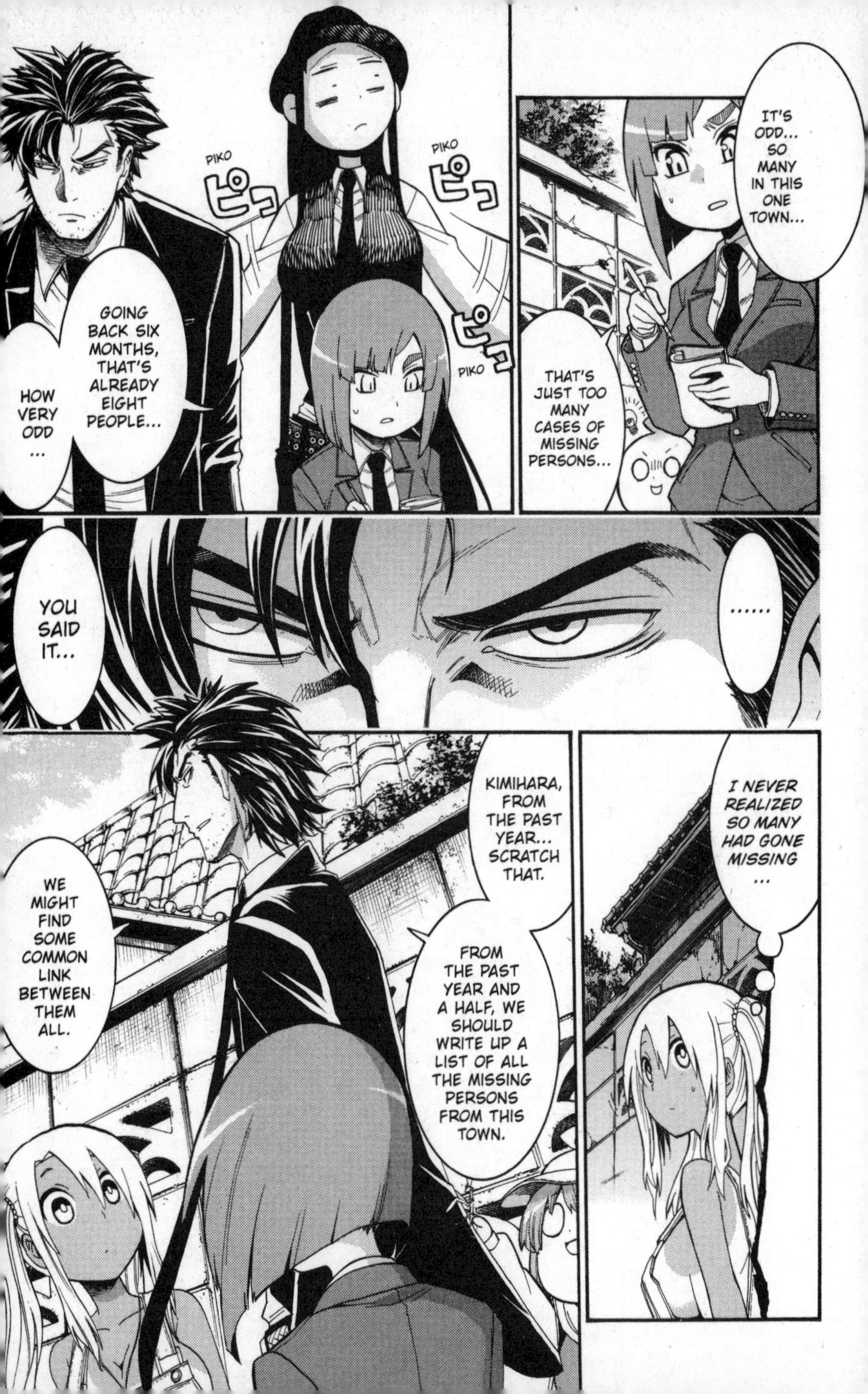
IT'S ODD... SO MANY IN THIS ONE TOWN...
THAT'S JUST TOO MANY CASES OF MISSING PERSONS...
PIKO ぴっ
PIKO ぴっ
PIKO ぴっ
GOING BACK SIX MONTHS, THAT'S ALREADY EIGHT PEOPLE...
HOW VERY ODD ...
......
YOU SAID IT...
I NEVER REALIZED SO MANY HAD GONE MISSING ...
KIMIHARA, FROM THE PAST YEAR... SCRATCH THAT.
FROM THE PAST YEAR AND A HALF, WE SHOULD WRITE UP A LIST OF ALL THE MISSING PERSONS FROM THIS TOWN.
WE MIGHT FIND SOME COMMON LINK BETWEEN THEM ALL.

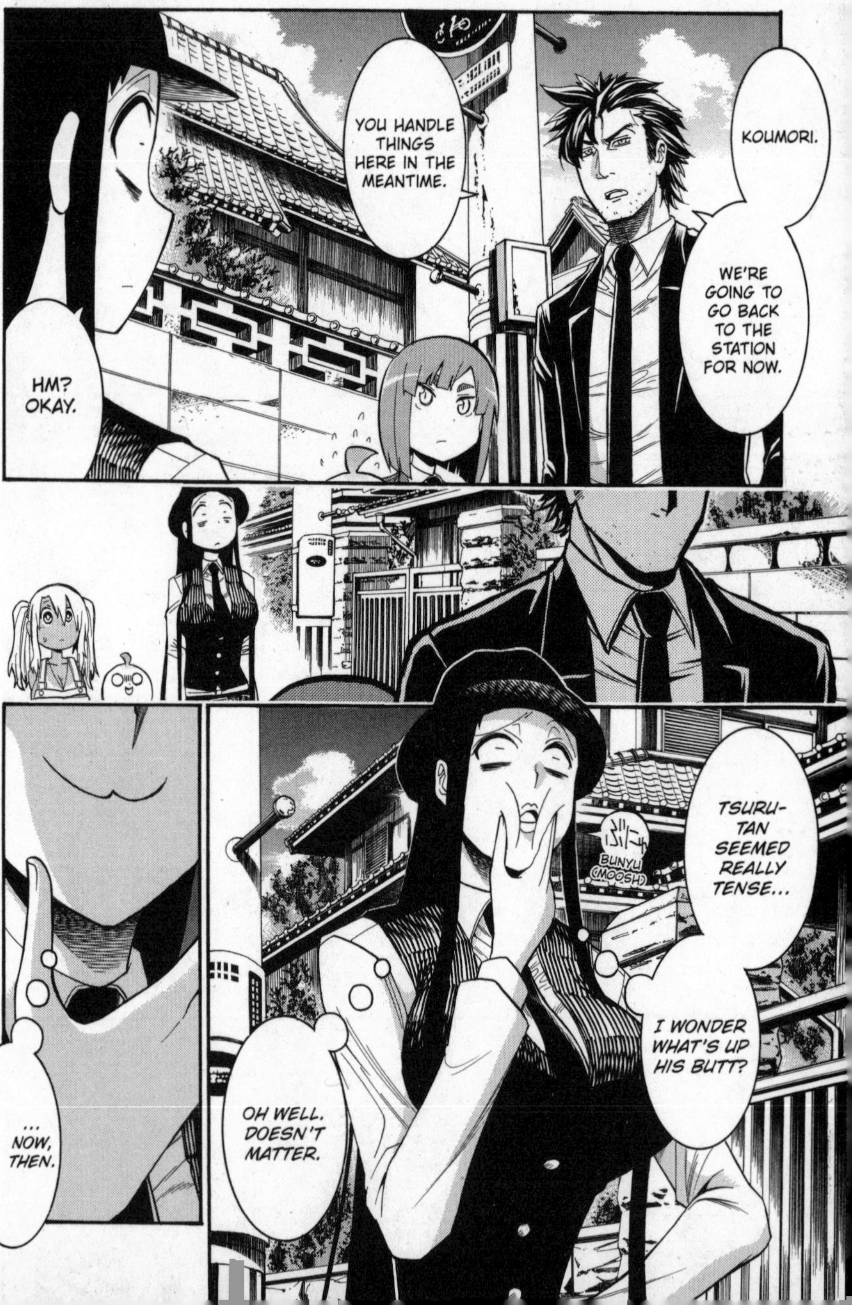
KOUMORI.
WE'RE GOING TO GO BACK TO THE STATION FOR NOW.
YOU HANDLE THINGS HERE IN THE MEANTIME.
HM? OKAY.
TSURU-TAN SEEMED REALLY TENSE...
BUNYU (MOOSH)
I WONDER WHAT'S UP HIS BUTT?
OH WELL. DOESN'T MATTER.
... NOW, THEN.

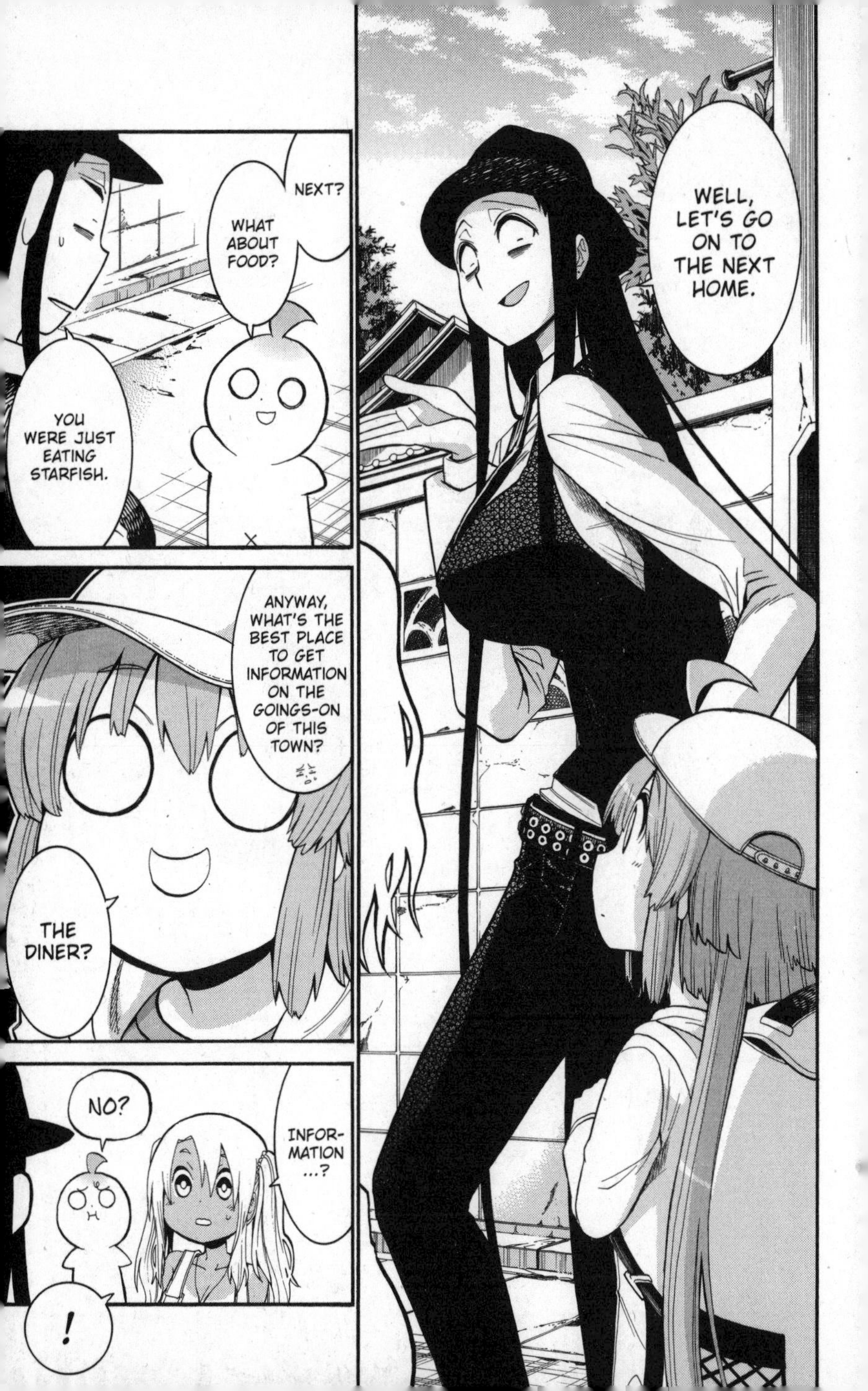
WELL, LET'S GO ON TO THE NEXT HOME.
NEXT?
WHAT ABOUT FOOD?
YOU WERE JUST EATING STARFISH.
ANYWAY, WHAT'S THE BEST PLACE TO GET INFORMATION ON THE GOINGS-ON OF THIS TOWN?
THE DINER?
INFOR-MATION ...?
NO?
!

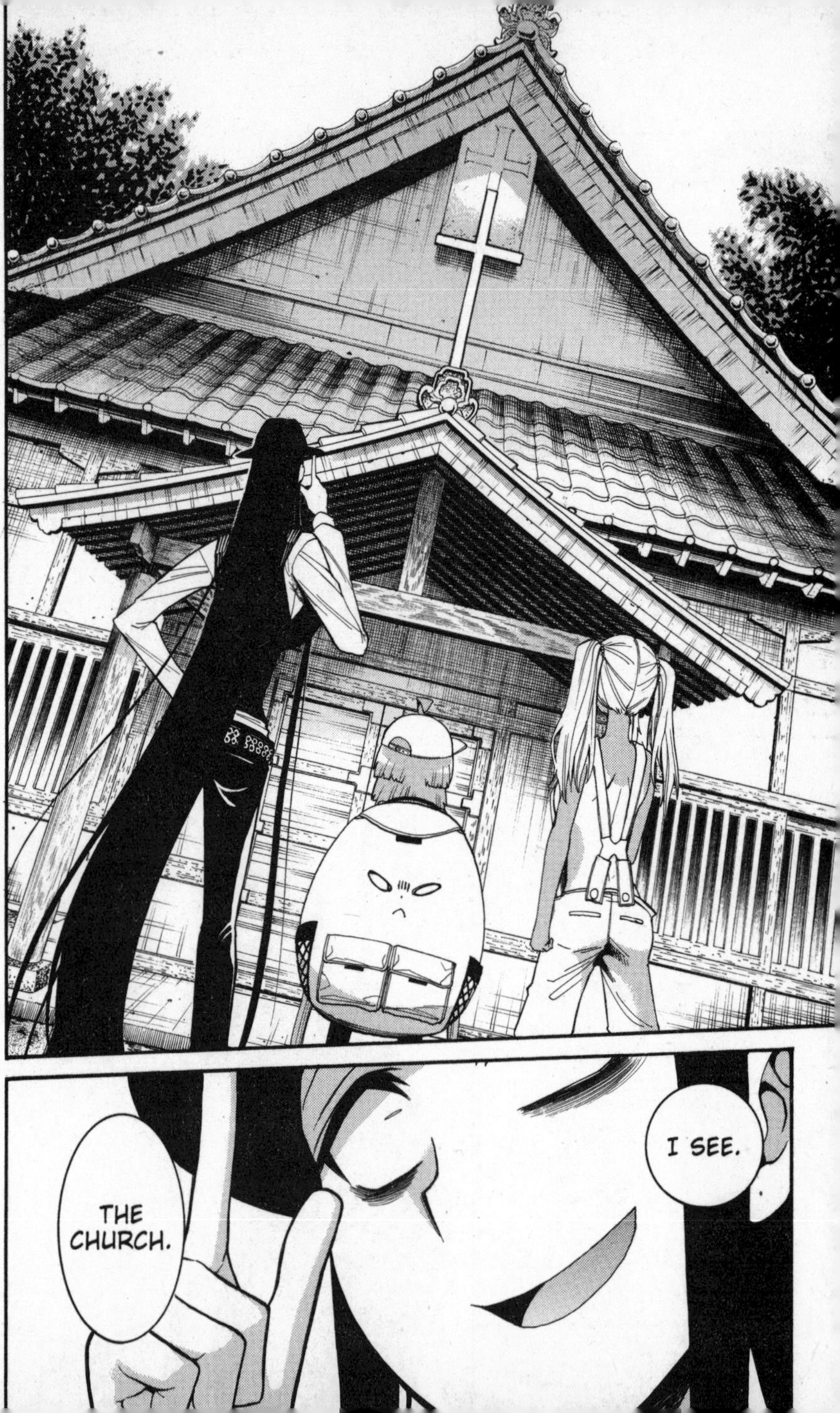
I SEE.
THE CHURCH.

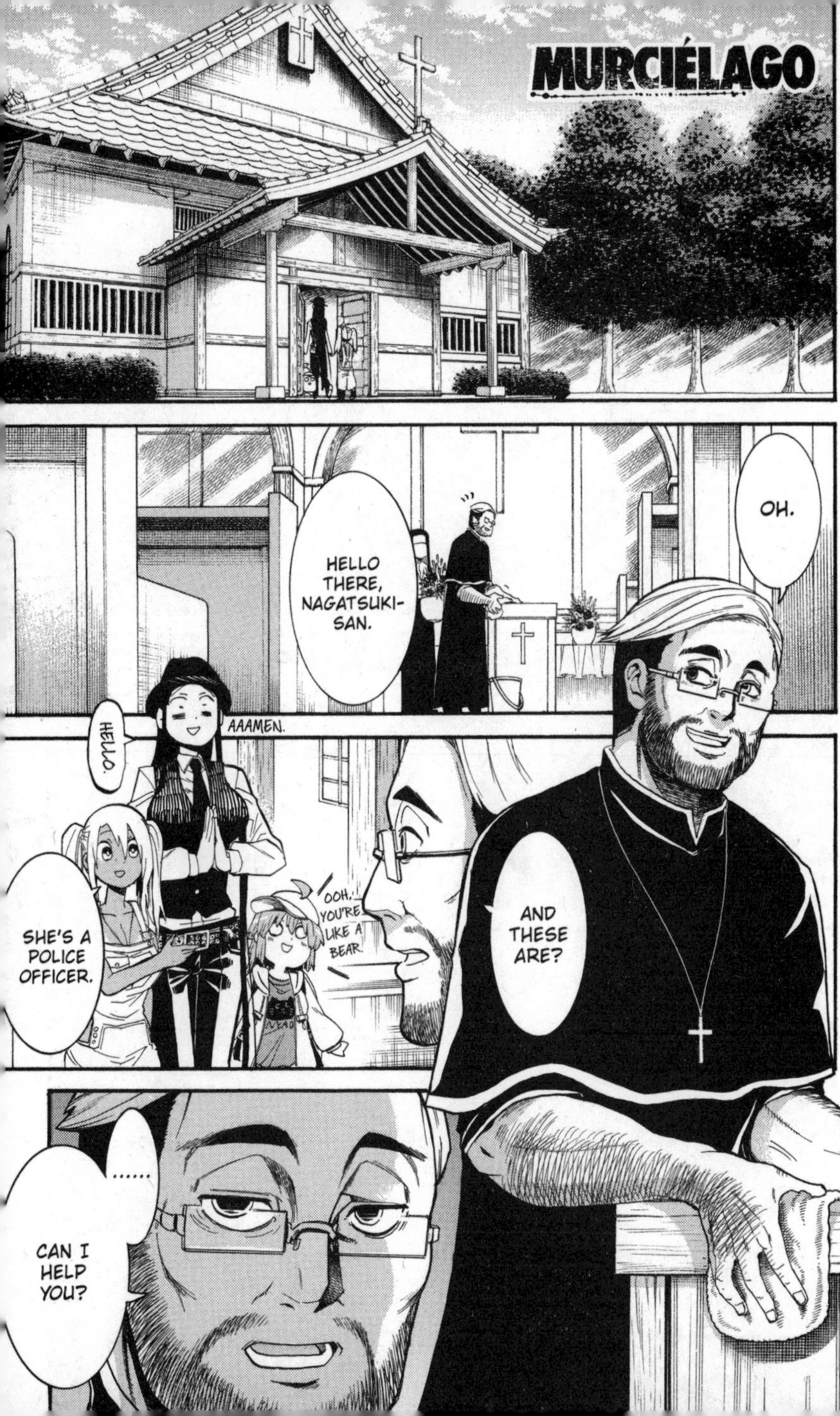
MURCIÉLAGO
OH.
HELLO THERE, NAGATSUKI-SAN.
HELLO.
AAAMEN.
AND THESE ARE?
OOH, YOU'RE LIKE A BEAR.
SHE'S A POLICE OFFICER.
......
CAN I HELP YOU?

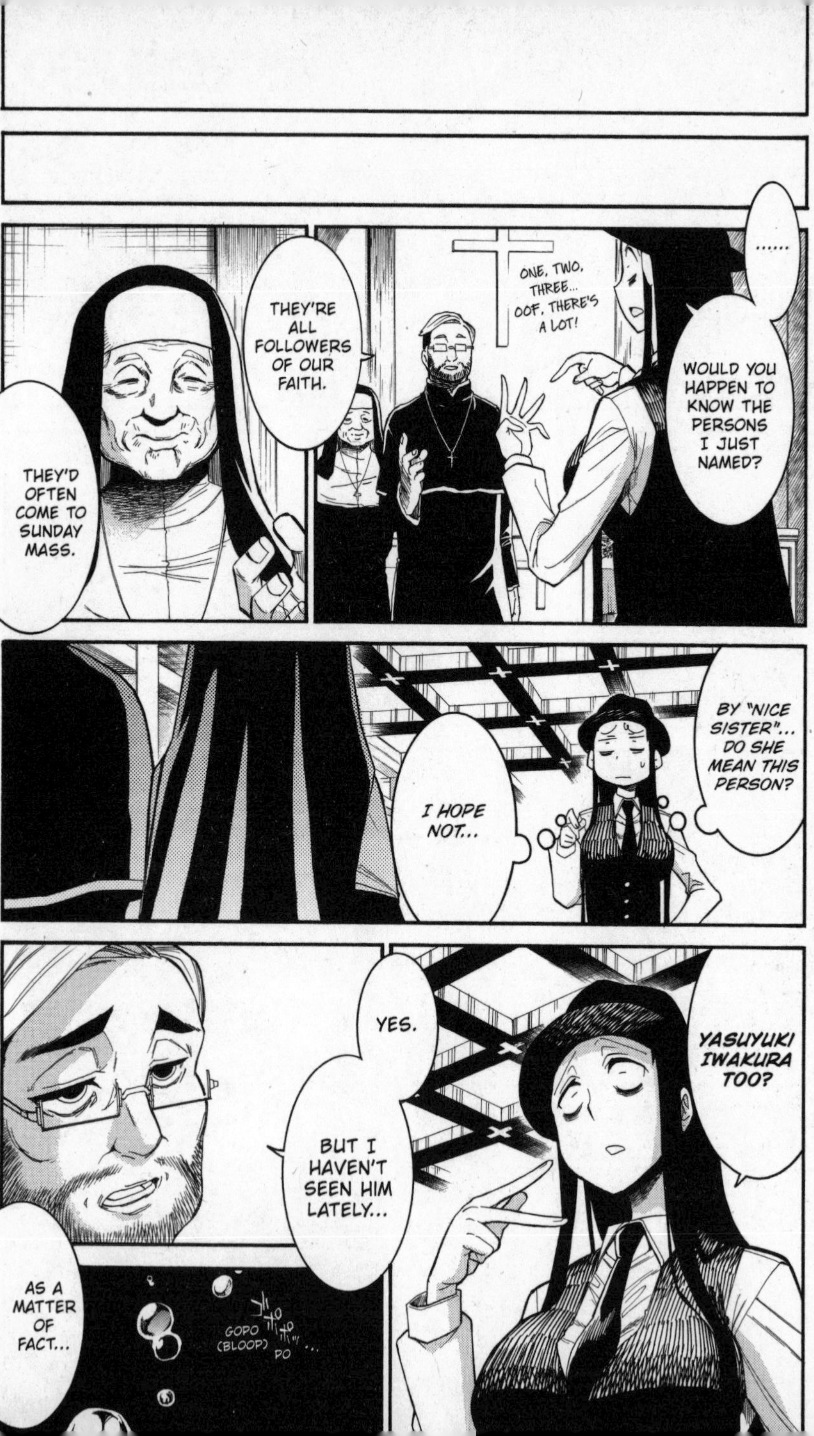
......
WOULD YOU HAPPEN TO KNOW THE PERSONS I JUST NAMED?
ONE, TWO, THREE... OOF, THERE'S A LOT!
THEY'RE ALL FOLLOWERS OF OUR FAITH.
THEY'D OFTEN COME TO SUNDAY MASS.
BY "NICE SISTER"... DO SHE MEAN THIS PERSON?
I HOPE NOT...
YASUYUKI IWAKURA TOO?
YES.
BUT I HAVEN'T SEEN HIM LATELY...
AS A MATTER OF FACT...
GOPO (BLOOP) PO

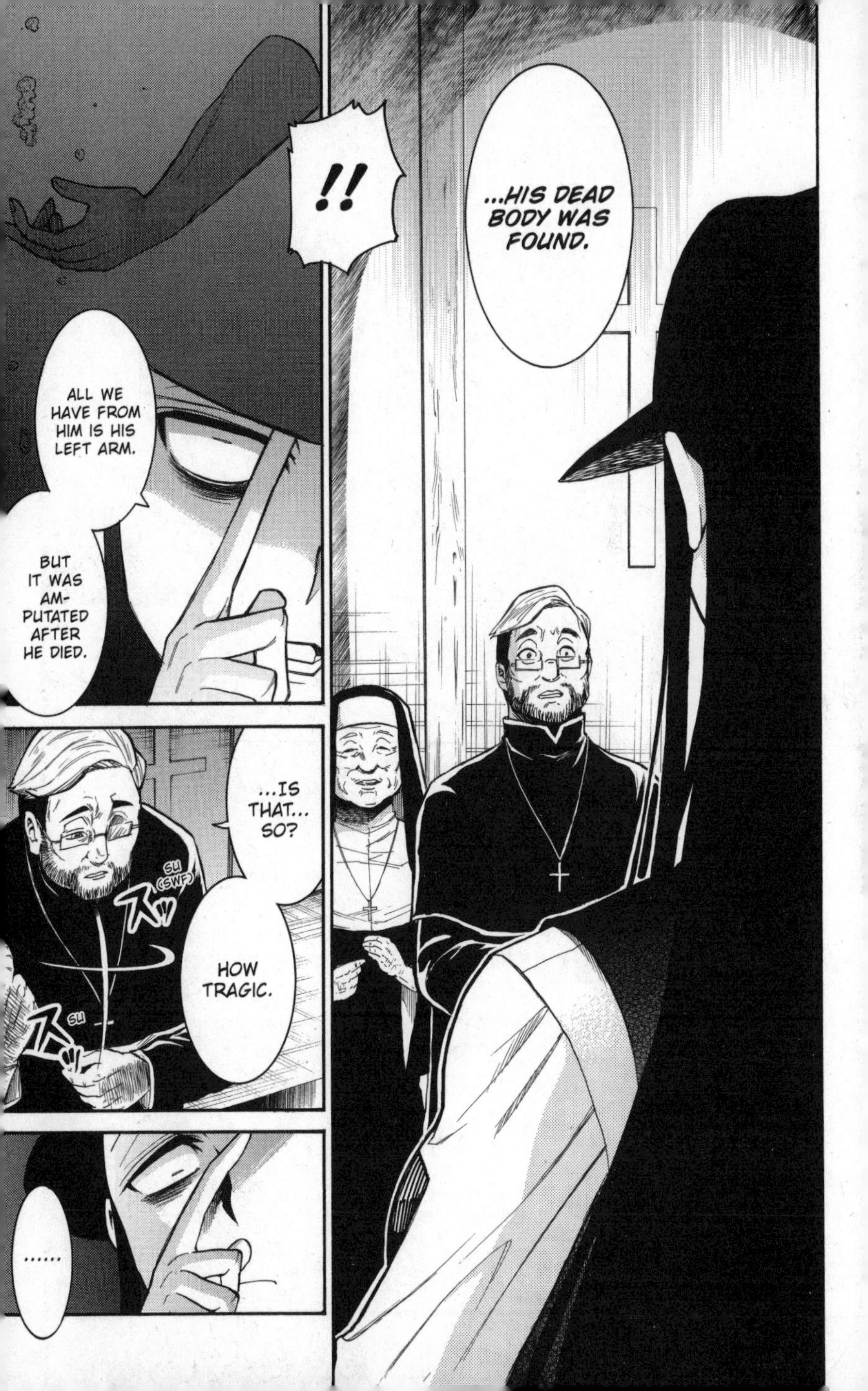
...HIS DEAD BODY WAS FOUND.
!!
ALL WE HAVE FROM HIM IS HIS LEFT ARM.
BUT IT WAS AMPUTATED AFTER HE DIED.
...IS THAT... SO?
SU (SWF)
SU
HOW TRAGIC.
......

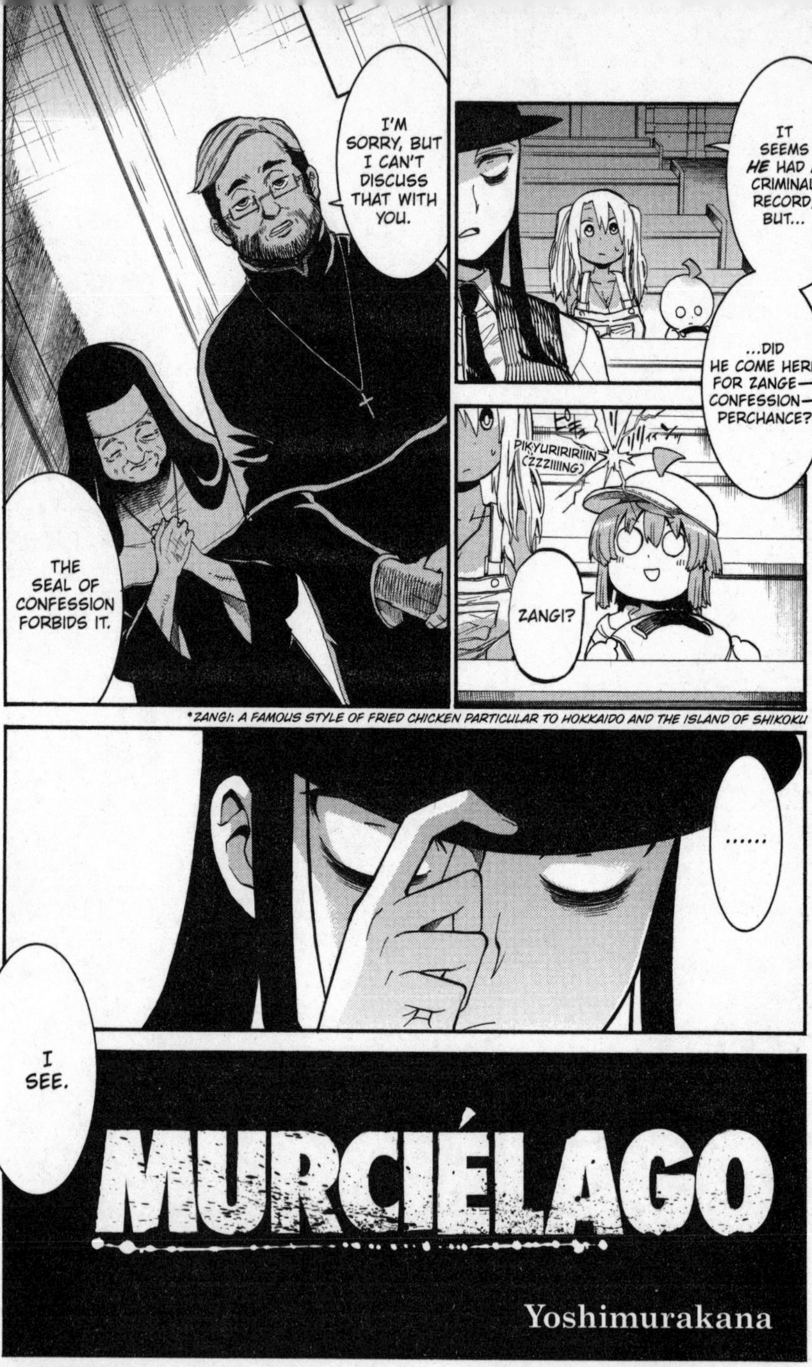
IT SEEMS *HE* HAD A CRIMINAL RECORD, BUT...
...DID HE COME HERE FOR ZANGE—CONFESSION—PERCHANCE?
PIKYURIRIRIIIN (ZZZIIIING)
ZANGI?
I'M SORRY, BUT I CAN'T DISCUSS THAT WITH YOU.
THE SEAL OF CONFESSION FORBIDS IT.
......
I SEE.
MURCIÉLAGO
Yoshimurakana

*ZANGI: A FAMOUS STYLE OF FRIED CHICKEN PARTICULAR TO HOKKAIDO AND THE ISLAND OF SHIKOKU

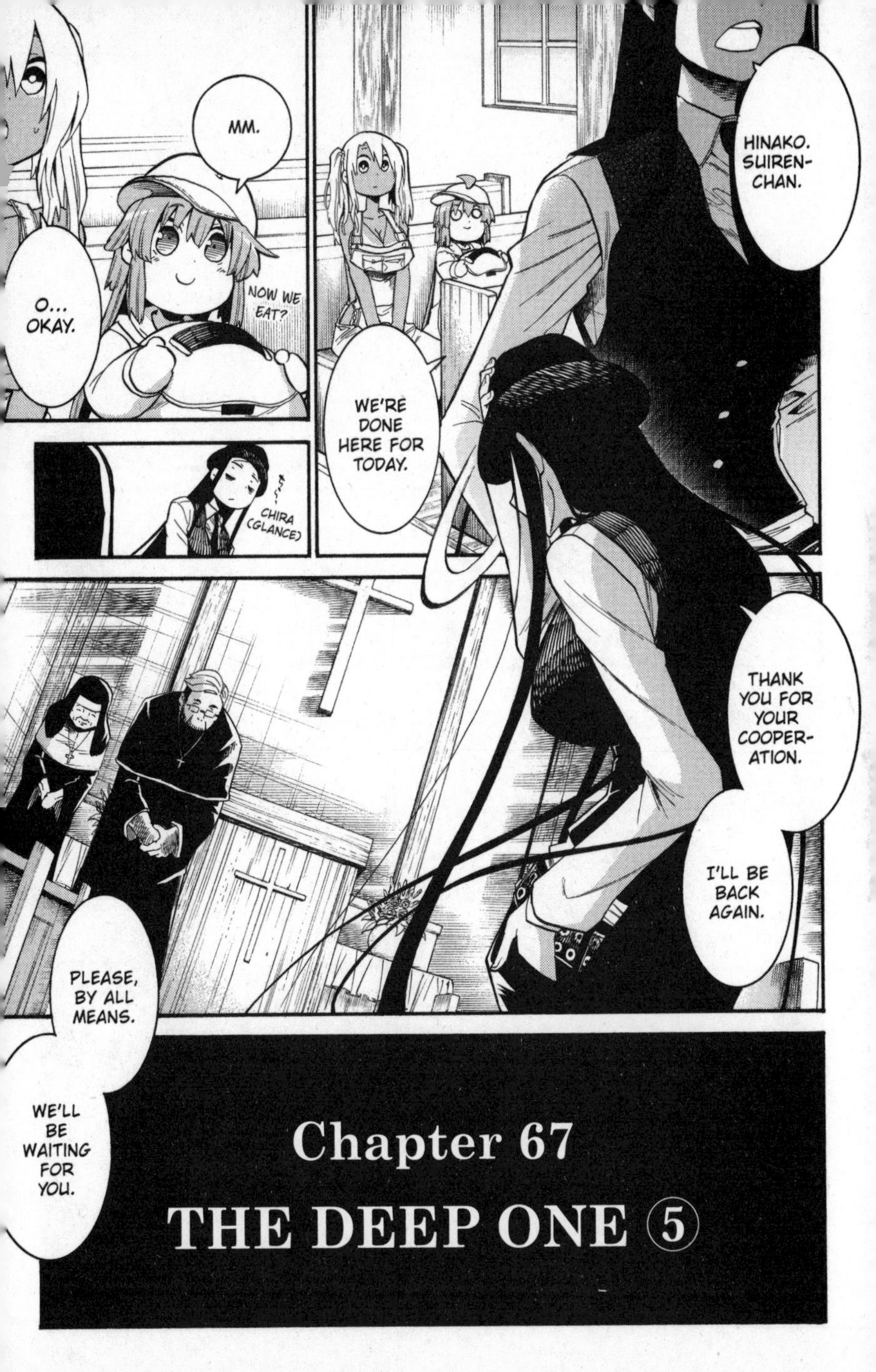
HINAKO. SUIREN-CHAN.
WE'RE DONE HERE FOR TODAY.
MM.
NOW WE EAT?
O... OKAY.
CHIRA (GLANCE)
THANK YOU FOR YOUR COOPERATION.
I'LL BE BACK AGAIN.
PLEASE, BY ALL MEANS.
WE'LL BE WAITING FOR YOU.

Chapter 67

THE DEEP ONE ⑤

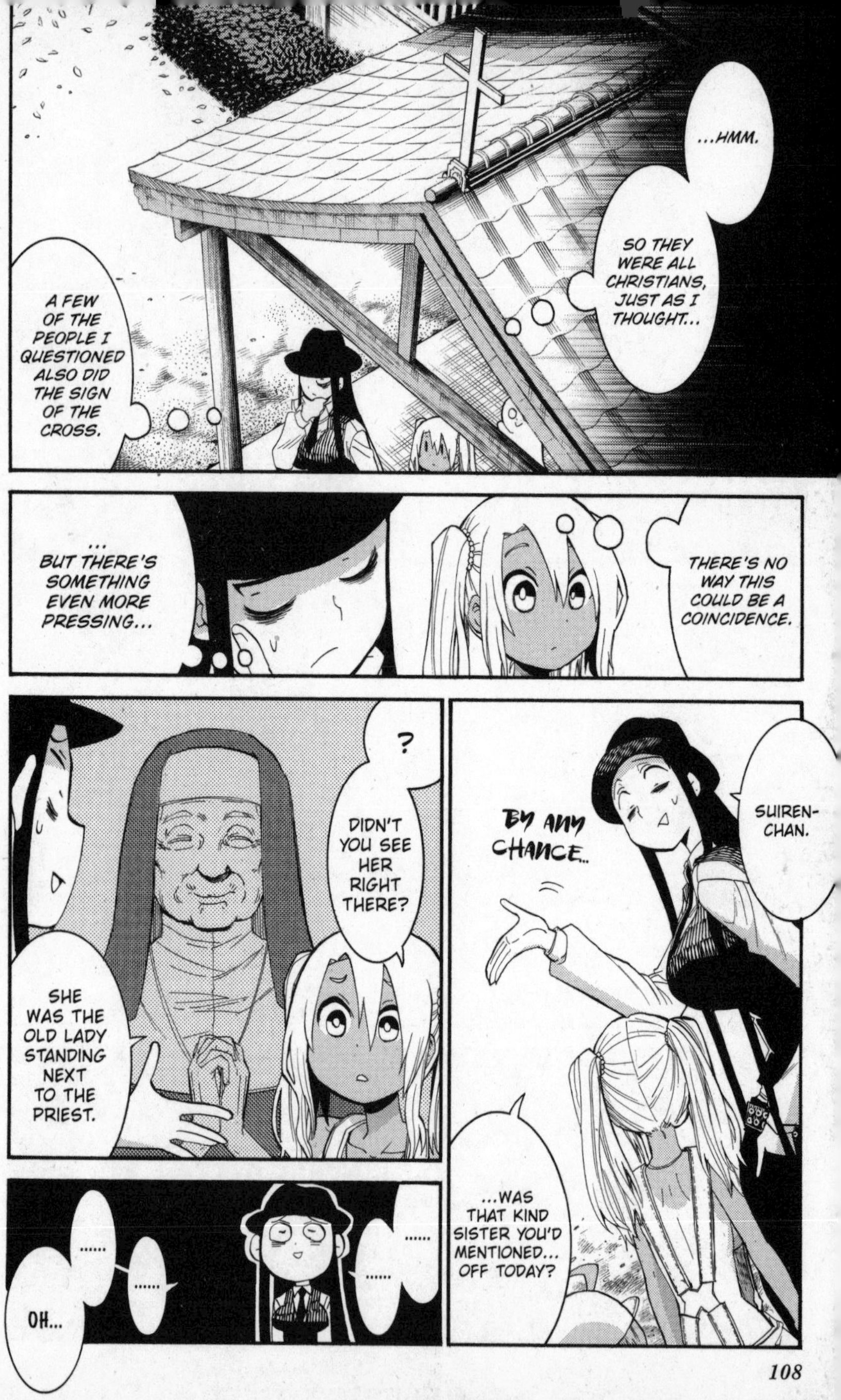
...HMM.
SO THEY WERE ALL CHRISTIANS, JUST AS I THOUGHT...
A FEW OF THE PEOPLE I QUESTIONED ALSO DID THE SIGN OF THE CROSS.
THERE'S NO WAY THIS COULD BE A COINCIDENCE.
...BUT THERE'S SOMETHING EVEN MORE PRESSING...
SUIREN-CHAN.
BY ANY CHANCE...
...WAS THAT KIND SISTER YOU'D MENTIONED... OFF TODAY?
?
DIDN'T YOU SEE HER RIGHT THERE?
SHE WAS THE OLD LADY STANDING NEXT TO THE PRIEST.
......
......
......
......
OH...

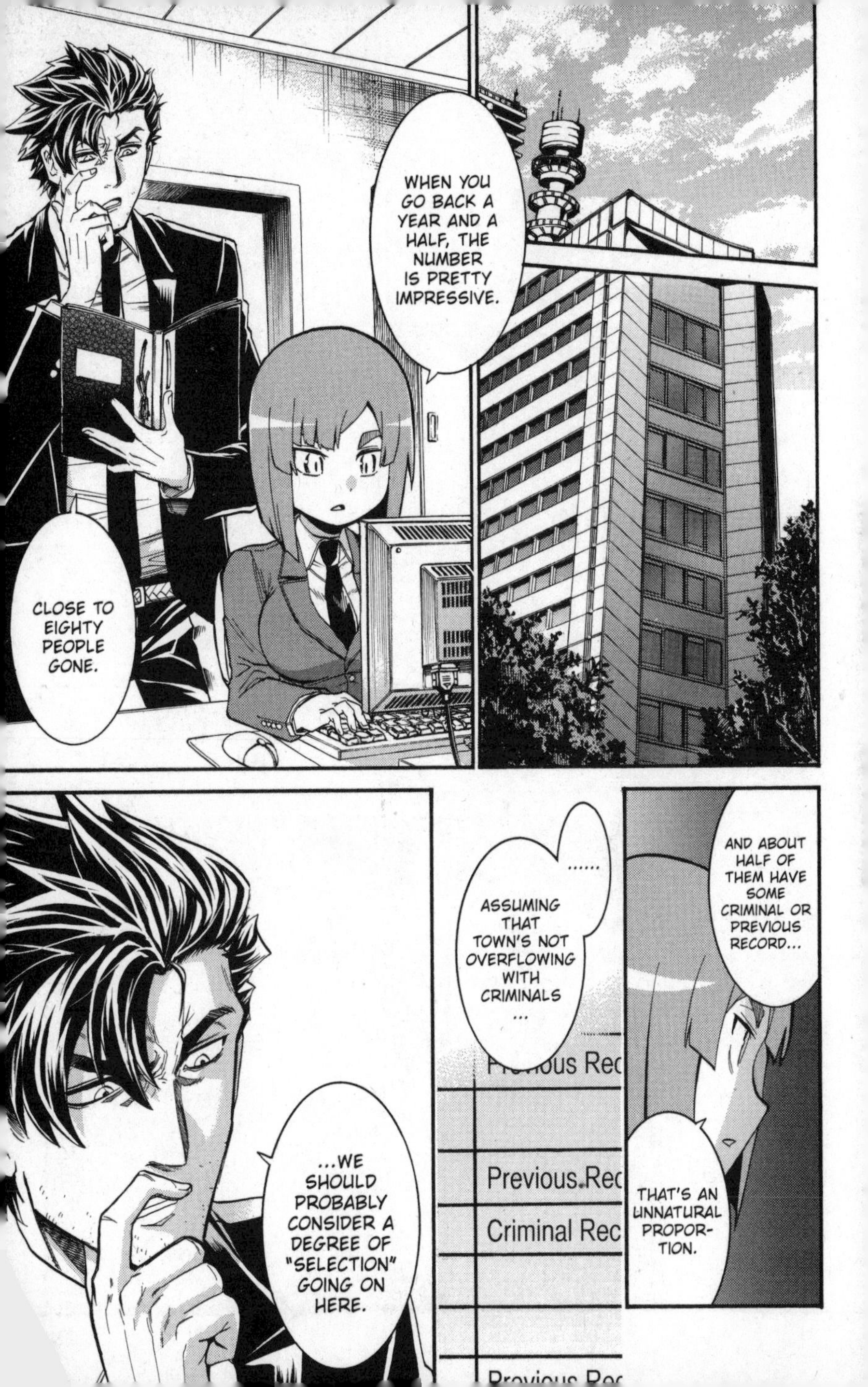
WHEN YOU GO BACK A YEAR AND A HALF, THE NUMBER IS PRETTY IMPRESSIVE.
CLOSE TO EIGHTY PEOPLE GONE.
AND ABOUT HALF OF THEM HAVE SOME CRIMINAL OR PREVIOUS RECORD...
THAT'S AN UNNATURAL PROPORTION.
......
ASSUMING THAT TOWN'S NOT OVERFLOWING WITH CRIMINALS...
...WE SHOULD PROBABLY CONSIDER A DEGREE OF "SELECTION" GOING ON HERE.

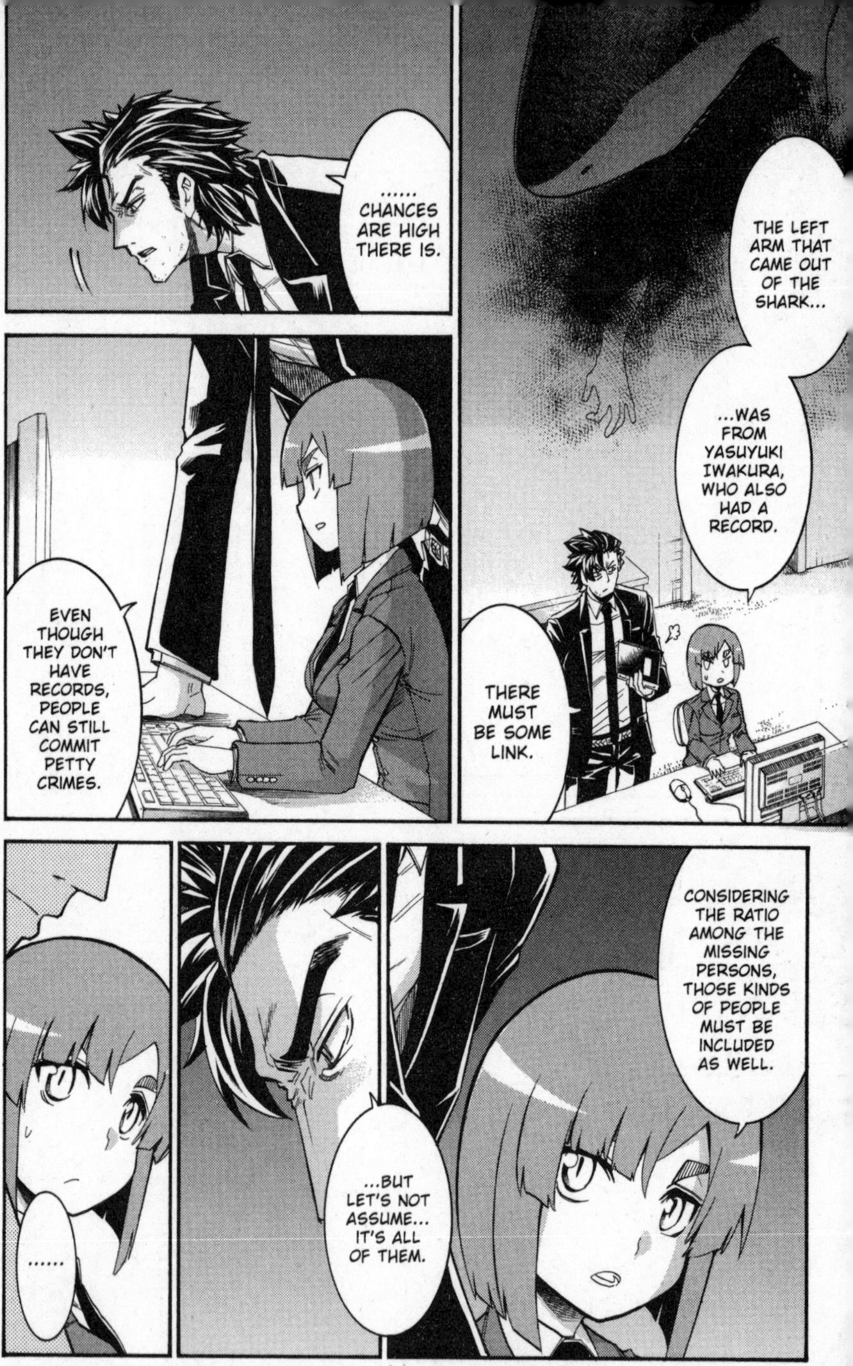
THE LEFT ARM THAT CAME OUT OF THE SHARK...
...WAS FROM YASUYUKI IWAKURA, WHO ALSO HAD A RECORD.
THERE MUST BE SOME LINK.
......CHANCES ARE HIGH THERE IS.
EVEN THOUGH THEY DON'T HAVE RECORDS, PEOPLE CAN STILL COMMIT PETTY CRIMES.
CONSIDERING THE RATIO AMONG THE MISSING PERSONS, THOSE KINDS OF PEOPLE MUST BE INCLUDED AS WELL.
...BUT LET'S NOT ASSUME... IT'S ALL OF THEM.
......

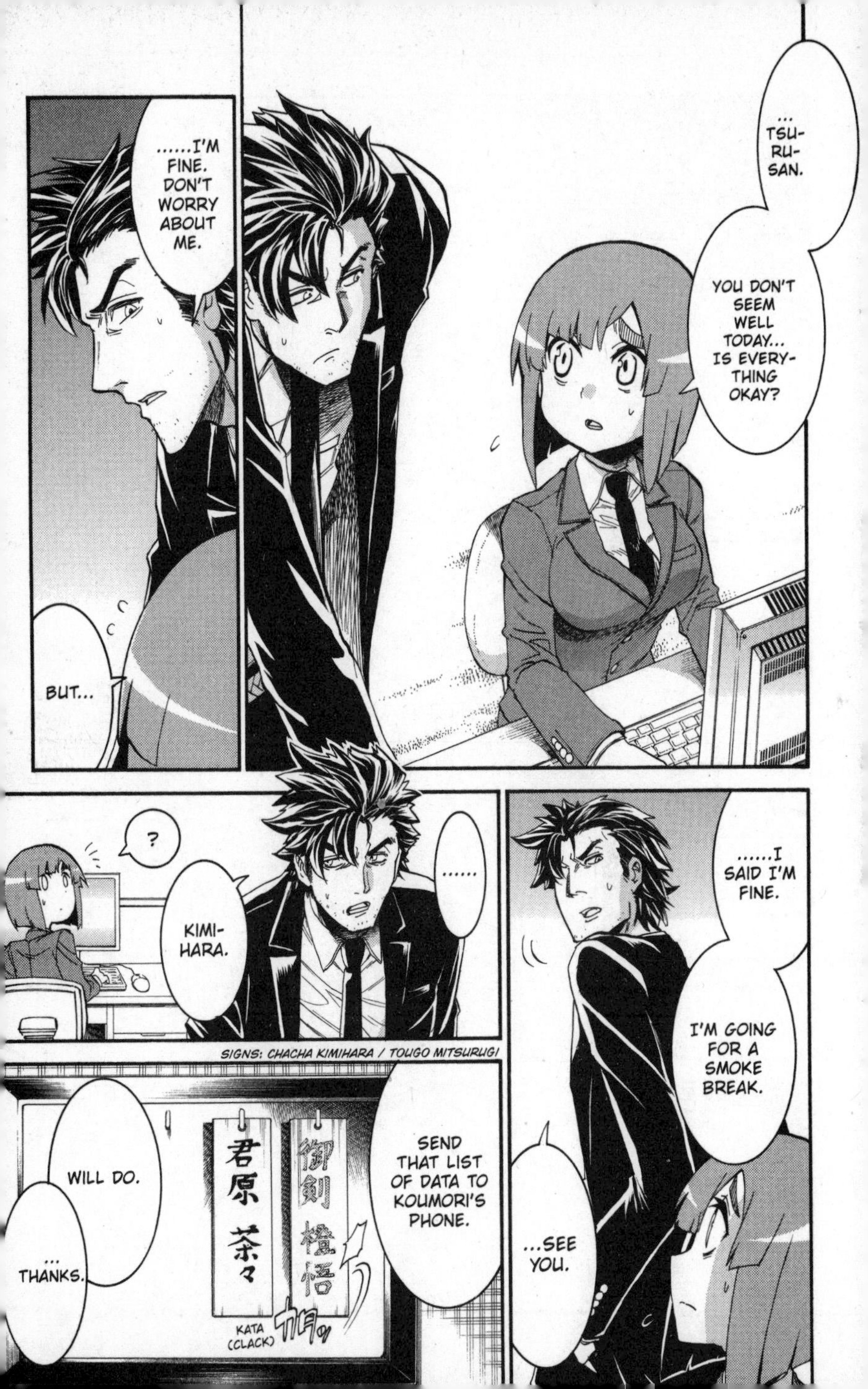
...TSU-RU-SAN.
YOU DON'T SEEM WELL TODAY... IS EVERY-THING OKAY?
......I'M FINE. DON'T WORRY ABOUT ME.
BUT...
......I SAID I'M FINE.
I'M GOING FOR A SMOKE BREAK.
...SEE YOU.
......
KIMI-HARA.
?
SIGNS: CHACHA KIMIHARA / TOUGO MITSURUGI
SEND THAT LIST OF DATA TO KOUMORI'S PHONE.
WILL DO.
...THANKS.
御剣 橙悟
君原 茶々
KATA (CLACK)

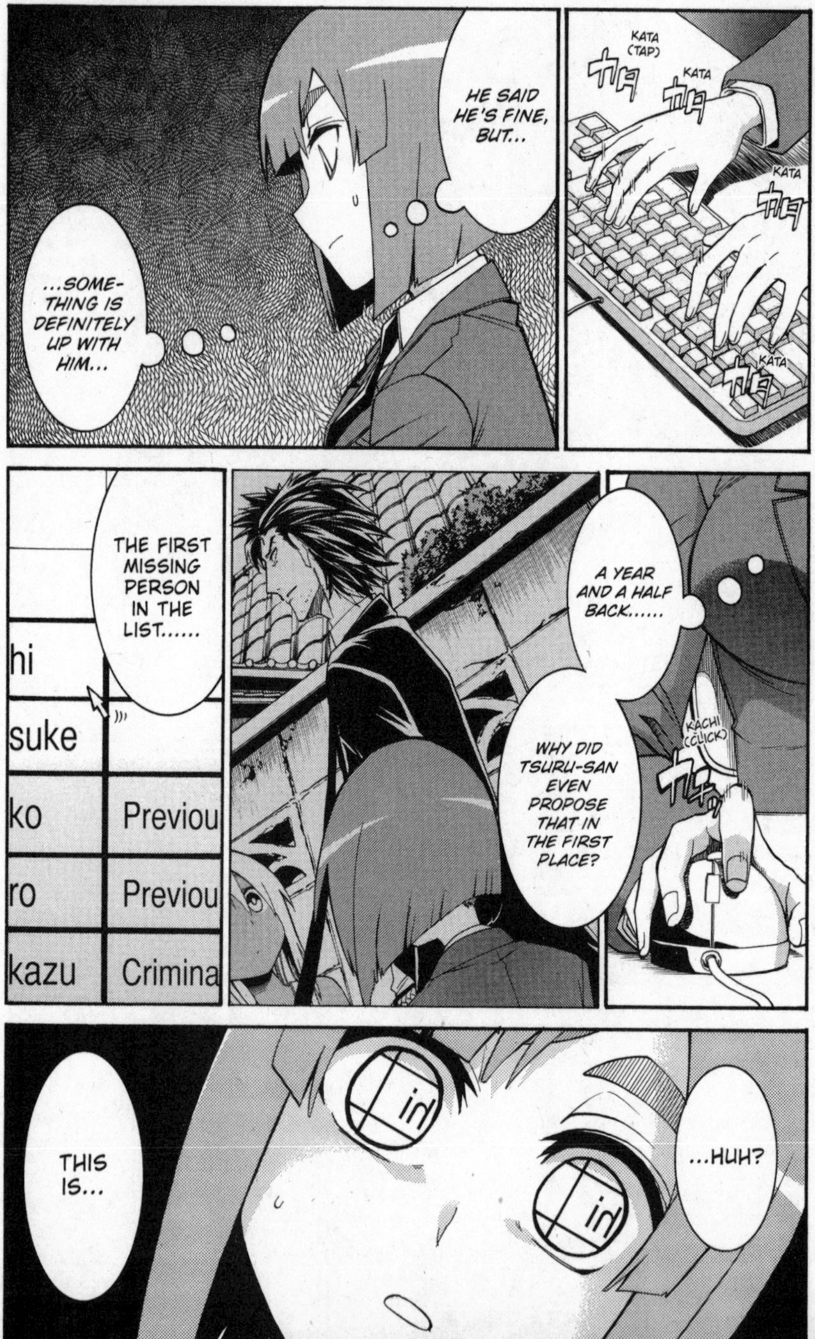
KATA (TAP)
KATA
KATA
KATA
HE SAID HE'S FINE, BUT...
...SOME-THING IS DEFINITELY UP WITH HIM...
A YEAR AND A HALF BACK......
WHY DID TSURU-SAN EVEN PROPOSE THAT IN THE FIRST PLACE?
KACHI (CLICK)
THE FIRST MISSING PERSON IN THE LIST......
hi
suke
ko Previou
ro Previou
kazu Crimina
...HUH?
THIS IS...

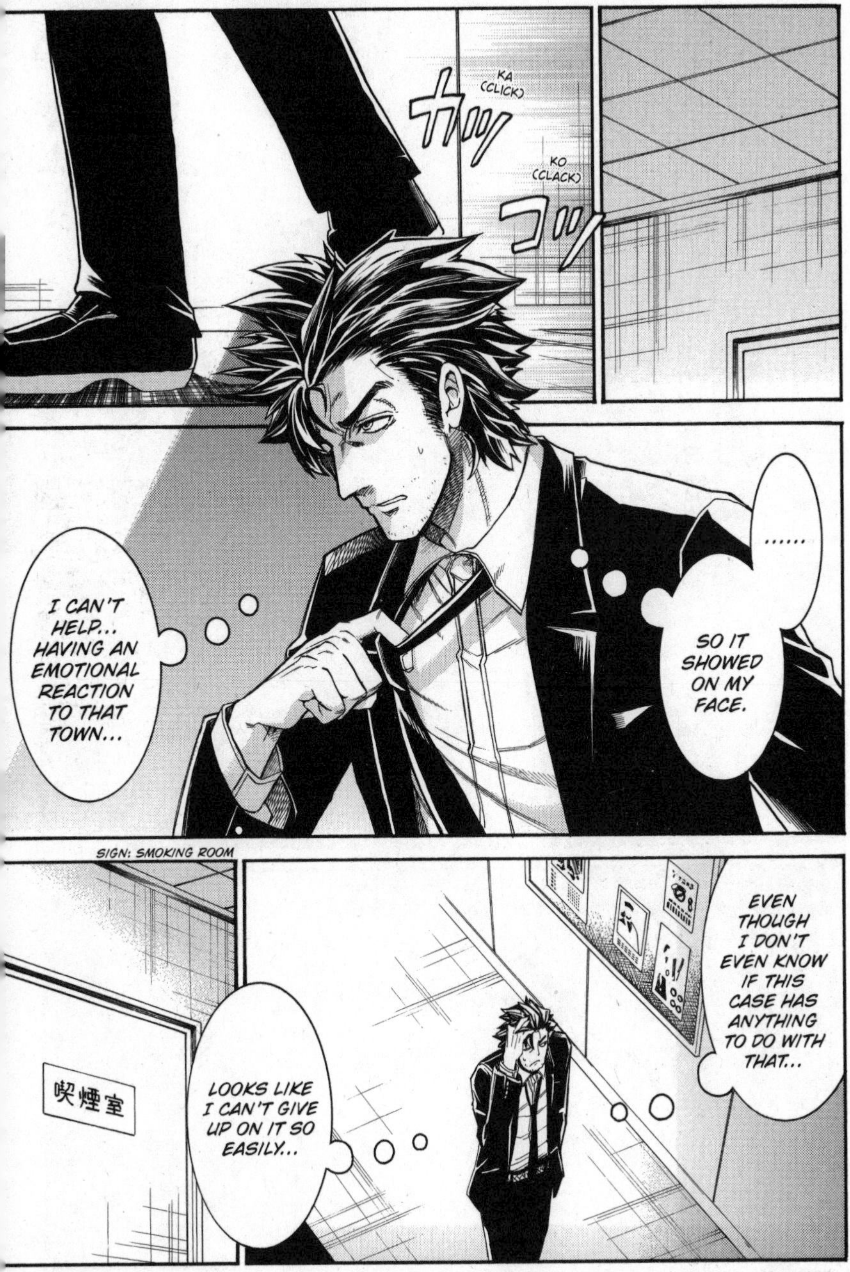
カッ
KA (CLICK)
コッ
KO (CLACK)
......
SO IT SHOWED ON MY FACE.
I CAN'T HELP... HAVING AN EMOTIONAL REACTION TO THAT TOWN...
EVEN THOUGH I DON'T EVEN KNOW IF THIS CASE HAS ANYTHING TO DO WITH THAT...
LOOKS LIKE I CAN'T GIVE UP ON IT SO EASILY...
SIGN: SMOKING ROOM
喫煙室

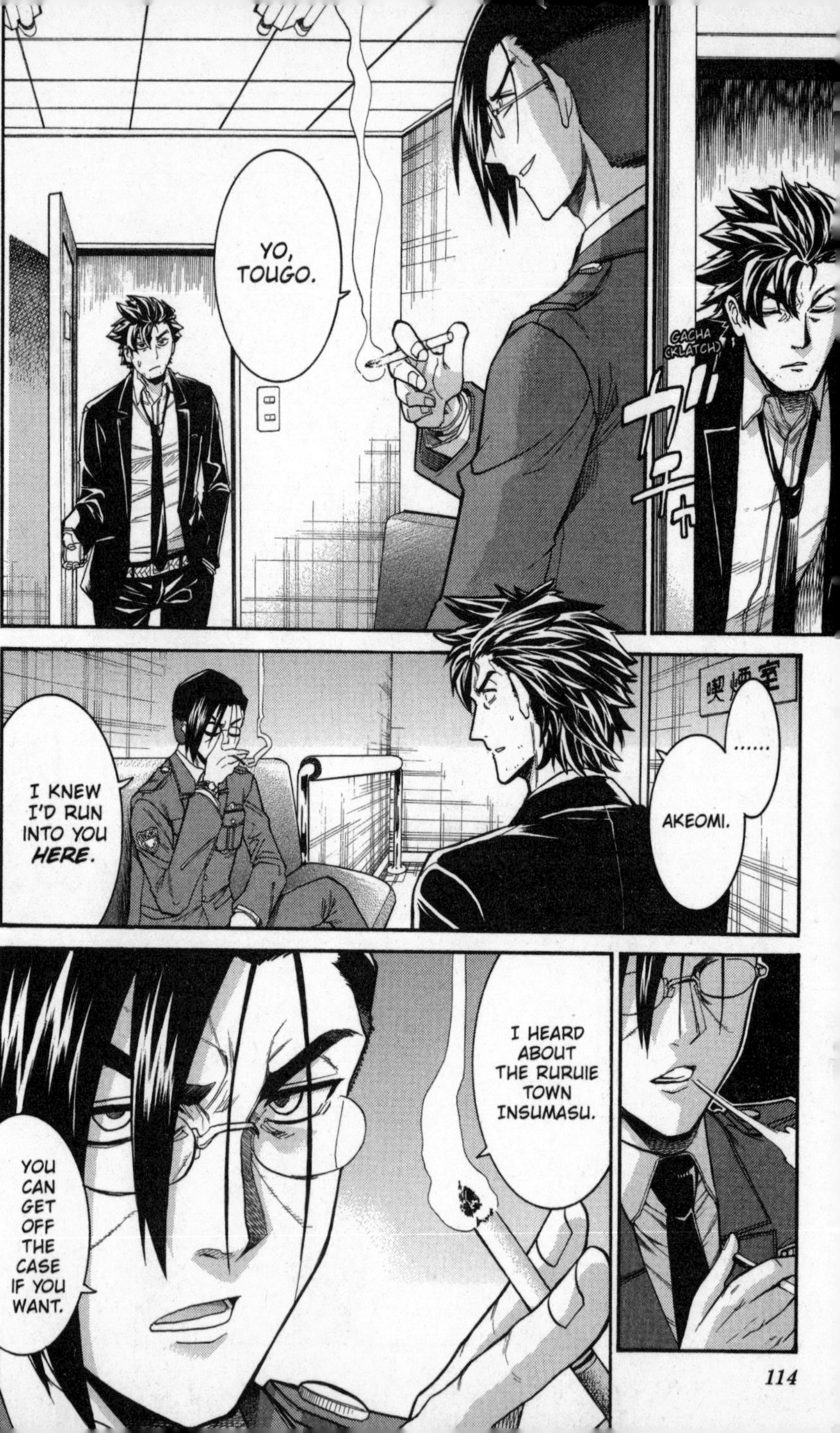
GACHA (KLATCH)
ガチャ
YO, TOUGO.
喫煙室
......
AKEOMI.
I KNEW I'D RUN INTO YOU ***HERE***.
I HEARD ABOUT THE RURUIE TOWN INSUMASU.
YOU CAN GET OFF THE CASE IF YOU WANT.

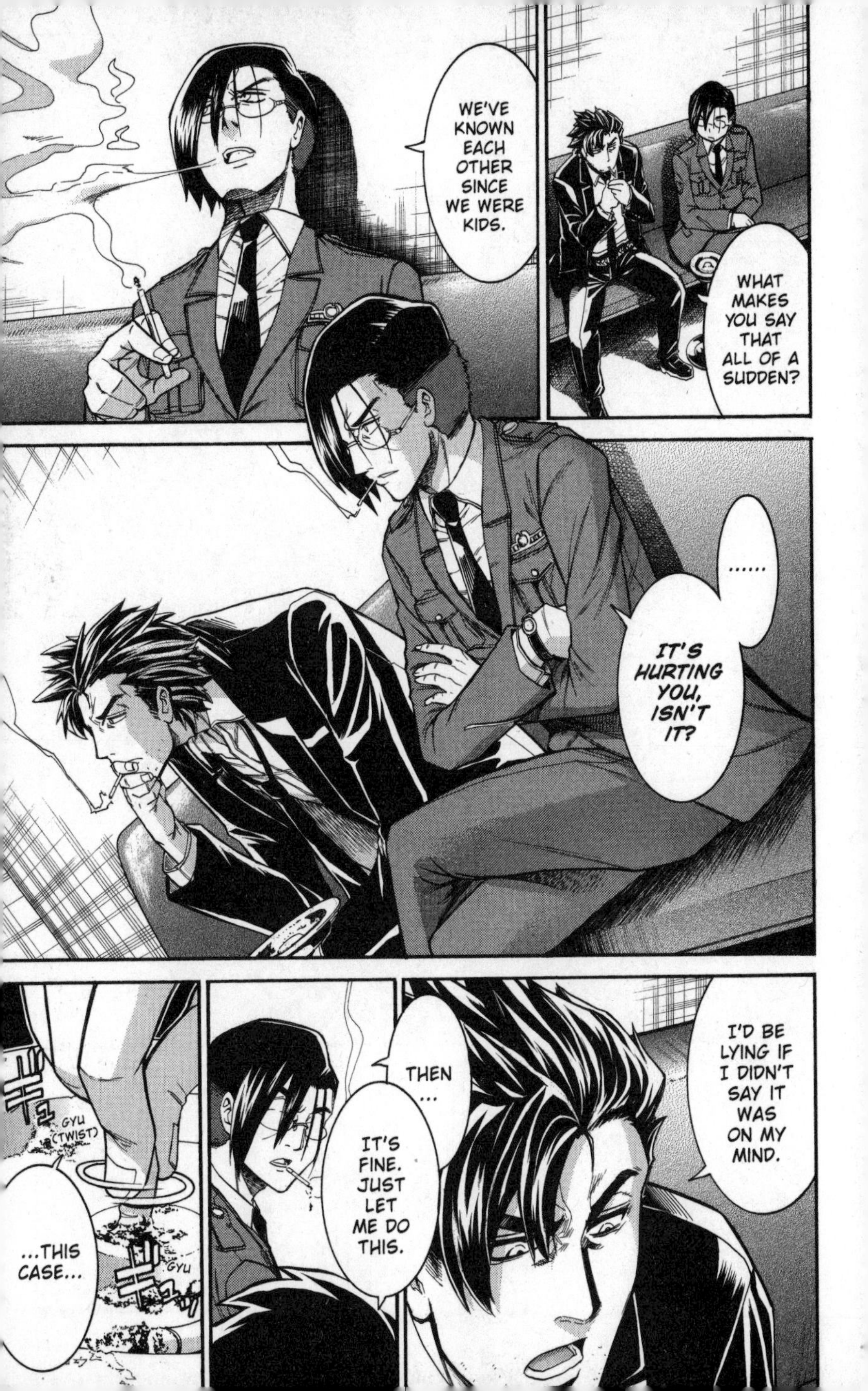
WHAT MAKES YOU SAY THAT ALL OF A SUDDEN?
WE'VE KNOWN EACH OTHER SINCE WE WERE KIDS.
......
IT'S HURTING YOU, ISN'T IT?
I'D BE LYING IF I DIDN'T SAY IT WAS ON MY MIND.
THEN...
IT'S FINE. JUST LET ME DO THIS.
GYU (TWIST)
...THIS CASE...
GYU

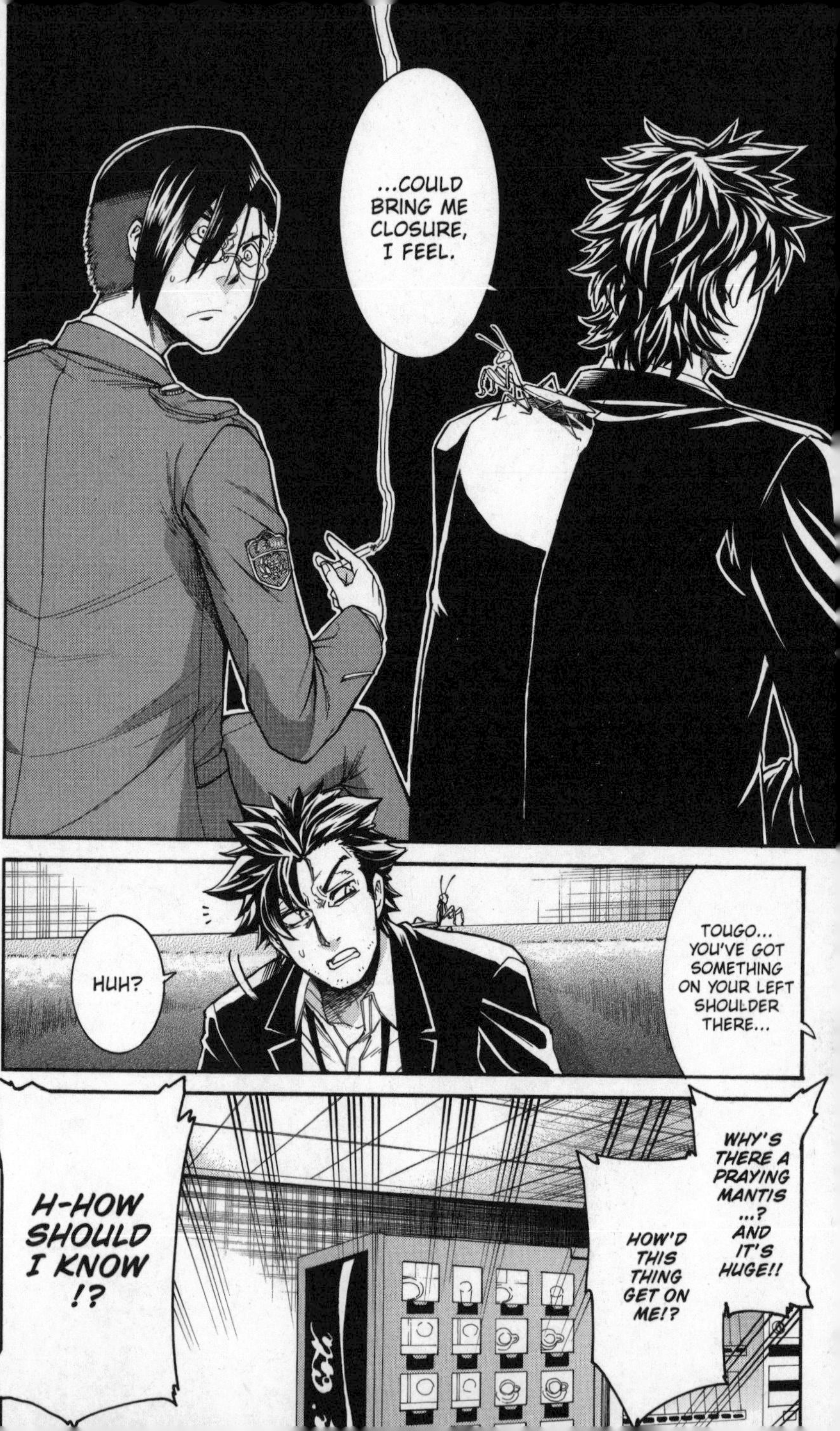
...COULD BRING ME CLOSURE, I FEEL.
TOUGO... YOU'VE GOT SOMETHING ON YOUR LEFT SHOULDER THERE...
HUH?
WHY'S THERE A PRAYING MANTIS ...? AND IT'S HUGE!!
HOW'D THIS THING GET ON ME!?
H-HOW SHOULD I KNOW !?

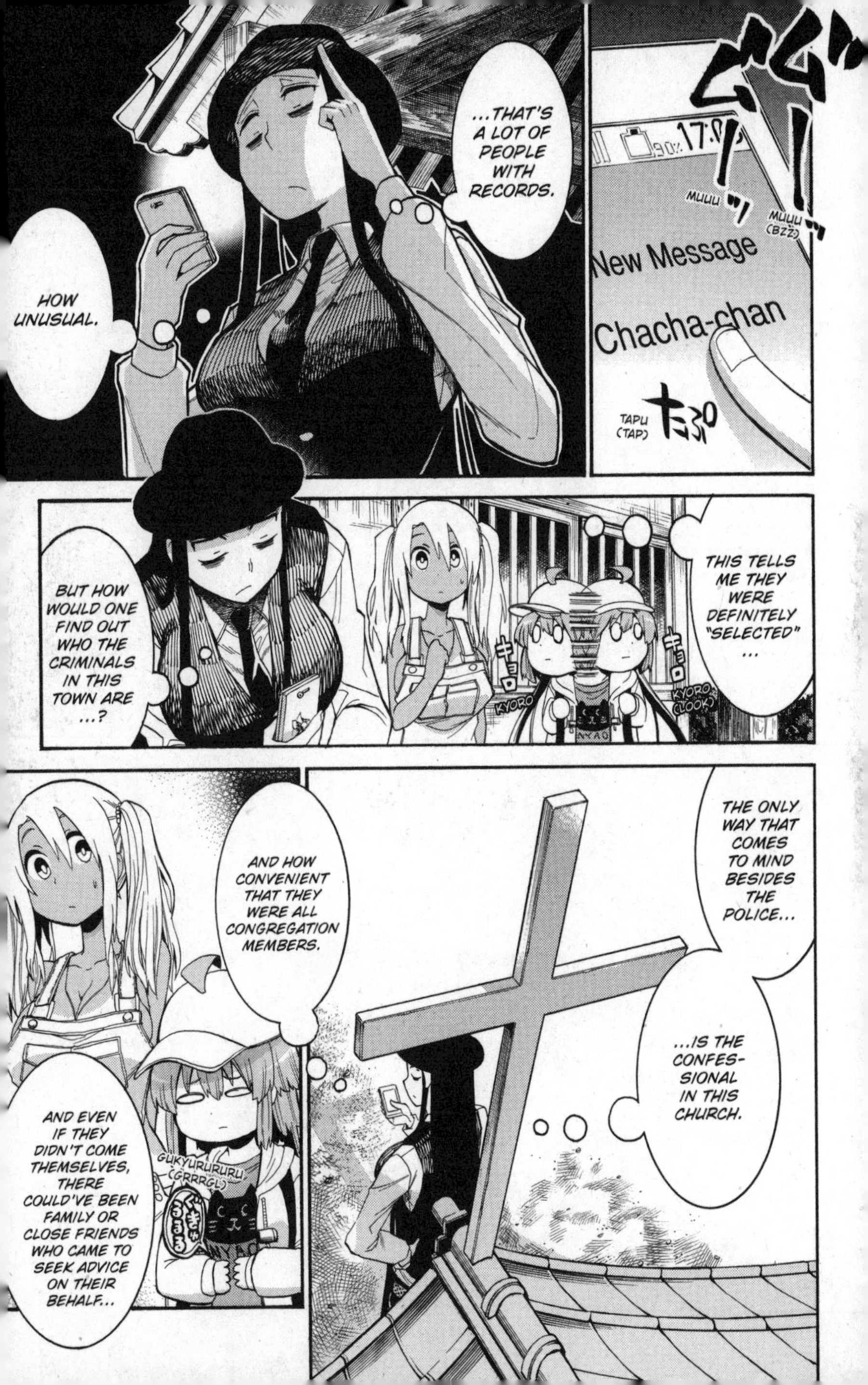
MUUU
MUUU (BZZ)
17:0
90%
New Message
Chacha-chan
TAPU (TAP)
...THAT'S A LOT OF PEOPLE WITH RECORDS.
HOW UNUSUAL.
THIS TELLS ME THEY WERE DEFINITELY "SELECTED"...
KYORO (LOOK)
KYORO
BUT HOW WOULD ONE FIND OUT WHO THE CRIMINALS IN THIS TOWN ARE...?
THE ONLY WAY THAT COMES TO MIND BESIDES THE POLICE...
...IS THE CONFESSIONAL IN THIS CHURCH.
AND HOW CONVENIENT THAT THEY WERE ALL CONGREGATION MEMBERS.
AND EVEN IF THEY DIDN'T COME THEMSELVES, THERE COULD'VE BEEN FAMILY OR CLOSE FRIENDS WHO CAME TO SEEK ADVICE ON THEIR BEHALF...
GUKYURURURU (GRRRGL)

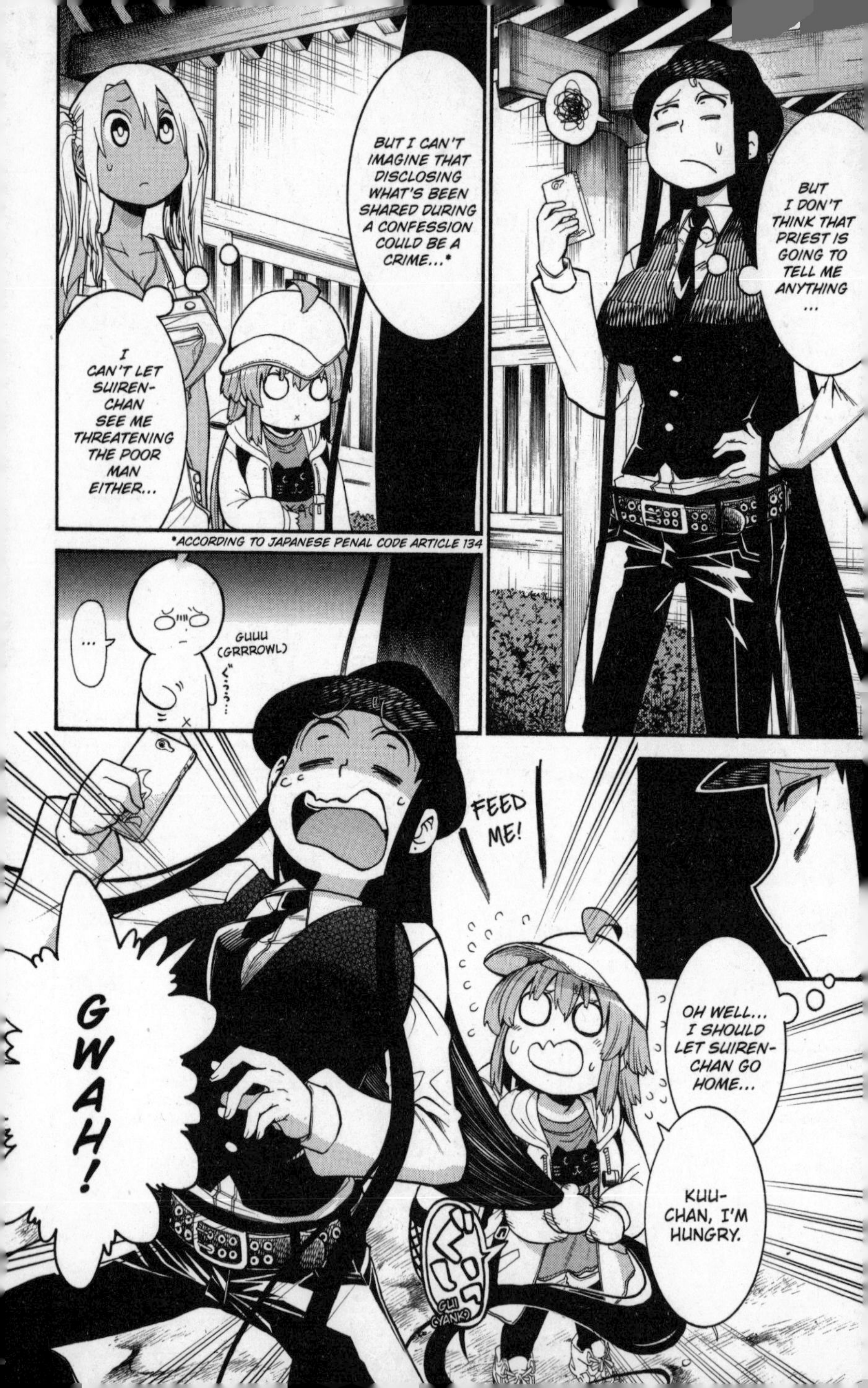
BUT I DON'T THINK THAT PRIEST IS GOING TO TELL ME ANYTHING...
BUT I CAN'T IMAGINE THAT DISCLOSING WHAT'S BEEN SHARED DURING A CONFESSION COULD BE A CRIME...*
I CAN'T LET SUIREN-CHAN SEE ME THREATENING THE POOR MAN EITHER...
*ACCORDING TO JAPANESE PENAL CODE ARTICLE 134
...
GUUU (GRRROWL)
OH WELL... I SHOULD LET SUIREN-CHAN GO HOME...
KUU-CHAN, I'M HUNGRY.
FEED ME!
GUI GYANK
GWAH!

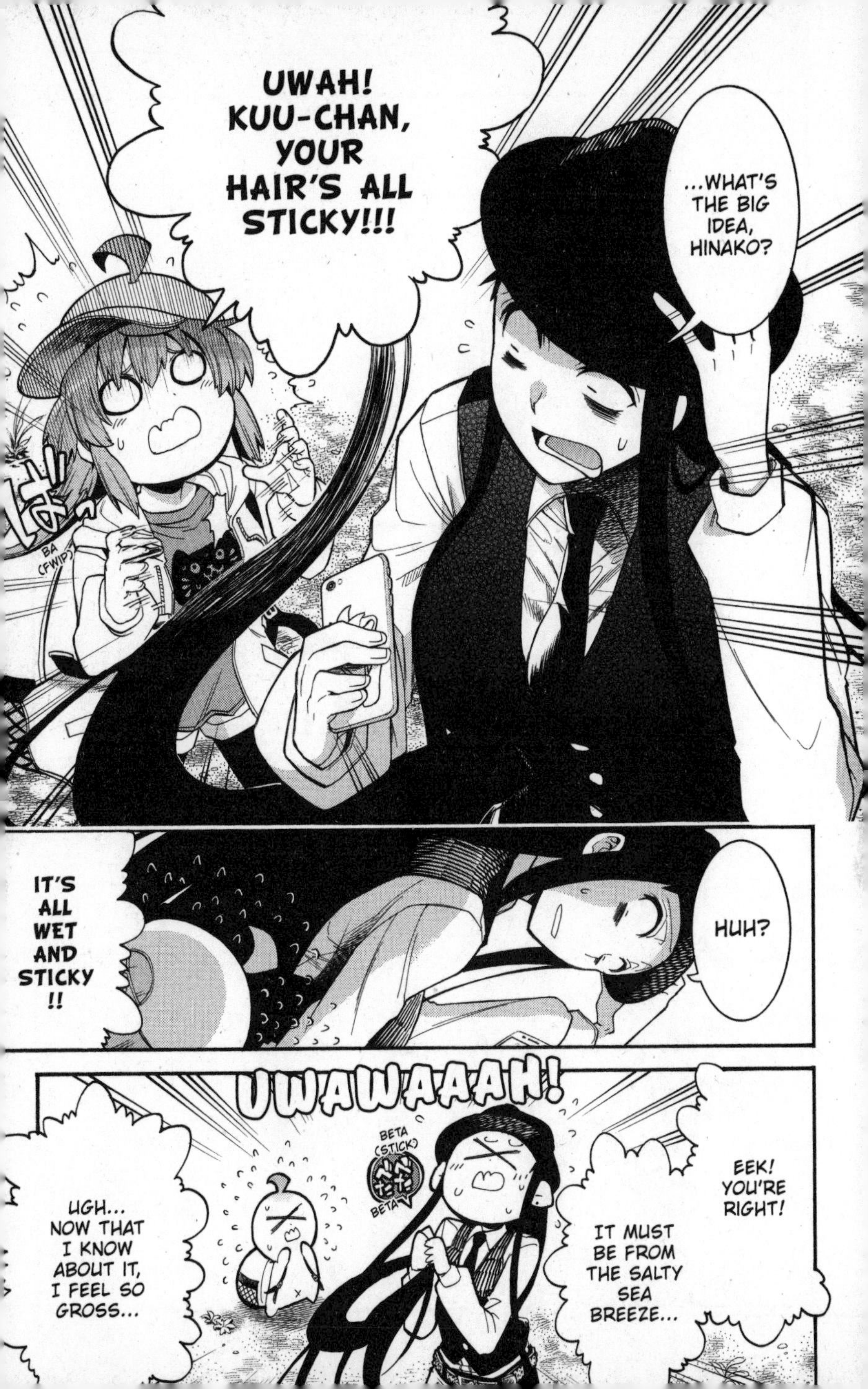
...WHAT'S THE BIG IDEA, HINAKO?
UWAH! KUU-CHAN, YOUR HAIR'S ALL STICKY!!!
ばっ
BA (FWIP)
HUH?
IT'S ALL WET AND STICKY!!
UWAWAAAAH!
EEK! YOU'RE RIGHT!
IT MUST BE FROM THE SALTY SEA BREEZE...
BETA (STICK) BETA
UGH... NOW THAT I KNOW ABOUT IT, I FEEL SO GROSS...

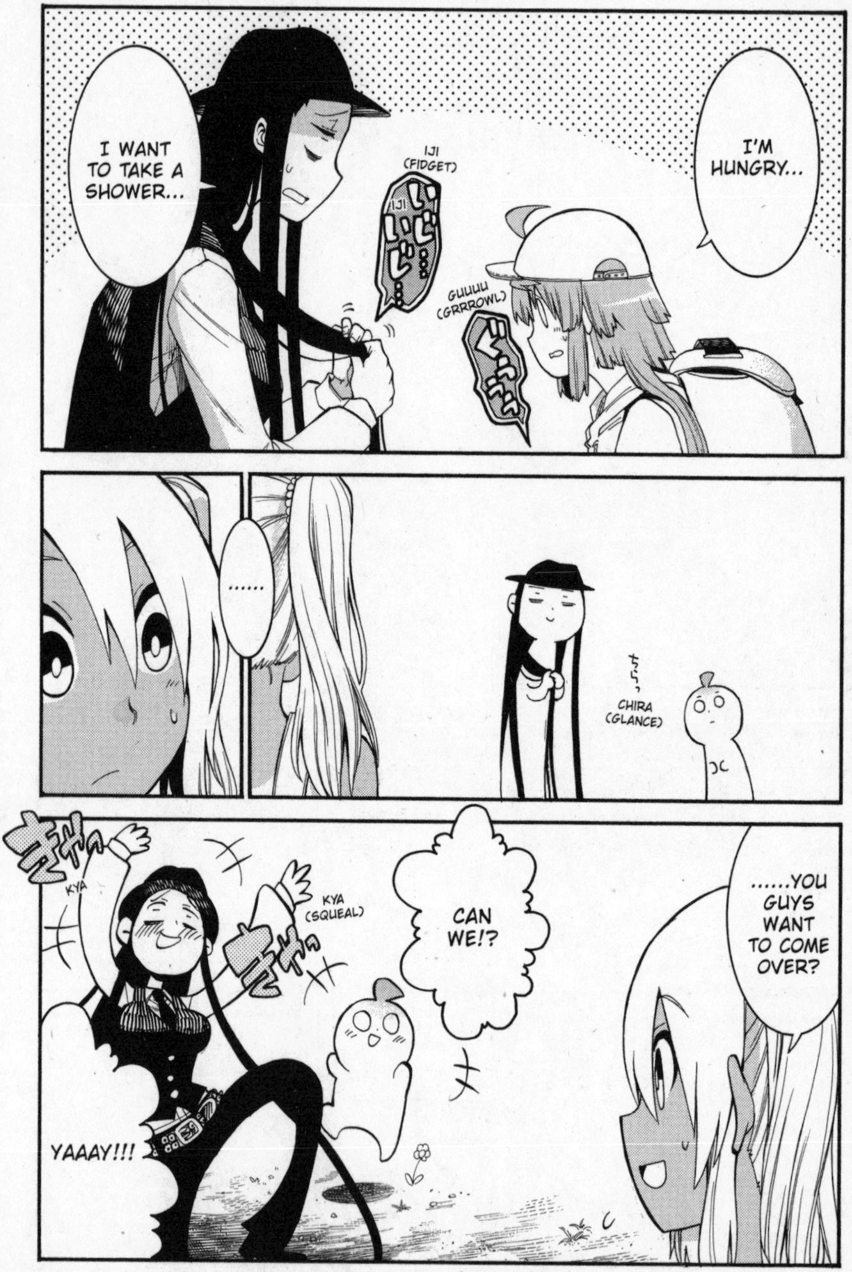
I'M HUNGRY...
GUUUU (GRRROWL)
IJI (FIDGET)
I WANT TO TAKE A SHOWER...
CHIRA (GLANCE)
......
......YOU GUYS WANT TO COME OVER?
CAN WE!?
KYA (SQUEAL)
KYA
YAAAY!!!

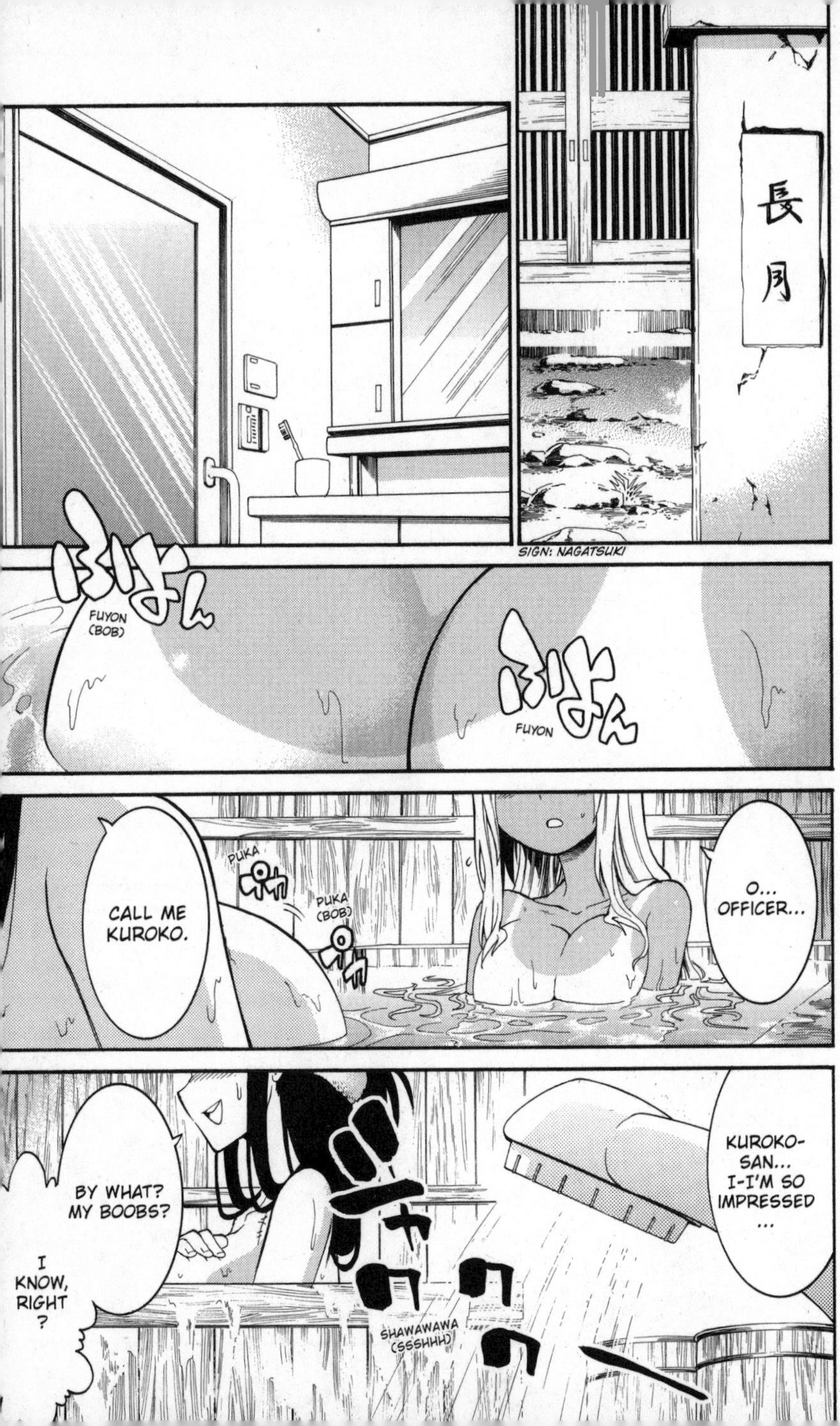
長月
SIGN: NAGATSUKI
ふよん
FUYON
ふよん
FUYON (BOB)
O... OFFICER...
PUKA (BOB)
PUKA
CALL ME KUROKO.
KUROKO-SAN... I-I'M SO IMPRESSED...
SHAWAWAWA (SSSHHH)
BY WHAT? MY BOOBS?
I KNOW, RIGHT?

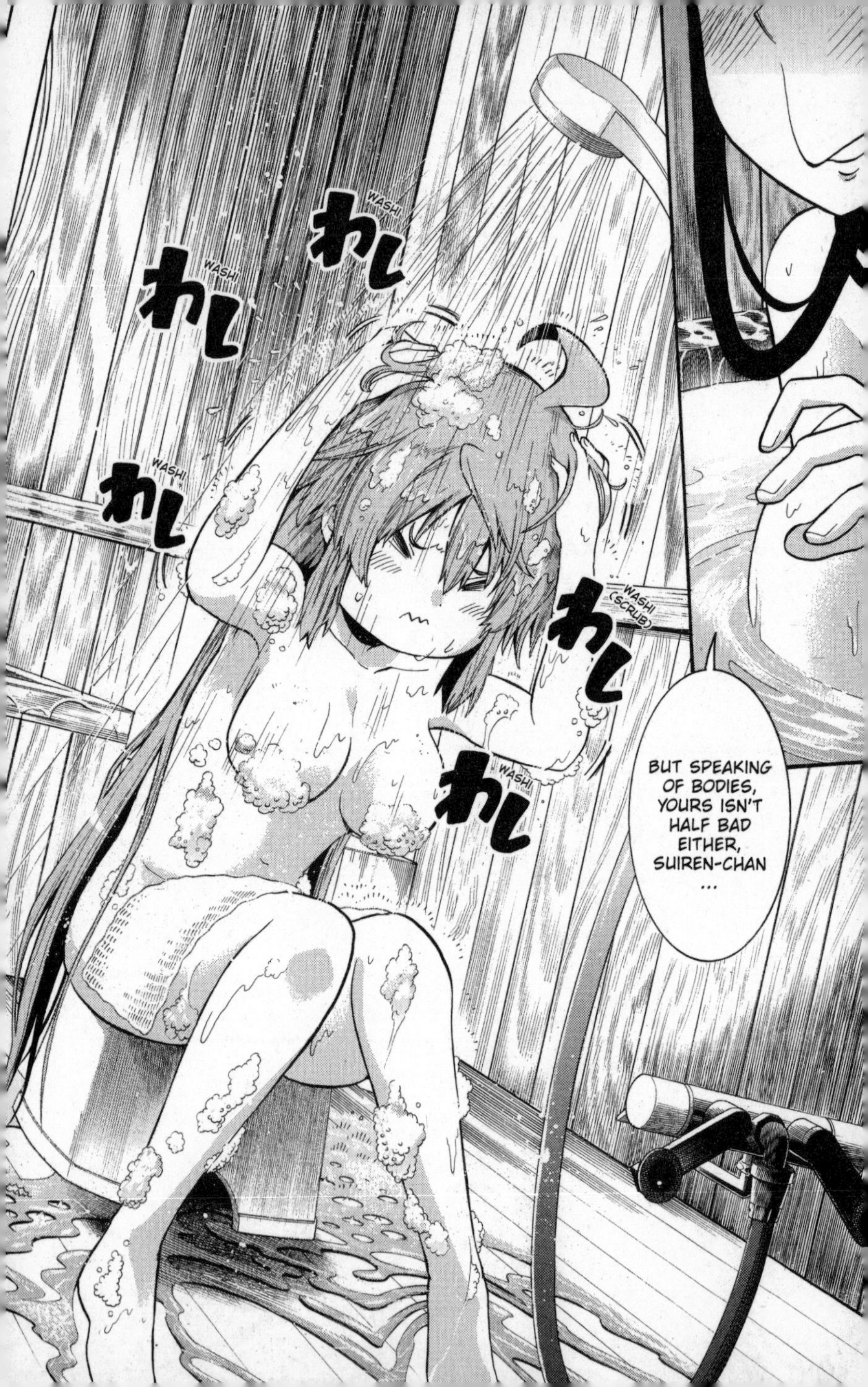
わし WASHI
わし WASHI
わし WASHI
わし WASHI (SCRUB)
BUT SPEAKING OF BODIES, YOURS ISN'T HALF BAD EITHER, SUIREN-CHAN ...
わし WASHI

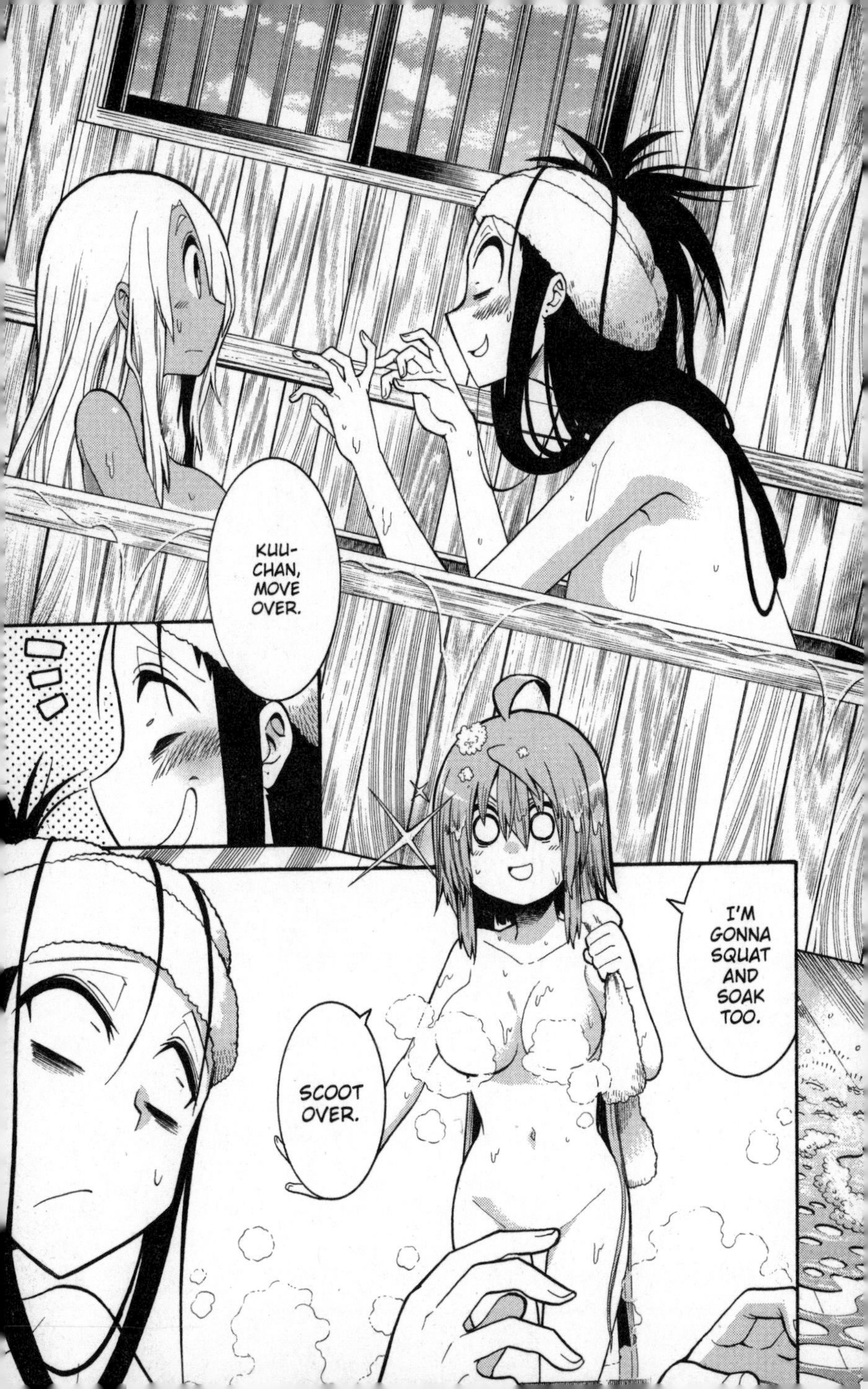
KUU-CHAN, MOVE OVER.
I'M GONNA SQUAT AND SOAK TOO.
SCOOT OVER.

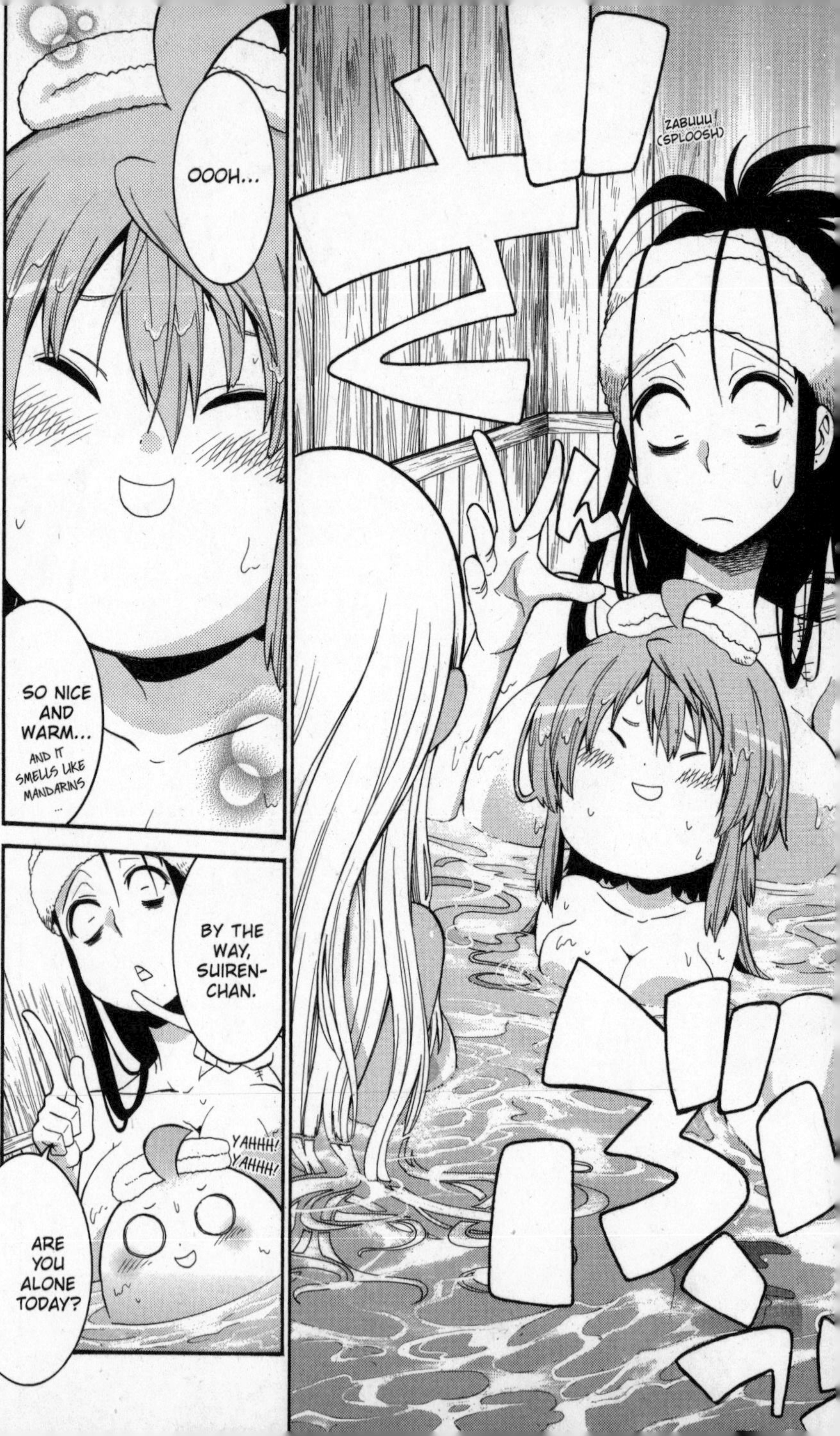
ZABUUU
(SPLOOSH)
OOOH...
SO NICE AND WARM...
AND IT SMELLS LIKE MANDARINS ...
BY THE WAY, SUIREN-CHAN.
YAHHH! YAHHH!
ARE YOU ALONE TODAY?

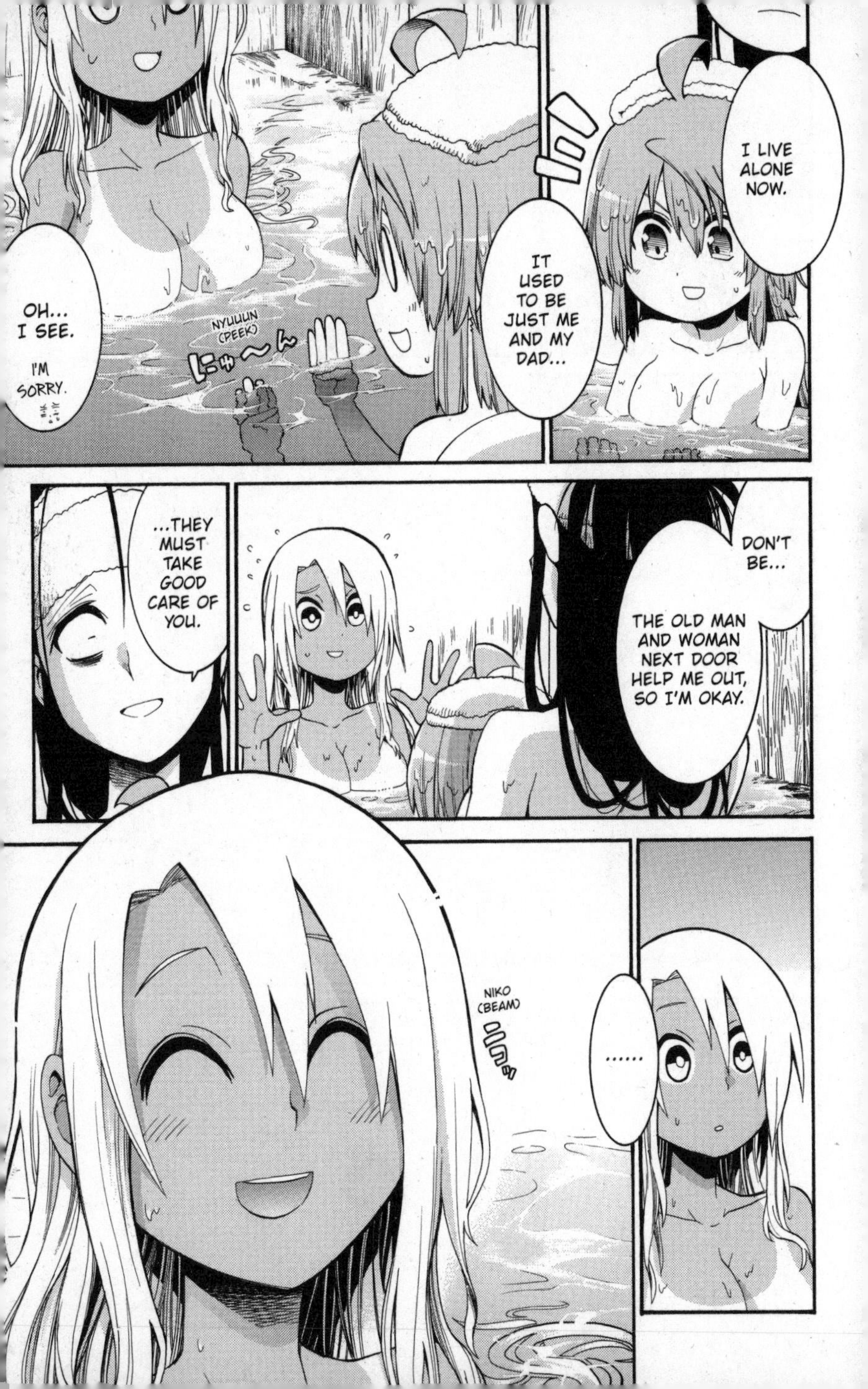
I LIVE ALONE NOW.
IT USED TO BE JUST ME AND MY DAD...
OH... I SEE.
I'M SORRY.
NYUUUN (PEEK)
にゅ～ん
DON'T BE...
THE OLD MAN AND WOMAN NEXT DOOR HELP ME OUT, SO I'M OKAY.
...THEY MUST TAKE GOOD CARE OF YOU.
......
NIKO (BEAM)
ニコッ

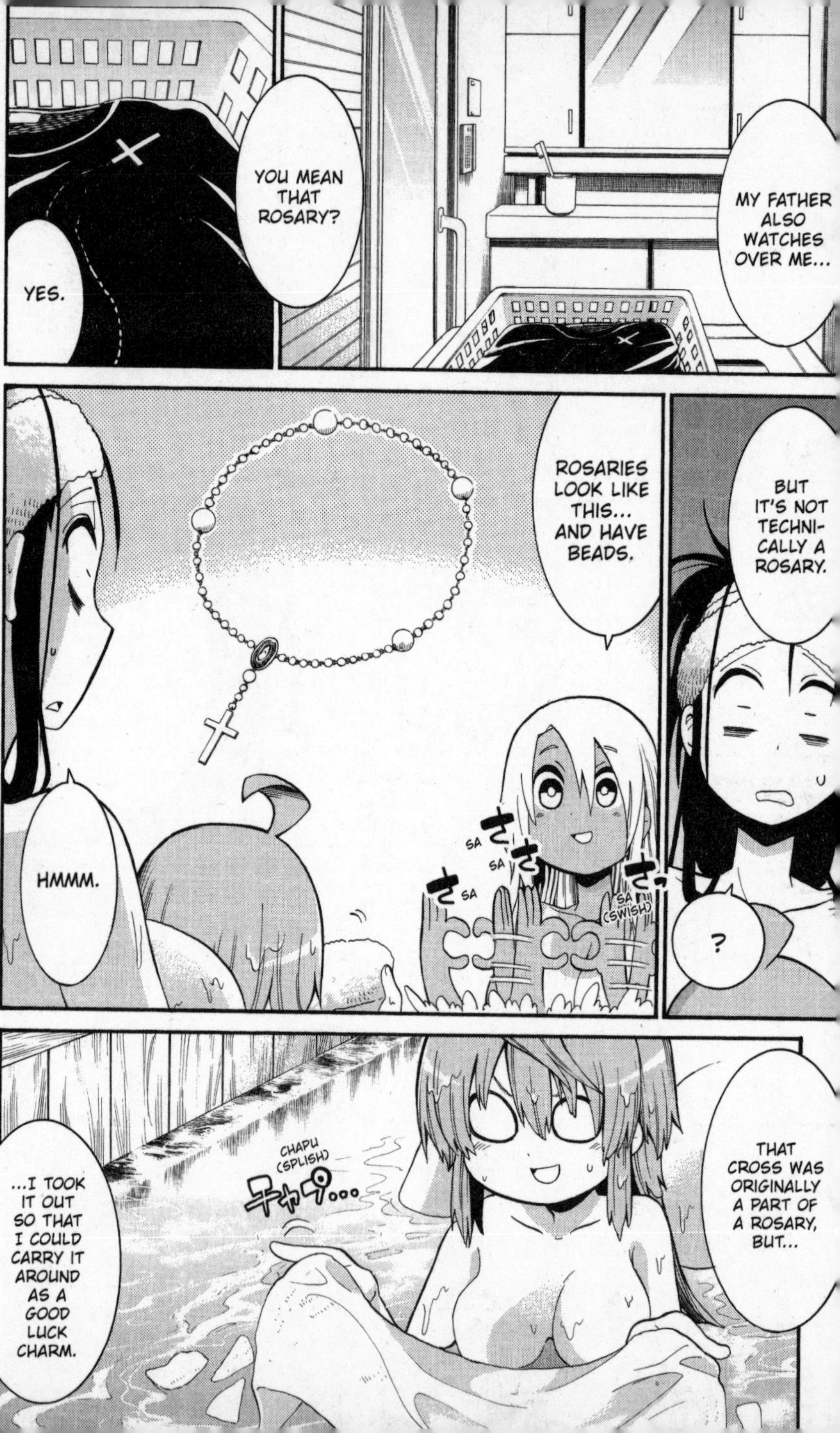
MY FATHER ALSO WATCHES OVER ME...
YOU MEAN THAT ROSARY?
YES.
BUT IT'S NOT TECHNICALLY A ROSARY.
?
ROSARIES LOOK LIKE THIS... AND HAVE BEADS.
SA SA SA SA (SWISH)
HMMM.
THAT CROSS WAS ORIGINALLY A PART OF A ROSARY, BUT...
CHAPU (SPLISH)
...I TOOK IT OUT SO THAT I COULD CARRY IT AROUND AS A GOOD LUCK CHARM.

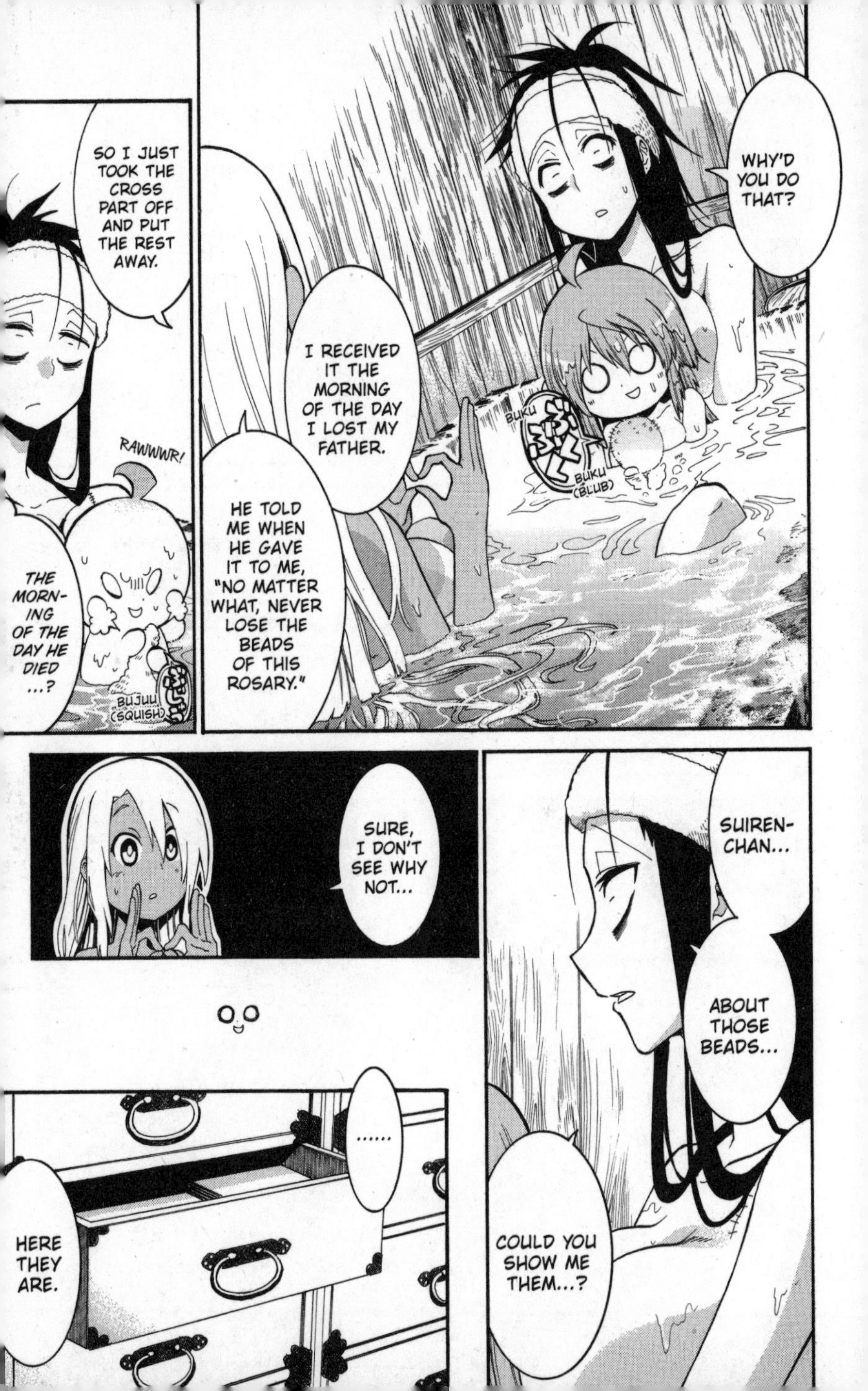
WHY'D YOU DO THAT?
I RECEIVED IT THE MORNING OF THE DAY I LOST MY FATHER.
BUKU
BUKU (BLUB)
HE TOLD ME WHEN HE GAVE IT TO ME, "NO MATTER WHAT, NEVER LOSE THE BEADS OF THIS ROSARY."
SO I JUST TOOK THE CROSS PART OFF AND PUT THE REST AWAY.
RAWWWR!
THE MORNING OF THE DAY HE DIED ...?
BUJUU (SQUISH)
SUIREN-CHAN...
ABOUT THOSE BEADS...
COULD YOU SHOW ME THEM...?
SURE, I DON'T SEE WHY NOT...
......
HERE THEY ARE.

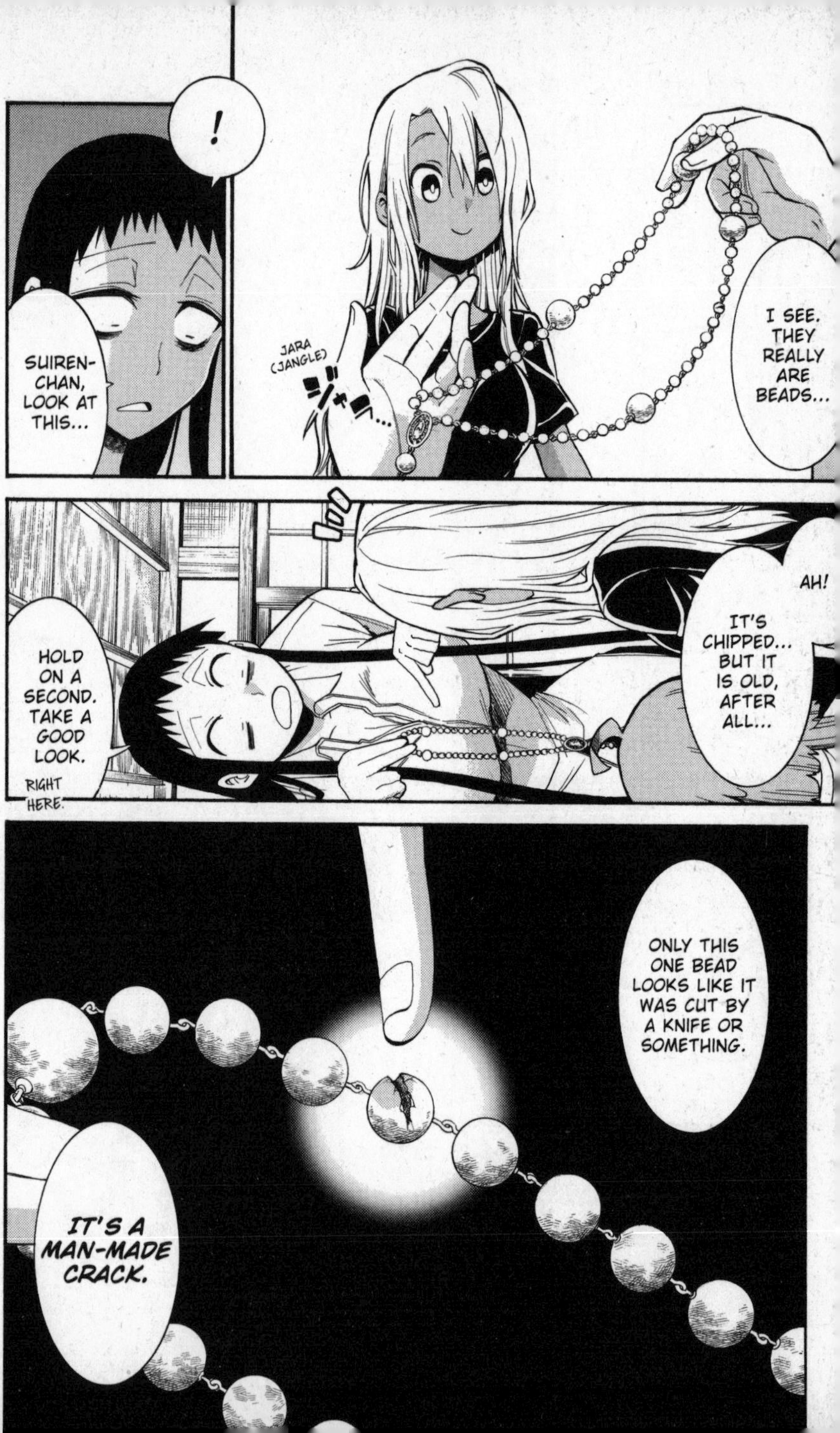
I SEE. THEY REALLY ARE BEADS...
JARA (JANGLE)
!
SUIREN-CHAN, LOOK AT THIS...
AH!
IT'S CHIPPED... BUT IT IS OLD, AFTER ALL...
HOLD ON A SECOND. TAKE A GOOD LOOK.
RIGHT HERE.
ONLY THIS ONE BEAD LOOKS LIKE IT WAS CUT BY A KNIFE OR SOMETHING.
IT'S A MAN-MADE CRACK.

MURCIÉLAGO

MURCIÉLAGO

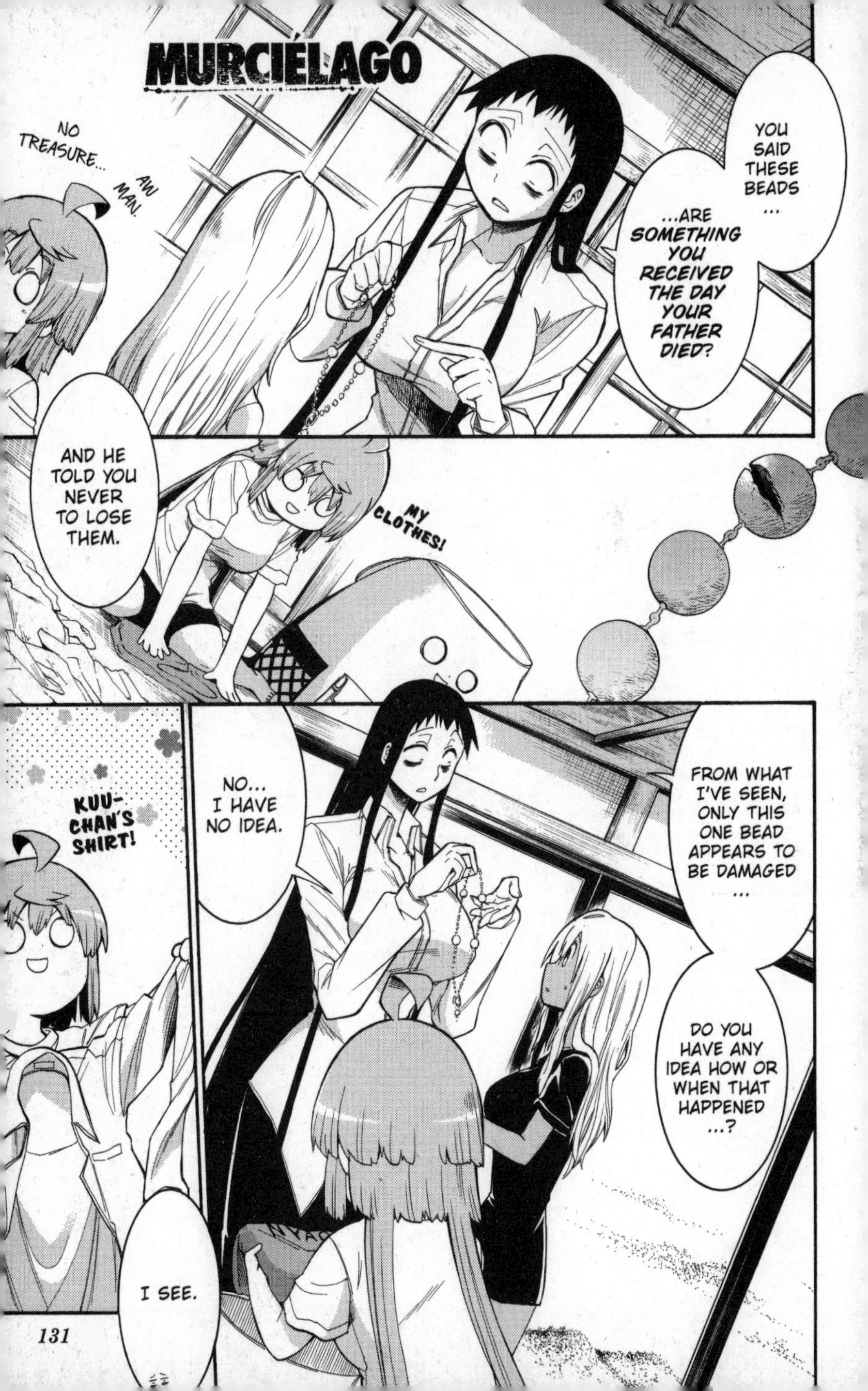
MURCIÉLAGO
YOU SAID THESE BEADS ...
...ARE SOMETHING YOU RECEIVED THE DAY YOUR FATHER DIED?
NO TREASURE...
AW MAN.
AND HE TOLD YOU NEVER TO LOSE THEM.
MY CLOTHES!
FROM WHAT I'VE SEEN, ONLY THIS ONE BEAD APPEARS TO BE DAMAGED ...
DO YOU HAVE ANY IDEA HOW OR WHEN THAT HAPPENED ...?
NO... I HAVE NO IDEA.
I SEE.
KUU-CHAN'S SHIRT!

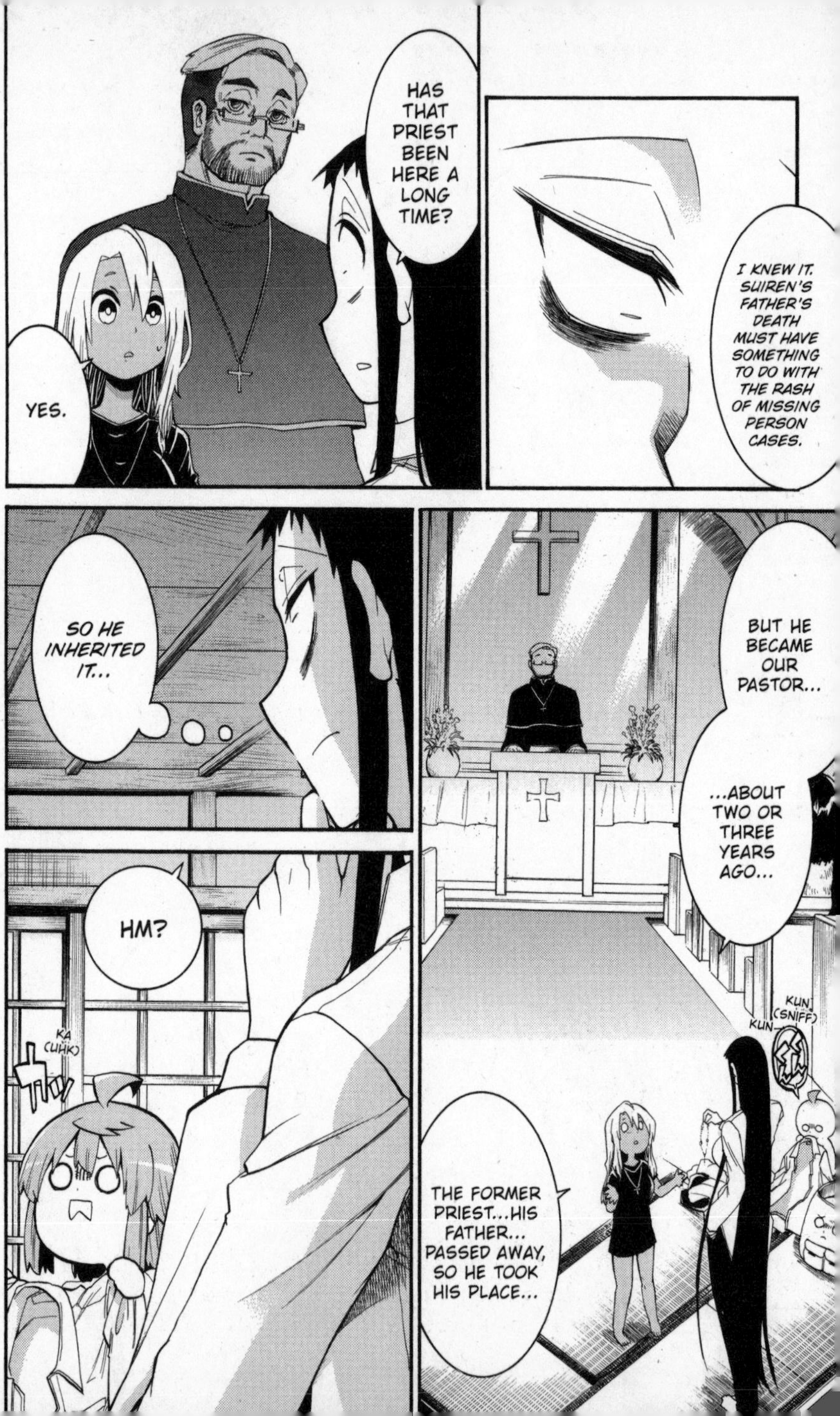
I KNEW IT. SUIREN'S FATHER'S DEATH MUST HAVE SOMETHING TO DO WITH THE RASH OF MISSING PERSON CASES.
HAS THAT PRIEST BEEN HERE A LONG TIME?
YES.
BUT HE BECAME OUR PASTOR...
...ABOUT TWO OR THREE YEARS AGO...
KUN KUN (SNIFF)
THE FORMER PRIEST...HIS FATHER... PASSED AWAY, SO HE TOOK HIS PLACE...
SO HE INHERITED IT...
HM?
KA (UHK)

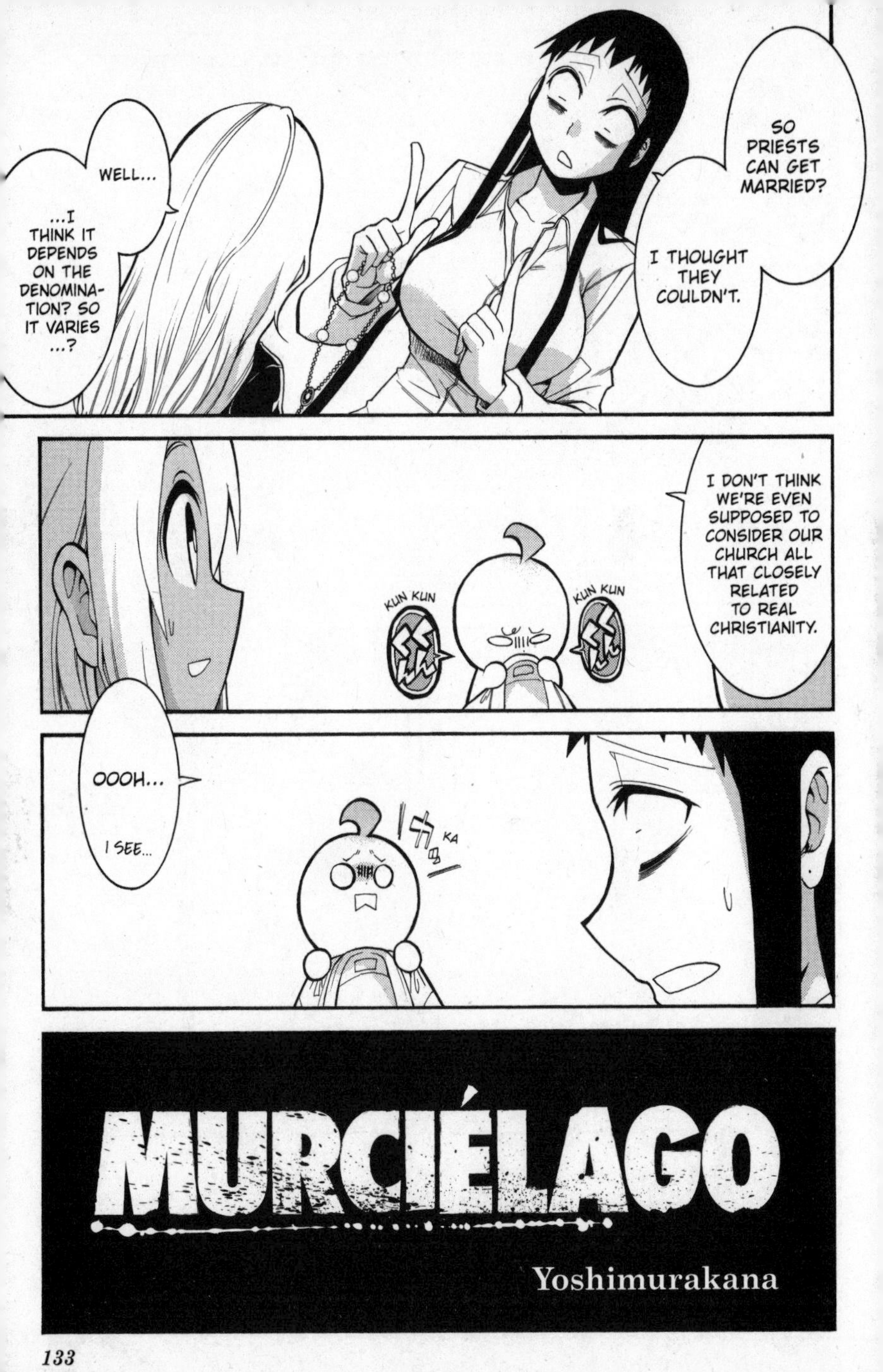
SO PRIESTS CAN GET MARRIED?
I THOUGHT THEY COULDN'T.
WELL...
...I THINK IT DEPENDS ON THE DENOMINATION? SO IT VARIES ...?
I DON'T THINK WE'RE EVEN SUPPOSED TO CONSIDER OUR CHURCH ALL THAT CLOSELY RELATED TO REAL CHRISTIANITY.
KUN KUN
KUN KUN
KA
OOOH...
I SEE...

MURCIÉLAGO

Yoshimurakana

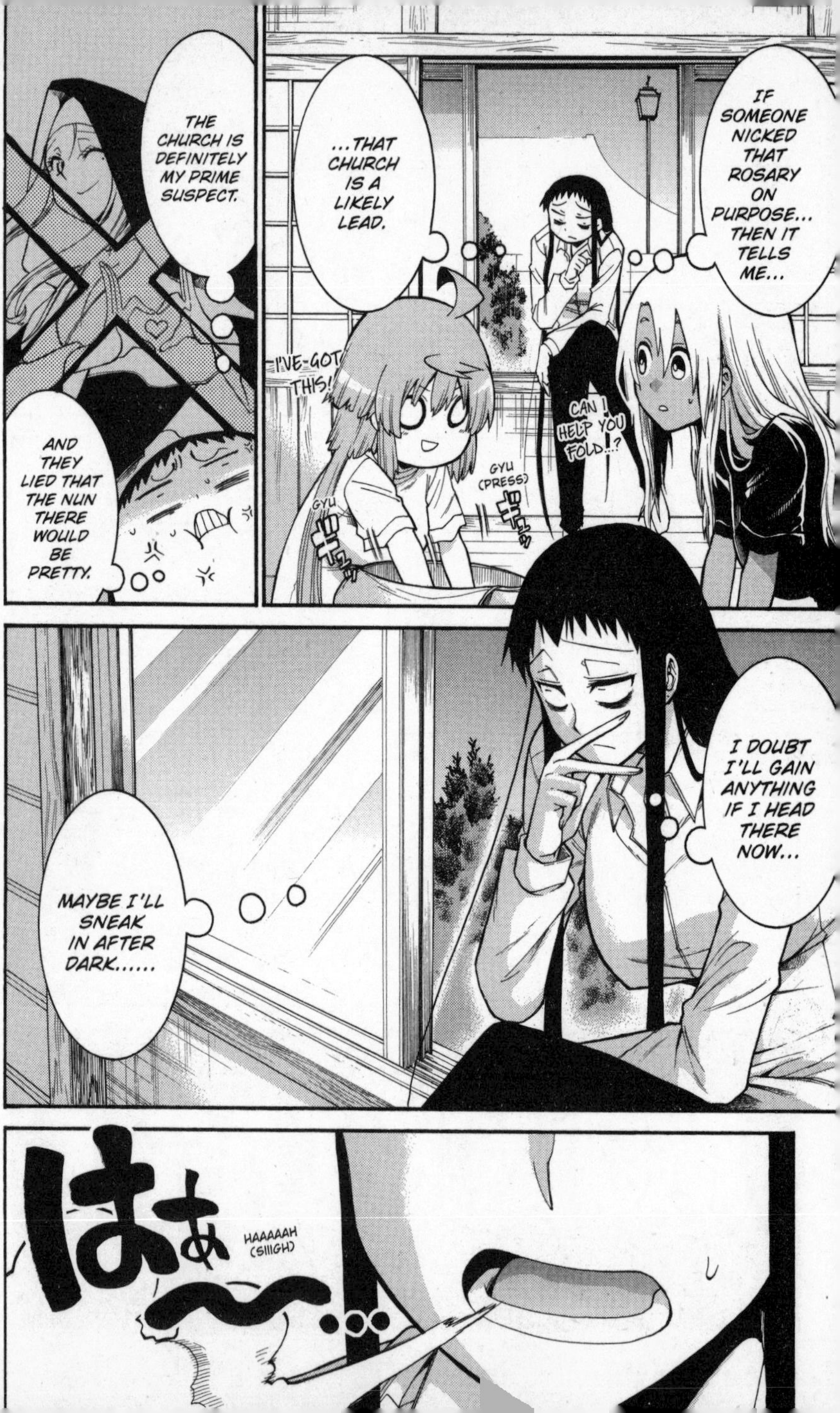
IF SOMEONE NICKED THAT ROSARY ON PURPOSE... THEN IT TELLS ME...
...THAT CHURCH IS A LIKELY LEAD.
CAN I HELP YOU FOLD...?
GYU (PRESS)
I'VE GOT THIS!
GYU
THE CHURCH IS DEFINITELY MY PRIME SUSPECT.
AND THEY LIED THAT THE NUN THERE WOULD BE PRETTY.
I DOUBT I'LL GAIN ANYTHING IF I HEAD THERE NOW...
MAYBE I'LL SNEAK IN AFTER DARK......
はぁ〜…
HAAAAAH (SIIIGH)

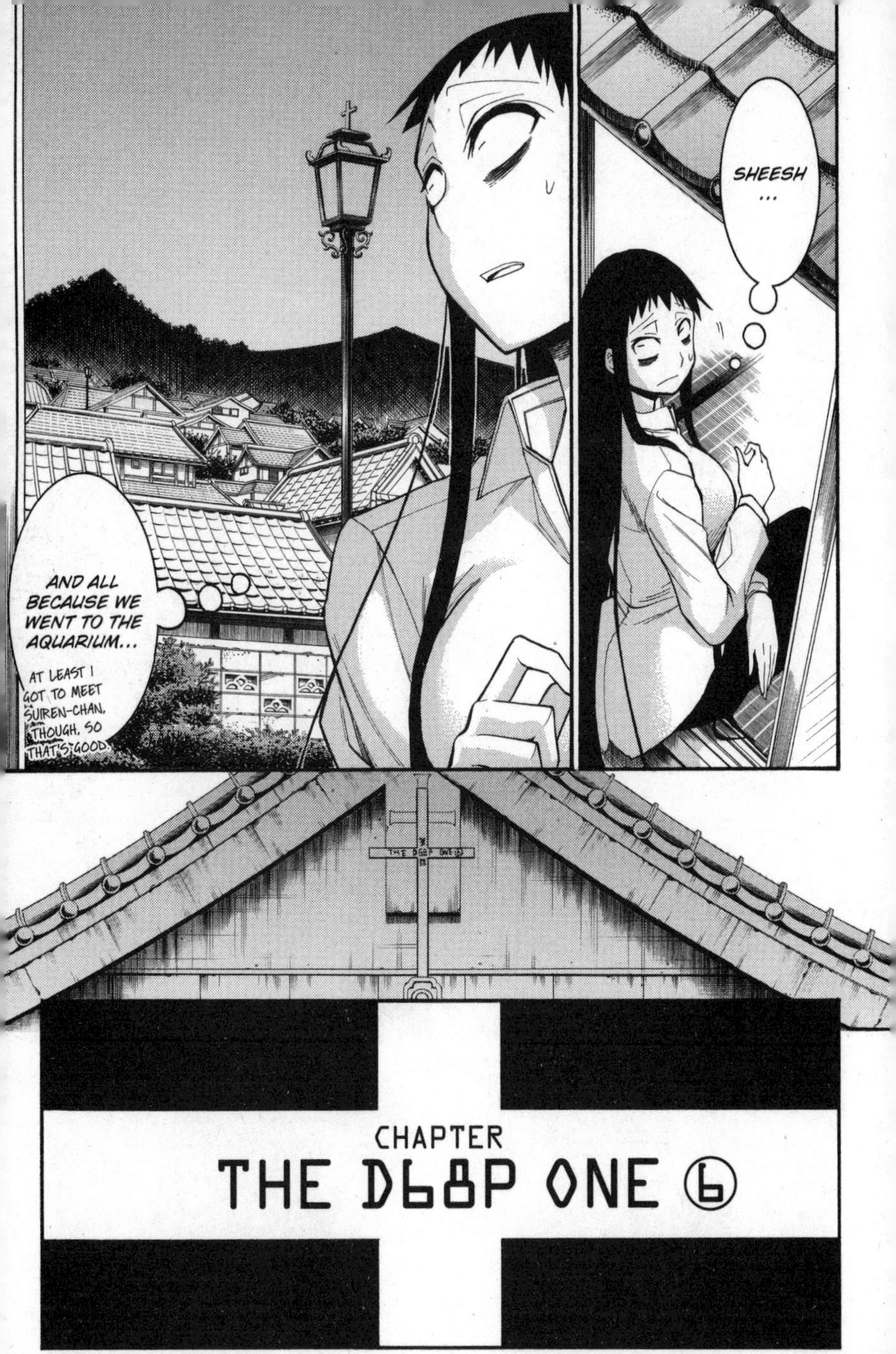
SHEESH ...
AND ALL BECAUSE WE WENT TO THE AQUARIUM...
AT LEAST I GOT TO MEET SUIREN-CHAN, THOUGH, SO THAT'S GOOD.
CHAPTER
THE DEEP ONE ⑥

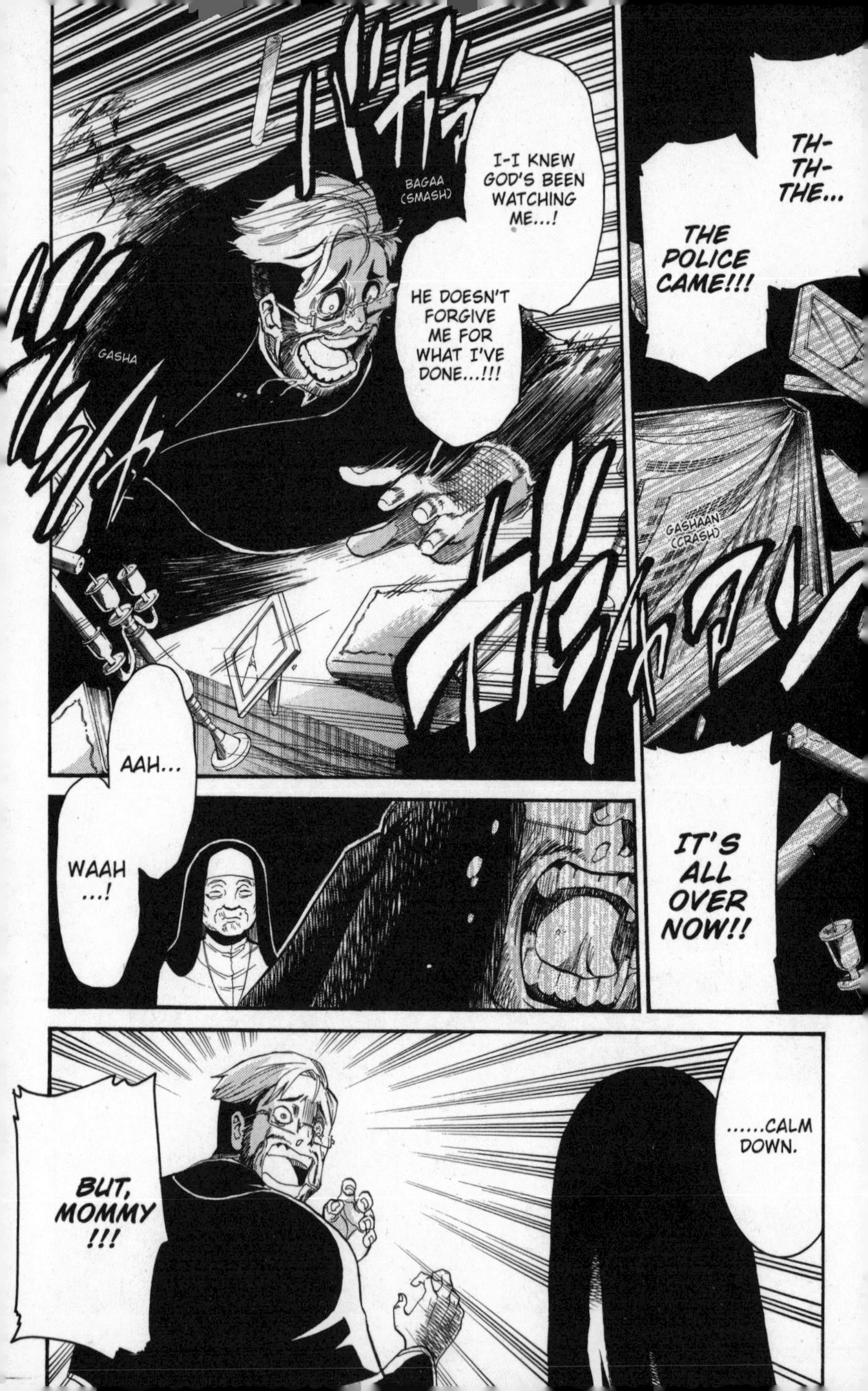
TH-TH-THE...
THE POLICE CAME!!!
IT'S ALL OVER NOW!!!
BAGAA (SMASH)
I-I KNEW GOD'S BEEN WATCHING ME...!
HE DOESN'T FORGIVE ME FOR WHAT I'VE DONE...!!!
GASHAAN (CRASH)
GASHA
AAH...
WAAH ...!
......CALM DOWN.
BUT, MOMMY !!!

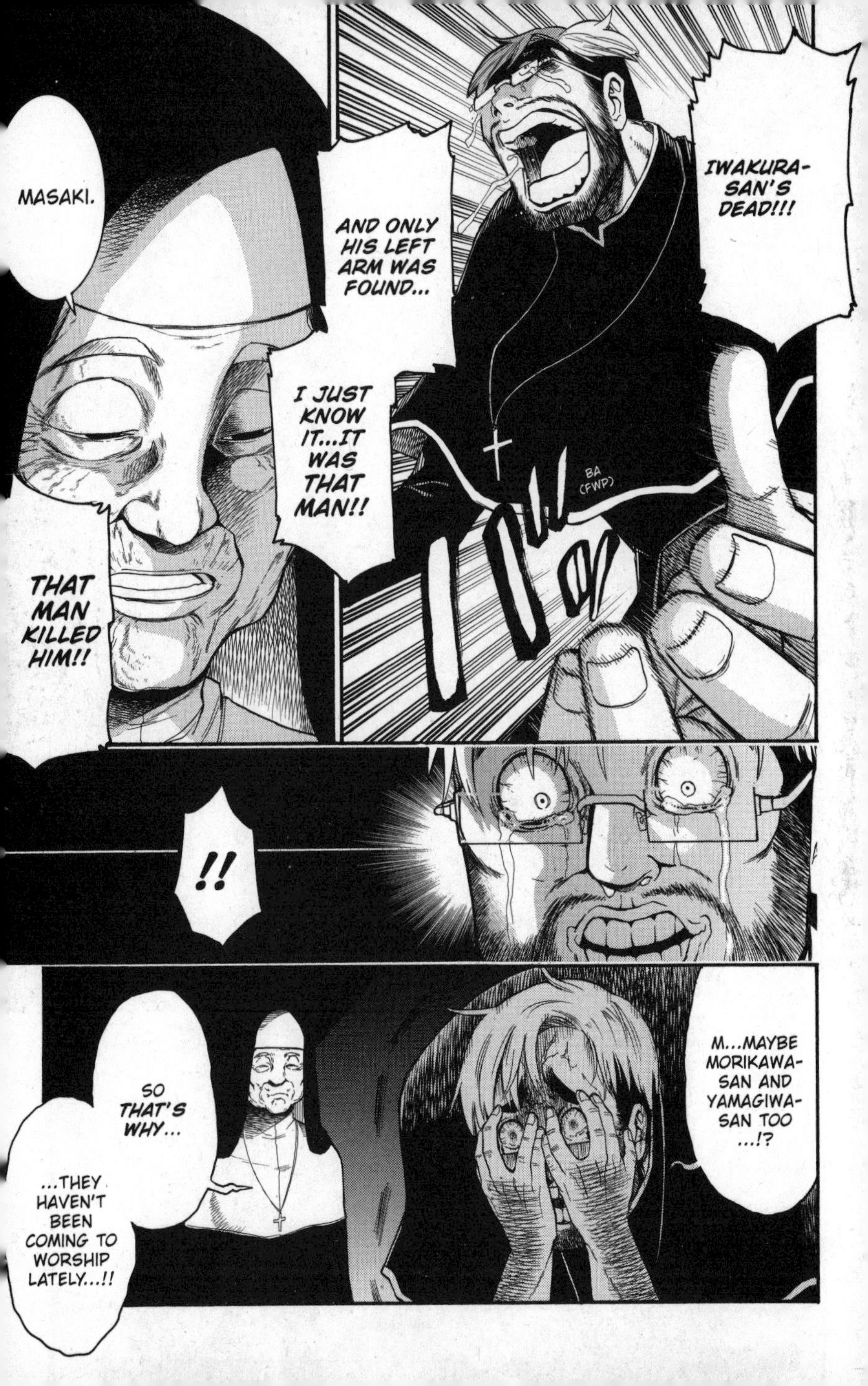
IWAKURA-SAN'S DEAD!!!
AND ONLY HIS LEFT ARM WAS FOUND...
I JUST KNOW IT...IT WAS THAT MAN!!
BA (FWP)
MASAKI.
THAT MAN KILLED HIM!!
!!
M...MAYBE MORIKAWA-SAN AND YAMAGIWA-SAN TOO ...!?
SO THAT'S WHY...
...THEY HAVEN'T BEEN COMING TO WORSHIP LATELY...!!

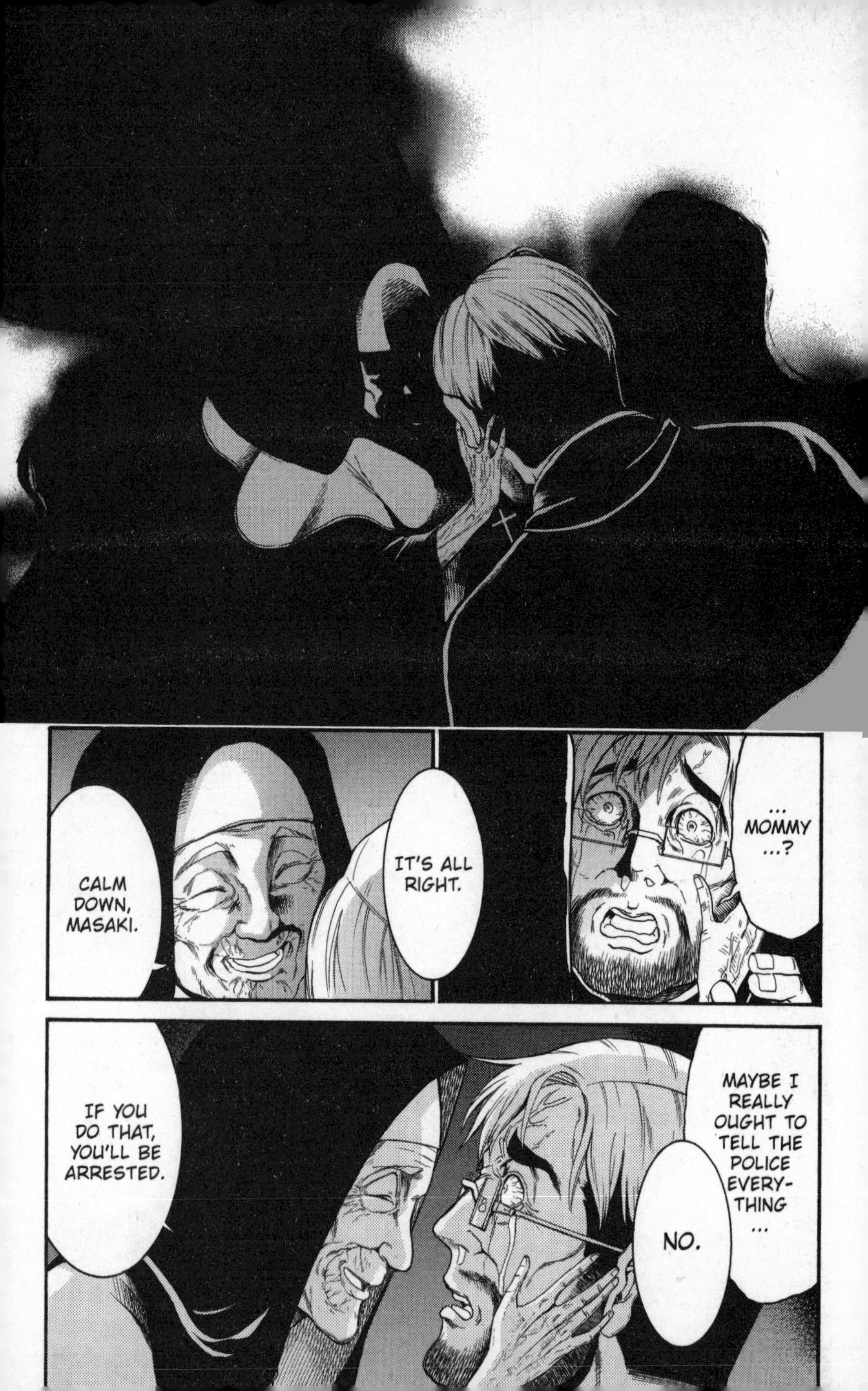
... MOMMY ...?
IT'S ALL RIGHT.
CALM DOWN, MASAKI.
MAYBE I REALLY OUGHT TO TELL THE POLICE EVERYTHING ...
NO.
IF YOU DO THAT, YOU'LL BE ARRESTED.

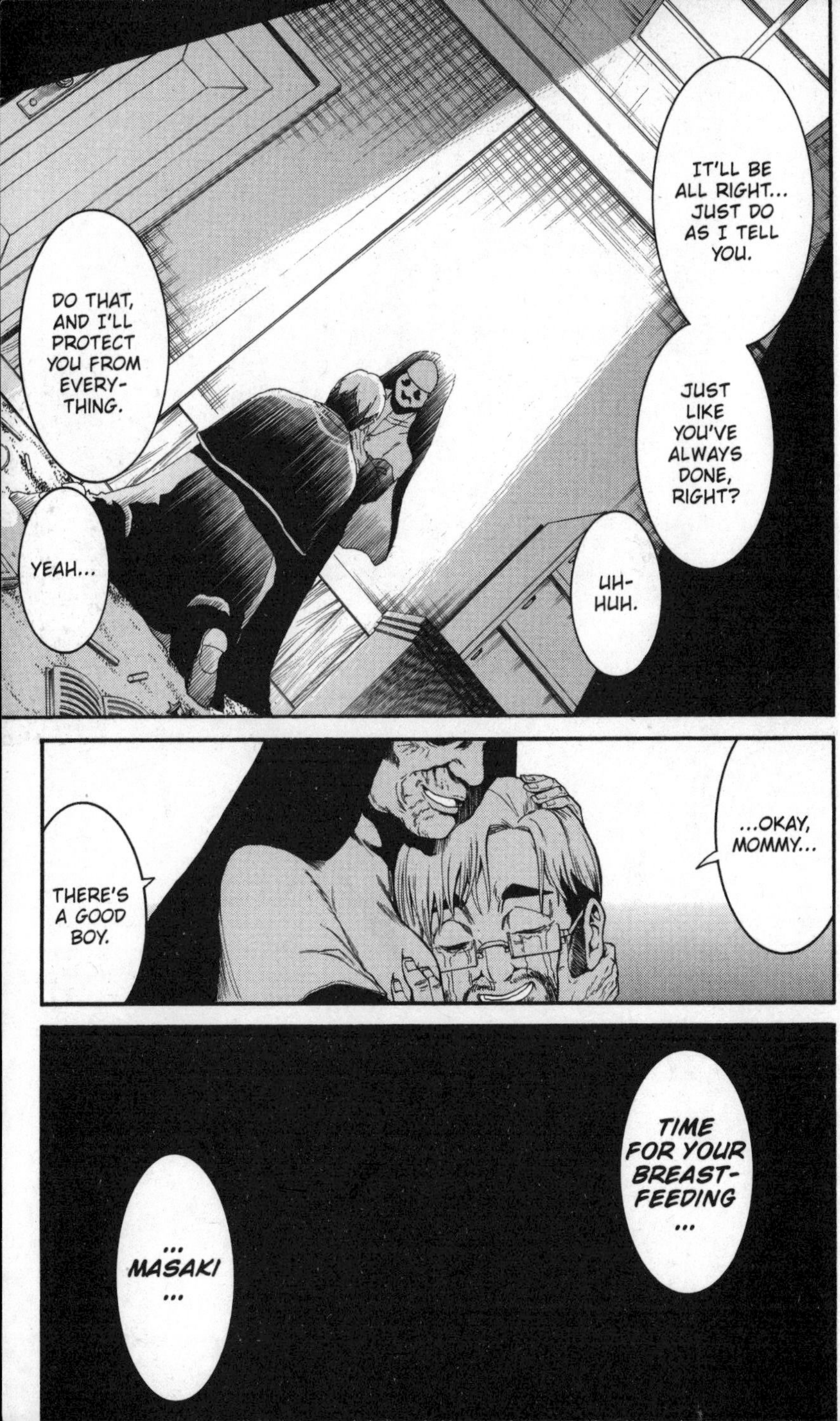
IT'LL BE ALL RIGHT... JUST DO AS I TELL YOU.
JUST LIKE YOU'VE ALWAYS DONE, RIGHT?
UH-HUH.
DO THAT, AND I'LL PROTECT YOU FROM EVERY-THING.
YEAH...
...OKAY, MOMMY...
THERE'S A GOOD BOY.
TIME FOR YOUR BREAST-FEEDING ...
... MASAKI ...

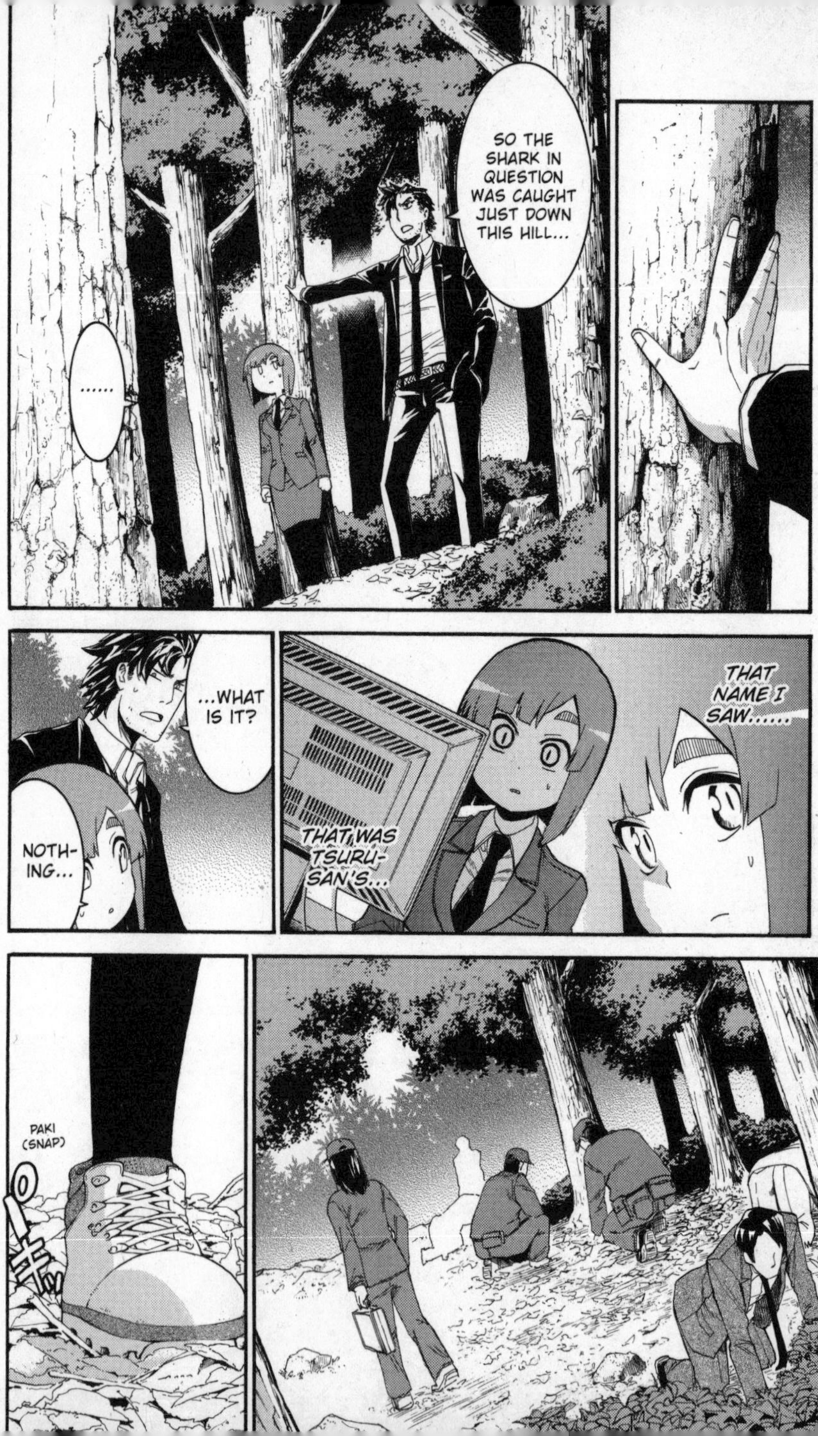
SO THE SHARK IN QUESTION WAS CAUGHT JUST DOWN THIS HILL...
......
THAT NAME I SAW......
THAT WAS TSURU-SAN'S...
...WHAT IS IT?
NOTH-ING...
PAKI (SNAP)

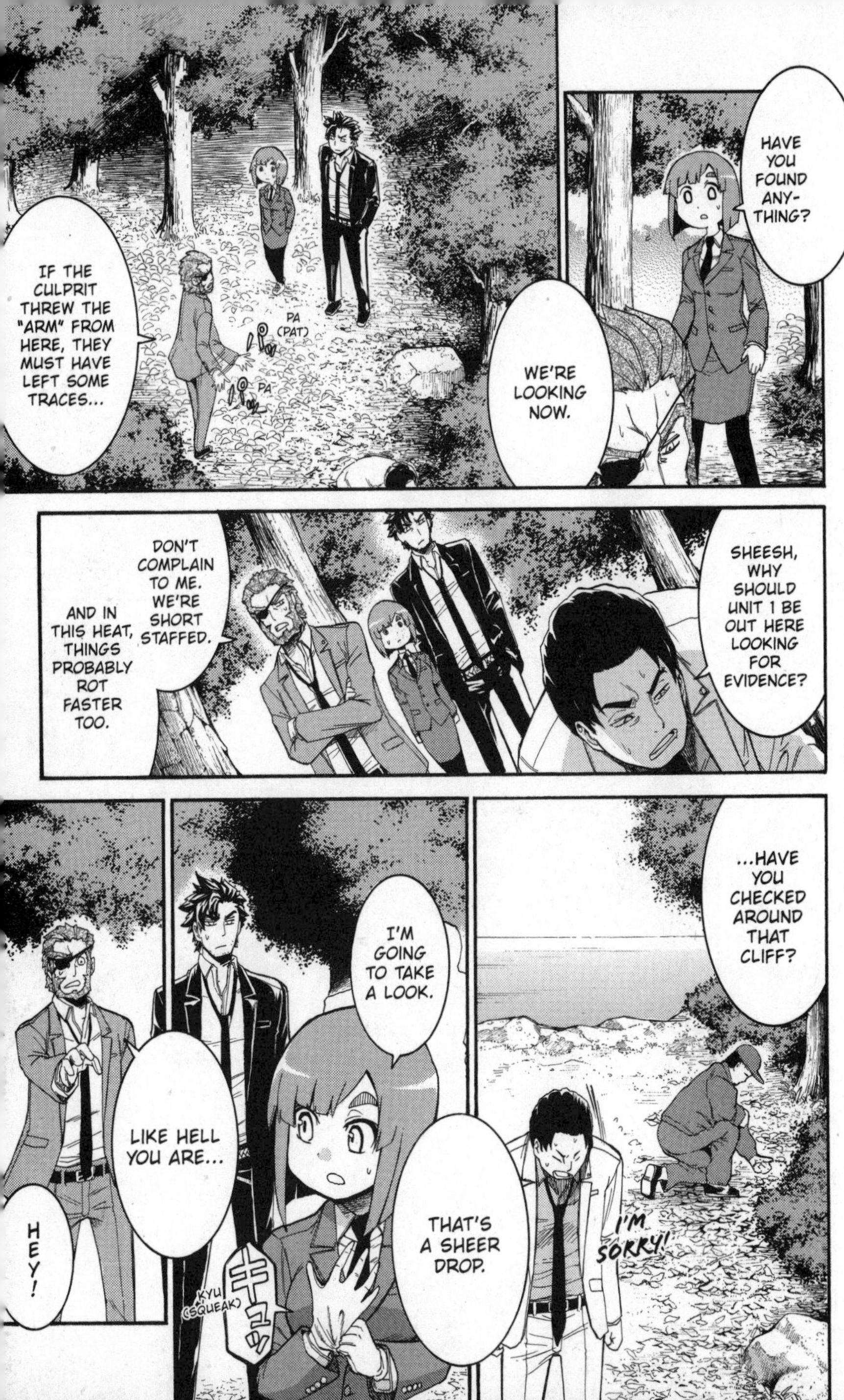
HAVE YOU FOUND ANY-THING?
WE'RE LOOKING NOW.
IF THE CULPRIT THREW THE "ARM" FROM HERE, THEY MUST HAVE LEFT SOME TRACES...
PA (PAT)
PA
SHEESH, WHY SHOULD UNIT 1 BE OUT HERE LOOKING FOR EVIDENCE?
DON'T COMPLAIN TO ME. WE'RE SHORT STAFFED.
AND IN THIS HEAT, THINGS PROBABLY ROT FASTER TOO.
...HAVE YOU CHECKED AROUND THAT CLIFF?
I'M SORRY!
THAT'S A SHEER DROP.
I'M GOING TO TAKE A LOOK.
LIKE HELL YOU ARE...
HEY!
キュッ
KYU (SQUEAK)

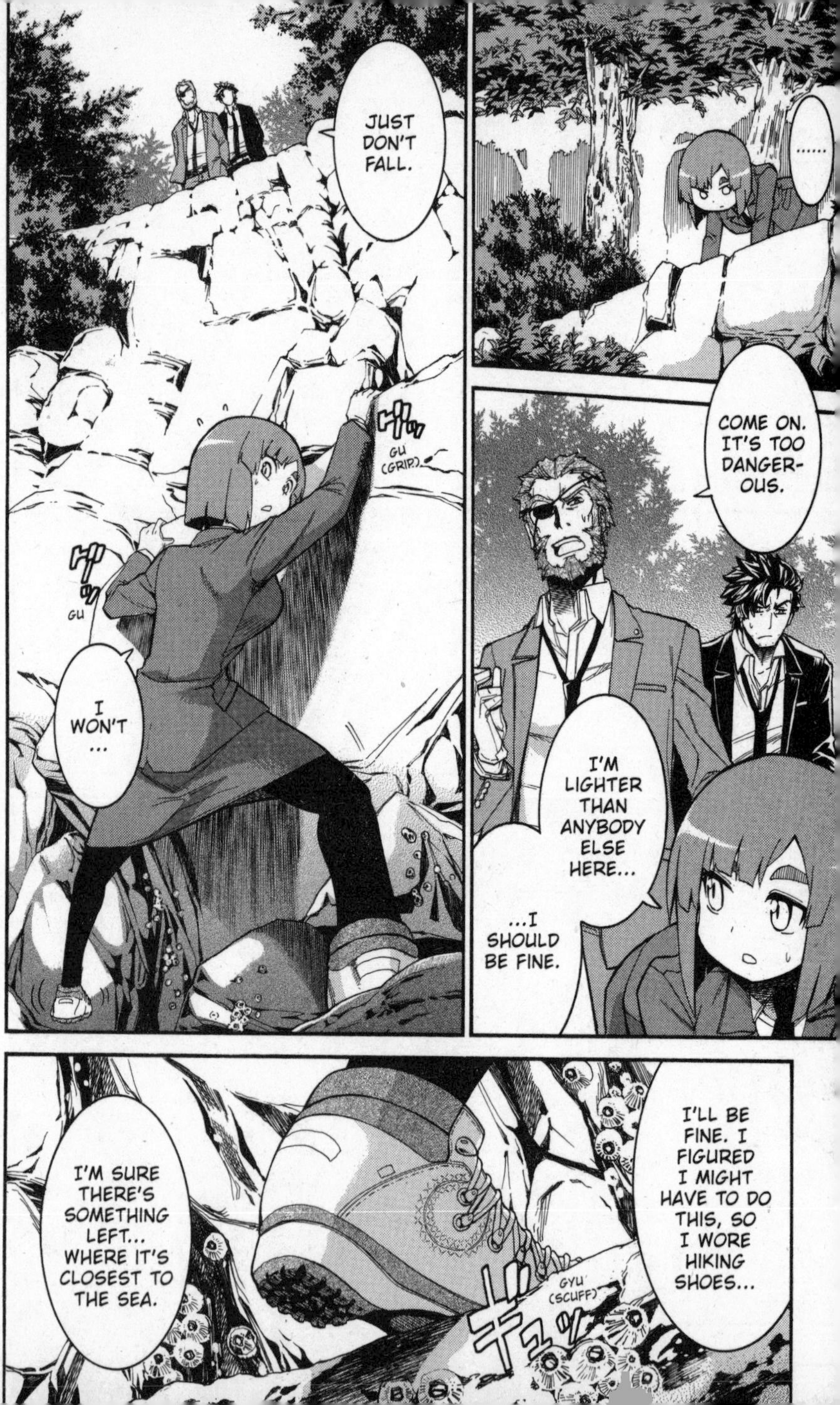
......
COME ON. IT'S TOO DANGER-OUS.
I'M LIGHTER THAN ANYBODY ELSE HERE...
...I SHOULD BE FINE.
JUST DON'T FALL.
GU (GRIP)
GU
I WON'T ...
I'LL BE FINE. I FIGURED I MIGHT HAVE TO DO THIS, SO I WORE HIKING SHOES...
GYU (SCUFF)
I'M SURE THERE'S SOMETHING LEFT... WHERE IT'S CLOSEST TO THE SEA.

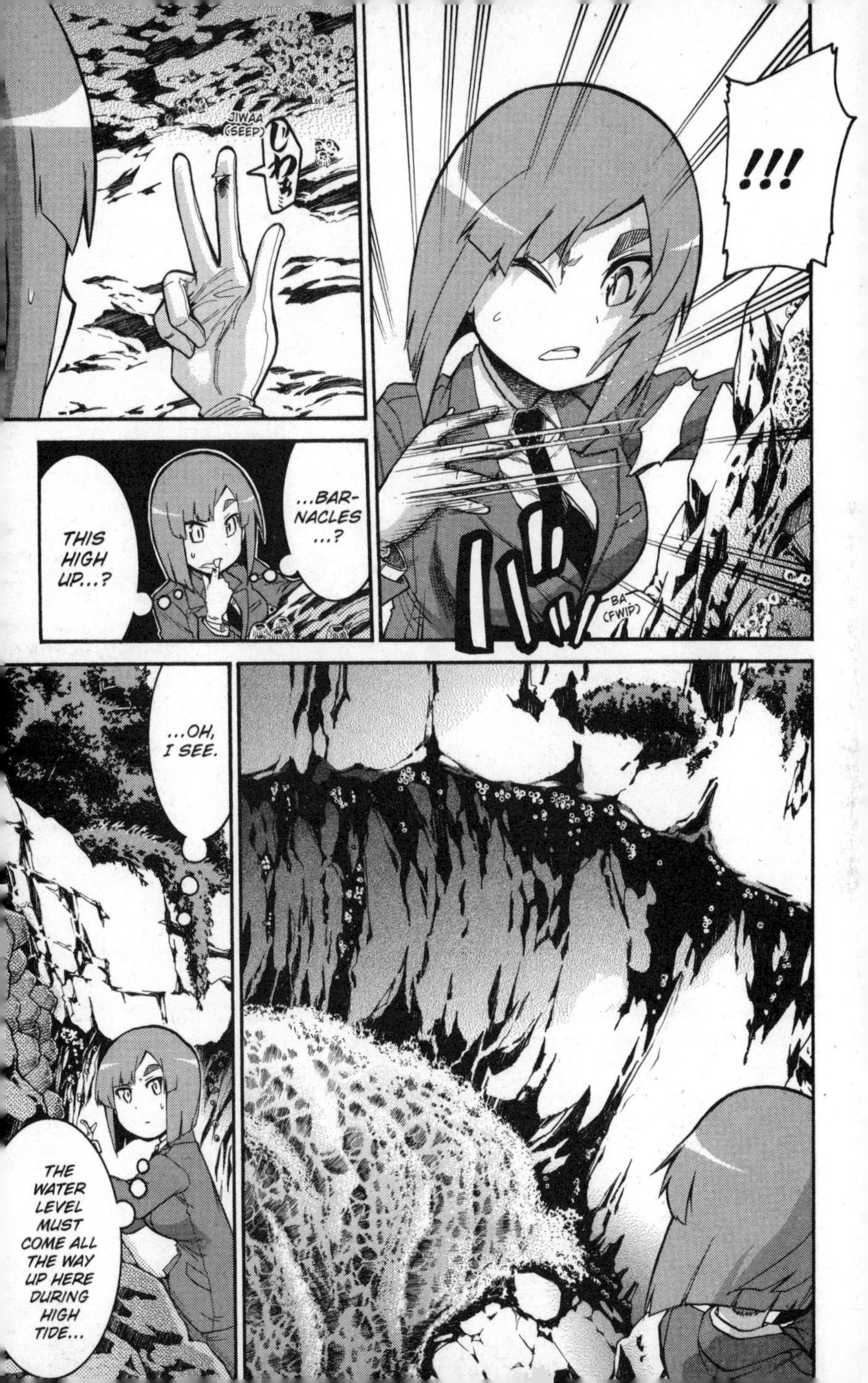
!!!
BA (FWIP)
JIWAA (SEEP)
じわぁ…
...BARNACLES...?
THIS HIGH UP...?
...OH, I SEE.
THE WATER LEVEL MUST COME ALL THE WAY UP HERE DURING HIGH TIDE...

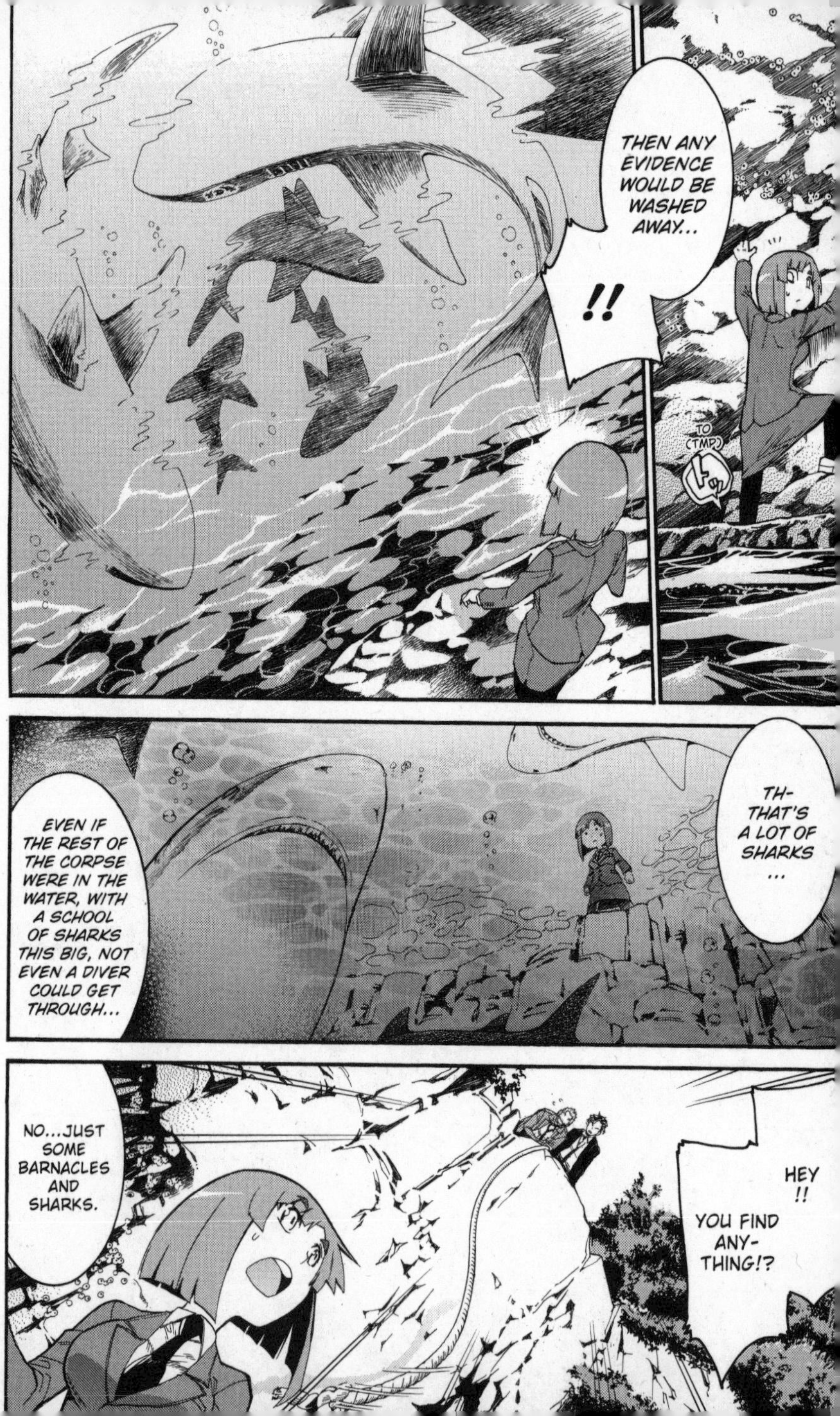
THEN ANY EVIDENCE WOULD BE WASHED AWAY...
!!
TO (TMP)
TH-THAT'S A LOT OF SHARKS ...
EVEN IF THE REST OF THE CORPSE WERE IN THE WATER, WITH A SCHOOL OF SHARKS THIS BIG, NOT EVEN A DIVER COULD GET THROUGH...
HEY !!
YOU FIND ANY-THING!?
NO...JUST SOME BARNACLES AND SHARKS.

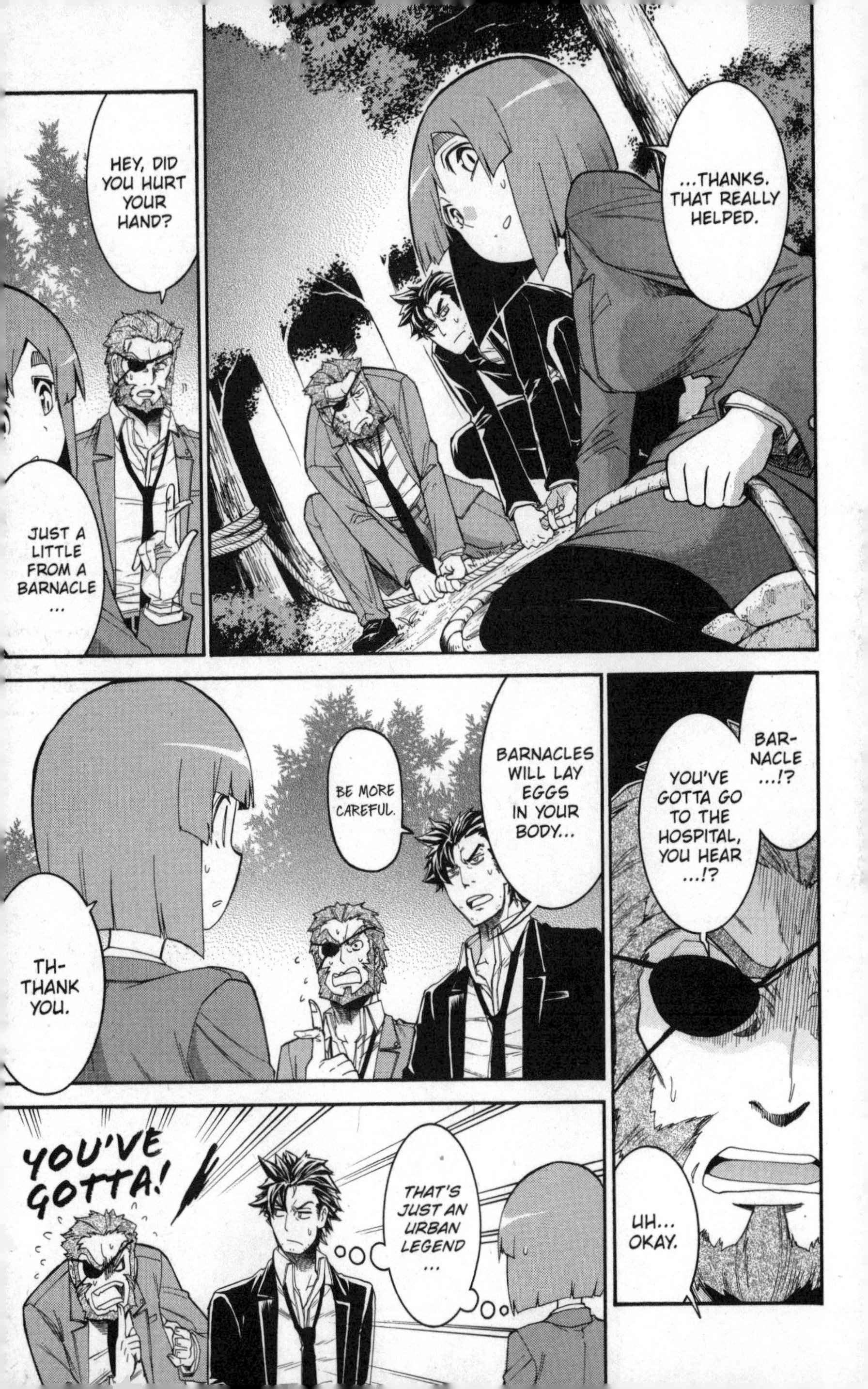
...THANKS. THAT REALLY HELPED.
HEY, DID YOU HURT YOUR HAND?
JUST A LITTLE FROM A BARNACLE ...
BAR-NACLE ...!?
YOU'VE GOTTA GO TO THE HOSPITAL, YOU HEAR ...!?
UH... OKAY.
BARNACLES WILL LAY EGGS IN YOUR BODY...
BE MORE CAREFUL.
TH-THANK YOU.
THAT'S JUST AN URBAN LEGEND ...
YOU'VE GOTTA!

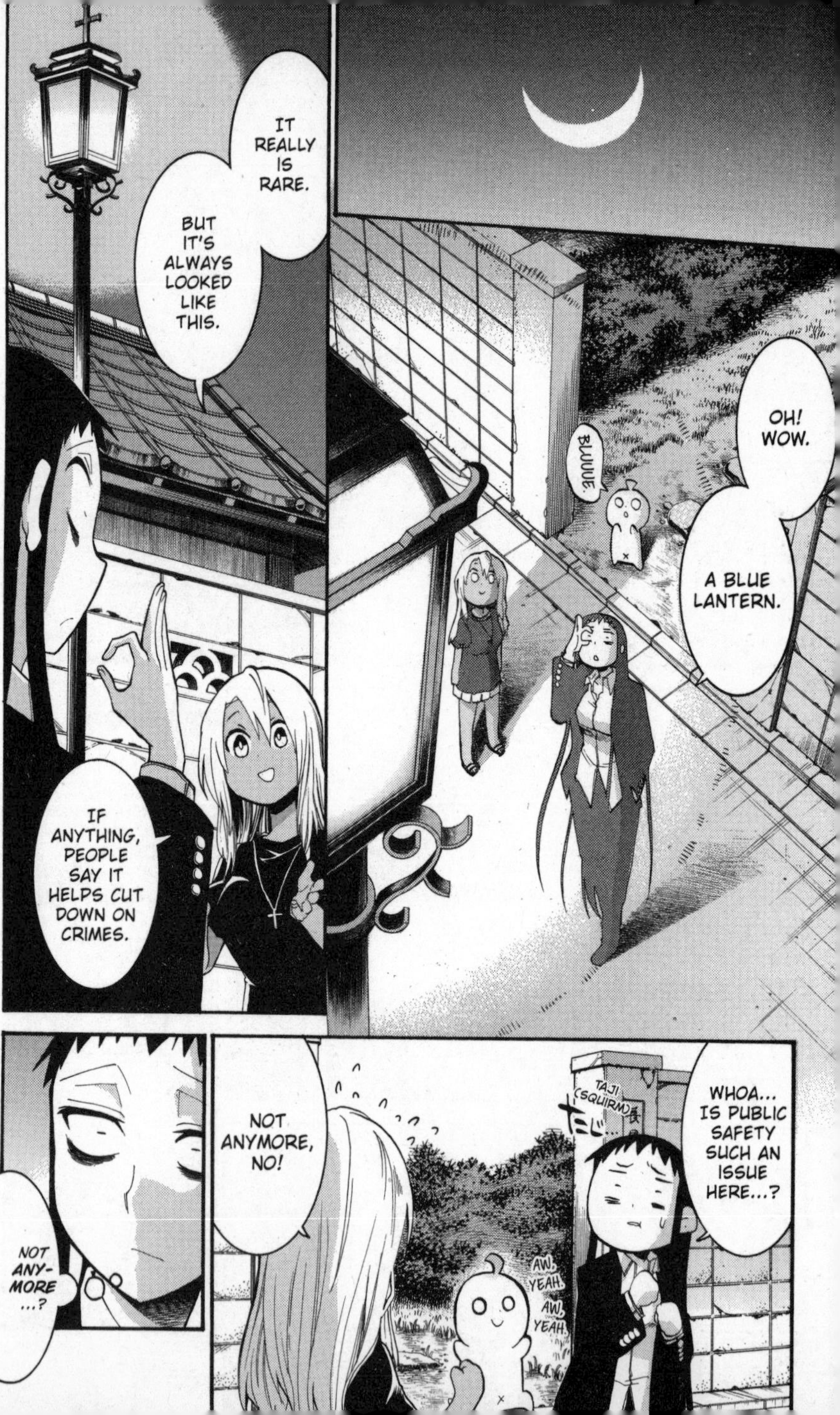
OH! WOW.
A BLUE LANTERN.
BLUUUE.
IT REALLY IS RARE.
BUT IT'S ALWAYS LOOKED LIKE THIS.
IF ANYTHING, PEOPLE SAY IT HELPS CUT DOWN ON CRIMES.
WHOA... IS PUBLIC SAFETY SUCH AN ISSUE HERE...?
TAJI (SQUIRM)
AW, YEAH. AW, YEAH.
NOT ANYMORE, NO!
NOT ANYMORE...?

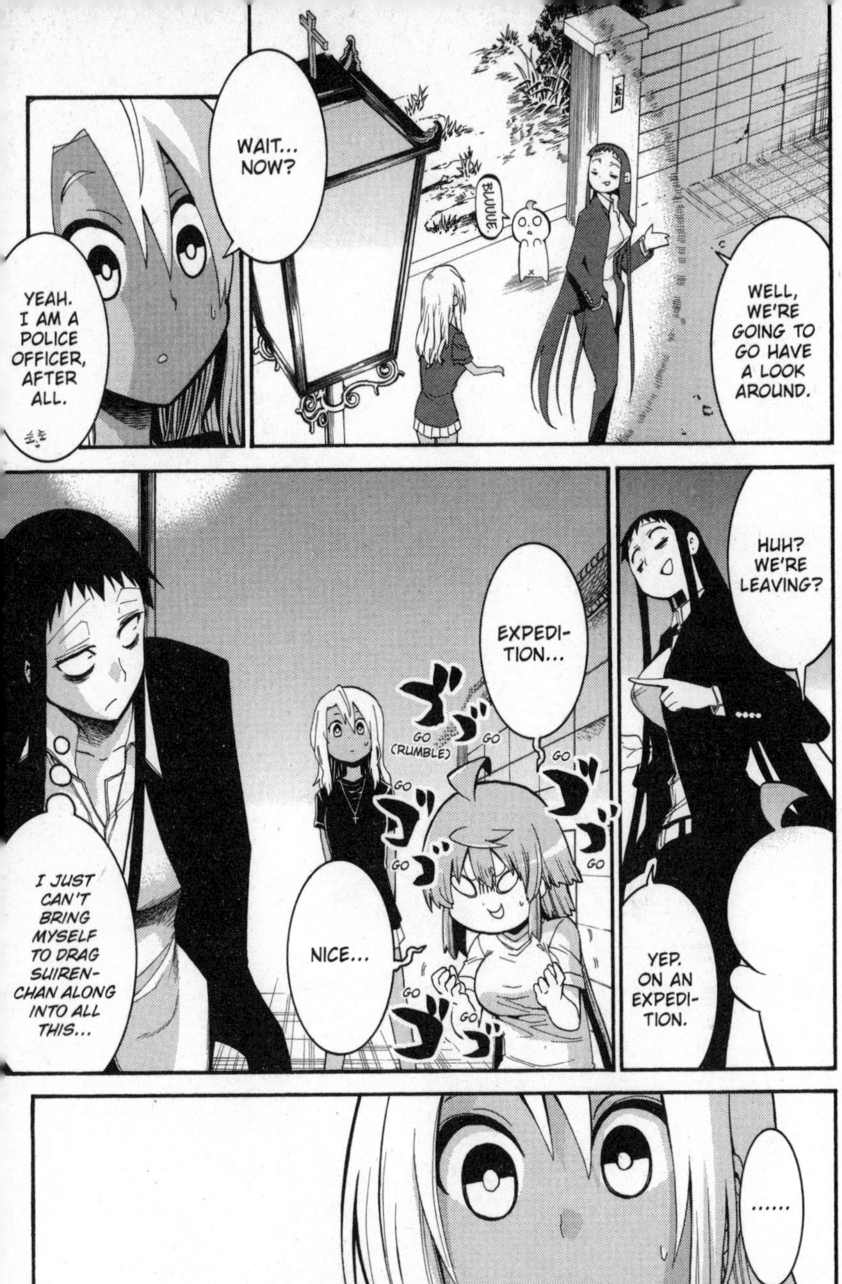
WELL, WE'RE GOING TO GO HAVE A LOOK AROUND.
BLUUUE
WAIT... NOW?
YEAH. I AM A POLICE OFFICER, AFTER ALL.
HUH? WE'RE LEAVING?
YEP. ON AN EXPEDITION.
EXPEDITION...
GO GO (RUMBLE) GO GO GO GO GO GO GO
NICE...
I JUST CAN'T BRING MYSELF TO DRAG SUIREN-CHAN ALONG INTO ALL THIS...
......

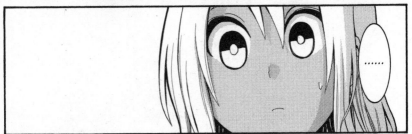

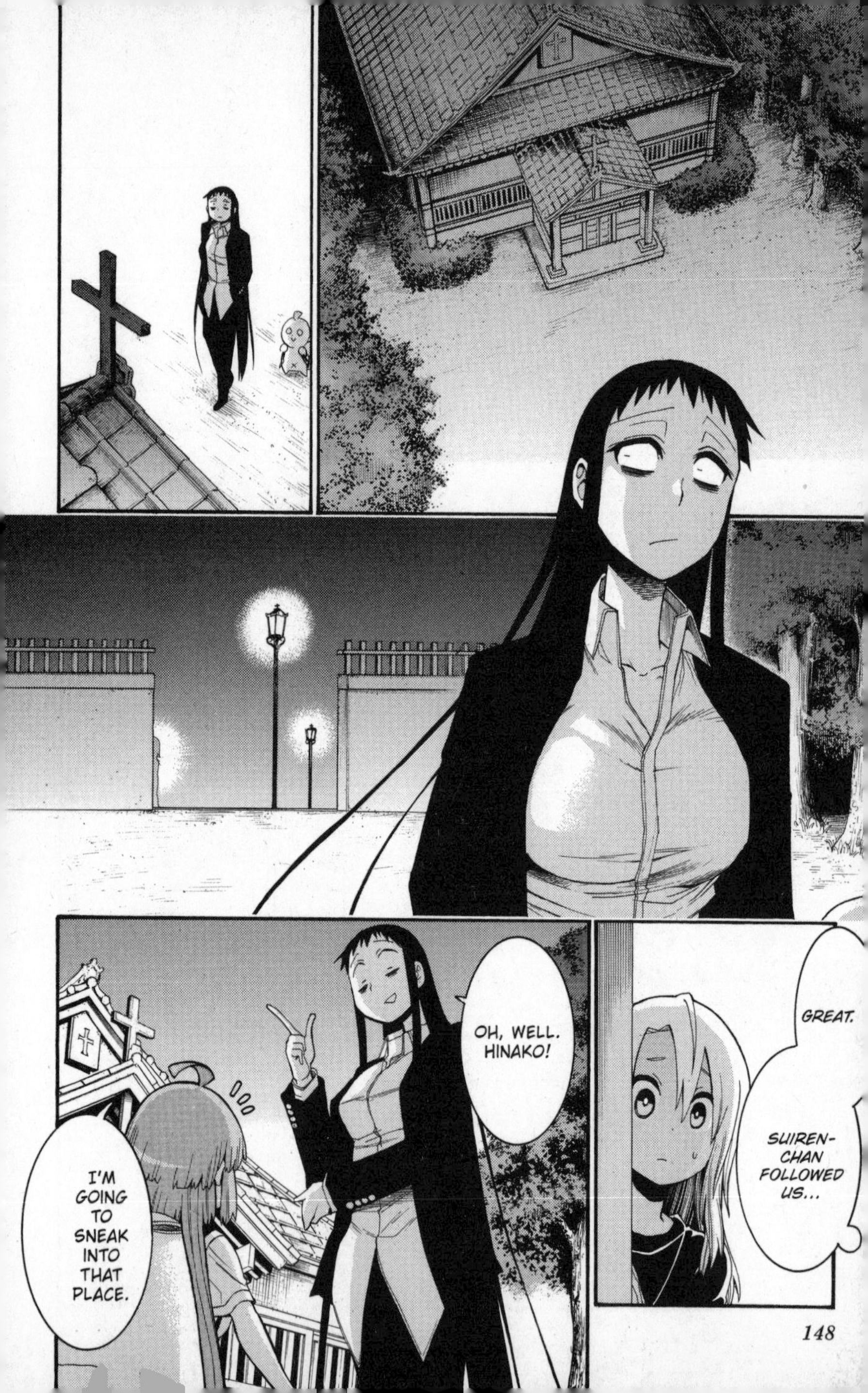
GREAT.
SUIREN-CHAN FOLLOWED US...
OH, WELL. HINAKO!
I'M GOING TO SNEAK INTO THAT PLACE.

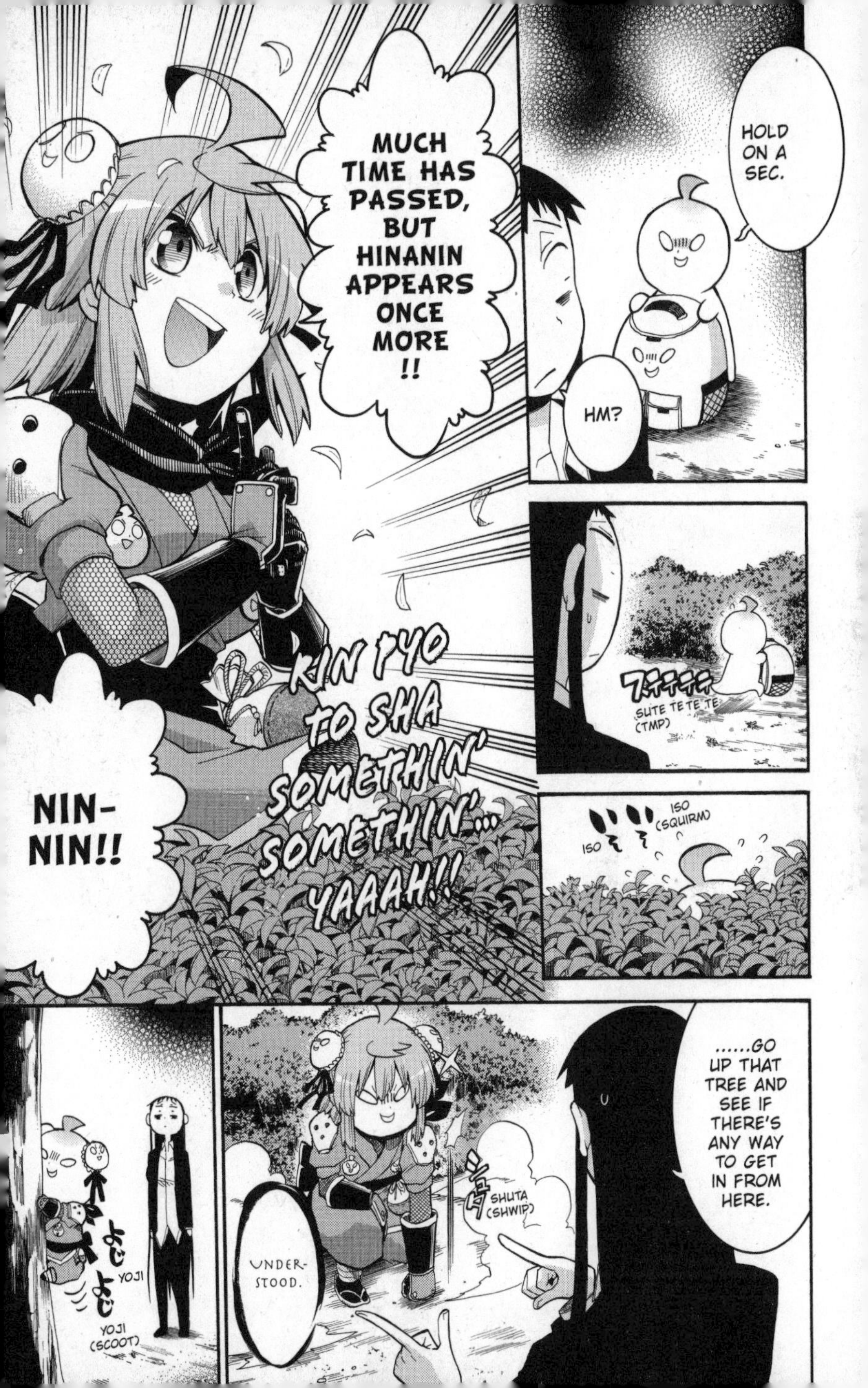
HOLD ON A SEC.
HM?
SUTE TE TE TE (TMP)
ISO
ISO (SQUIRM)
MUCH TIME HAS PASSED, BUT HINANIN APPEARS ONCE MORE !!
KIN PYO TO SHA SOMETHIN' SOMETHIN'... YAAAH!!
NIN-NIN!!
......GO UP THAT TREE AND SEE IF THERE'S ANY WAY TO GET IN FROM HERE.
SHUTA (SHWIP)
UNDER-STOOD.
よじ
YOJI
よじ
YOJI (SCOOT)

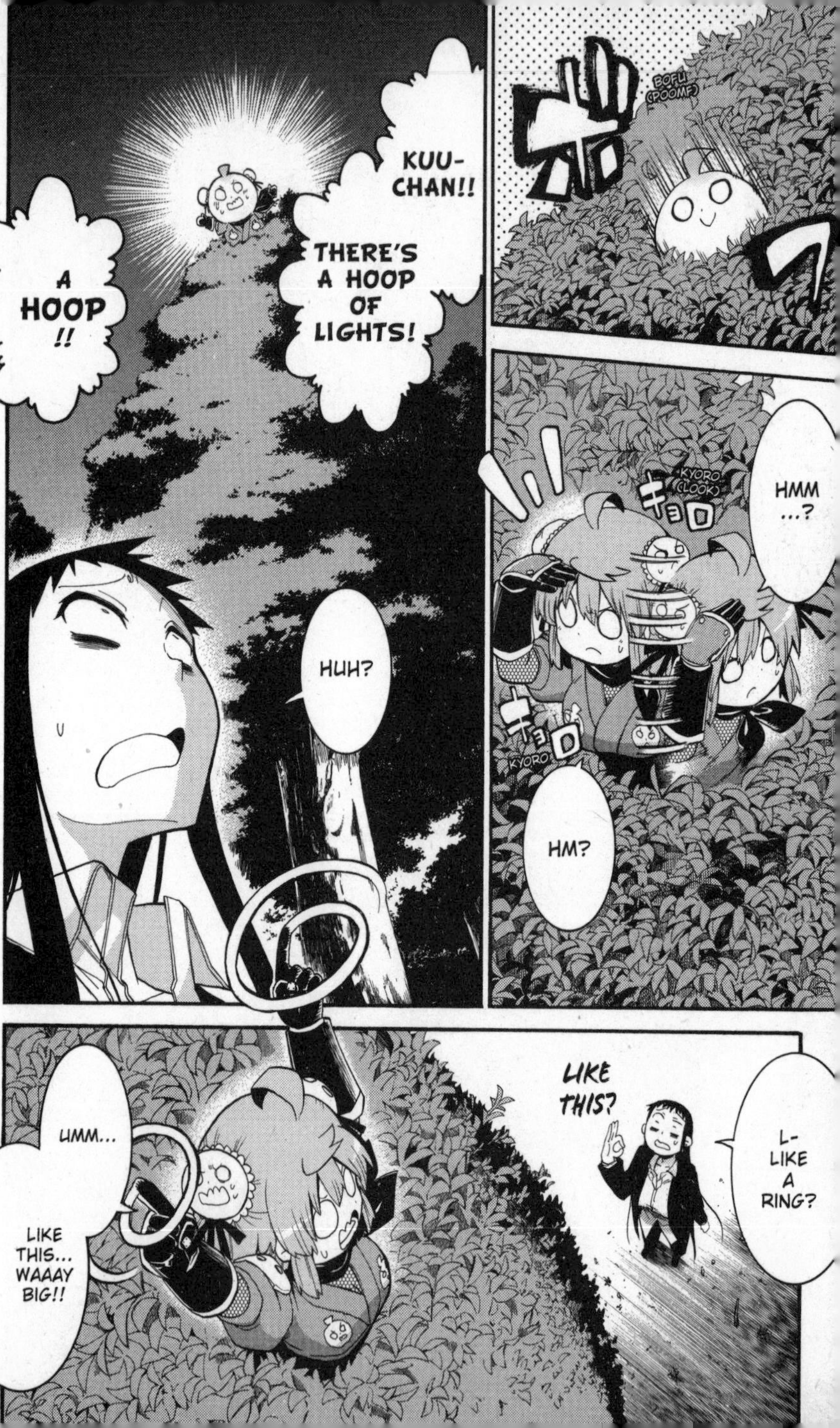
BOFU (POOMF)
KYORO (LOOK)
HMM ...?
KYORO
HM?
KUU-CHAN!!
THERE'S A HOOP OF LIGHTS!
A HOOP !!
HUH?
L-LIKE A RING?
LIKE THIS?
UMM...
LIKE THIS... WAAAY BIG!!

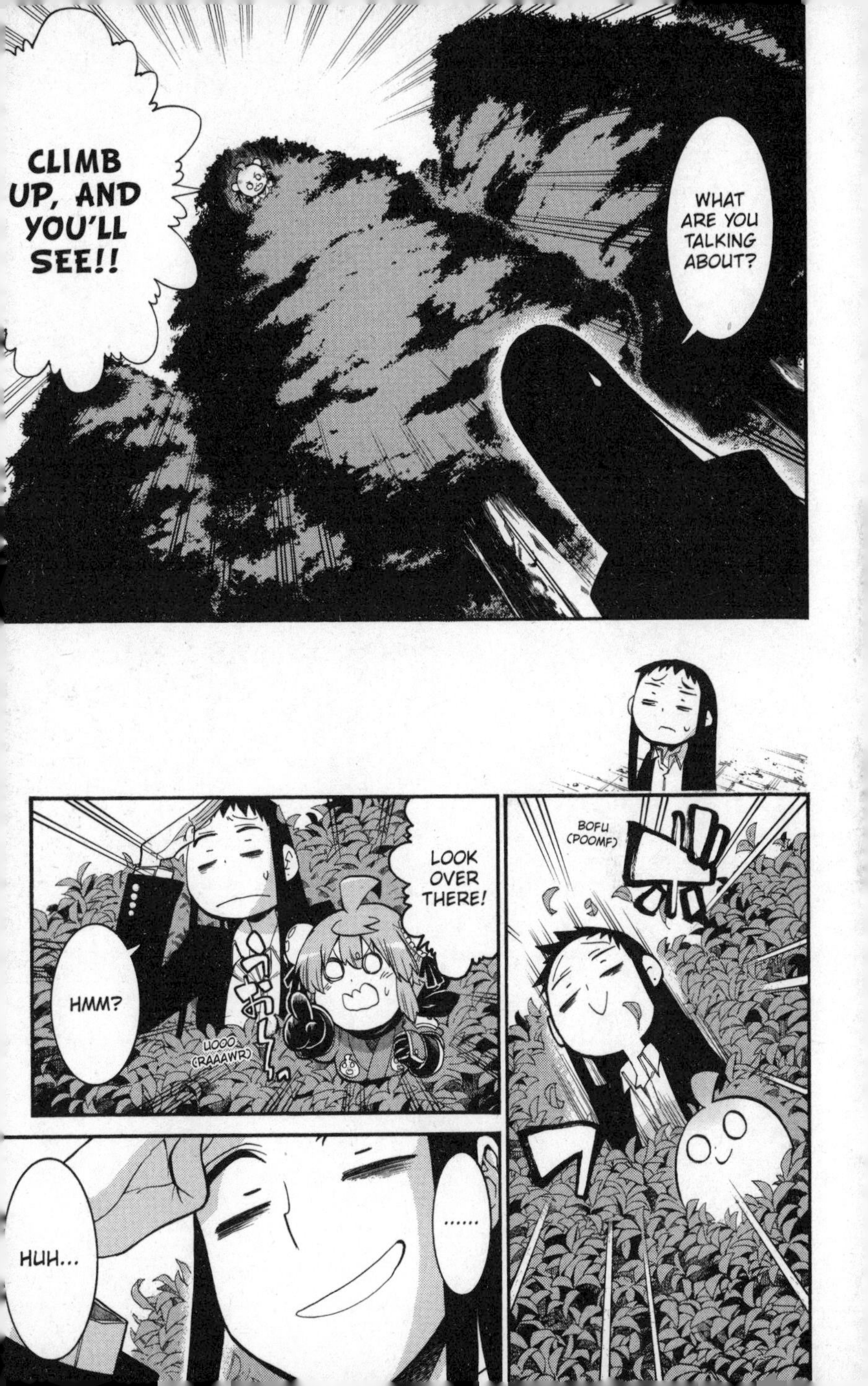
WHAT ARE YOU TALKING ABOUT?
CLIMB UP, AND YOU'LL SEE!!
BOFU (POOMF)
LOOK OVER THERE!
HMM?
UOOO (RAAAWR)
......
HUH...

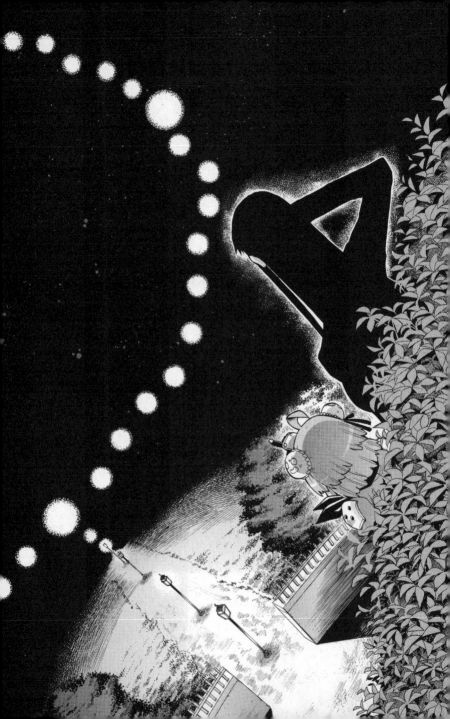

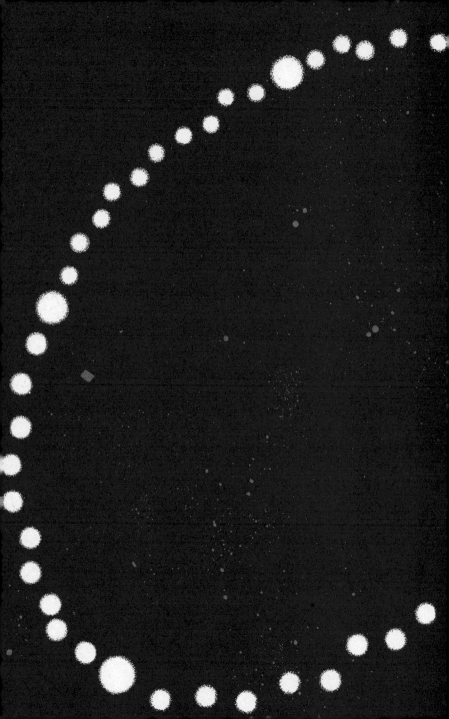

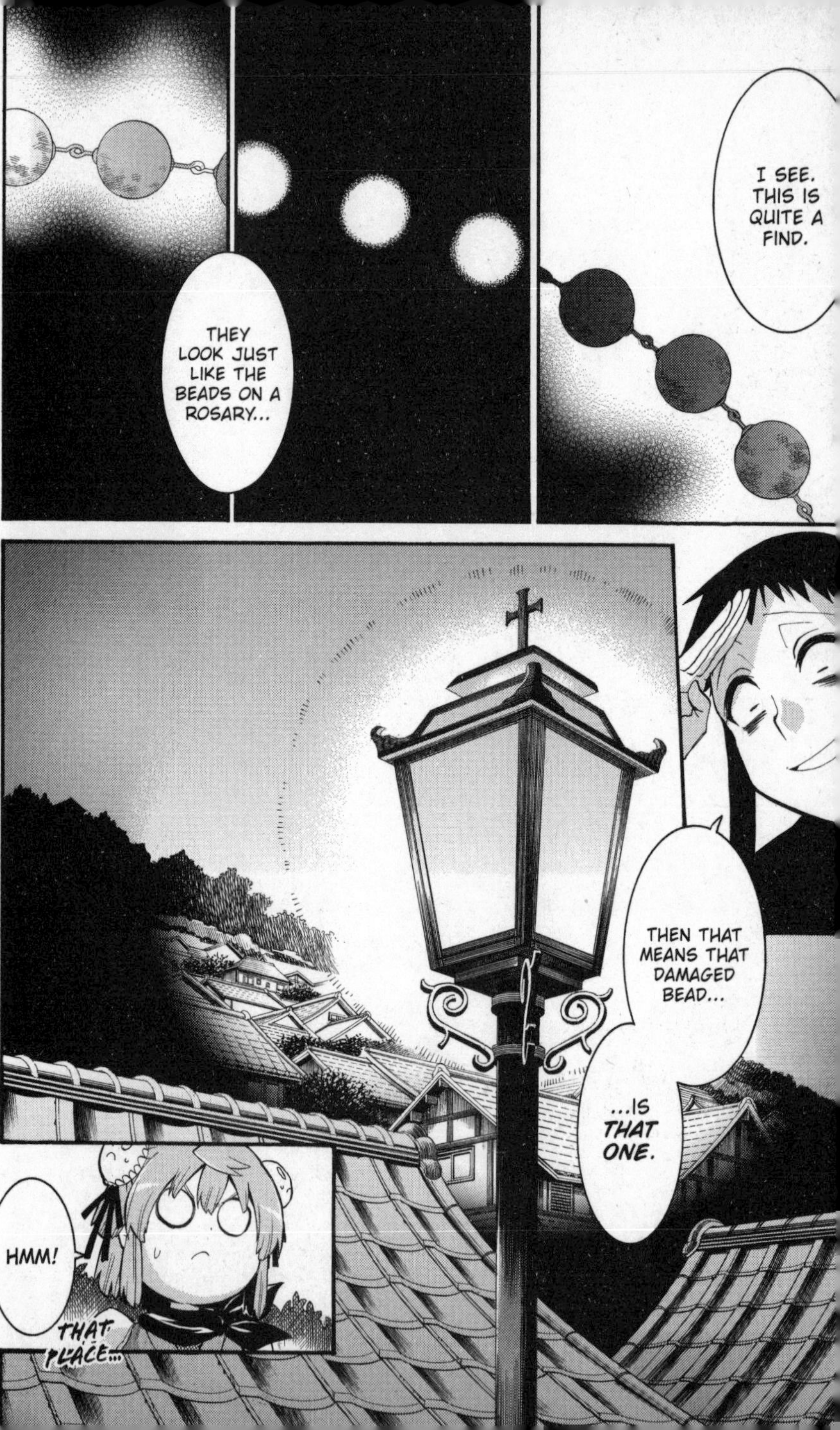
I SEE. THIS IS QUITE A FIND.
THEY LOOK JUST LIKE THE BEADS ON A ROSARY...
THEN THAT MEANS THAT DAMAGED BEAD...
...IS *THAT ONE*.
HMM!
THAT PLACE...

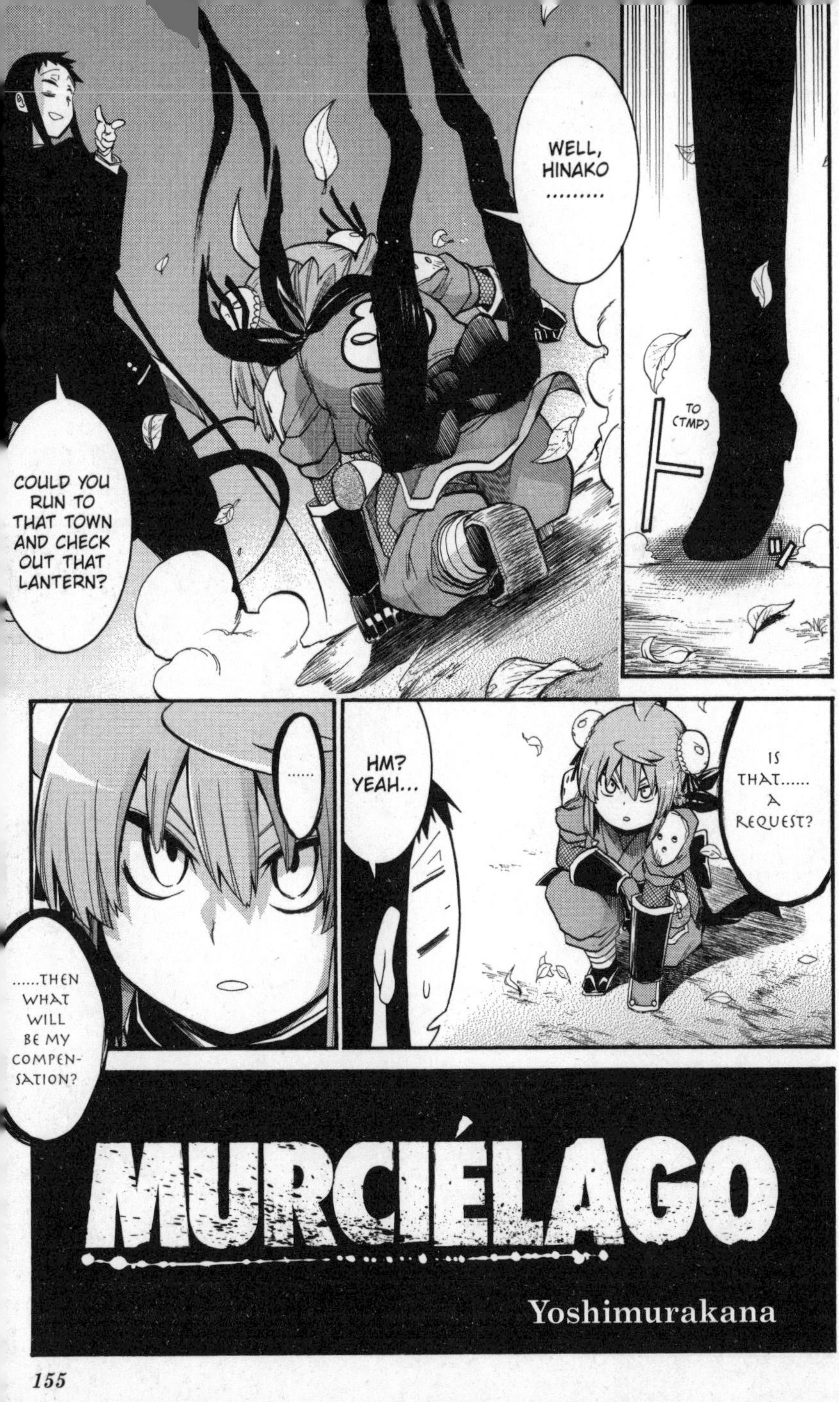
TO (TMP)
WELL, HINAKO ....
COULD YOU RUN TO THAT TOWN AND CHECK OUT THAT LANTERN?
IS THAT...... A REQUEST?
HM? YEAH...
......
......THEN WHAT WILL BE MY COMPEN-SATION?
MURCIÉLAGO
Yoshimurakana

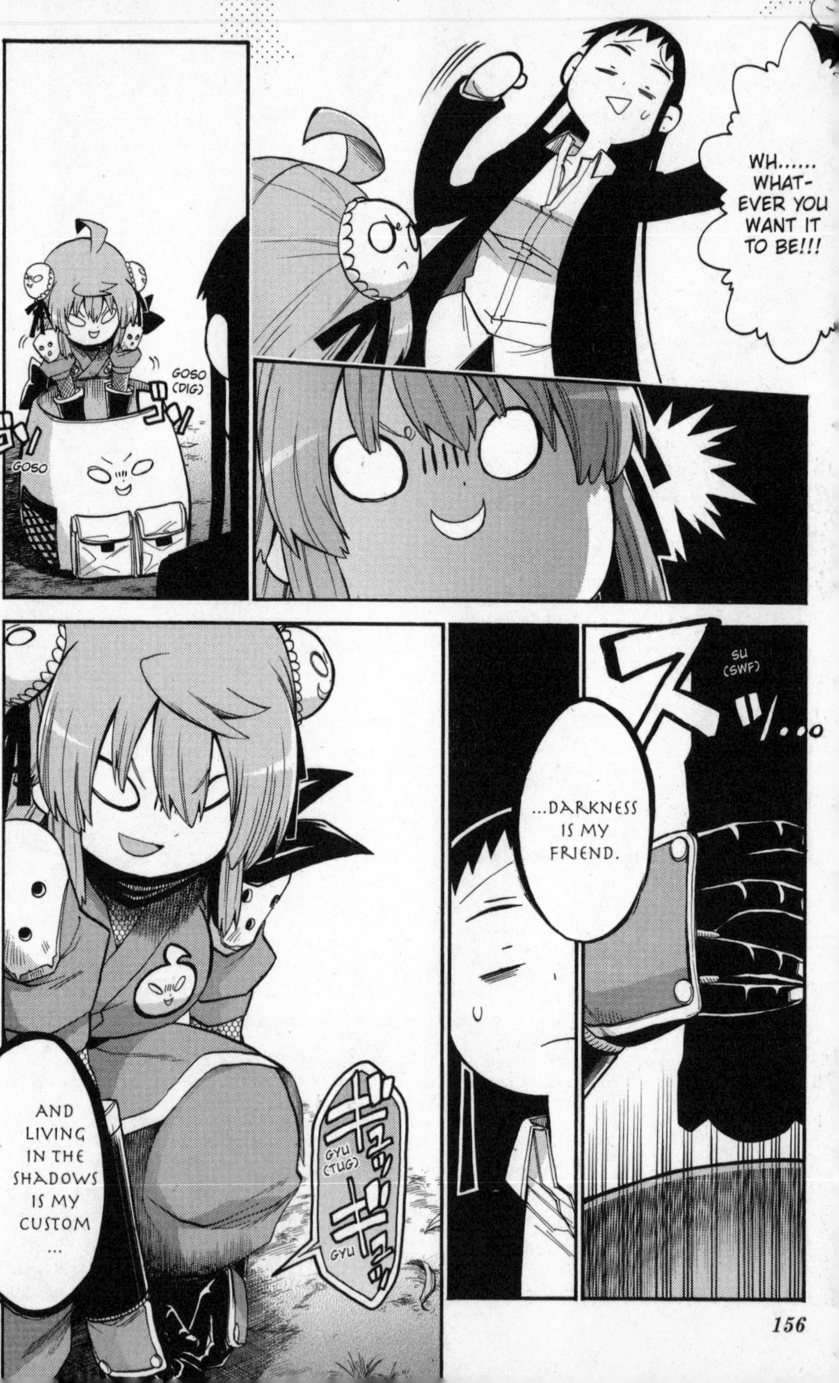
WH...... WHAT-EVER YOU WANT IT TO BE!!!
GOSO (DIG)
GOSO
SU (SWF)
...DARKNESS IS MY FRIEND.
AND LIVING IN THE SHADOWS IS MY CUSTOM ...
GYU (TUG)
GYU

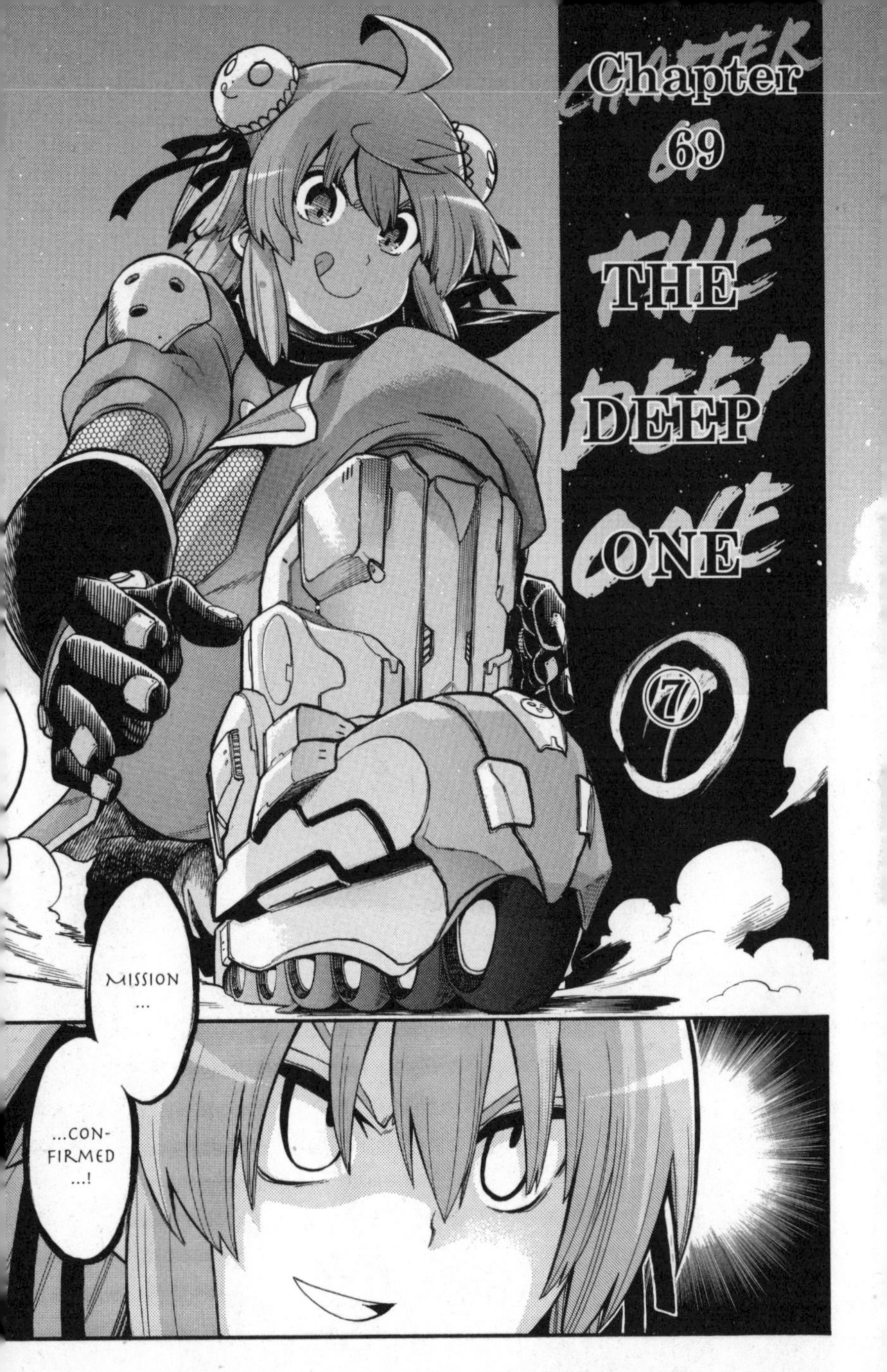
Chapter 69
THE DEEP ONE
7
MISSION ...
...CON-FIRMED ...!

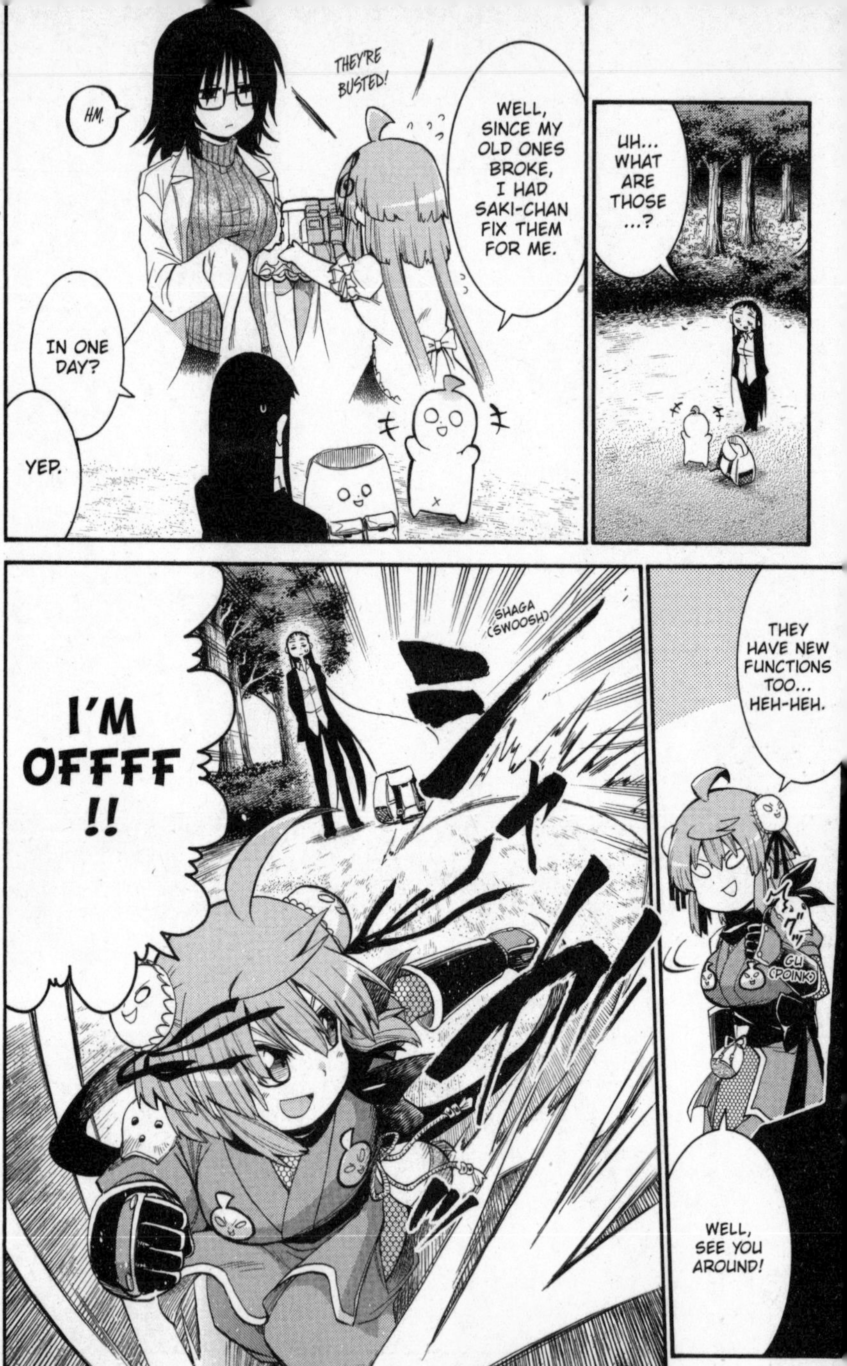
UH... WHAT ARE THOSE ...?
WELL, SINCE MY OLD ONES BROKE, I HAD SAKI-CHAN FIX THEM FOR ME.
THEY'RE BUSTED!
HM.
IN ONE DAY?
YEP.
THEY HAVE NEW FUNCTIONS TOO... HEH-HEH.
GU (POINK)
WELL, SEE YOU AROUND!
SHAGA (SWOOSH)
I'M OFFFF !!

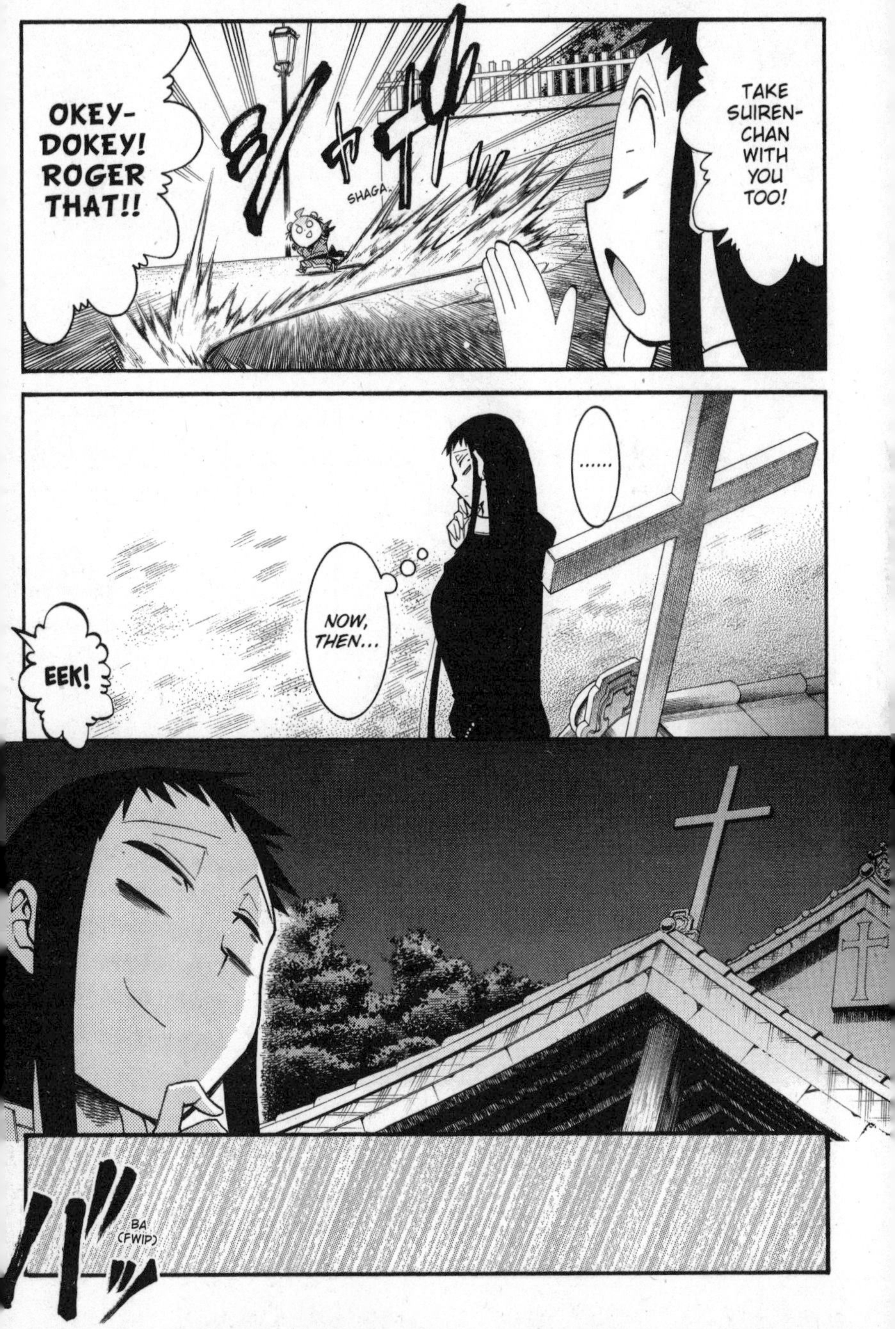
TAKE SUIREN-CHAN WITH YOU TOO!
SHAGA
OKEY-DOKEY! ROGER THAT!!
......
NOW, THEN...
EEK!
BA (FWIP)

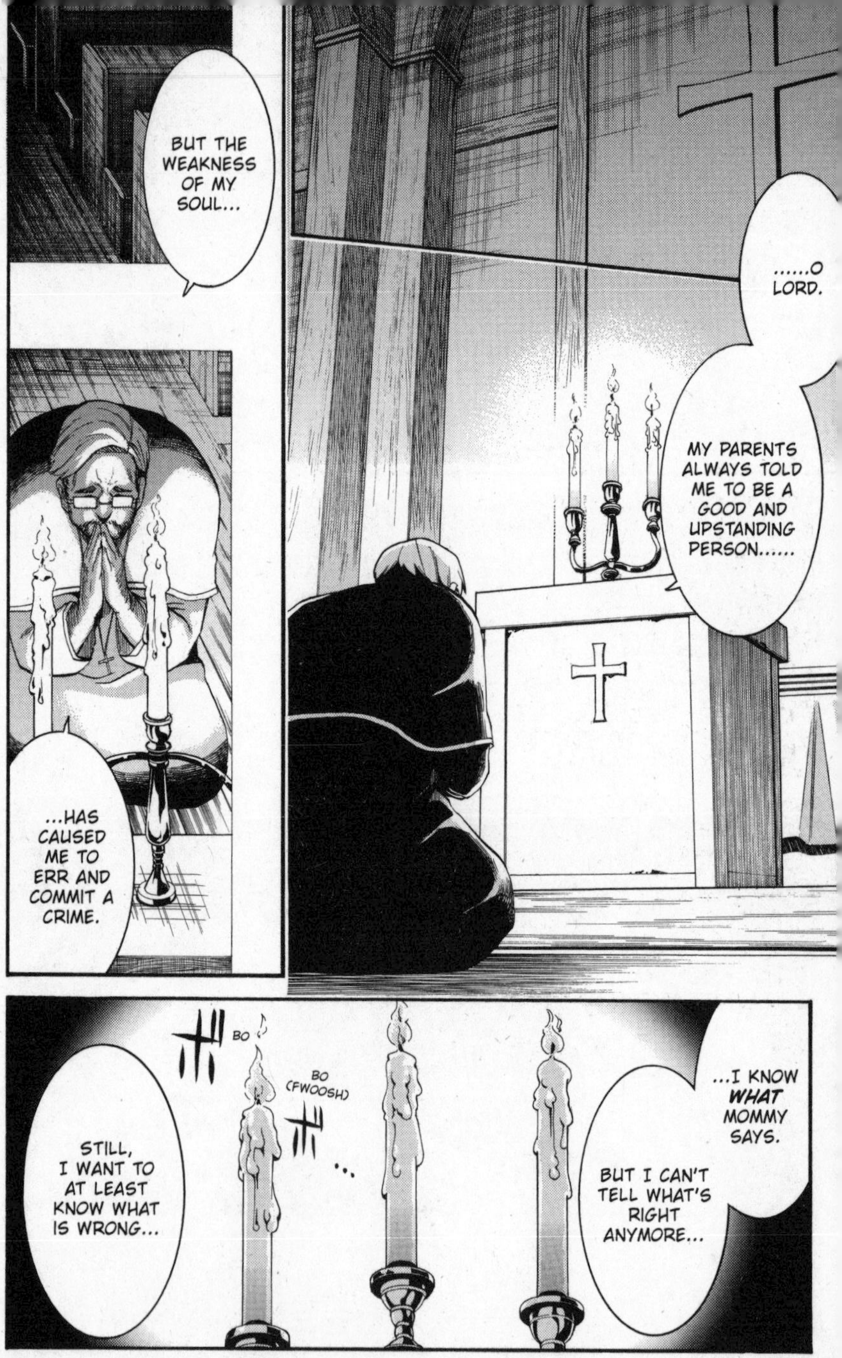
......O LORD.
MY PARENTS ALWAYS TOLD ME TO BE A GOOD AND UPSTANDING PERSON......
BUT THE WEAKNESS OF MY SOUL...
...HAS CAUSED ME TO ERR AND COMMIT A CRIME.
...I KNOW *WHAT* MOMMY SAYS.
BUT I CAN'T TELL WHAT'S RIGHT ANYMORE...
BO (FWOOSH)
BO
...
STILL, I WANT TO AT LEAST KNOW WHAT IS WRONG...

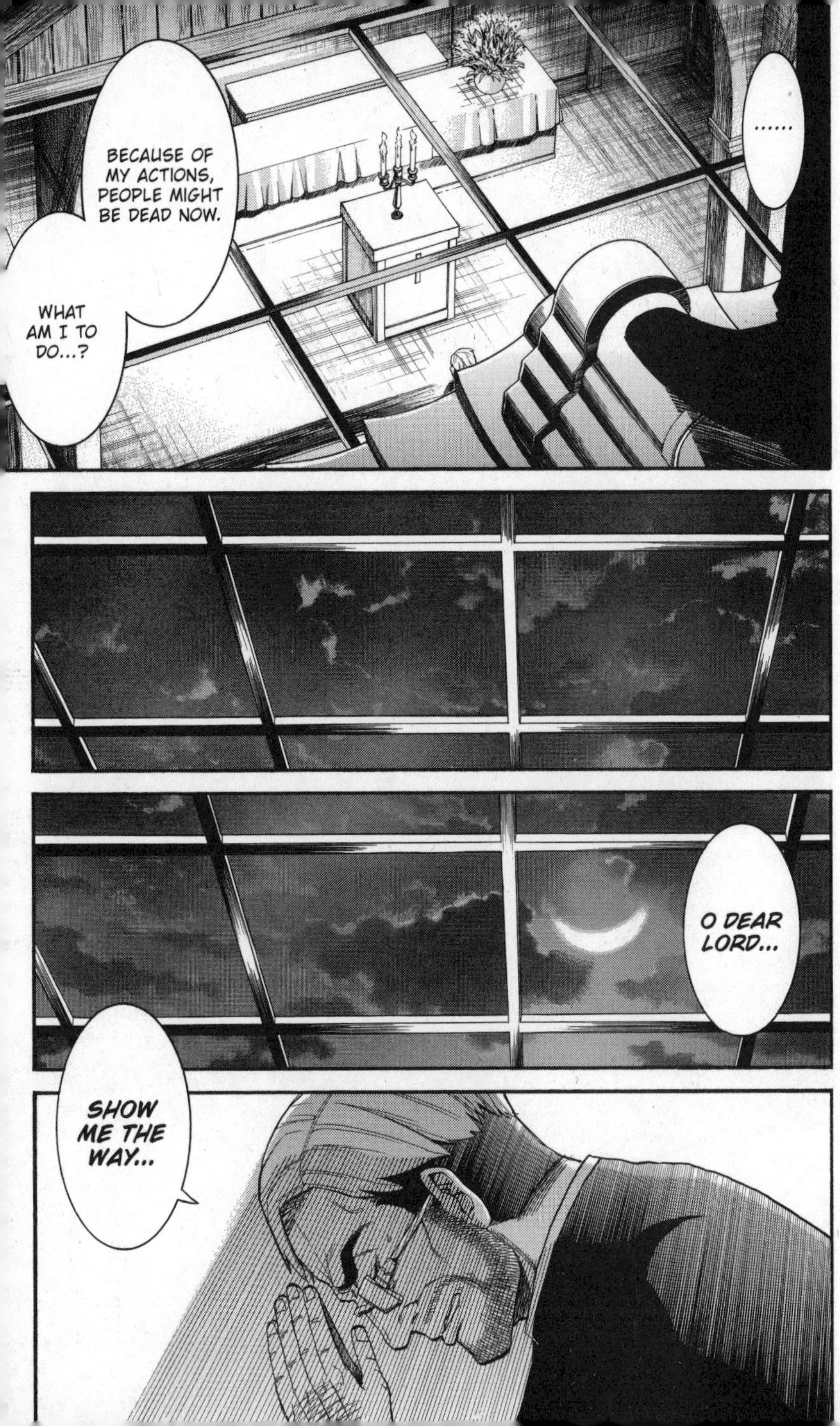
……
BECAUSE OF MY ACTIONS, PEOPLE MIGHT BE DEAD NOW.
WHAT AM I TO DO…?
O DEAR LORD…
SHOW ME THE WAY…

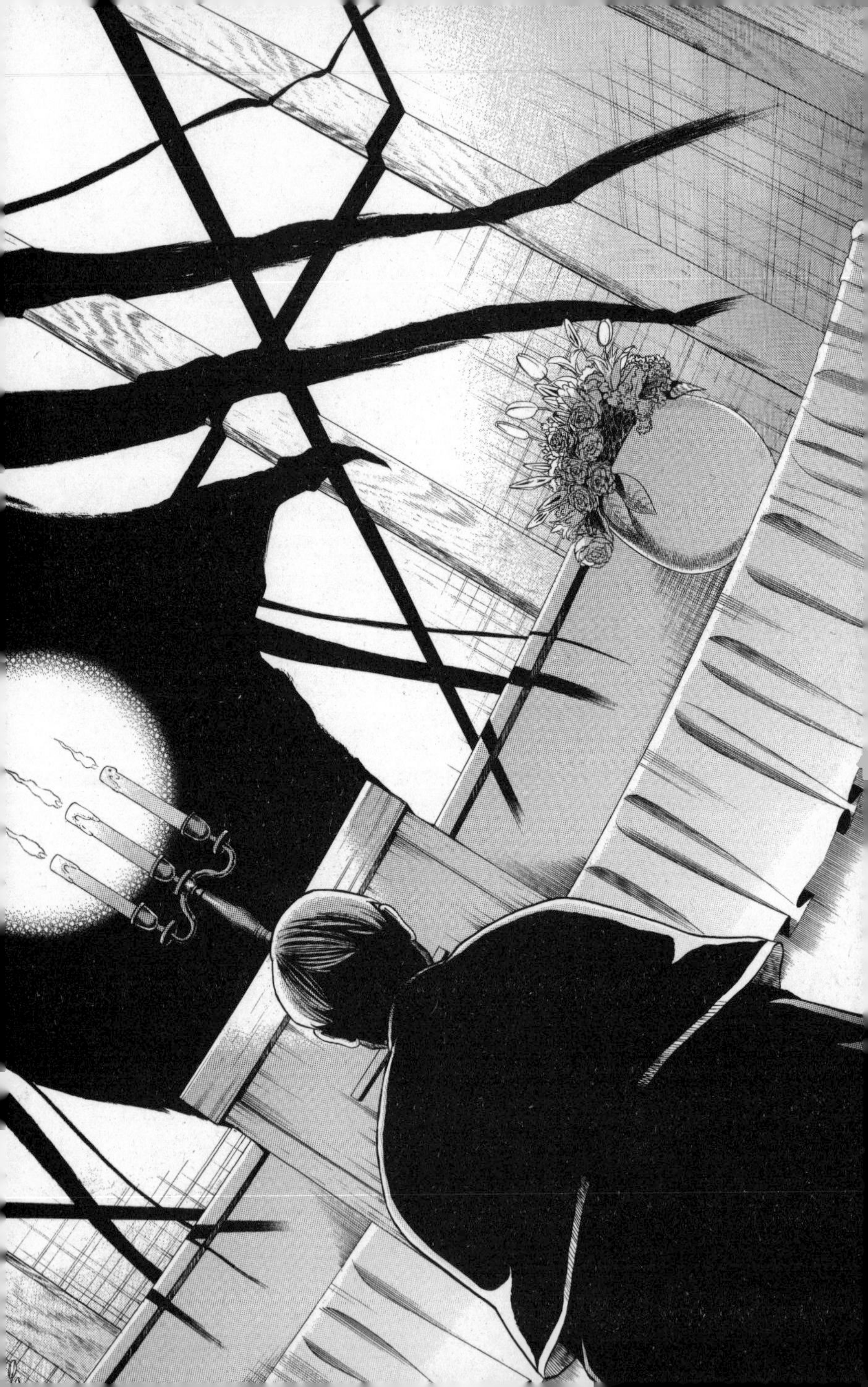

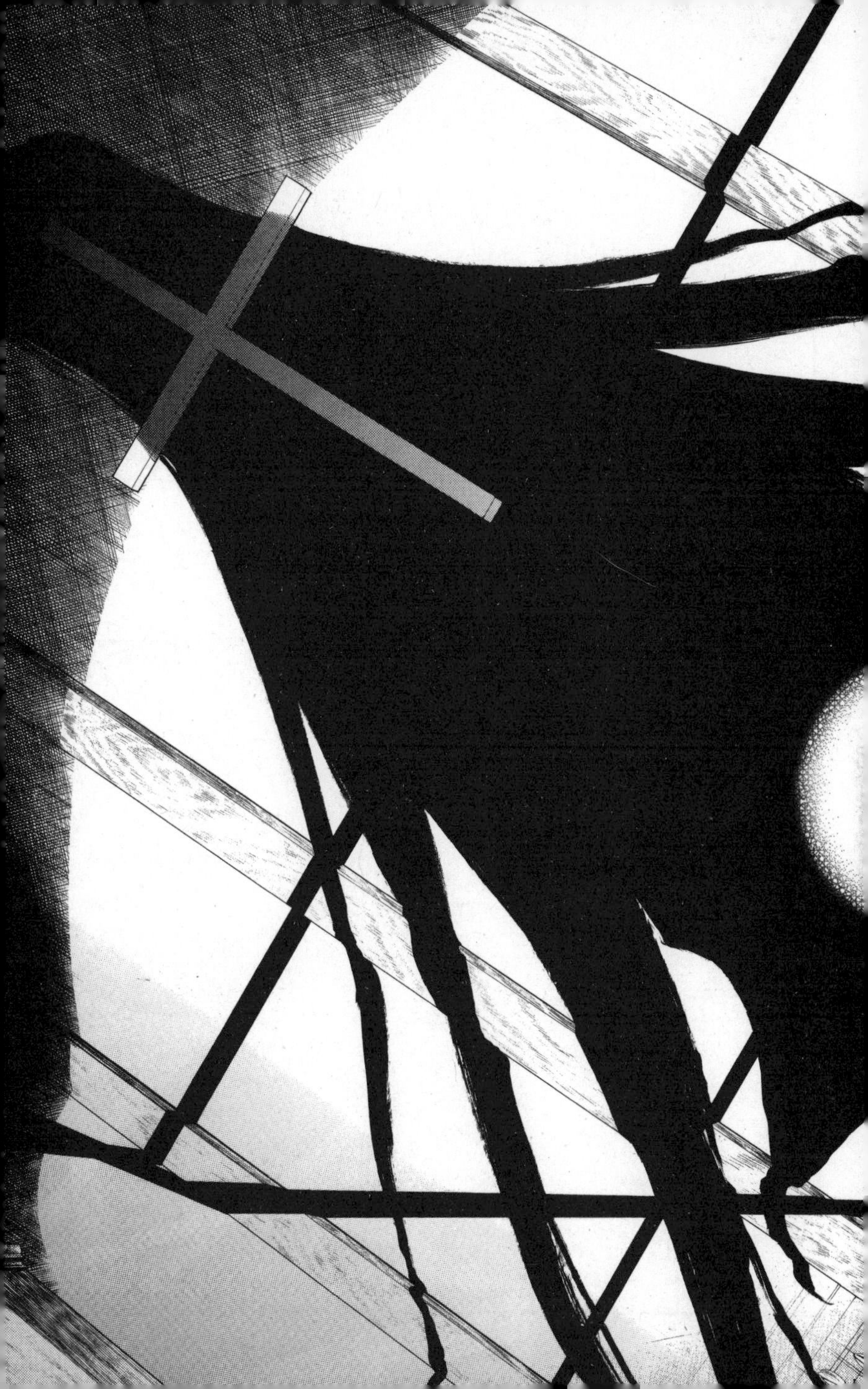

AH
...!

THE
DEVIL
...!?

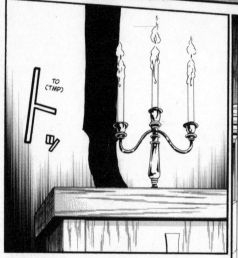

PARIN
(SHATTER)

TO
(TMP)

EEE
!!

GASHAN
(SHATTER)

PARDON
ME.

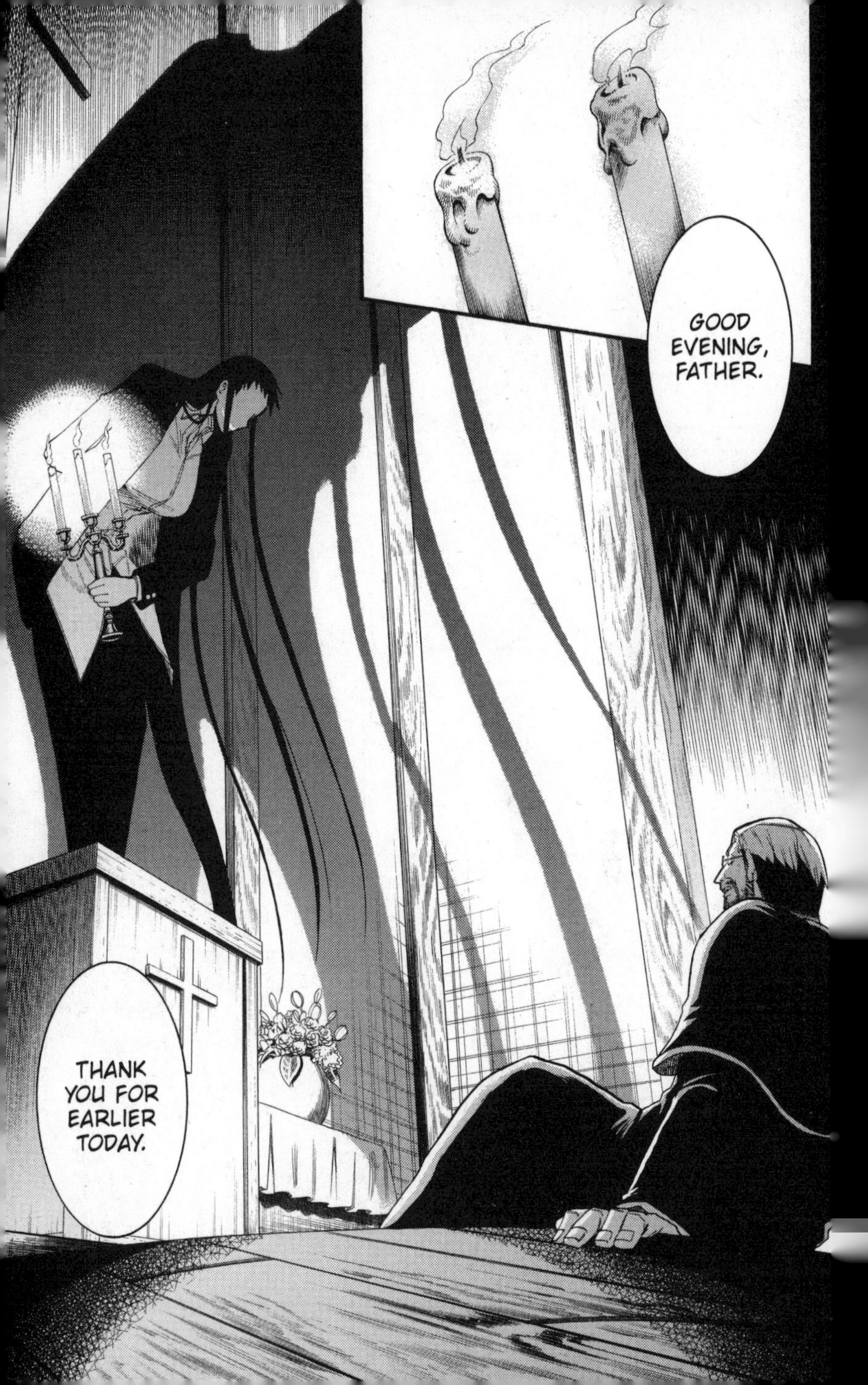
GOOD EVENING, FATHER.
THANK YOU FOR EARLIER TODAY.

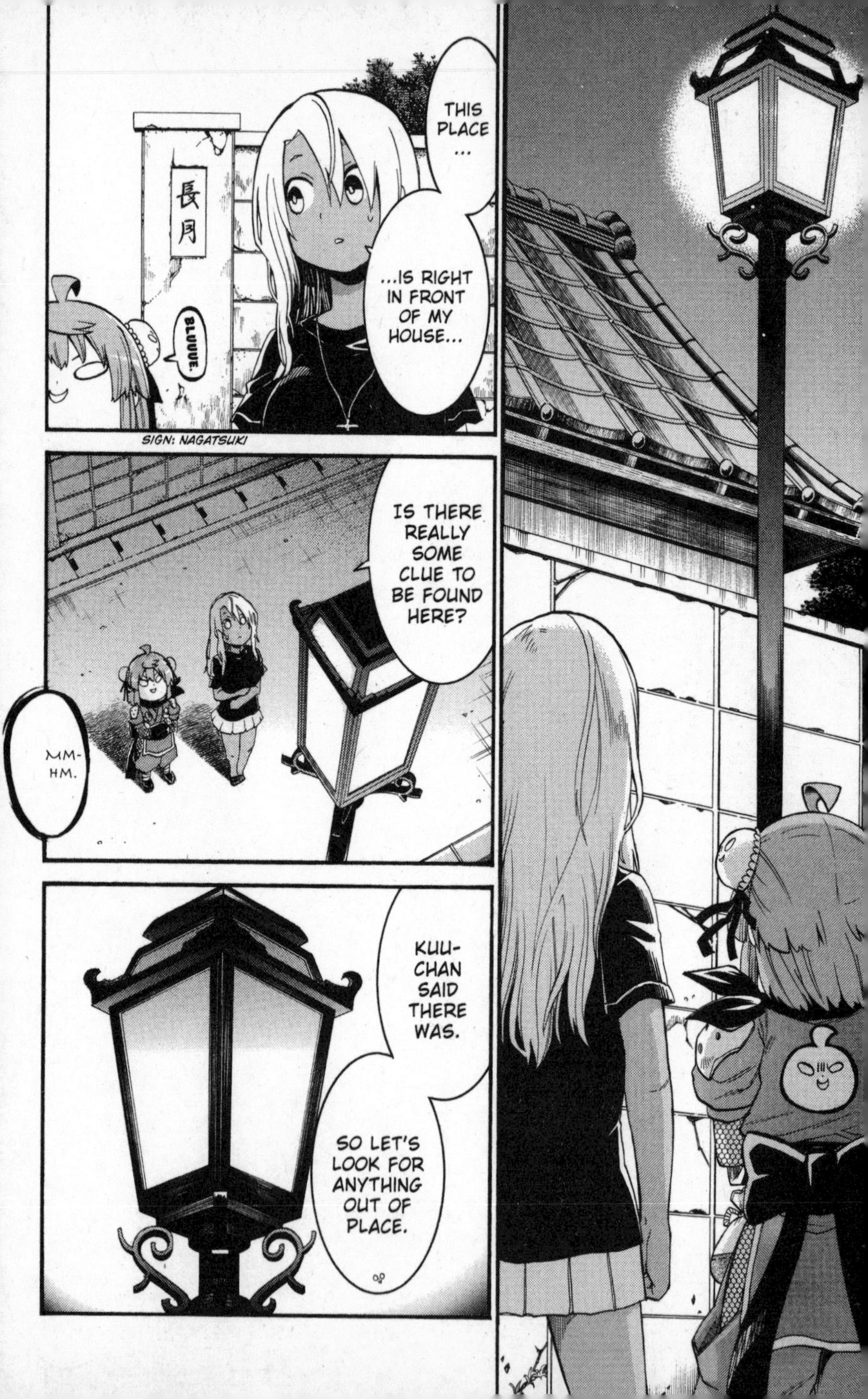
THIS PLACE ...
...IS RIGHT IN FRONT OF MY HOUSE...
長月
BLUUUE.
SIGN: NAGATSUKI
IS THERE REALLY SOME CLUE TO BE FOUND HERE?
MM-HM.
KUU-CHAN SAID THERE WAS.
SO LET'S LOOK FOR ANYTHING OUT OF PLACE.

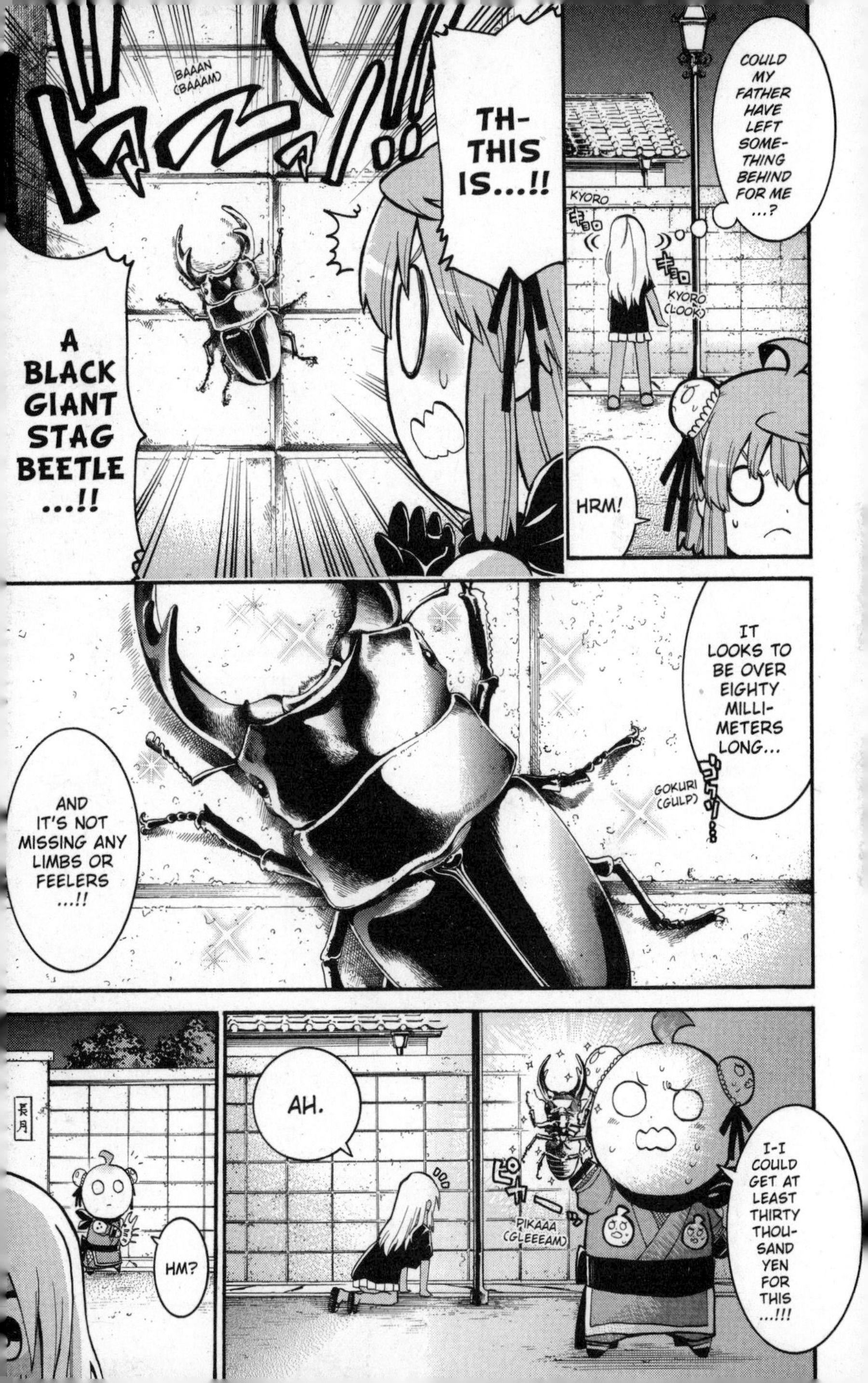
COULD MY FATHER HAVE LEFT SOMETHING BEHIND FOR ME ...?
KYORO
KYORO (LOOK)
HRM!
BAAAN (BAAAM)
TH-THIS IS...!!
A BLACK GIANT STAG BEETLE ...!!
IT LOOKS TO BE OVER EIGHTY MILLIMETERS LONG...
GOKURI (GULP)
AND IT'S NOT MISSING ANY LIMBS OR FEELERS ...!!
I-I COULD GET AT LEAST THIRTY THOUSAND YEN FOR THIS ...!!!
PIKAAA (GLEEEAM)
AH.
長月
HM?

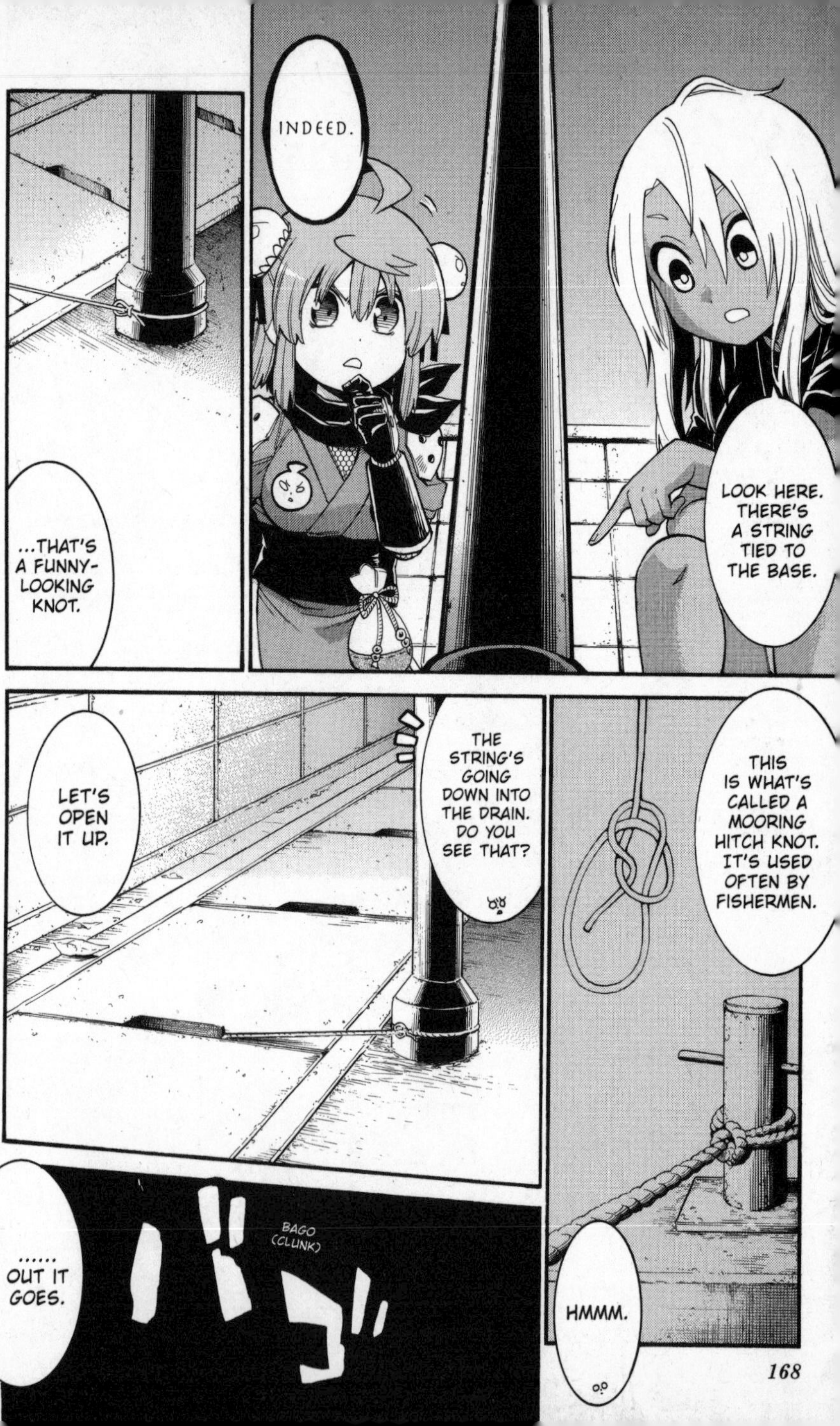
LOOK HERE. THERE'S A STRING TIED TO THE BASE.
INDEED.
...THAT'S A FUNNY-LOOKING KNOT.
THIS IS WHAT'S CALLED A MOORING HITCH KNOT. IT'S USED OFTEN BY FISHERMEN.
HMMM.
THE STRING'S GOING DOWN INTO THE DRAIN. DO YOU SEE THAT?
LET'S OPEN IT UP.
BAGO (CLUNK)
...... OUT IT GOES.

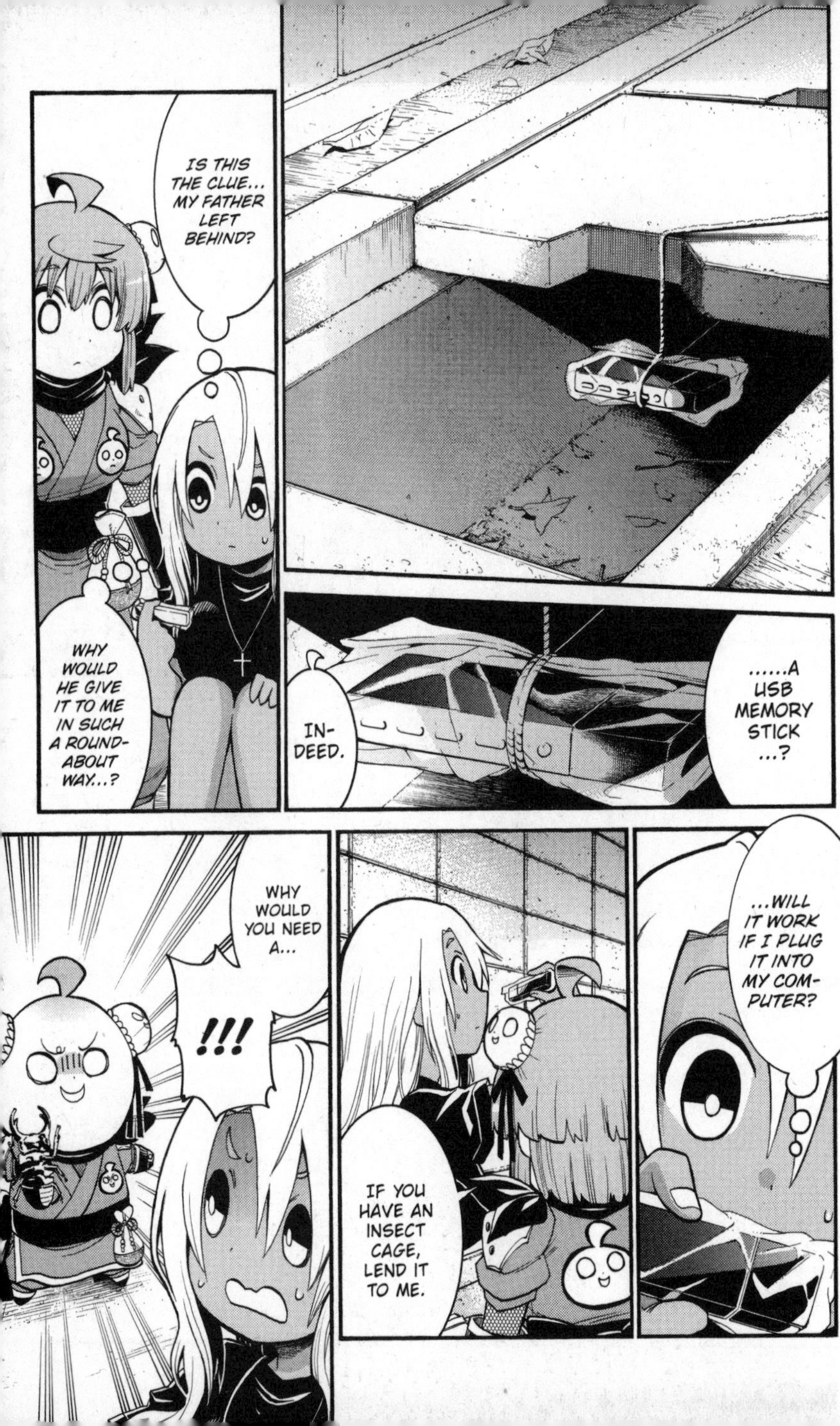
......A USB MEMORY STICK ...?
IN-DEED.
IS THIS THE CLUE... MY FATHER LEFT BEHIND?
WHY WOULD HE GIVE IT TO ME IN SUCH A ROUND-ABOUT WAY...?
...WILL IT WORK IF I PLUG IT INTO MY COM-PUTER?
IF YOU HAVE AN INSECT CAGE, LEND IT TO ME.
WHY WOULD YOU NEED A...
!!!

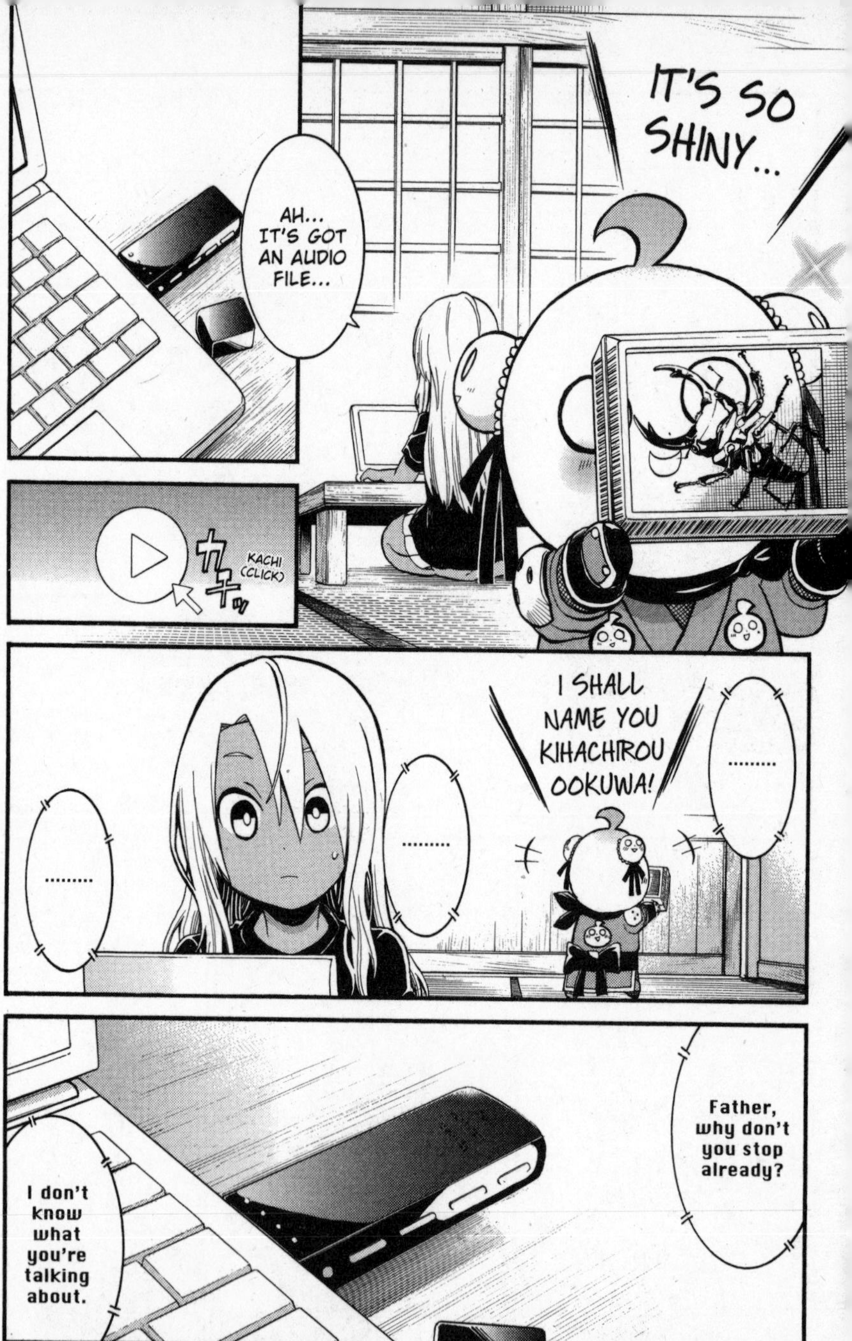
IT'S SO SHINY...
AH... IT'S GOT AN AUDIO FILE...
KACHI (CLICK)
....
I SHALL NAME YOU KIHACHIROU OOKUWA!
....
....
Father, why don't you stop already?
I don't know what you're talking about.

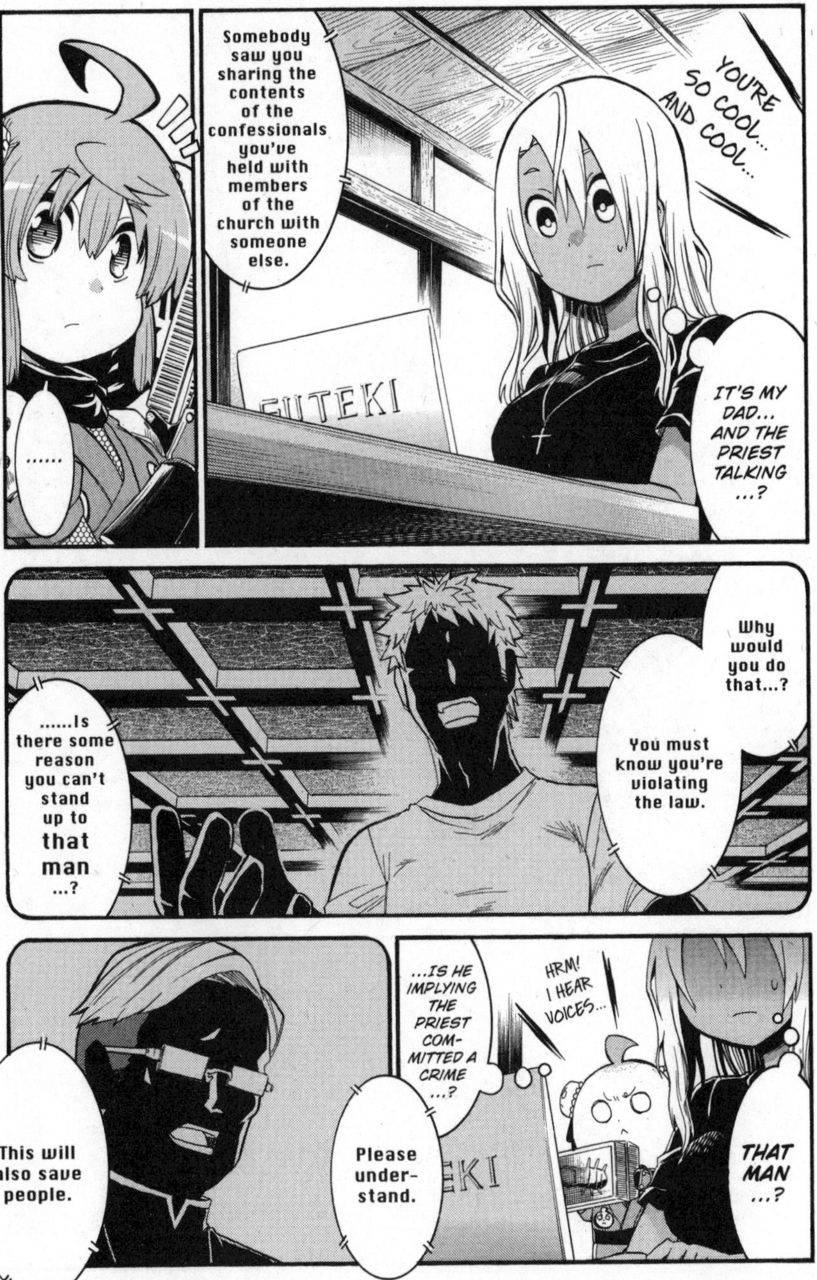
YOU'RE SO COOL... AND COOL...
Somebody saw you sharing the contents of the confessionals you've held with members of the church with someone else.
IT'S MY DAD... AND THE PRIEST TALKING ...?
......
Why would you do that...?
You must know you're violating the law.
......Is there some reason you can't stand up to that man ...?
THAT MAN ...?
HRM! I HEAR VOICES...
...IS HE IMPLYING THE PRIEST COM-MITTED A CRIME ...?
Please under-stand.
This will also save people.

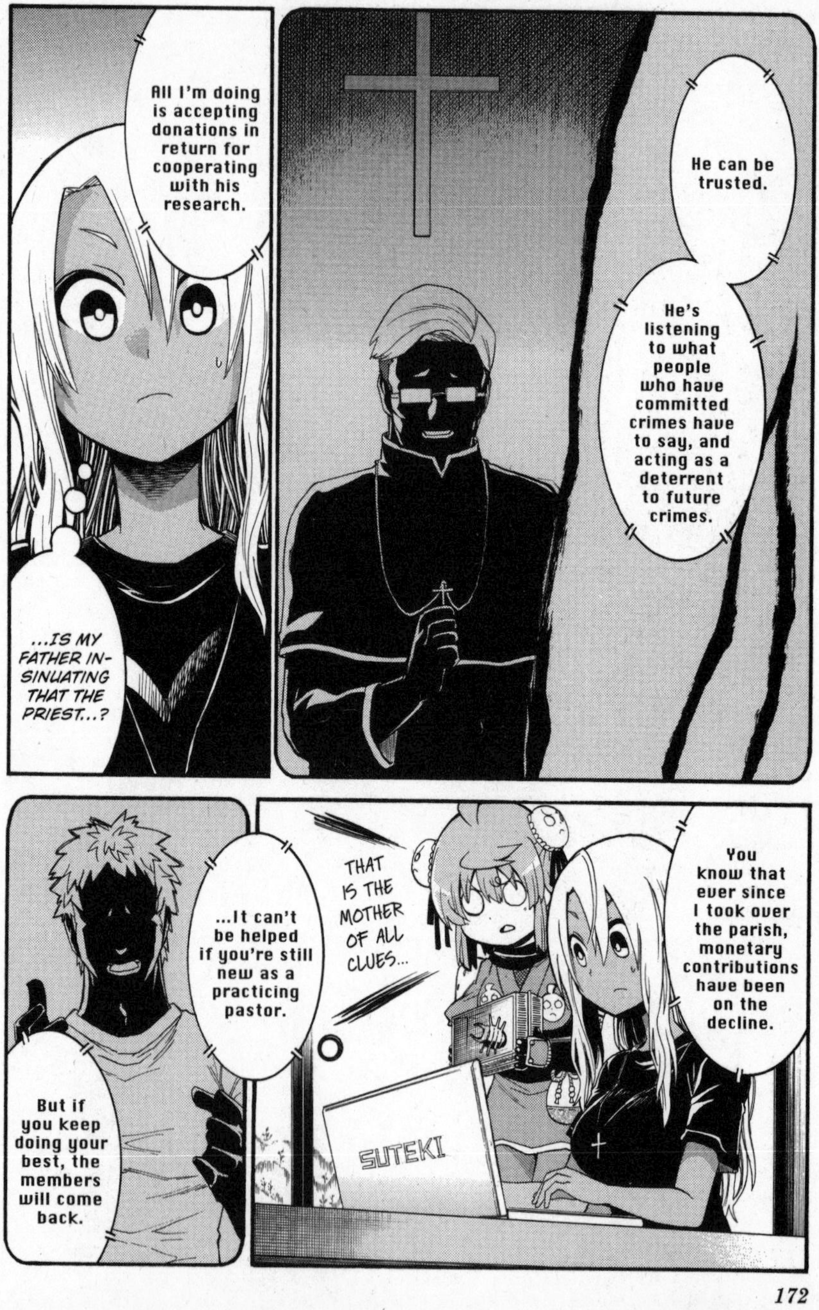
He can be trusted.
He's listening to what people who have committed crimes have to say, and acting as a deterrent to future crimes.
All I'm doing is accepting donations in return for cooperating with his research.
...IS MY FATHER IN-SINUATING THAT THE PRIEST...?
You know that ever since I took over the parish, monetary contributions have been on the decline.
THAT IS THE MOTHER OF ALL CLUES...
SUTEKI
...It can't be helped if you're still new as a practicing pastor.
But if you keep doing your best, the members will come back.

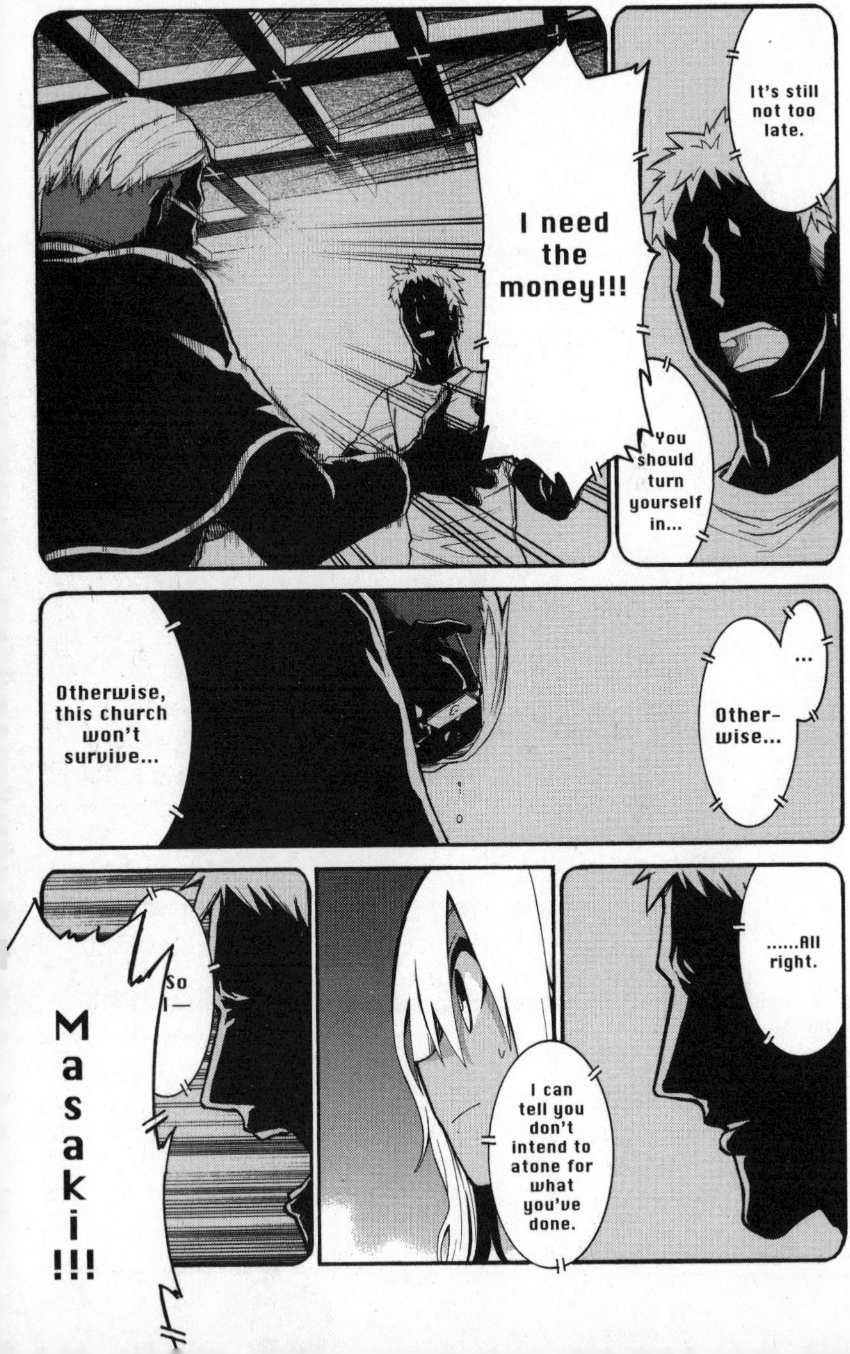
It's still not too late.
You should turn yourself in...
I need the money!!!
...
Other-wise...
Otherwise, this church won't survive...
......All right.
I can tell you don't intend to atone for what you've done.
So I—
Masaki!!!

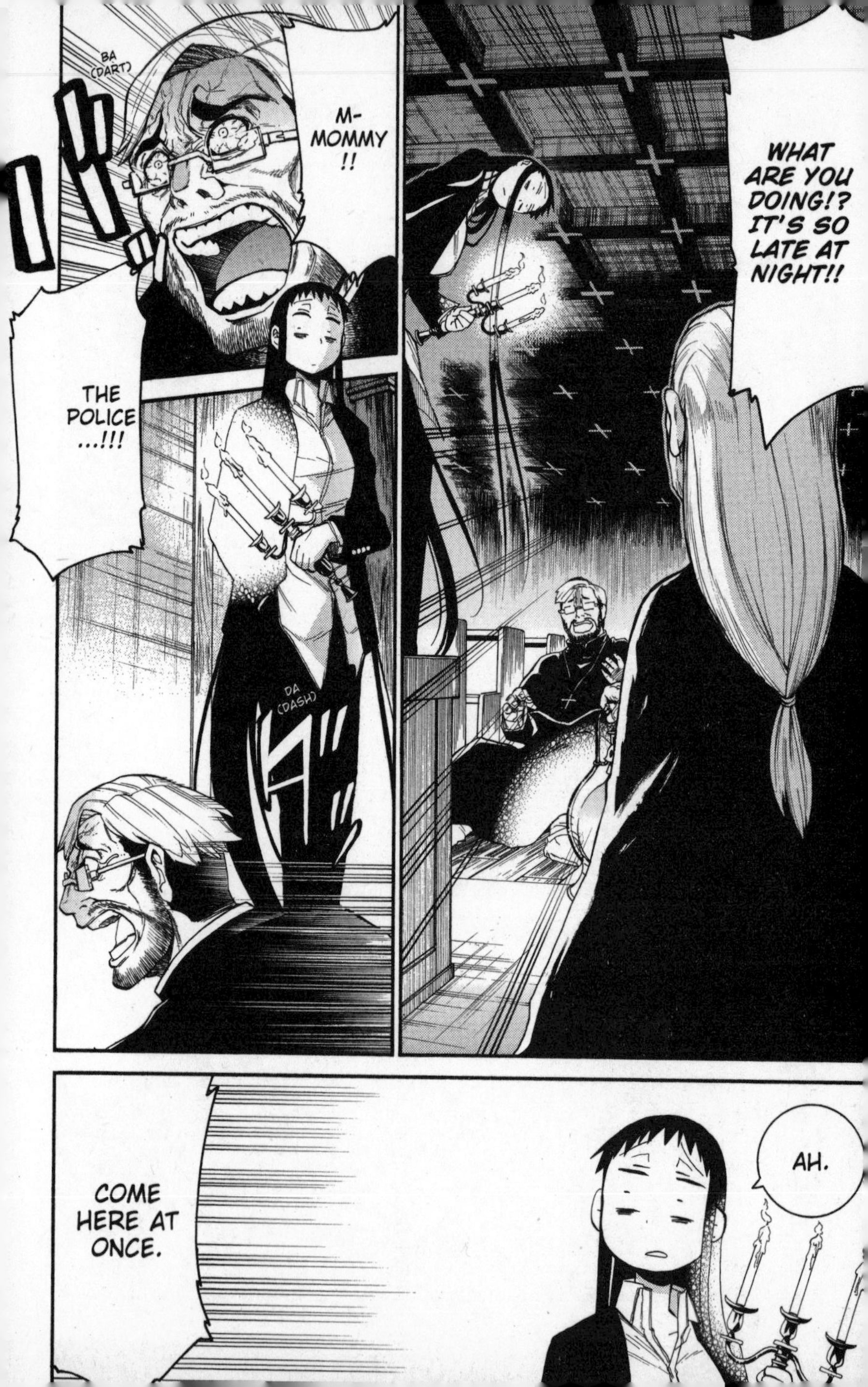
WHAT ARE YOU DOING!? IT'S SO LATE AT NIGHT!!
M-MOMMY!!
BA (DART)
THE POLICE ...!!!
DA (DASH)
AH.
COME HERE AT ONCE.

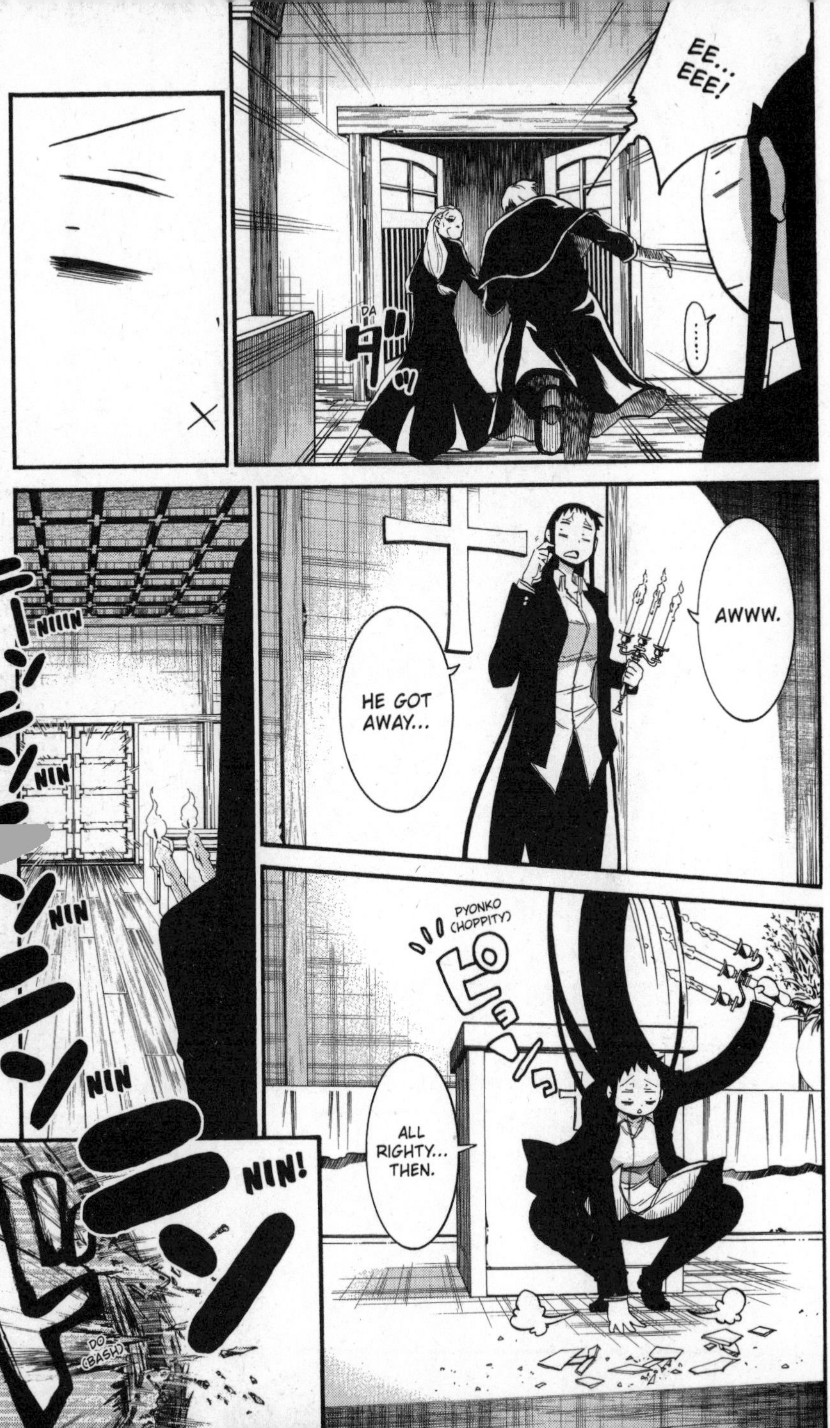
EE... EEE!
......
DA
AWWW.
HE GOT AWAY...
PYONKO (HOPPITY)
ALL RIGHTY... THEN.
NIIIN
NIN
NIN
NIN
NIN!
DO (BASH)

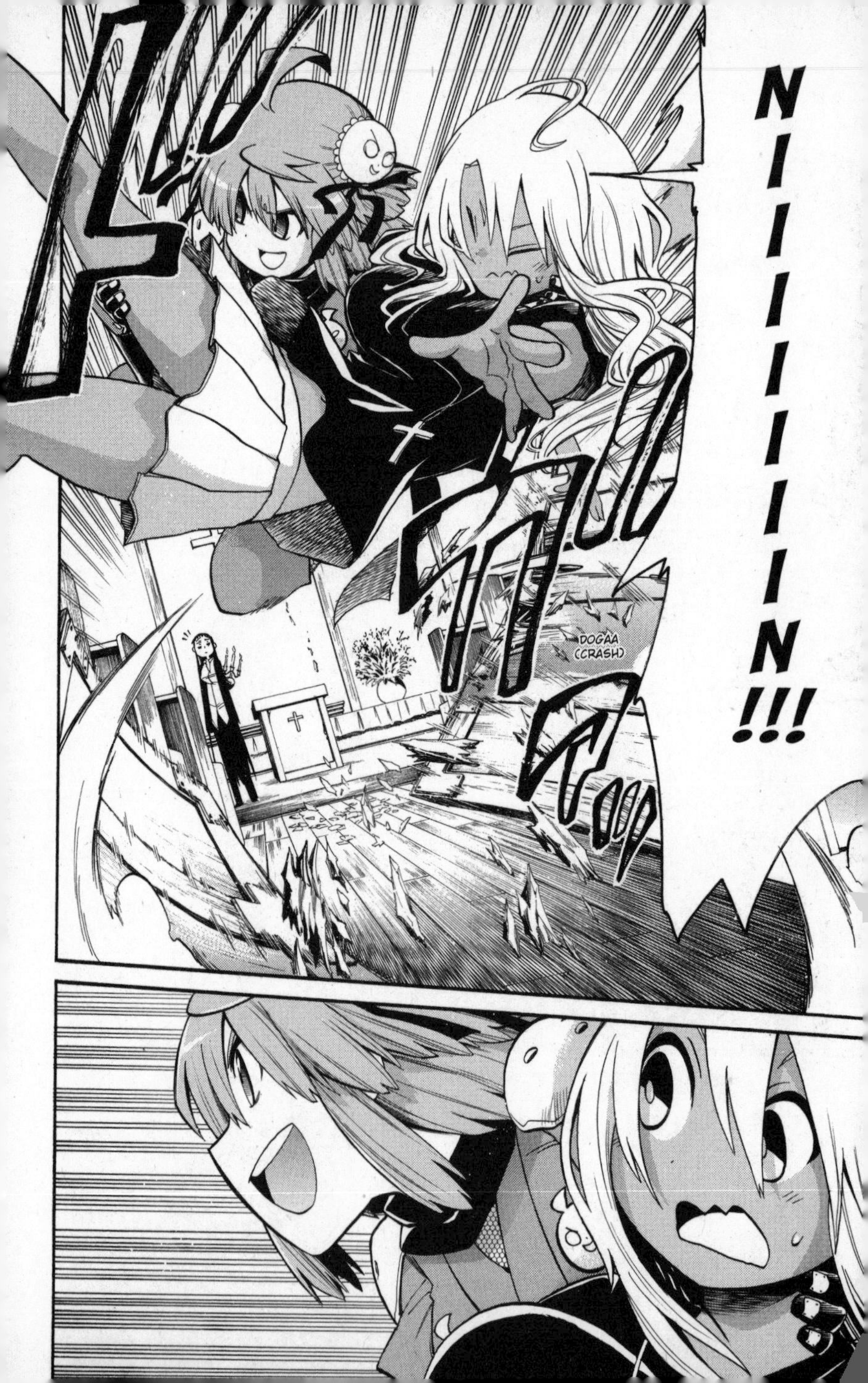
NIIIIIN!!!
DOGAA
(CRASH)

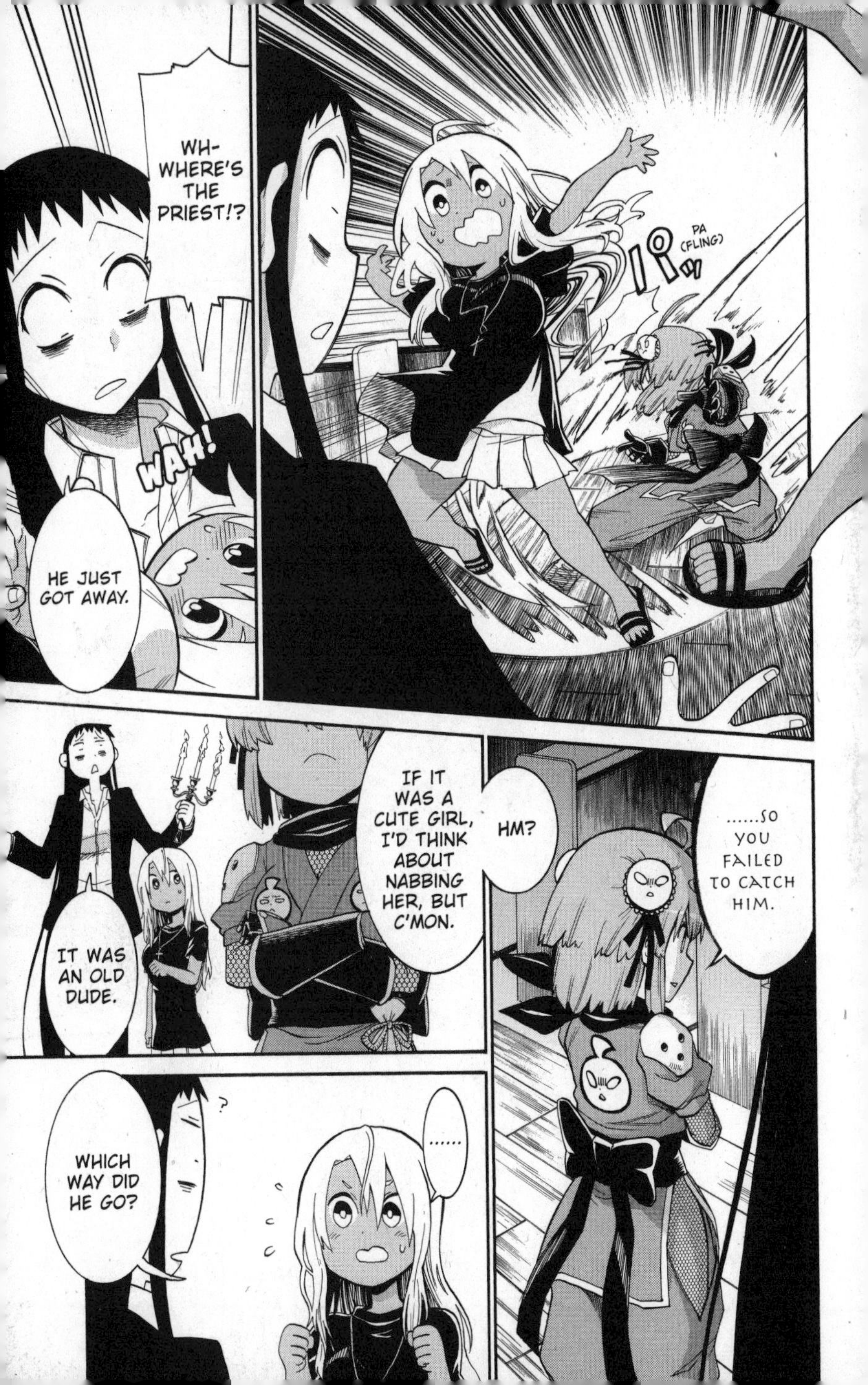
PA (FLING)
WH- WHERE'S THE PRIEST!?
WAH!
HE JUST GOT AWAY.
......SO YOU FAILED TO CATCH HIM.
HM?
IF IT WAS A CUTE GIRL, I'D THINK ABOUT NABBING HER, BUT C'MON.
IT WAS AN OLD DUDE.
......
?
WHICH WAY DID HE GO?

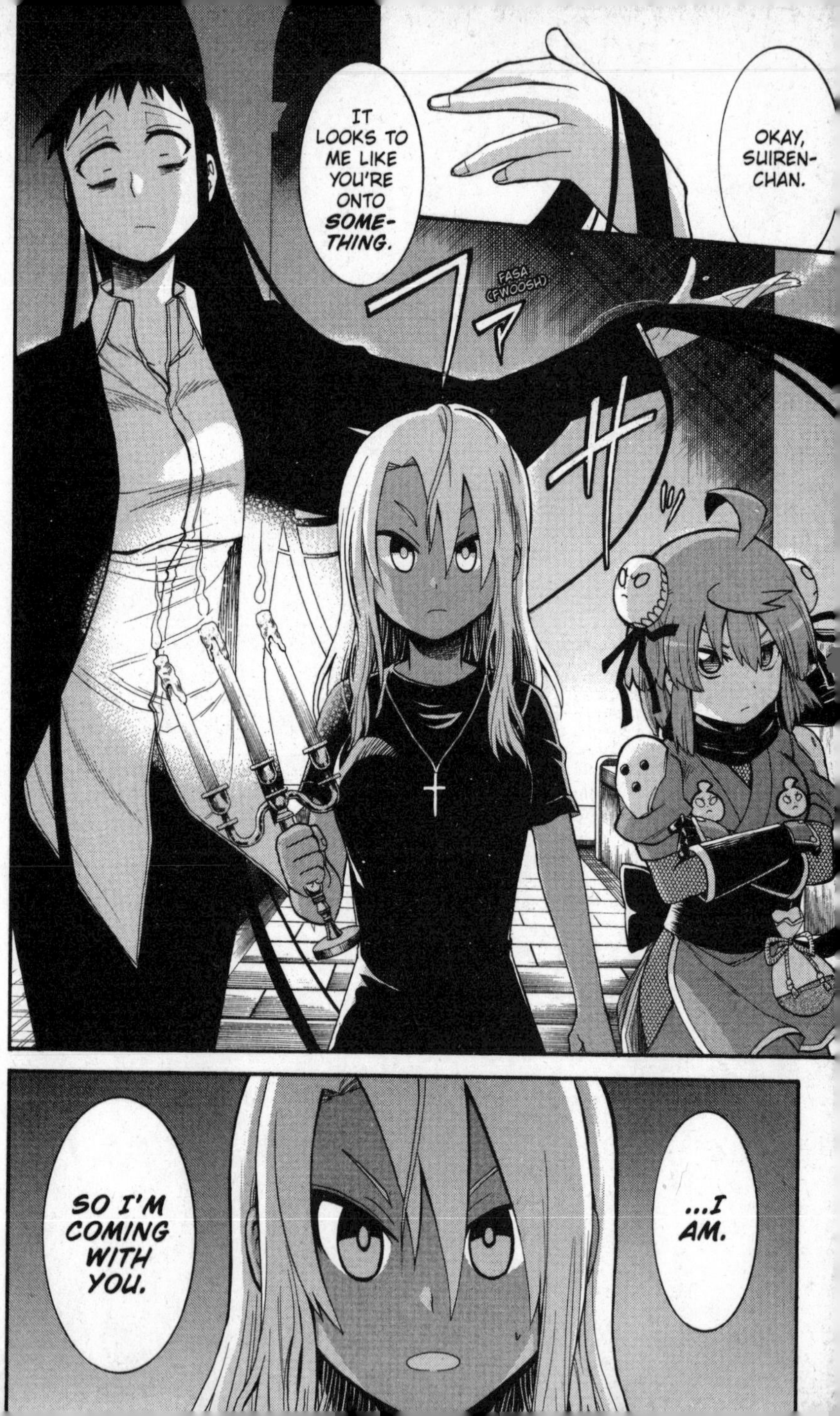
OKAY, SUIREN-CHAN.
IT LOOKS TO ME LIKE YOU'RE ONTO *SOME-THING.*
FASA (FWOOSH)
...I AM.
SO I'M COMING WITH YOU.

MURCIÉLAGO

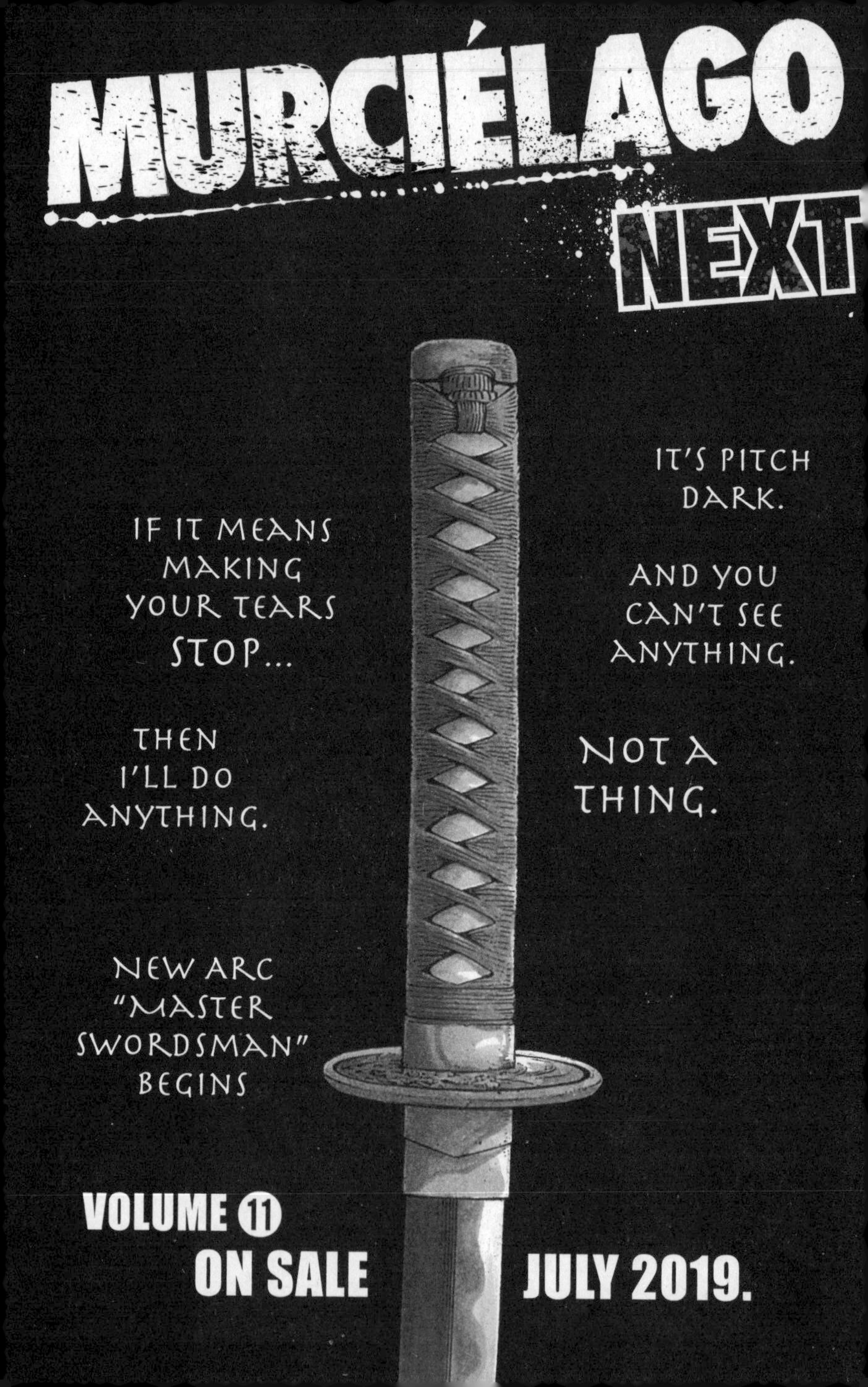

MURCIÉLAGO
NEXT
IT'S PITCH DARK.
AND YOU CAN'T SEE ANYTHING.
NOT A THING.
IF IT MEANS MAKING YOUR TEARS STOP...
THEN I'LL DO ANYTHING.
NEW ARC "MASTER SWORDSMAN" BEGINS
VOLUME 11 ON SALE JULY 2019.

MURCIÉLAGO

MURCIÉLAGO

SIGNS: PUB FUJI JUKAI / HIGHBALL / YUUHI

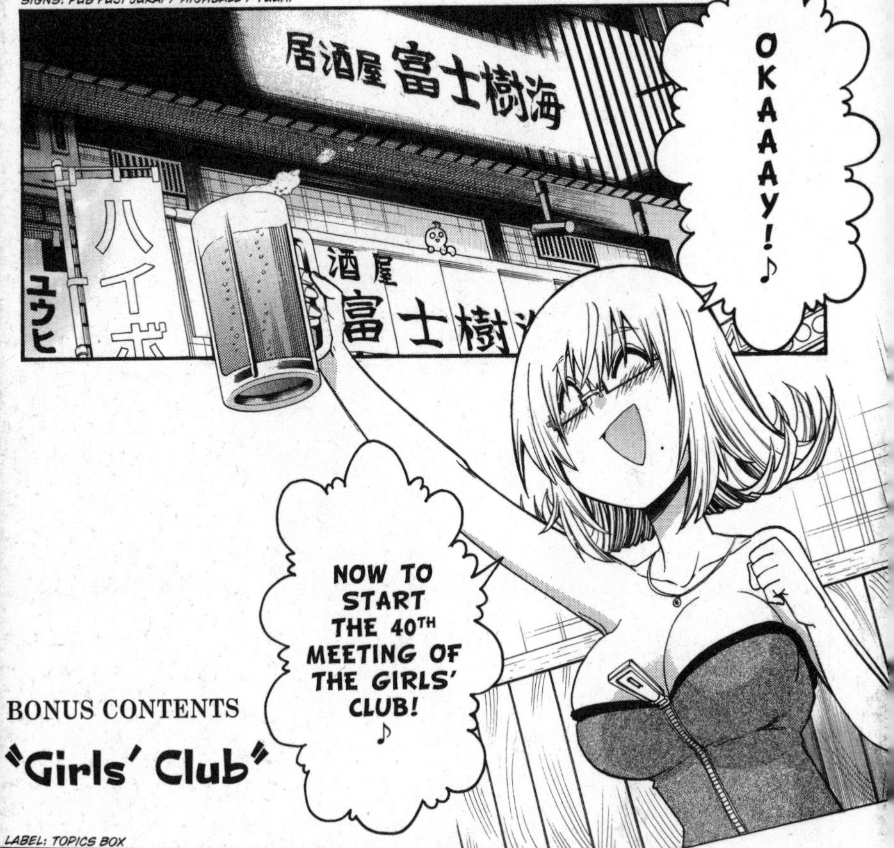
居酒屋 富士樹海
ハイボ
ユウヒ
OKAAAAY!♪
NOW TO START THE 40TH MEETING OF THE GIRLS' CLUB! ♪

BONUS CONTENTS

"Girls' Club"

LABEL: TOPICS BOX

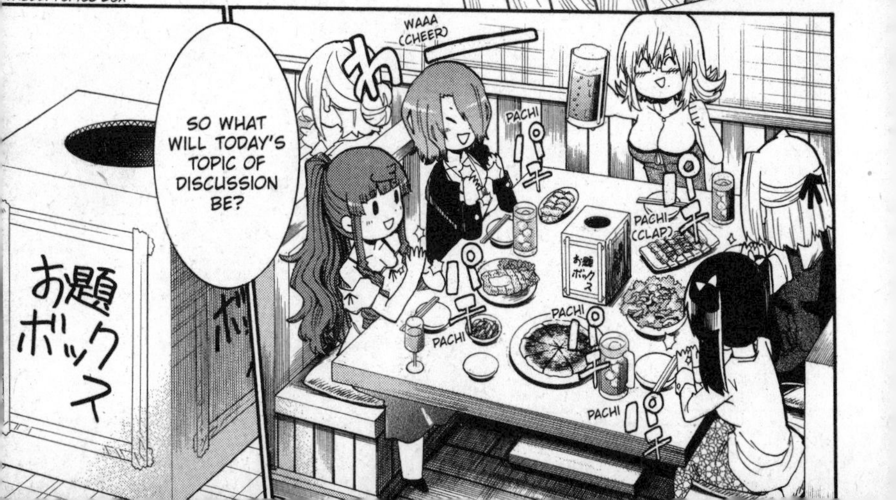
WAAA (CHEER)
SO WHAT WILL TODAY'S TOPIC OF DISCUSSION BE?
PACHI
PACHI (CLAP)
PACHI
PACHI
PACHI
お題ボックス

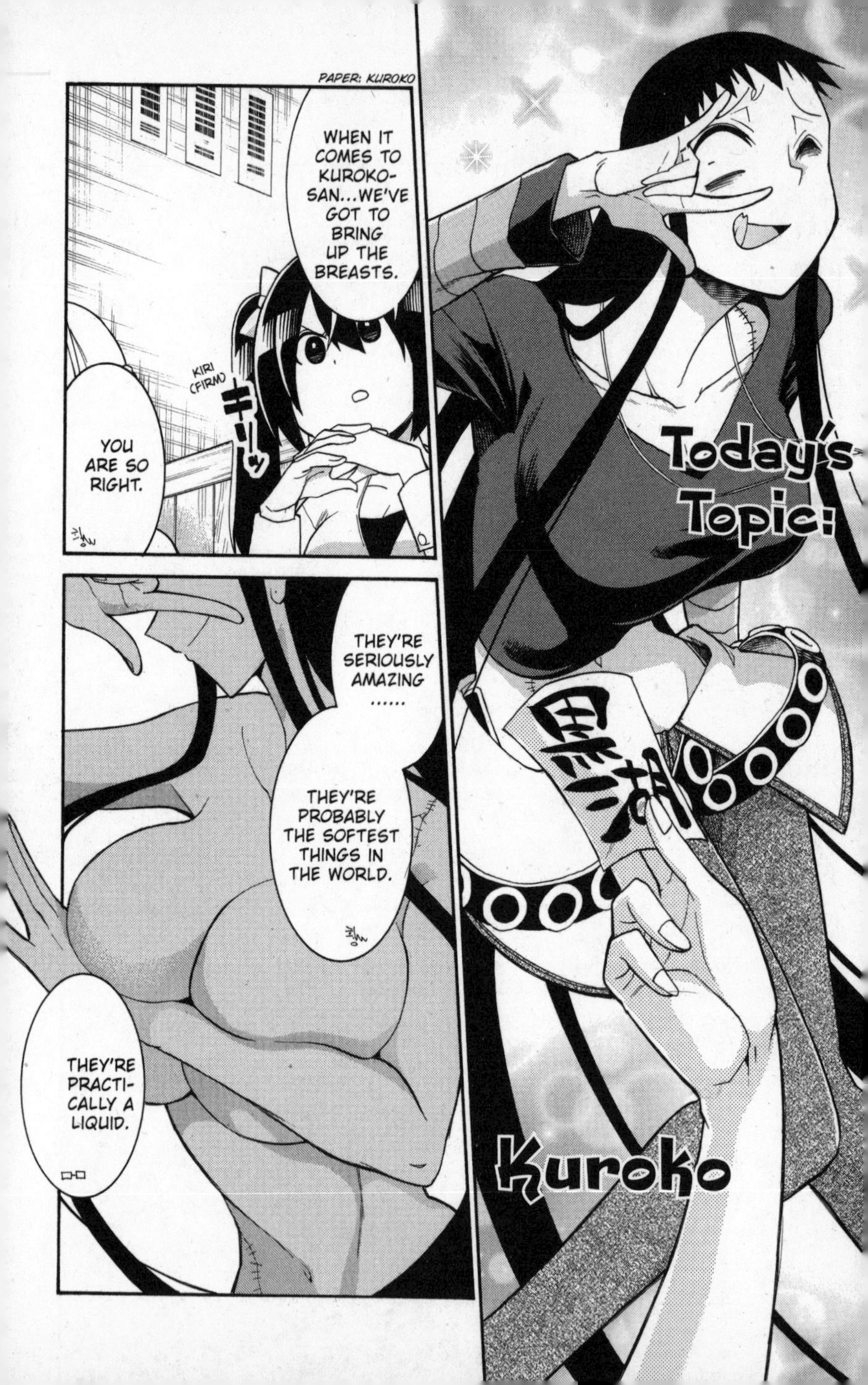
Today's Topic:
Kuroko
PAPER: KUROKO
WHEN IT COMES TO KUROKO-SAN...WE'VE GOT TO BRING UP THE BREASTS.
KIRI (FIRM)
YOU ARE SO RIGHT.
THEY'RE SERIOUSLY AMAZING ......
THEY'RE PROBABLY THE SOFTEST THINGS IN THE WORLD.
THEY'RE PRACTICALLY A LIQUID.

SIGN: MEAT BUNS, 300 YEN

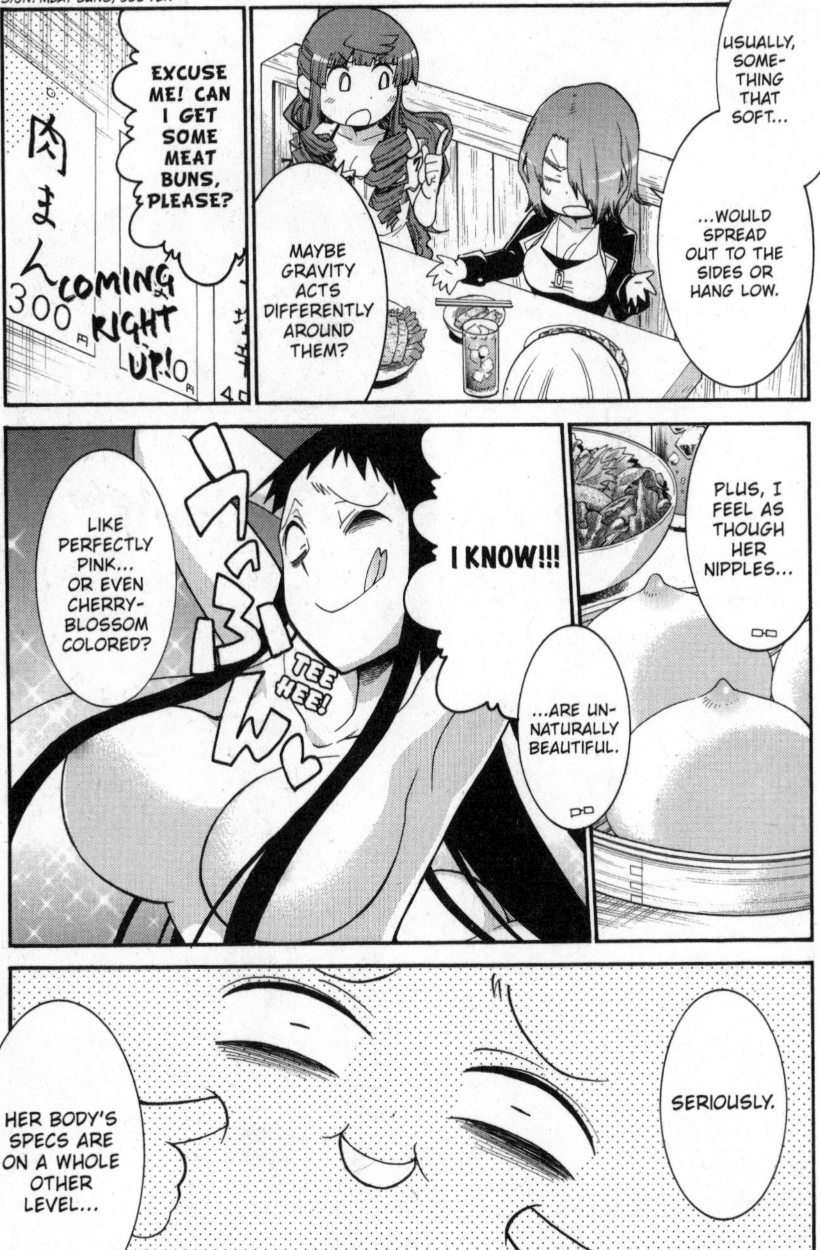
USUALLY, SOMETHING THAT SOFT...
...WOULD SPREAD OUT TO THE SIDES OR HANG LOW.
MAYBE GRAVITY ACTS DIFFERENTLY AROUND THEM?
EXCUSE ME! CAN I GET SOME MEAT BUNS, PLEASE?
COMING RIGHT UP!
肉まん
300円
PLUS, I FEEL AS THOUGH HER NIPPLES...
...ARE UNNATURALLY BEAUTIFUL.
I KNOW!!!
LIKE PERFECTLY PINK... OR EVEN CHERRY-BLOSSOM COLORED?
TEE HEE!
SERIOUSLY.
HER BODY'S SPECS ARE ON A WHOLE OTHER LEVEL...

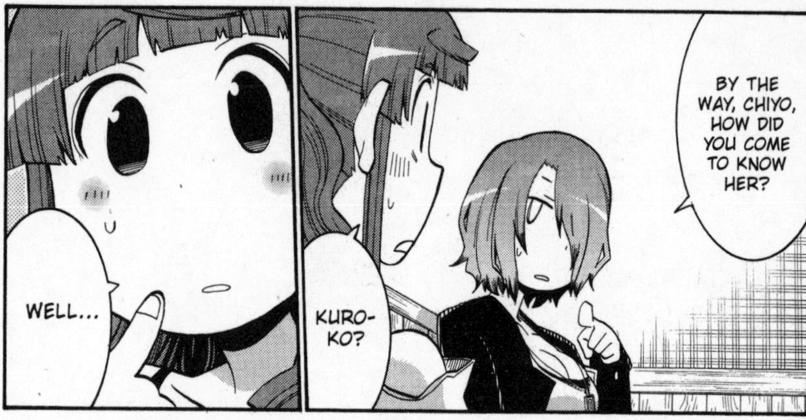
BY THE WAY, CHIYO, HOW DID YOU COME TO KNOW HER?
KURO-KO?
WELL...

Chiyo Yanaoka's Story

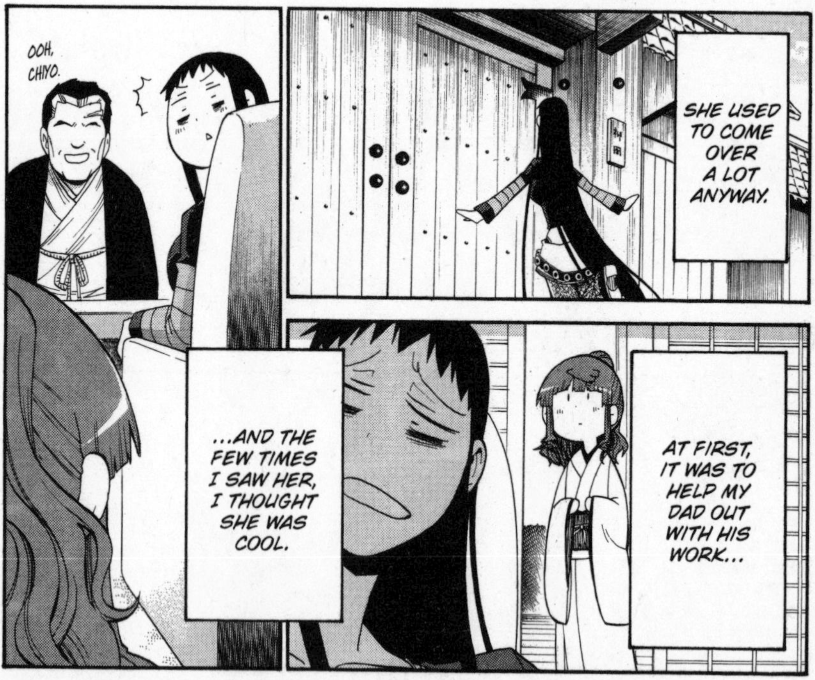
SHE USED TO COME OVER A LOT ANYWAY.
AT FIRST, IT WAS TO HELP MY DAD OUT WITH HIS WORK...
...AND THE FEW TIMES I SAW HER, I THOUGHT SHE WAS COOL.
OOH, CHIYO.

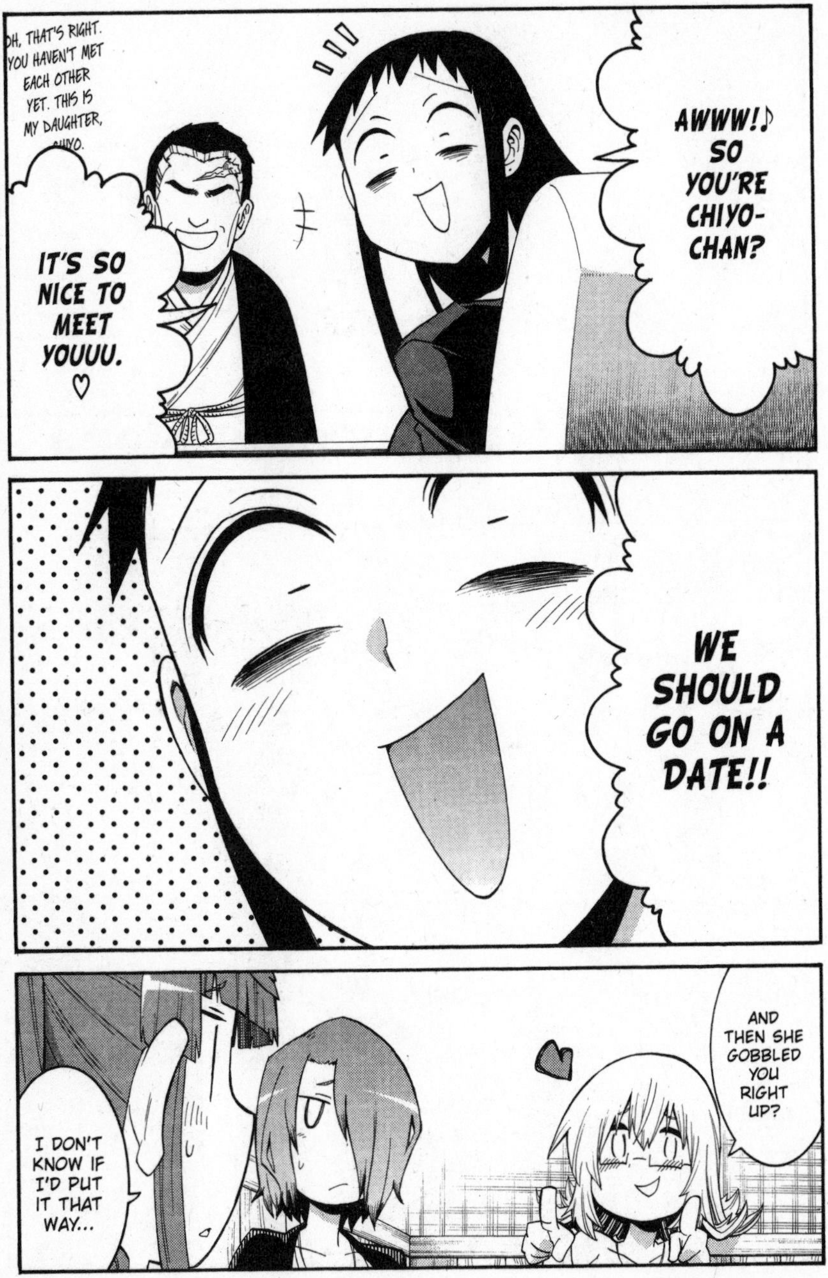
AWWW!♪ SO YOU'RE CHIYO-CHAN?
OH, THAT'S RIGHT. YOU HAVEN'T MET EACH OTHER YET. THIS IS MY DAUGHTER, CHIYO.
IT'S SO NICE TO MEET YOUUU. ♡
WE SHOULD GO ON A DATE!!
AND THEN SHE GOBBLED YOU RIGHT UP?
I DON'T KNOW IF I'D PUT IT THAT WAY...

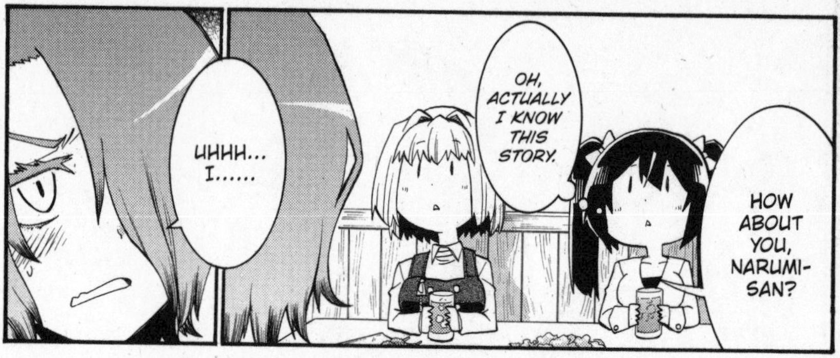
HOW ABOUT YOU, NARUMI-SAN?
OH, ACTUALLY I KNOW THIS STORY.
UHHH... I......

Narumi Momoyama's Story

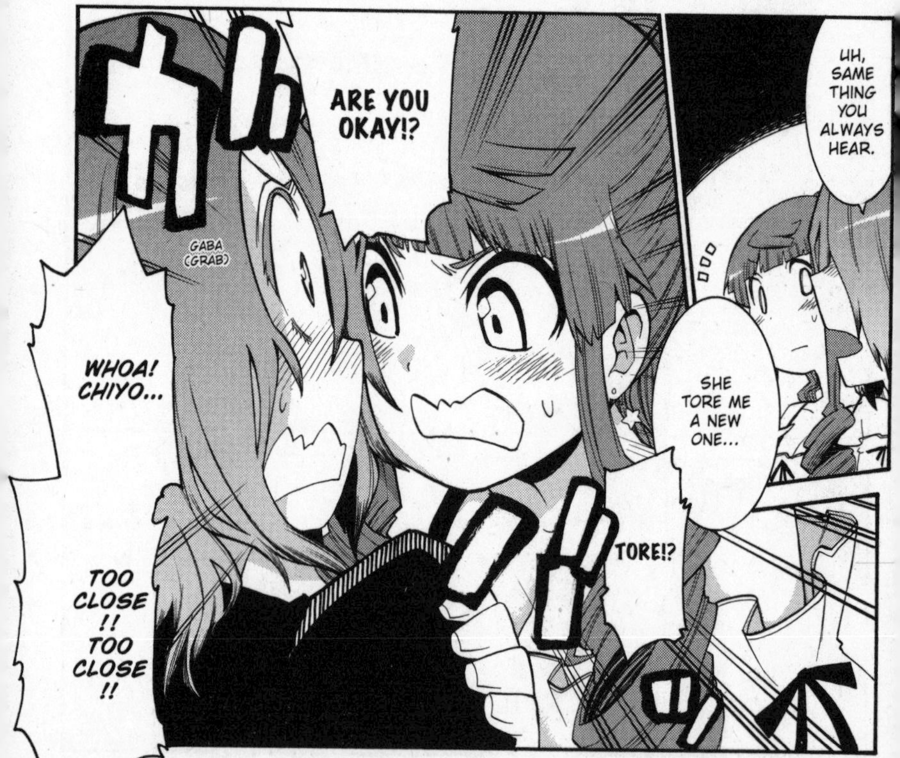
UH, SAME THING YOU ALWAYS HEAR.
SHE TORE ME A NEW ONE...
TORE!?
ARE YOU OKAY!?
GABA (GRAB)
WHOA! CHIYO...
TOO CLOSE!! TOO CLOSE!!

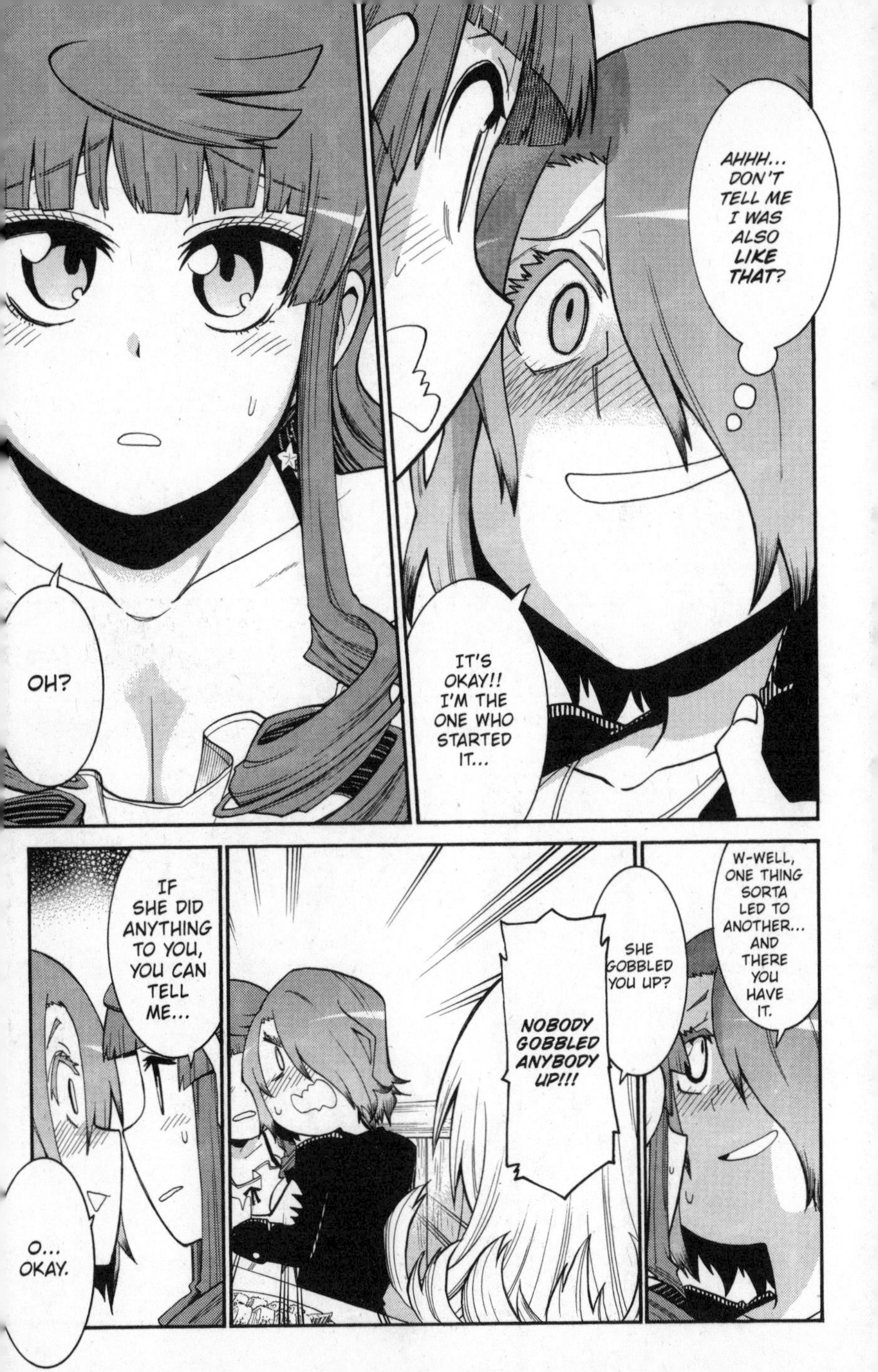
AHHH... DON'T TELL ME I WAS ALSO LIKE THAT?
IT'S OKAY!! I'M THE ONE WHO STARTED IT...
OH?
W-WELL, ONE THING SORTA LED TO ANOTHER... AND THERE YOU HAVE IT.
SHE GOBBLED YOU UP?
NOBODY GOBBLED ANYBODY UP!!!
IF SHE DID ANYTHING TO YOU, YOU CAN TELL ME...
O... OKAY.

Yuria Fujinami's Story

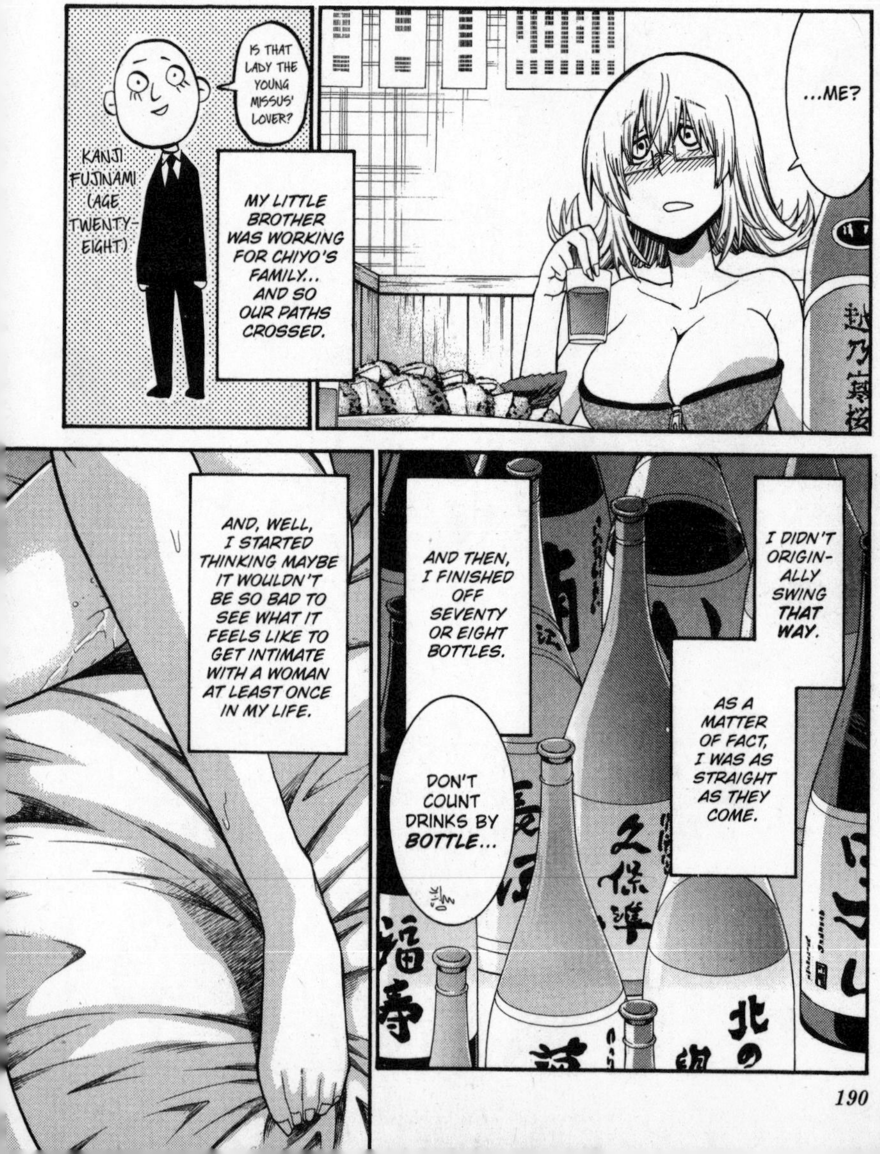
...ME?
IS THAT LADY THE YOUNG MISSUS' LOVER?
MY LITTLE BROTHER WAS WORKING FOR CHIYO'S FAMILY... AND SO OUR PATHS CROSSED.
KANJI FUJINAMI (AGE TWENTY-EIGHT)
I DIDN'T ORIGIN-ALLY SWING THAT WAY.
AS A MATTER OF FACT, I WAS AS STRAIGHT AS THEY COME.
AND THEN, I FINISHED OFF SEVENTY OR EIGHT BOTTLES.
DON'T COUNT DRINKS BY BOTTLE...
AND, WELL, I STARTED THINKING MAYBE IT WOULDN'T BE SO BAD TO SEE WHAT IT FEELS LIKE TO GET INTIMATE WITH A WOMAN AT LEAST ONCE IN MY LIFE.

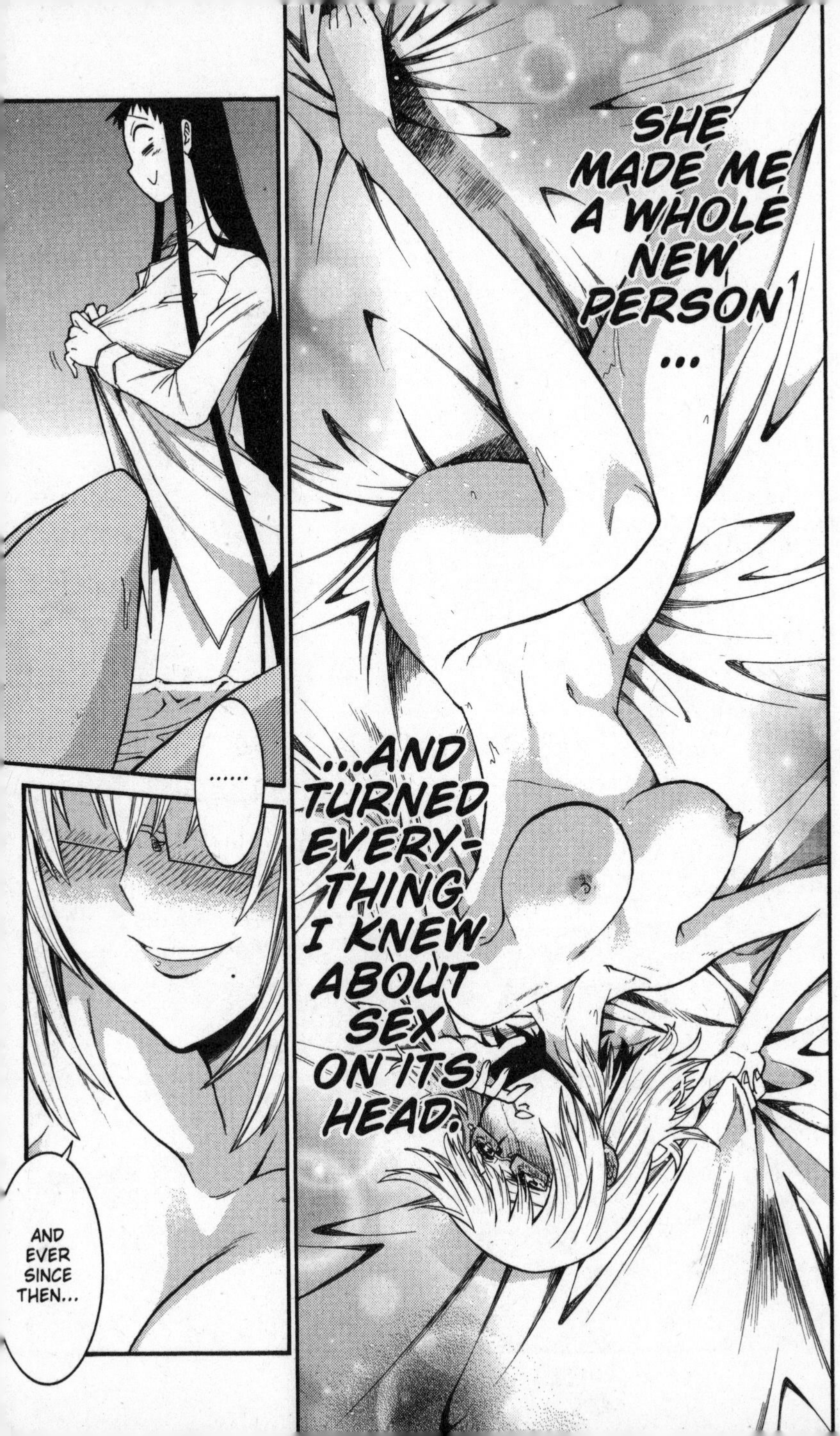
SHE MADE ME A WHOLE NEW PERSON...
...AND TURNED EVERY-THING I KNEW ABOUT SEX ON ITS HEAD.
......
AND EVER SINCE THEN...

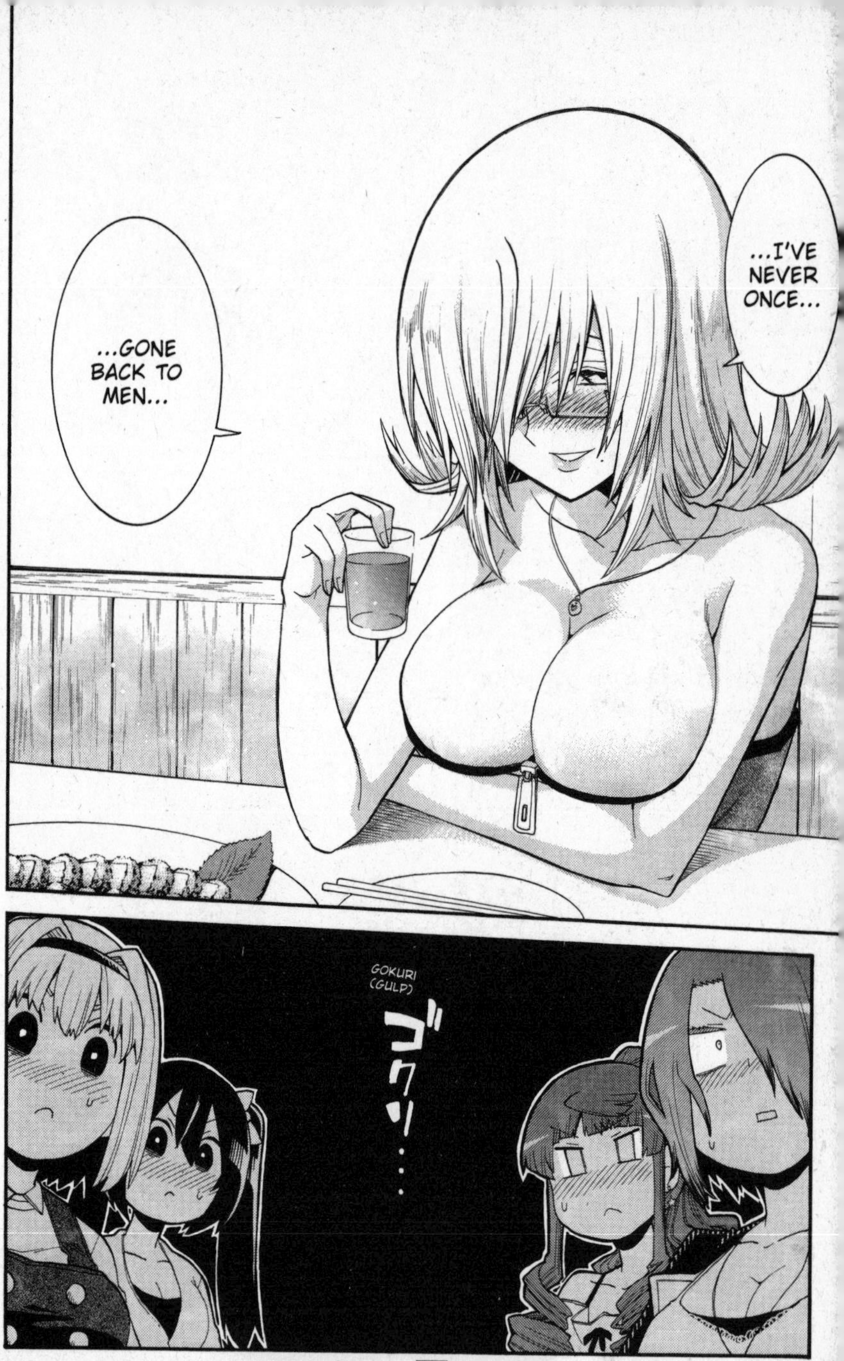
...I'VE NEVER ONCE...
...GONE BACK TO MEN...
GOKURI (GULP)
ゴクッ...

MURCIÉLAGO 10 THE END

Translation Notes

General
Murciélago is Spanish for "bat."

Suteki is Japanese for "lovely."

Kuroko means "black lake" in Japanese, and is a Cthulhu Mythos reference to the Lake of Hali, where the Dark God Hastur dwells.

The city of **Ruruie** is a reference to R'lyeh, a fictional lost city in H. P. Lovecraft's "The Call of Cthulhu."

Page 6
Enjoy and exciting is the motto of the *Berserk* manga character Wyald and his group, the Black Dog Knights.

Page 11
In Japanese culture, circles mean "good;" round flowers (*hanamaru*) mean "great."

Page 38
One Cup, or One Cup Ozeki, a Japanese brand of single-serving sake.

Page 44
Mamekan is a Japanese dessert made of agar jelly and served without fruit.

Page 47
Umami is a savory-like taste sensation and literally means "good flavor."
In Japanese, Hinako says the somewhat redundant *"Umami ga umai...!!!"*

Page 67
Gal (or "*gyaru*") is a Japanese fashion style that commonly involves (artifically) tanned skin, though in Suiren's case the tan appears to be natural.

Page 79
Hidden Christians in Japan originated in the Edo period because Christianity was banned until 1873. One way of obscuring their faith involved disguising Christian statues as Buddhist ones, as shown on page 96.

Page 94
In Japanese, instead of **"porno good reason,"** Kuroko originally mishears *midari* (recklessly) and responds with *midara* ("obscene").

Page 106
Pyukuriririiin, along with the spark visual effect, is a reference to the Newtype flashes— essentially psychic signals—from the Gundam franchise.

Page 114
Insumasu is based on the fictional town of Innsmouth from H. P. Lovecraft's Cthulhu mythos, which is characterized by being in a state of ruin and decay.

Page 123
Squat and soak is translated from the Japanese word *tsukumoru*, which means "to squat down and soak in a bath up to the shoulders."

Page 170
Ookuwa essentially means "big beetle" and is a play on *kuwagata* ("stag beetle").

Page 183
Fuji Jukai ("Mt. Fuji Sea of Trees") is a reference to Aokigahara forest—a common spot for suicides in Japan.

Yuuhi is a brand of Japanese beer.

MURCIÉLAGO

Yoshimurakana

Translation: Christine Dashiell ✦ Lettering: Alexis Eckerman

MURCIÉLAGO vol. 10
© 2017 Yoshimurakana / SQUARE ENIX CO., LTD.
First published in Japan in 2017 by SQUARE ENIX CO., LTD.
English translation rights arranged with SQUARE ENIX CO., LTD. and Yen Press, LLC
through Tuttle-Mori Agency, Inc.

English translation © 2019 by SQUARE ENIX CO., LTD.

Yen Press
1290 Avenue of the Americas
New York, NY 10104

Visit us at yenpress.com
facebook.com/yenpress
twitter.com/yenpress
yenpress.tumblr.com
instagram.com/yenpress

Yen Press is an imprint of Yen Press, LLC.
The Yen Press name and logo are trademarks of Yen Press, LLC.

The publisher is not responsible for websites (or their content) that are
not owned by the publisher.

First Yen Press Edition: April 2019

Library of Congress Control Number: 2016958266

ISBNs: 978-1-9753-0249-8 (paperback)
978-1-9753-0255-9 (ebook)

10 9 8 7 6 5 4 3 2 1

WOR

Printed in the United States of America